ROCKNE & JONES

ROCKNE
& JONES

Notre Dame, USC, and the Greatest Rivalry of the Roaring Twenties

Thomas Rupp

Black Squirrel Books®
Kent, Ohio

BLACK SQUIRREL BOOKS® 🐿®
Frisky, industrious black squirrels are a familiar sight on the Kent State
University campus and the inspiration for Black Squirrel Books™, a trade
imprint of The Kent State University Press. www.KentStateUniversityPress.com

© 2017 by Thomas Rupp
Foreword © 2017 by The Kent State University Press

Library of Congress Catalog Card Number 2016055040
ISBN 978-1-60635-330-1
Manufactured in the United States of America

Library of Congress Cataloging-in-Publication Data
Names: Rupp, Thomas, 1957- author.
Title: Rockne and Jones : Notre Dame, USC, and the greatest rivalry of the roaring
    twenties / Thomas Rupp.
Description: Kent, Ohio : The Kent State University Press, 2017. | Includes biblio-
    graphical references and index.
Identifiers: LCCN 2016055040 (print) | LCCN 2017004134 (ebook) | ISBN
    9781606353301 (pbk. : alk. paper) | ISBN 9781631012624 (ePub) | ISBN
    9781631012631 (ePDF)
Subjects: LCSH: Rockne, Knute, 1888-1931. | Jones, Howard H., 1885-1941. |
    University of Notre Dame--Football--History--20th century. | Notre Dame
    Fighting Irish (Football team)--History--20th century. | University of South-
    ern California--Football--History--20th century. | Southern California Trojans
    (Football team)--History--20th century.
Classification: LCC GV939.R6 R86 2017 (print) | LCC GV939.R6 (ebook) | DDC
    796.3320922 [B] --dc23
LC record available at https://lccn.loc.gov/2016055040

21 20 19 18 17   5 4 3 2 1

Contents

Foreword

      If you were to ask students of the University of Notre Dame or the University of Southern California how the intense rivalry between their two football teams began, most probably wouldn't have a clue—but they do know that it is real! If you asked them why the rivalry exists, my guess is that they would have their own stories to tell. There are probably as many reasons for the quest for supremacy between these two opponents as there are years since it first started. This book chronicles the origin of the rivalry between the Fighting Irish and the Trojans that underlies the endless trash-talking between their supporters. The tug-of-war that began in 1926 persists nationwide today, and certainly continues in my family!

      While the rivalry between Notre Dame and USC holds a special place in college football history, for me it is very personal. Watching Notre Dame football on Sunday mornings was a tradition in the Browner household. Saturday games were televised on Sunday mornings, and the Browner clan was front and center as we watched some of the best schools in the nation play against Notre Dame. As a youngster, I had no knowledge of any special rivalry; the other teams were all just opponents of Notre Dame.

      The way I learned about the rivalry is another story. For me, it dates back to 1972, my senior year of high school. Although I am from the small town of Warren, Ohio, my football skills gained national attention and I was fortunate enough to be recruited by more than thirty Division 1 colleges across the country. With no limit on the number of college visits permitted at the time, I seized the opportunity and visited all thirty university campuses. In the process, I met some of the nation's best players and formed friendships that have lasted a lifetime.

Gary Jeter of Cleveland and I were considered the best linemen in the state of Ohio in 1972. Finding that we liked each other, we coordinated our schedules so we could view the same colleges at the same time, visiting Ohio State, Michigan, Michigan State, Penn State, Nebraska, and Notre Dame together. We got along so well that we hoped to play on the same team. Gary became one of my best friends.

Gary and I both were invited to visit USC, but since I had also been invited to visit the University of Pittsburgh, I postponed my visit to USC until the week after Gary's visit. The Monday morning after I returned from Pittsburgh, I received a call from John Jackson, the USC recruiting coach and assumed he was calling to reschedule my campus visit.

"Ross," Coach Jackson told me, "I have good news and I have bad news." I asked for the good news first. He said, "We signed Gary Jeter during his weekend visit." I replied, "Great! That is wonderful news, because we are talking about going to the same school!" But the next thing Coach Jackson said was a total shocker. The bad news was that Gary had been awarded USC's last out-of-state scholarship! My visit had to be canceled because no other scholarship was available.

I paused, thought for a minute, and then responded to Coach Jackson with a question: Which teams were on Southern California's schedule for the 1973 football season? He told me that USC's team would play all of the Pac 8 teams and also Notre Dame. I answered him with a smile on my face. "Well, Coach," I said, "then look for me on Notre Dame's team! I'll be playing against you!" So for me, 1973 marked the beginning of the rivalry between Notre Dame and USC. However, it never occurred to me that the rivalry would later extend to my very own family.

In my large and close-knit family of six boys and two girls, we were our own best friends, playmates, and teammates. As a result, all six boys became talented football players. As the oldest boy, I was the first to leave home for college. My brother Jimmie Browner was right on my heels. He, too, was heavily recruited by major universities and accepted a scholarship to play for Notre Dame. The following year, my next brother, Willard Browner, who also had the privilege of choosing from among the finest schools in the nation, made the wise decision to join Jimmie and me at Notre Dame and play for the "best." With three of us playing for Notre Dame, we were making history and creating a tradition that made the university, our parents, and our family proud.

In 1978, my family moved to Atlanta, Georgia. While Jimmie, Willard, and I had all been high school All-Americans in Ohio who went on to Notre Dame, my three youngest brothers, Joey, Keith, and Gerald, became high school All-Americans in Atlanta.

When Joey was heavily recruited like his older brothers, we expected him to follow in our footsteps and attend Notre Dame. He chose USC instead. While we were shocked that he didn't choose Notre Dame, we were still excited that Joey was awarded a college scholarship. Keith, a year younger than Joey, was the next brother to graduate, and the two created a new family tradition by playing at USC together, while our youngest brother, Gerald, struck out on his own, attending the University of Georgia.

For many years, the Browner household had been loyal to one team—Fighting Irish through and through. Now that loyalty and respect is divided, as the Trojans have earned an equal place of honor in the family. "Go Irish!" and "Fight On!"

Recently, when I called my brother Keith to ask him for the Notre Dame versus USC record stats during his playing years, he was quick to tell me that the Trojans had beaten the Irish three out of four of the years he played, while Notre Dame had won only two of the four games in which I'd played. While we talked, I received an e-mail from him with the record of all the Notre Dame versus USC games. Keith also proudly pointed out that during a span from 2002 to 2009, Notre Dame lost to USC eight years in a row. Fortunately, I noticed that those same stats showed the overall record of Notre Dame wins as 46–36–5. Need I say more?

The thrill of victory and the agony of defeat in the rivalry between Notre Dame and USC still create memorable moments for the Browner family. Thomas Rupp's carefully researched account of the historic basis for that rivalry justifies its impact over the years on thousands of other Irish and Trojan fans, who probably have their own personal stories to tell.

Ross Browner
Notre Dame, 1978
Go Irish!

Preface: Rivalry

"A vying with others for victory or supremacy."

—*The American Heritage Roget's Thesaurus*, 2014

The first known use of the word *rivalry* in the English language occurred not long after the Spanish Armada foundered in the North Atlantic in 1588. The Latin word *rivus,* meaning "brook," has been offered as one possible origin of the term. Some suggest that as the language of the Romans began to percolate into the culture of the British Isles, the tales of competing tribes battling over a river's life-sustaining water supply spawned a new word.

The Spanish Armada was lost in a much larger body of water, but that decisive battle was a key point in the ongoing rivalry between the great powers of England and Spain. At stake was the future of Europe, for had Spain's King Philip II emerged victorious, the Iberian monarch would have dethroned England's Queen Elizabeth I and installed a puppet ruler in her place. The complete domination desired by King Philip would have resolved the conflict, replacing the rivalry between the two nations with the subjugation of one over the other. In a classic rivalry, conflict persists over an extended period of time, with successes and defeats on both sides.

History has known many rivalries akin to the conflict between England and Spain. From ancient empires, to medieval kingdoms, to modern nation-states, countries have fought one another through the ages. Rivalries can form on the national, institutional, or personal level, in politics or the world of business, among artists and musicians, between colleagues, friends, or siblings, even in matters of the heart. In today's world, athletics are notorious for spawning great rivalries.

Rivalries in sports arise from more than just the record of wins and losses between teams. An intense hunger for victory, a shared feeling that the success of the season is defined simply by the outcome of that one game, must be present. A sense of tradition and continuity from year to year keeps the rivalry vibrant and alive. There must be excellence as well, so that the competition is of the highest caliber, with public attention rising accordingly. Finally, success must be somewhat even between the two teams, or one side dominates and the opposing side is dismissed as little more than a free spot on the bingo board.

In America, college football has many rivalries. Perhaps the oldest is Harvard versus Yale. Other prominent examples are Army versus Navy, Ohio State versus Michigan, and Texas versus Oklahoma, yet they represent only a few of the dozens of annual rivalries formed between colleges large and small. These rivalries typically share obvious characteristics. Geographic proximity is the most common, whether between colleges from bordering states, within the same state, or even within the same city. Only the service academies are exceptions, sharing not geography but rather membership in the same national military establishment.

On the other hand, all reflect some basic conflict that extends beyond the two schools to some larger opposing interests that the teams represent. The rivalry between the Buckeyes and Wolverines is a case in point. A border dispute between the state of Ohio and the adjoining Michigan territory fueled the animus long before the two schools began playing football.

Only one major rivalry in college football forms an exception to this pattern. In this rivalry, no borders are disputed. No conference championships are at stake. No prize is bestowed by the military commander in chief. No trophy of any kind was awarded until twenty-six years after the first game, when a jeweled shillelagh became the symbol of pride and honor for the victor. For almost a century, mutual respect has been the ideal in this rivalry, where hatred normally prevails amid such heated competition.

This rivalry began not in the earliest days of football, as did the one between Harvard and Yale, but in the second decade of the twentieth century. It was a time of rapid industrial development that made regular long-distance travel practical. Only then could two widely separated foes form such a strong bond. Later the college football system would become too fixed, and national attention too distracted, to allow a similar rivalry to develop. No series begun after this one remains the same sort of major annual tradition decades later.

This unique rivalry is the football series between the Fighting Irish of Notre Dame (also known in the early days as the Ramblers) and the Trojans of the University of Southern California. It exists because the right two people, from two very different backgrounds, faced off at exactly the right time in history.

Acknowledgments

I would like to express my appreciation to all those who provided support and assistance in the creation of this book. Charles Lamb at Notre Dame, Tim Tessalone at the University of Southern California, and Jeremy Brett at the University of Iowa were instrumental in making their archival material available. Emily Nusbaum at Yale likewise helped access materials from that school's holdings. To everyone at the Central Branch of the Los Angeles Public Library, the Orange County Public Library System, and the USC Library, I give thanks. Lizz Zitron of the Pacific Lutheran University Library went out of her way for me. I should also note the service provided by the companies operating the websites Newspapers.com and Newspaperarchive.com. The depth and breadth of detail in this book would have been impossible without their archives.

I have made many new acquaintances during this journey who allowed me into their homes or otherwise granted access to family members who lived through the events in this book. Among these are Bernadette Vargas, Jacque and Rod Swerdfeger, and Charles Schindler. Joyce Nelson and Milo Sweet Jr. were also very generous in sharing their families' legacies. My great thanks go to Ross Browner for sharing his perspective on the football rivalry in his foreword. Many people helped obtain images to be reproduced within these pages. Among them are Dawn Childress at the UCLA Library, Cari Hillman at the MidPointe Library System, Karen and John Hickey, Steven Shook, Steve Cantamessa, and Susan Cheas.

The work of many authors inspired me, including Jim Dent, Michael Rosenberg, Ray Robinson, Jim Lefebvre, Jack Cavanaugh, Todd

Tucker, and Murray Sperber. Don Lechman not only recorded history in his own writing but also proved instrumental in supporting mine.

My unending gratitude is extended to everyone at Kent State University Press. William Underwood, Mary Young, Susan Cash, and Christine Brooks were all professional and supportive throughout the path to publication. I'm sure there are others there whose names I never learned. Joyce Harrison has moved on to greener pastures at another university, but it was she who saw the potential in my ideas and encouraged me to stick with it. Marian Buda's editing was instrumental in hammering out the final product.

Among the family and friends I should acknowledge are my late parents, who raised me on stories of Los Angeles in the Roaring Twenties, my sister Susannah and my brothers Bill and John, for helping me with research and advice, Mark Alberici, for always believing in the project, and George Chumo, for providing support and encouragement when it was sometimes in short supply. My wife's parents, Bob and Kathy Nelson, were always there to lend a helping hand when it was needed. There were others providing encouragement along the way, including Marc Burdell, Sean Keneally, and Paul McDonald. Above all, I am thankful that my wife, Cindy, supported me through thick and thin. I forgive her for rooting for the Irish when they play the Trojans.

Finally, my gratitude to the readers. Without you, there is no reason to write.

1

The Beginning of the New

The uncertainties of 1919 were over. America was on the greatest, gaudiest spree in history.

—F. Scott Fitzgerald, 1920

It was a time unlike any that had come before. Begun in sorrow, it would end in ruin, with the days between contrasting the innocence of the old with the shock of the new. Bold ideas arose to clash with backward thinking, as modern science developed alongside outbreaks of mass hysteria. People yearned to cast aside worry and doubt amid upheaval and uncertainty, and live life in the moment. Frivolity was king. It was the "Era of Wonderful Nonsense."[1]

Money and success spilled over the seething cauldron of change until a roiling cloud of unrepentant decadence wafted across the nation. It stung the senses and inflamed simmering passions. It teased the eye with hemlines cut above the knee and shook the ground as a Duesenberg rumbled down the boulevard. It moved you with a crazy beat, and quenched your thirst with the bitter sting of bootleg hooch. Exuberance was everywhere, driven by limitless optimism amid the celebration of unbridled excess. It seemed that everything was awash in bright lights and wrapped in polished chrome. It was the time of Gatsby, of speakeasies, when everyone was hip to the jive. People called it the Roaring Twenties, or the Jazz Age. They were good times, maybe the best times—while they lasted.

Having fun became America's pastime, and the passion for having a good time burned twice as hot as a firecracker on the Fourth of July.

Americans had grown tired of being tired. They were starving for fun, thirsty for thrills, and desperate to suppress all the bad memories of the worst days the nation had seen since the Civil War.

This desperate quest for pleasure had been brewing almost since the day Congress declared war in the spring of 1917. By the time an armistice was signed toward the end of 1918, the world had been fighting for more than four years. Europe was shattered. Although the Yanks had come to the battle later than most nations, the Great War had also left its scars on America. There was enough sorrow around the globe to scar a whole "Lost Generation," as Gertrude Stein had dubbed the listless souls who'd survived the carnage.

Well before the guns had fallen silent, the death and decay of war had spawned an influenza virus that morphed into a worldwide pandemic. It was a scourge that snatched more souls from hospital beds than had been cut down on the battlefield.[2] Economic collapse followed the end of hostilities, both in 1918 and again in 1920, to pile financial ruin on top of the already devastating cost of lost and shattered lives.

When it was over, Americans were looking for change and were desperate for better days. President Warren Harding won his electoral victory in 1920 with the slogan "A Return to Normalcy."[3] In reality the world would never really be "normal" again—at least, never the same as it had been before. The transformation that would come in the decade of the 1920s marked the end of the old world and the beginning of the new.

World War I had toppled kings and potentates, dissolved three great empires, and redrawn the maps of Europe and the Middle East. It had spawned political movements that persist a century later. Science and modern engineering had revolutionized the art of war through the efficiency of the assembly line, but it also had stimulated the development of technologies that would change the peacetime world. The automobile and the airplane increased mobility, and radio waves brought distant people together without travel. Industrialization enticed people from the farm into the factory, making city dwellers out of country folk. Even the roles of men and women began a fundamental shift.

Everyone started hustling. By 1925, "40 percent of workers in the United States earned at least $2,000 annually—which would adequately if not extravagantly support a family of four."[4] Ten years before it had been half that.[5] Soon everyone felt like a high roller. Eventually, even shoeshine boys were trading stock tips.

Industry demanded efficiency, and efficiency brought prosperity, and with it a shorter workweek. People needed something to do with the spare time that the relentless routine of farm life had never allowed.[6] So they gathered around the radio, danced the Charleston, or played exotic board games like mah-jongg. They were going crazy for fads—pogo sticks, roller skates, yo-yos—and entering all kinds of absurd contests, like goldfish eating and kissing marathons. Everyone wanted to feel young, live fast, and stay on the make. Nothing expressed that ideal of youth and vitality better than the heroic exploits of the athletic champion. The love of sport grew so fast and became so widespread that the Roaring Twenties also became known as the Golden Age of Sports.

The mania for games helped suppress the bitter memories of war and despair still fresh in the public mind. Football, a sport so brutal that it had nearly been outlawed a decade earlier, suddenly became a wholesome activity, at least compared to combat. Even before America had been drawn into the war, the *New York Times* had expressed this changing attitude toward football by comparing "Europe distorted with war real and awful" to the "exhibition of friendly rivalry within a big-hearted neutral nation" displayed in the annual Harvard-versus-Yale football game.[7]

Grantland Rice, a syndicated columnist and a war veteran, wrote a piece in 1919 that explained the growing love of sport in the context of a world scarred by hot lead and cold steel. "With the return of peace it was only natural that there should be . . . an almost universal desire for recreation and for play" he wrote, " . . . where it was more man against man, rather than man against machine."

Rice foresaw "the greatest international competition that sport and outdoor life have ever known."[8] His prediction soon came true. Athletics grew so popular, and were portrayed so dramatically by writers such as Rice, that in the 1920s sports became a metaphor for life itself.

Sportswriters practiced a "gee whiz" brand of journalism that projected the hopes and struggles of common people onto the exhilarating triumphs and tragic failures of flamboyant ballplayers, dashing gridiron heroes, and rough-hewn pugilists.[9] Men with everyday names like

Babe Ruth, Red Grange, and Jack Dempsey became the Bambino, the Galloping Ghost, and the Manassa Mauler.

A quick thinking go-getter by the name of Christy Walsh did the scribes one better by signing those top athletes and then leveraging their reputations to rake in endorsements and generate all manner of revenue off the field. Walsh controlled a carefully crafted narrative that the public adored. Ty Cobb, Lou Gehrig, Babe Ruth, Glenn "Pop" Warner, and many others became his clients. All were legends in their own right, but one man among his pantheon of stars stood alone atop not only the sports world but also perhaps even celebrity itself. That man was Knute Rockne of Notre Dame.

Notre Dame's Knute Rockne was more than a football coach. On or off the gridiron, he was always the ultimate salesman. (Image courtesy of Notre Dame Archives.)

Today, hearing the name Rockne rekindles the flame of nearly extin-guished memories that cast a warm glow on legendary exploits of the past. Like all legends, Rockne's was built on the life of a real man who lived and breathed, who won and lost, who erred at times yet made good again. So much of this man's life has been recorded, studied, de-bated, and celebrated for so long that single facets of his character have filled entire volumes.

His exploits, which even at face value stand unequaled in many cases, have been so embellished over the years that at times it is very difficult to separate truth from myth. Like the tale of George Wash-ington cutting down the cherry tree, the old stories live on: Rockne invented the forward pass, his backfield shift was inspired by a theat-rical chorus line, he was so brilliant that he might have been a world-famous chemist instead of the nation's leading football coach, and so on. None of these tales is strictly factual, yet they all contain a germ of truth, and retelling them sustains Rockne's legend long after the verac-ity of details has been discredited. Even his first name, Knute, is usu-ally pronounced incorrectly today, with the *K* rendered silent instead of properly voiced, as in the Danish name Canute.

On the other hand, the basic facts of Rockne's birth in Norway, child-hood in Chicago, and adult life in Indiana are widely known and easy to document. Rockne's growth from standout track athlete and foot-ball player in his youth to winning and innovative coach and teacher; sought-after public speaker, columnist, and author; and effective prod-uct pitchman, broadcaster, and filmmaker; as well as successful sales manager, sporting goods designer, stockbroker, administrator, busi-nessman, and entrepreneur, is attributable to the sheer force of his in-tellect and personality.

In many ways, Rockne *was* Notre Dame, at least in the public's mind. Despite the best efforts of those at the college who stressed its more aca-demic achievements, Knute Rockne's very being came to personify the Notre Dame mystique. The scriptural passage "Upon this Rock," with which Catholic theology buttresses the office of the papacy, could just as accurately describe the foundation of renown that Rockne's famous foot-ball program had brought the school. Notre Dame's growth was often tied to the success of Rockne's football teams, starting from his days as a student athlete there and culminating in his tenure as America's most famous and successful head coach. By the time of Rockne's death, Notre Dame football had become the embodiment of Catholic righteousness, in an act of transubstantiation as mystical as the mysterious conversion of a communion wafer.

Before Rockne, Notre Dame was hardly synonymous with the game of football. Rev. Edward Sorin, a French priest within the Congregation of Holy Cross, founded the school in 1842.[10] Excellence in the classroom was the primary goal, but while the accomplishments of the most brilliant of academics might go largely unnoticed outside ivy-covered walls, headlines on Sunday mornings extolling the previous day's exploits on the football field cast the glory of the team's latest victory upon the whole school. In the Golden Age of Sports, it was the gridiron, not the lecture hall, that captured the public's imagination. This was a troublesome reality at times for the school's administration, and the struggle between athletics and academics would continue at Notre Dame well past Rockne's era and at least through Frank Leahy's tenure two decades later.[11]

Before Notre Dame's devotion to football rose to this near-veneration, its raison d'être was simply to serve the educational needs of the country's Catholic population, which had been a minority even from colonial times. Though many of the earliest explorers claiming territory in North America during the Age of Discovery did so for the Catholic monarchies of Spain and France, the English colonization of the Atlantic coast meant that Protestants soon became the majority in what would later become the United States. Friction with that Protestant majority, reflecting a history of religious strife in Europe, left Catholics chafing at what they considered second-class status. The fact that many Catholics who came to America in the great migrations of the late nineteenth and early twentieth centuries were poor, uneducated, and did not understand English only increased the prejudice against them.

As the Notre Dame football team began to score victories over the titans of the day, many of them East Coast colleges perceived as symbols of the Protestant power structure, the school's popularity grew until it became the standard-bearer for Catholics everywhere. Many of the team's fans were city dwellers, most famously Irish from New York City and Chicago, who would never set foot on the grounds of Notre Dame or any other campus. It was largely through these "subway alumni" that Rockne touched the public far beyond football and, in the process, rose well above the field of play.

Of course Rockne shared the spotlight with other famous football coaches of his day. Pop Warner, Fielding Yost, and Amos Alonzo Stag likewise made headlines and enjoyed great renown. While none were equals, many aspired to be rivals. Only one of Rockne's contemporaries could truly make that claim, if a rivalry must be forged not just with competing newspaper headlines but through direct opposition on the field of play. Only one coach who earned such high acclaim also scheduled Rockne's teams year after year. He was a man as different from Rockne as could be imagined. That man was Howard Harding Jones.

Jones was another of the very first professional football coaches to emerge from the ranks of the gentleman amateur who dominated sports

Howard Harding Jones, Southern California's Headman, c. 1925. (Image courtesy of USC Digital Library.)

in the early 1900s. In that era, many colleges relied on volunteer coaches, chosen by the team captain and often retained only on a yearly basis. It was not until later that the old amateur ideal yielded to the hard reality of professionalism and money.

Unlike Rockne's, Jones's fame did not increase upon his death. While a famous youth league bears Pop Warner's name and a college championship game is called the Amos Alonzo Stagg Bowl, little is left to remind us that Howard Jones was once one of the biggest names in the sport.

While Jones's contributions to the game are seldom noted today, he was a pioneer and an innovator in his own right. He was an excellent defensive coach, who was "probably better than Rockne" in that regard, according to a former Trojan player.[12]

Sometimes dismissed as an imitator of other offensive systems, Jones added ideas of his own to build his system of power football. Warner himself credited Jones with inventing the trap play—just one example of his innovations.[13]

Jones oversaw the implementation of his dictates with the firm hand of a stern taskmaster. His commandments were considered as immutable as those on the stone tablets that Moses carried down from the mountain, and his ire as feared as the wrath of God himself. Yet he seldom meted out punishment in anything approaching biblical fashion, instead showing displeasure in the same stoic fashion he displayed in almost every facet of his life. It was said that he "never barks at his men."[14] A simple glance or quiet demotion to the second team spoke louder than words. Yet Jones's expectations were so strict and uncompromising that they eventually earned him a nickname as simple and strong as his beliefs—"Headman."

As a person, Howard Jones was everything Rockne was not, and every descriptive term that failed to define Rockne fit Jones to a T.[15] A simple comparison of their backgrounds reveals that while the title "All-American" became associated with Rockne through a film released nearly a decade after his death, the moniker actually fit Jones better.

Jones was born in Ohio to a prominent family, while Rockne was born the son of Lars Rockne, a carriage maker of modest means in Voss, Norway. Jones lived an idyllic "Huckleberry Finn" childhood, hunting, fishing, and exploring the hills and woods of southwest Ohio,[16] before attending the finest Eastern schools, while Rockne grew up on the

rough-and-tumble streets of Chicago and worked for the post office before enrolling at Notre Dame, which was not considered an elite school
at the time.[17]

Jones never had to assimilate into a foreign culture, nor was he forced
to adopt a new language as had Rockne. Born into money, Jones never
had to concern himself with finances, unlike Rockne, whose family had
modest means. Long after the poor immigrant boy grew into a wildly

Rockne's family left tranquil Voss, Norway, to settle just a few miles from this urban
canyon, Chicago's Randolph Street, shown here c. 1900. The Windy City likewise
contrasted sharply with the rural peace of Jones's childhood home in Excello, Ohio.
(Image from author's collection.)

successful and financially secure adult, Rockne remained overly concerned with matters of money.

The two men diverged politically as well. Howard Jones belonged to a prominent Republican family. His uncle, John Eugene Harding, was elected to the Ohio Senate in 1902 and then to the U.S. House of Representatives in 1906. In contrast, Rockne, after converting to Catholicism, was pressured to support fellow Catholic Al Smith during that Democrat's run for the White House in 1928, though, aside from a few examples such as his name appearing on campaign posters, there was little evidence of outspoken support.[18]

The stability of their coaching careers also differed. Rockne stayed with the same school where he had been a player, and though he would often flirt with other opportunities, he remained loyal to Notre Dame to the end. By contrast, Jones coached at Syracuse, Yale, Ohio State, Iowa, and Trinity (today's Duke) before ending his career at the University of Southern California.

Howard Jones's boyhood home in Excello, Ohio, c. 1895. The dwelling was located across the street from the family paper mill. (Image courtesy of Middletown Library.)

Rockne, shown here as a student at Notre Dame, c. 1913, lettered in both football and track. (Image courtesy of Notre Dame Archives.)

The two men were also very different in appearance and manner. Jones stood taller and trimmer than Rockne, had a more prominent nose, and would retain a full head of hair throughout his life, while Rockne's famously squashed beak and bald head were the most outstanding features of his instantly recognizable visage. Deep creases would etch Jones's face as he grew older, but he was a handsome man in his youth, with the dignified air befitting his patrician breeding. Rockne looked more like a working stiff and already seemed almost middle-aged not long after he left college.[19]

However, it was not their outward differences but the inner workings of the two men's personalities that stood in sharpest contrast. Howard Jones, a man of few words and little visible emotion, would remain something of a mystery to even his closest associates,[20] while Rockne, personifying the charm and charisma of a superstar salesman, was a master of emotional manipulation, so likable that almost everyone in America seemed to count him as a friend, regardless of whether they'd ever met the man.[21] Jones married twice, with both unions filled with unhappiness, while Rockne remained a devoted husband to the only woman he ever loved, raising four children with her.

In short, if one were to seek out the exact opposite of Knute Rockne among his fellow coaches, it would be hard to find a more compelling example than Howard Jones. From the very beginning, the two men followed different paths, although their separate roads would cross even before the two had met and well before the impact of that intersection was fully understood.

Prelude to Greatness

The duty of the man of wealth . . . set an example of modest,
unostentatious living, shunning display or extravagance.
—Andrew Carnegie, 1899

Howard Jones was born in Excello, Ohio, in 1885, as the era historians call the Gilded Age was drawing to a close. The country was growing, pushing west, and breaking new ground. Factories were humming across America, railroad tycoons were crisscrossing the continent with ribbons of steel, and the first skyscrapers were rising above the nation's cities.

Jones was three years old when Rockne was born in Norway, and he was eight when Rockne arrived in the United States to join the hordes of immigrants pouring into America's growing cities. As Rockne's parents worked to carve out a niche in their new world, Jones was enjoying the secure place his family had already built. They owned the paper mill along the canal running through town, and if he had wanted to, Howard could have settled into a comfortable career within the family business instead of pursuing coaching.[1]

Howard was the first of five children born to Thomas Albert Jones and Sarah Adelaide Harding. Young Howard began playing football with the neighborhood kids and then at nearby Middletown High School until he was packed off to an exclusive boarding school in Exeter, New Hampshire, with his brother Thomas Albert Dwight ("Tad") Jones, who was two years his junior.[2] After their days at Phillips Exeter

Academy, both Howard and Tad would go on to play for Yale, and still later, both brothers would become famous college football coaches.

Like Rockne, Jones played two sports, but while Rockne ran track, Howard's other game was baseball.[3] On the gridiron, Jones lined up at left end, the same position that Rockne would play a few years later at Notre Dame, one of several parallels in the lives of Jones and Rockne that involved football. A vastly different rule book governed Jones's playing days, however, than the one Rockne played under.

Gridiron football evolved from the English game of rugby, which itself emerged in an officially sanctioned form in 1871 from a mishmash of different versions, each with its own rules. Ball games featuring kicking and tackling date back at least to the ancient Roman game of harpastum, and some forms of rugby were being played in America for decades before the 1870s, many specific to individual colleges, such as Princeton University's ballown (dating from the 1820s) and Dartmouth University's Old Division football (dating from the 1830s). The game became more widely popular in the United States in the 1870s, when Ivy League colleges began having intercollegiate matches.[4] In 1880, Walter Camp devised the line of scrimmage and down sequence rules that cleaved American "gridiron" football from its British precursor.

In the United States before 1910, the game featured the same 110-yard field and three-down sequence still used in Canada. The form played in those early days, however, unlike that played in Canada today, had no end zones, so the ball had to be carried over the end line to score a touchdown. Also, a touchdown earned just five points then, compared to four points for kicking a field goal.[5] During this period of Jones's youth, the game was a primitive forerunner of its current incarnation, but over the next three decades, Jones would see these and many other aspects of the game change, maturing—often with his input on various rule committees—into something more recognizable to football fans today.

During Jones's three varsity years at Yale, from 1905 through 1907, his football teams never tasted defeat, beating Yale's archrival, Harvard, in all three matches and claiming a trio of national championships. But though Howard Jones was a good athlete, it was his "more famous" brother, the All-American quarterback Tad Jones, who became the star.[6] While Howard and Tad did not quite embody the fictional George and Harry Bailey in the film *It's a Wonderful Life,* in which George lived in the shadow of younger brother Harry, the football star, Howard did toil in relative obscurity while his sibling earned acclaim in the backfield.[7]

Though Howard, like Rockne, was made a team captain, the *New York Times* described his athletic career at Yale as "substantial, although not brilliant," adding that a "right arm ruined by pitching" in baseball and a "shoulder . . . badly damaged" in football—both at Exeter—had left him "a crippled athlete." However, the same article foreshadowed his future in coaching by judging him "one of the brainiest of baseball and football players."[8]

Upon his graduation in 1908, though, with injuries limiting his professional prospects in athletics and the low pay common in sports careers hardly attractive to a man of his breeding, Jones initially planned to pursue a career in business instead. Then an offer to become the head coach at Syracuse University persuaded him to forgo that idea, through the football season at least. His record that rookie year was a respectable 6–3–1, including a 28–4 drubbing of Michigan in the season finale.

In those days, the Yale coach was selected by the captain and normally given just a one-year term; only once between 1900 and 1916 did Yale enjoy the continuity of the same head coach serving two consecutive years. In late 1908, Yale captain Ted Coy sought Jones's services as coach for the 1909 season, an offer that may have reflected the Syracuse Orangemen's strong performance in a close loss to Yale that season. There were rumors that the Naval Academy had made a competing offer to Jones, but in the end he made his way back to New Haven.[9]

The Bulldogs marched through their first nine games of 1909, including a win over Syracuse, Jones's former team of the prior season. That 15–0 win came at the expense of his brother Tad, who had followed Howard as coach at Syracuse. Identical 17–0 shutouts of Army and Princeton highlighted the Bulldogs' remaining games before the showdown with Harvard in "The Game" in the final contest of the season.

That 1909 game against Harvard was Jones's first real taste of the new kind of blockbuster football "events" that would become almost commonplace a few years later. Harvard and Yale were, and remain today, two of the most prestigious universities in America. At the time they were also two of the biggest powers in college football. Both teams were undefeated. Harvard's team had outscored its opponents 103–9, while Yale's had bested their foes 201–0. Their matchup drew national attention. Tickets were scalped for many times face value, and the New Haven Railroad was forced to add fifteen trains to handle the flow of rabid fans heading into Cambridge, Massachusetts. On game day, thirty-eight thousand fans filled the stadium to capacity.[10]

Howard Jones's squad bested the Crimson 8–0, and the first perfect season of his coaching career was complete. Yale had not been scored upon all season, an astounding feat not to be repeated in all his years on the sideline.

At season's end, Howard Jones was faced with a choice. He could remain in coaching or choose a more conventional business career that would pay enough to marry and raise a family. Sport as a profession was still in the formative stages. Few could support a family on the wages that were offered. However, the process of industrialization was starting to change things. As mechanized factories increased productivity, requiring fewer hours for better wages than farm jobs, the public could enjoy more free time than ever before—time that could be spent on leisure activities, including sports. With more ticket sales came more revenue and higher pay for those involved, but things evolved slowly.[11] Pro boxing purses were not really big enough for most athletes to make ends meet in the ring alone. Barnstorming baseball teams had been around for almost half a century, but Major League Baseball as we know it had only begun in 1903 when the first modern World Series was arranged between the champions of the older National League and the upstart American League. As for football, not many college coaches were paid, and those who did draw salaries were not enriching themselves by any means, while public opinion held, as Jimmy Breslin later put it, that pro football was good only "to keep coal miners off the streets."

Faced with these realities, Jones made his decision and resigned from Yale at the end of the year. "I will not go back to Yale," he declared in a statement to the *Syracuse Herald* published on December 17, 1909, adding "I am done with coaching, and while I will continue to take a great deal of interest in football and may go back for a day or two before the big games next fall, I will not do any more coaching. It is time for me to get down to work."[12]

Despite these strong pronouncements, the same Syracuse newspaper printed hints of Jones's lingering desire to return to coaching just three days later: "Right on top of the announcement from Howard Jones that he is through with coaching comes the report from Columbus, O[hio], that he has been elected coach of the Ohio State University eleven for next fall and will probably accept."[13]

Howard did spend the 1910 season in Columbus, recording a 6–1–3 mark, with every game played in his native state, Ohio. The one loss that year was to Case Institute of Technology, the only game not played on the Buckeyes' home field.

Throughout this period, Howard retained his permanent residence in Excello. During the summer of 1911, he met a young society girl from Denver named Leah Clark, who was visiting friends in nearby Middletown. Their courtship was notable enough to make the newspapers clear out on the West Coast. The *Los Angeles Times* ran an article on the whirlwind engagement, calling it "a case of love at first sight," with the announcement coming just one day after they met.

The story quoted his brother's enthusiastic approval. "That's the stuff," Tad said. "That brother of mine has shown himself to be as good in love as he is on the gridiron." Opining further on the state of modern romance, he added, "You can't handle them with sweet talk as it used to be done. The modern girl wants to be taken by storm." Tad credited Howard's romantic prowess to his football training. "A woman has to be rushed off their [*sic*] feet," he explained.[14]

The couple married on September 14, 1911. They settled down to life at the Hotel St. George in Brooklyn on October 1,[15] and for two years Howard worked in New York City for the American Writing Paper Company, which owned the Excello paper mill at the time.[16]

Leah Jones may have looked forward to a comfortable position as a successful businessman's wife enjoying the glittering nightlife of New York City, but it was not to be. Unfortunately for her, football was his "first love," and his mind was preoccupied with the game.[17]

Talk of bringing back Jones to resurrect the flagging Yale football program began as soon as the final whistle sounded in the Bulldogs' 20–0 loss to Harvard at the end of the 1912 season.[18] It had been Yale's fourth straight loss to the Crimson and the third in a row in which the Elis had failed to score against their archrivals. Around that same time, rumors began spreading that Yale was considering dropping Army from their schedule, a move that would buck a twenty-year tradition of scheduling Army in late October or early November.[19]

In January 1913, Yale formally announced decisions on both these issues. Despite adding a tenth game to their season, the Bulldogs confirmed scheduling changes in which they dropped Syracuse for Maine and replaced Army with Lehigh. Then Yale announced that Howard Jones would become the first paid coach in the Bulldogs' history. It was a one-year assignment, but it came at an unforeseen but crucial time in the history of football.[20]

Yale's moves left Army coach Charlie Daly in a bind. With the other major Eastern powers already booked, he would have to scramble to fill the open date Yale had created. He knew any available school was bound to be second rate, and he left the job of finding a worthy opponent to his student manager, Hal Loomis. Loomis answered an inquiry from a small college in Indiana, eventually agreeing to the school's demand for a $1,000 guarantee for coming to play Army at West Point. Notre Dame's coach, Jesse Harper, insisted on that financial detail, and the deal was eventually signed.[21]

The game between Army and Notre Dame turned out to be a shocker, a milestone in the evolution of football. Rockne, playing left end, and his quarterback, Gus Dorais, made history by stunning the heavily favored Cadets with a dazzling display of a passing game that had not been seen in an era of football dominated by the ground attack. "Notre Dame's Open Play Amazes Army," ran the headline on the game in the *New York Times* the next day. The unnamed writer marveled at the visitors' unstoppable offensive attack. Calling it "the most sensational football that has been seen in the East this year," he noted that "the yellow leather egg was in the air half the time," adding, "the Army players were hopelessly confused." Although the article singled out the play of quarterback Dorais, Rockne's pass catching on offense and his tackling on defense also drew praise. This was the first time that Rockne really grabbed the attention of New York sportswriters, but it was not the last occasion that he'd make headlines in the Big Apple.[22]

The upset of Army marked the first step in transforming Knute Rockne from mortal to legend. It also linked Rockne to Jones for the first time. The bridge between the two was Yale. The school had put

Rockne into the spotlight by making the famous game possible when it dropped Army, and it had put Jones into the spotlight by making him the coach of an Ivy League power at the exact same time.

The game with Army helped propel Rockne to third team All-American honors his senior year. He was the first Notre Dame player to win that honor.[23] After graduation, Rockne, like Jones before him, considered coaching offers. He looked at possibilities elsewhere but stayed at Notre Dame as an assistant coach to Jesse Harper. With a full-time job to support him, and with side income from coaching local professional teams, he married Bonnie Skiles, a "pious and devout young lady" (as the priest who married them described her), on July 15, 1914.[24] The wedding took place just two weeks after Archduke Ferdinand was shot in Bosnia, setting in motion the crisis that launched the First World War.

Rockne met his future bride while both were working vacation jobs at a resort in Wisconsin between college terms. That summer, Rockne had divided his free time between wooing Bonnie and working on passing techniques with teammate Gus Dorais, a preparation that paid off handsomely when Notre Dame faced Army in the fall.[25]

A few months before Rockne's wedding, in February 1914, Howard and Leah Jones celebrated the birth of their son, Clark Harding Jones. After coaching at Yale, Howard spent the next two years in business and away from coaching, except for helping with the Eli squad on a volunteer basis as his schedule allowed.[26] His business career was short-lived, for although he tried to leave it behind, football could never abandon Howard Jones. In 1916, Howard quit the business world as his full-time vocation for good, and the family left for Iowa.

Reed Lane, a classmate of Howard's from his days at Exeter, was a local businessman there and a member of the State University of Iowa Athletic Board, which was seeking to replace part-time coach Jesse B. Hawley with someone willing to work full-time. Reed suggested approaching Jones, and on December 20, 1915, the university announced Jones's appointment as the new man in charge of the Hawkeyes, with a five-year contract reportedly paying $4,500 per year.[27]

Iowa's dean of pharmacy, Wilber Teeters, called Jones "a quiet, modest, unassuming young man, filled with life and vitality and a natural leader." A reference letter from Thomas French, president of the athletic

Howard Jones in 1917, shortly after arriving at the University of Iowa. (Image courtesy of the University of Iowa.)

board at Ohio State, described Jones as "an exceedingly close student of the game . . . [whose] actions rather than words [provided] evidence of this," adding that Jones, "does no talking in regard to his ability."[28]

Howard Jones soon moved his wife Leah and son Clark to Iowa City, lodging at the Jefferson Hotel there until a permanent home for the family could be found.[29] Jones would later describe the job as "anything but promising."[30]

The task at hand was making the Hawkeyes competitive in the Western Conference, as the Big Ten (actually nine schools then) was known at the time. Iowa had finished in seventh place in 1915, with a record of 3–4–0, and had failed to place any players on All-Conference teams when the selections were announced at season's end. At least one of those all-stars, Laurens Shull, was an Iowa native, so Jones's first priority was keeping local talent at home, although he would need to develop better material wherever it could be found.

Jones's first campaign at Iowa got off to a good start, with his team winning its first three games, against Cornell, Grinnell of Iowa, and Purdue, by a total of 72–19. The bottom fell out the following week, when

Jones took his team to Minnesota to face the Golden Gophers. They handed Jones the worst defeat of his career, overwhelming his under-manned squad by 67–0.

With a week off between games, and powerhouse Nebraska sched-uled for the final week, Jones traveled to Lincoln to scout the Cornhusk-ers on the fifth weekend of the season. Big Red was facing Iowa State that day, and several coaches looking for an edge in upcoming games against Nebraska crowded into the press box at Nebraska Field to take notes. Among them was Notre Dame assistant Knute Rockne. His boss, Jesse Harper, had sent Rockne to gather the dope on the Cornhuskers while Harper traveled to West Point to oversee the game with Army.[31]

Neither Iowa nor Notre Dame benefited from their coaches' scout-ing trips. Both teams were blown out by Nebraska later in the season, but something more important came out of that press box in Lincoln— Howard Jones and Knute Rockne were introduced to one another. Five years later they would meet again and start down parallel roads. Their paths would cross a third time a decade after their first encounter, with Nebraska again playing a key role.

Jones was made the second athletic director in Iowa's history the fol-lowing year, replacing Nelson A. Kellogg. Kellogg, an Army reservist, was called up for duty in 1917 to serve with the American forces en-tering World War I.[32] Jones's own draft card had a registration date of September 12, 1918, the day of the Third Registration of the Selective Service Act of 1917, which required men aged thirty-one to forty-five to sign up. Jones's status as a local official would have made him Class III—"exempted, but available for military service."[33] In any case, the war ended on November 11, 1918, just two months after Jones registered.

Jones was finishing his third season at Iowa as the war came to a close, while Rockne was completing his first year as the new head coach at Notre Dame. Jesse Harper, Rockne's mentor and his coach during his playing days, had left Notre Dame earlier in the year to take over for a deceased relative who had been running the family ranch in Kansas. Harper recommended his protégé for the job, and, like Jones, Rockne was also named to the post of athletic director, a position Harper had also held. With one child already, three-year-old William, and another on the way, Rockne welcomed the raise in pay. By the first kickoff of 1918, he was the proud father of a second son, Knute Jr.[34]

Jones had not shown much improvement at Iowa up to that point, having gone just 7–9–0 in his first two years. Rockne, on the other hand, was about to take the second step on his road to glory. This time he'd get a little help from a speedy halfback from Larium, Michigan. That halfback was another South Bend hero destined to become a legend.

Almost Ready to Roar

Well, what are we waiting for?

—Knute Rockne, 1928

George Gipp was lanky for a football player, standing six feet tall and weighing no more than 180 pounds. He was a naturally gifted athlete, with so much raw talent that he never really had to expend much effort to succeed. When he arrived from his hometown in Michigan, he could effortlessly run one hundred yards fully clothed in 10.2 seconds, without the benefit of training.[1] At Notre Dame, he often would stay out all night before a game and still be the best player on the field the next day.[2] He was Rockne's problem child—a coach's dream on the field and a pain in the ass off it. A preacher's son, he drank, gambled, hustled pool, and generally caroused till all hours. The one thing he seldom did was go to class, but Rockne was always able to pull enough strings to keep his star pupil eligible for Saturdays in the fall.

Gipp joined the varsity in 1917, while Rockne was still an assistant. Rockne's debut as head coach came a year later, on September 28, 1918, when Notre Dame played against the Case Institute of Technology in Cleveland, Ohio. The venue was a less than majestic setting in which to showcase two future Notre Dame icons. Van Horn Field was a modest facility with low wooden bleachers perhaps twelve rows high, plus a central section twice that size covered with a barnlike roof supported by steel girders that blocked the view of the game every five yards or so.[3] The hardscrabble playing field was a patchwork of dirt and grass, but the footing proved good enough for Gipp and his teammates. In the

Rockne made his 1918 debut as head coach at Van Horn Field in Cleveland, Ohio, just before the football craze took off after World War I. A decade later, he would face his rival Howard Jones before crowds exceeding 100,000 fans. (Image property of Case Western Reserve University Archives.)

second half of the game, Notre Dame pulled away to easily win the game 26–6. Fortunately for Gipp and his coach, the war year of 1918 was ruled "unofficial." Gipp's transcripts didn't record a single credit for the year, so the fact that participation was not counted against the players' four years of eligibility allowed him to return to the field in 1919.[4]

Meanwhile, Howard Jones was making steady, if slow, progress toward installing his system at Iowa. Despite lackluster results in his first two years there, things began looking up in 1918. Jones was bringing in a new crop of players, among them a promising freshman lineman by the name of Frederick Wayman Slater. Like Gipp, Slater was a preacher's son, although he wasn't the hell-raiser Gipp was. Also like Gipp, he became one of the greatest players of the early days of football.

Slater, like another of Jones's linemen years later, had picked up the nickname "Duke," and both he and the guy at USC had taken that moniker from the family dog. Unlike Trojan Marion Morrison, however, Slater earned his fame both on and off the field. Slater stood out for other reasons in addition to his athletic talent, and the difference was obvious the instant you saw him. Slater was African American.

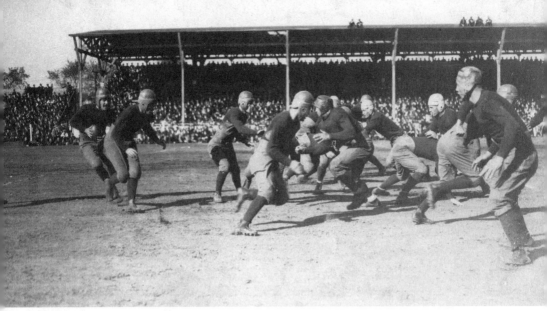

Rockne's first big star, George Gipp, carries the ball c. 1919. (Image courtesy of Notre Dame Archives.)

Slater was born on the south side of Chicago in December 1898. Despite being poor and black in an age of open discrimination, and despite having been uprooted to Iowa at the age of thirteen, Duke Slater rose to prominence, first in college football, then in the NFL, and finally as a trailblazing attorney and judge back in his native Illinois.[5] Slater was the first of a handful of black players that Jones would coach over the years, with two of them earning All-American honors. Rockne's teams, on the other hand, never had a single black player on the roster in all his years at Notre Dame.

Among the notable events in Slater's freshman year of 1918 was a bizarre game between Iowa and Coe College played at the height of the influenza scare, at which spectators were banned completely, a decision enforced by "locked gates and armed guards," according to Iowa City's *Press-Citizen*. "If anyone watches the battle from the Iowa river bridges, or from the over-towering west side hills, they may not escape a bayoneting by the soldiers," the newspaper warned. "The game is absolutely barricaded against all non-playing customers."[6] Inside the stadium the stands were empty, save for a contingent of military trainees who were the only ones on hand not directly involved with the contest.

The reporting after the game was understandably sparse, but the 27–0 outcome in favor of Howard Jones's eleven was recorded. It was ever

NOTRE DAME vs
SOLDIER

In stark contrast to earlier days at places like Van Horn Field, Chicago's Soldier Field was the site where the Irish hosted the Trojans in 1927, before a mammoth crowd of well over one hundred thousand fans, including the mayors of Los Angeles, New York, and Chicago and the underworld boss of the Windy City, Al Capone. (Image courtesy of Notre Dame Archives.)

thus with Coach Jones: he won games but sometimes failed to make the same kind of headlines that Rockne did. Like a game played in an empty stadium, Howard Jones's triumphs never seemed to get the same fanfare as Notre Dame's, denying him a level of fame that would echo well past his lifetime.

In 1918, however, people were taking notice. Overall, both coaches were building momentum during the season, recruiting freshmen who were made eligible because of the wartime shortage of talent. Rockne went just 3–1–2 for the year, but a loss to Michigan State in mid-November would be his last defeat until the third game of 1921. Howard Jones fared better in 1918, rebounding from an early loss to a military team from the Great Lakes Naval Training Center to go 6–2–1 for the campaign. An especially satisfying win occurred when his Hawkeyes outfought Minnesota's Golden Gophers in a tough 6–0 victory, avenging

UTHERN CALIFORNIA
LD CHICAGO
26, 1927

the worst drubbing of Jones's career, suffered two years earlier, when Minnesota beat Iowa 67–0.

The worst fears of war and disease were dissipating as the 1919 season approached. With the war over, established players were returning to school and young athletes were enrolling in college instead of leaving for military training. Meanwhile, better coaching and a wider effort to build successful football programs helped schools all over the country to field quality teams. It soon became evident that the supremacy of college football's "Big Three"—Princeton, Harvard, and Yale—was waning. Notre Dame had already proven itself equal to an Eastern power by beating Army, and now little Boston College had done the same when its team upset Yale's. Dominance of the game was no longer limited to the Ivy League; soon the best teams would be found in other parts of the country.

Rockne was well placed to capitalize on the westward migration of football dominance. He had a good roster of talent to work with, led by his star running back. Before the first kickoff of the 1919 season, a publicity writer for Rockne asserted that "Gipp is expected to be a prime factor in bringing the championship of Indiana to the Gold and Blue archives."[7] Notre Dame marched through the schedule, mixing hard-fought victories over Nebraska and Army with a string of lopsided wins over the rest of their less formidable opponents. Gipp's nonchalant, effortless style and flair for the dramatic built his reputation, and his team's, as the best in the Midwest.

The size of the crowds at the games grew as word of Notre Dame's prowess spread. Cullum Hall Field at West Point was filled to its capacity of fifteen thousand to witness Gipp lead a comeback win over Army in November 1919. The spectators included some of the first of the "subway Irish"—Notre Dame fans from nearby New York City who flocked to that game to root for the team they considered their own.[8]

Rockne's breakout season of 1919 proved to be the same year that Jones turned the corner at Iowa. Led by Slater, his fellow All-Conference selections Aubrey Devine at quarterback and Fred Lohman at fullback, and All-American end Lester Belding, the Hawkeyes lost just two games by a total of five points.

Conditions in the country at large remained uneven. On the one hand, public health was improving as the decade came to a close, with influenza on the wane. The worst of the pandemic had peaked the year before, and a dwindling number of new cases was being reported in 1919. On the other hand, the nation's economy was barely treading water. Business had slowed with the end of wartime expansion, and although conditions had improved temporarily by the spring of 1919, they collapsed again in January 1920. The struggle to adjust to a peacetime economy caused a depression that was deep and devastating. The collapse in the monetary base was the largest in U.S. history up to that time.[9] So it appeared initially that the new decade might not offer any better opportunities than the last. It must have seemed ironic that just when people might really need a drink, Congress had outlawed their refreshment.

With war and disease behind it, the country applied the crusading spirit that had marched the doughboys off to the "war to end all wars" back in 1917 to a new target: demon alcohol. The temperance movement had triumphed, and in October 1919, Congress overrode President Wilson's veto to pass the Volstead Act, which set out guidelines for the enforcement of the Eighteenth Amendment, passed the previous January. Americans had until midnight, January 17, 1920, to legally buy booze. After that, the country would go dry. At least, it was sup-posed to be that way. For hoodlums like Al Capone, Prohibition would be a tidal wave of opportunity.

By March 1920, Rockne would have been justified in falling into his own personal depression. His best player and team captain, All-Amer-ican George Gipp, had been expelled. Gipp's high living finally had caught up with him. Too many cut classes and too many appearances at unsavory nightspots had done him in. Rockne was not the type to wallow in misfortune, however, and he wasted no time in setting out to restore the eligibility of his greatest weapon.

While rival coaches like Yost and Warner, and General Douglas Mac-Arthur, the superintendent of West Point, vied to obtain Gipp's services for their schools, Rockne made his move. He lobbied local business lead-ers, who in turn pressured Notre Dame's president, Father James Burns, warning him that the loss of a drawing card such as Gipp threatened the planned expansion of Cartier Field.[10] While Burns valued the study hall over the scrimmage field, he also appreciated the value of a dollar and eventually gave in. By the end of April, Gipp was restored to eligibil-ity. To combat the spreading perception of Notre Dame as a "football factory," the story arose that Gipp was reinstated only after passing a rigorous special examination. In one version of the story, Notre Dame's president personally conducted the test. Years later, Notre Dame history professor Robert Burns proclaimed such tales "total fabrications."[11]

Whatever the details of Gipp's redemption, Rockne had one last ob-stacle to overcome. Restored eligibility was one thing. Getting Gipp back in uniform was another. The coach tracked Gipp down in Michigan dur-ing the summer, where he was playing semi-pro baseball, to make sure he would return in the fall. Fielding Yost was after Gipp too, but Rockne was not about to lose his best player to the Wolverines if he could help it. Gipp finally did return to South Bend that fall, just in time for the first game of the 1920 fall season, after skipping training camp.[12]

Rockne and his team powered through the first six games, including a come-from-behind victory over Army. Gipp's incredible performance on the field that day made plenty of noise, but quiet words in the locker room at halftime said more about his character. After Rockne had given the team a pep talk, Gipp assured his coach that while he may have seemed indifferent to Rockne's oration, he was in fact quite interested in the game. After all, Gipp casually informed his coach, he had $500 wagered on the outcome.[13]

By the time Notre Dame traveled to Indianapolis to play Indiana, the seemingly invincible Gipp was showing signs of mortality, resulting in a performance that was undeniably below par. He was nursing injuries, said to be a dislocated shoulder and a broken collarbone. Whether the damage was incurred on or off the field is still debated. Employing a sidearm throwing motion to deal with the pain, and using himself as a decoy to hand off the winning touchdown run, Gipp came off the bench to deliver another come-from-behind victory, extending Notre Dame's winning streak to eighteen games.

In his usual lone wolf style, Gipp got off the team train on the return trip. He had planned to meet up with a former Notre Dame teammate who was playing for the Chicago Tigers of the NFL, supposedly to help coach some high school players. Instead, the two went on a drinking binge across Chicago that lasted "several days." By the time he made it back to South Bend he had a fever, sore throat, and was coughing up phlegm.[14]

Moe Aranson, a lifetime resident of South Bend, stated that the story later told by Gipp's old pals in the pool rooms in town was that Gipp "got so drunk one night, he passed out in the snow and they found him the next morning. That's how he got the pneumonia."[15]

With Gipp pale and weak, it was decided that he should be held out of the next game at Northwestern, despite the fact that Notre Dame had declared the event "George Gipp Day." The crowd in Evanston didn't share Notre Dame's caution, and, with the visitors enjoying a big lead in the third quarter, they began to chant, "We want Gipp! We want Gipp!" Always game, Gipp said he was ready, so in he went. He did not disappoint either, setting a passing record in the second half.[16] It was the last time Gipp would set foot on a football field.

He was in the hospital by the time of Notre Dame's final game of the season against Michigan State at East Lansing the following week. After ups and downs in his condition, the doctors diagnosed his illness as tonsillitis, but soon after they released him, Gipp returned to the hospital. This time, he was diagnosed with pneumonia and within a few hours was put on the critical list. While a streptococcus infection was spreading though his body, rumors were raging across campus. George Gipp was dying.

The end came on December 14, 1920. Gipp was only twenty-five years old. He had just been named first team All-American, the first player at Notre Dame so honored.[17] The headlines announcing his death would not be the last time the name of George Gipp would capture public notice: his name would live on in the memory of football fans for decades to come.

While the year had not been as tumultuous for Jones as for Rockne, it had been eventful. His system was working well. Brothers Aubrey and Glenn Devine, Hawkeyes since 1918, had become standout players. Sophomore Gordon Locke provided power running inside, while Aubrey Devine dashed to the corners. Iowa went 5–2, with only road losses to the University of Illinois and the University of Chicago marring the seven-game schedule.

The new year of 1921 would bring change to both Rockne and Jones. Rockne would have to ready himself for the coming season without Gipp. Jones would have to get ready for Rockne: Iowa would be hosting Notre Dame for the third game of the season. In October, the two coaches who had met in the press box at Nebraska a few years earlier would go head-to-head on the field.

Change was also coming to the wider world. In Washington, D.C., a new president would take office in 1921, bringing a shift in the political climate. The Gilded Age had bled out on the battlefields of Europe, and a new age was on the horizon. What it would bring was uncertain, but people were ready for change. The twenties were finally ready to roar. It was going to be a wild ride.

Heading for a Showdown

Are we ready, gang?

—*Daily Iowan*, October 8, 1921

The murmurs of the milling crowd were growing louder. Suddenly, shouts of "Here they come!" and "Get ready" rose above the noise, stirring the already restless gathering into a spasm of excitement. Vibrations shook the tracks along the platform, confirming that the train was only moments away from its destination. One last shrill blast of the whistle sounded, then the steady rhythm of the clanging bell atop the locomotive rang a warning call as the train drew into the station. The brake blocks engaged, emitting a piercing metallic squeal as they pressed against the treads of the spinning drivers to force the wheels to slow their rotation. With one final lurch forward the massive engine came to a stop, exhaling a long blast of billowing steam as excess pressure inside the boiler was bled off. It was 3:41 P.M.[1] The Notre Dame team and its entourage had arrived.

Rockne and his assistant coach Walter Halas, the players, reporters, dignitaries including the mayor of South Bend, and other assorted camp followers had climbed aboard almost four hundred miles away. They had followed the route of the Chicago, Rock Island, and Pacific Railroad through the Windy City, across Illinois, and then on into Iowa, with stops along the way to replenish water and top off fuel.[2] Tired from the long trip but brimming with confidence, the Notre Dame team had made it to Iowa City. The boys were ready to take on whatever attack Iowa could muster.

Even without Gipp, Rockne's team boasted a number of stars. The line formed a solid foundation for Rockne to build on. Three of his linemen, Fred Larson, Heartley "Hunk" Anderson, and Arthur Garvey, were future NFL players. Larson and Anderson hailed from the same Michigan town as their fallen teammate Gipp, and Garvey from Massachusetts.

There was speed aplenty in the backfield, with converted track star Chester Wynne and Daniel Coughlin, called "perhaps the best open field runner on the squad."[3] Fellow halfback August Desch had been a Bronze Medal–winning Olympic hurdler the year before in Antwerp.[4] Third halfback John Mohardt, another multisport letterman, would later shine in Major League Baseball. As a football player, he was called a "second George Gipp" by Iowa's student newspaper.[5]

A trio of steamrollers provided power running that punished defensemen with jabs at the interior of the line. There was Paul Castner, later a baseball pitcher for the Chicago White Sox; Earl Walsh, deemed to be "the hardest hitting half-back"[6]; and—the third blasting up the middle—standout fullback Robert Phelan.

Passing the ball was mostly the job of starting quarterback Chet Grant. A twenty-nine-year-old native of Ohio, Grant originally came to Notre Dame to play for Jesse Harper in 1915, while working as a sportswriter for the *South Bend Tribune*. After a stint in the army during World War I, he returned to school and began playing for Rockne in 1920.[7]

Catching Grant's passes were ends Roger Kiley and Eddie Anderson. Anderson, also a team captain, was an Iowa native who would return to his home state to become the Hawkeyes' head coach in 1939. He was hailed as a "real Notre Dame man" in the *Notre Dame Scholastic* season review for 1921.[8] At season's end, Anderson would be awarded various All-American honors by different selectors, including two first team nods as well as a second team selection on Walter Camp's All-America squad.

Overall, going into the third game of Rockne's fourth year as head coach, Notre Dame was on a roll. Rockne had lost only one game since taking over back in 1918, and he was defending an unbeaten streak going back twenty-two games. The first two games of 1921 had been blowouts, with Rockne's eleven outscoring the opposition 113–10. It was claimed, at least in Indiana, that Hawkeye supporters expected to lose by two touchdowns.[9]

Despite Irish claims of their opponents' lack of confidence, the Hawk-eyes' own lineup offered reason for optimism in Iowa City. Jones had let Rockne pluck Eddie Anderson from under his nose, but his team still boasted plenty of talent. Duke Slater led the way up front, while Aubrey Devine, Lester Belding, and Gordon Locke continued to pile up yardage out of the backfield. Jones was now 25–14–1 at the University of Iowa, with a more modest five-game winning streak of his own. On game day, of course, all that would be set aside. Only what happened on the field would matter, and it would soon be time to discard paper comparisons and actually play the game.

As the Notre Damers stepped down onto the station platform, the welcoming committee that had gathered to greet them quickly sprang into action. A contingent of Hawkeye students and fans, including fifty members of the "Howling 300," an all-male student cheering section formed two years before, was on hand for the festivities. Outside the station, a big army truck, festooned with a large banner reading "Wel-come Notre Dame," formally announced the greetings of the Hawkeye faithful. A caravan of automobiles waited outside to shuttle the thirty players and their entourage to the Jefferson Hotel. Sixteen rooms had been booked for the visitors, each decorated in the Hawkeyes' colors of black and gold, with smaller banners reading "Welcome to Iowa."[10]

It was Friday, October 7, 1921. Prohibition had been in effect for nineteen months. Warren G. Harding had been sworn in as the twenty-ninth president of the United States the previous March. Over the summer, Harding had signed a joint congressional resolution formally ending the state of war with Germany, Austria, and Hungary. Two weeks after that, Adolf Hitler was named Führer of the Nazi Party, an action propelling Germany on the first dark step back toward war—a war that would break out nearly two decades later. On this day, how-ever, the only thoughts of combat in Iowa City would be those cen-tered on the contest scheduled for the following day.

There were still a few events scheduled before that battle could take place. There was the aforementioned welcome for the Notre Dame con-tingent at the Wright Street Station, a tour of the city and the university campus, followed by a pep rally to which the visiting team was invited—a custom that had become the norm in college sports. A "college craze" was sweeping the nation, and was well under way by 1921; enthusiastic participation in organized cheering sections, pep rallies or "mass meetings" as they were called, were weekly fixtures of the football season. Everyone wanted in on the party. Local businesses took out supportive ads in Iowa University's school paper; Reich's Chocolate Shop, for example, urged supporters to help the team "Beat Notre Dame."[11]

Just one week later, an article in the *New York Times* would illustrate the growing frenzy for college life, trumpeting the "Greatest Rush to American Universities" and backing the claim with evidence of increasing enrollment at schools across the country.[12] Part of the period's college ideal was a sense of good sportsmanship, as exhibited by the warm welcome the Hawkeyes were offering their guests.

More serious preparations for the big game had to be completed before the Iowa players could join the campus frivolities. Jones was using every available moment to get ready. He conducted one last practice, even as Rockne and his charges were motoring to their hotel. It was a secret session held behind locked gates, away from the prying eyes of fans who had been welcomed just the day before. By 5:00 P.M., the workout had wrapped up,[13] ending a week of drills that had included the freshman team standing in for the opposition to ready the varsity for Rockne's famous backfield shift.[14]

Rockne preferred to waste no time with trivialities on campus. He led his squad directly onto Iowa Field as soon as the Hawkeyes had cleared out, conducting a walk-through in lieu of a formal practice; the late arrival of trunks holding the team's equipment had spoiled plans for a last-minute practice session before the game.[15]

With the walk-through finished and all possible preambles delivered, Rockne had little left to do save to guard his team against overconfidence. Rockne counseled his boys not to underestimate their opponent. He warned that the Iowa team was a "tough squad" that would "be out for blood."[16]

There was a history behind that passion. For years, Rockne had flirted with the idea of having Notre Dame join the Big Ten, but the Western Conference had rebuffed his many overtures. Some members may have looked down on a Catholic school as unworthy. Certainly Fielding Yost of Michigan seemed to hate the Notre Dame coach, perhaps because of

an anti-Catholic bias.[17] He was among those who considered Rockne to
be a bit of a charlatan, the puppet master of a shady "football factory," a
view that worked against Notre Dame's acceptance.[18] The attitude was
rather hypocritical, given widespread efforts within the Big Ten to skirt
eligibility rules, but the persistent rumors of Gipp's professionalism and
lack of academic rigor lent a veneer of credence to the righteous indigna-
tion of Notre Dame's opponents.[19]

Rockne's disappointment was reduced by his ability to schedule
games with conference teams, such as this game with Iowa, even though
the sanctimonious Western Conference had rebuffed Notre Dame's efforts to join. He had arranged the game with Howard Jones at the Big
Ten coaches' meeting held in Chicago[20] back in December 1920.[21] Other
than Purdue, Indiana, and Michigan State, Iowa was the first Big Ten
school Rockne had been able to schedule. Now he just needed to win.

Rockne was a competitive man and would have certainly relished the
chance to upend another symbol of the Eastern establishment. Howard
Jones was, after all, an Ivy Leaguer. The game was also another opportunity to beat a team from the Big Ten. Rockne was described by Iowa's
student newspaper as "extremely anxious to win," but with typical
guile he revealed no hint of extra motivation.

When pressed about the upcoming game, he said, "It will certainly
be a tough battle."[22] Always hoping to sandbag the opposition, he un-
derplayed his own team's chances by saying, "If my boys hold the
Iowa eleven even I'm going to be satisfied." Then he added, "Of course
we don't expect to run away from Old Gold."[23]

In reality, Rockne desperately wanted to win. "Rock had taunted the
Big Ten for years in order to grab [that] date with Iowa," Chet Grant
recalled.[24] The coach was certainly taking no chances in his preparation.
He had sent a scout to spy on Iowa. While Rockne was said to have "uncovered nothing" in Notre Dame's first two games, Jones was thought
to have "opened up all his stuff" for scouts to see in Iowa's game against
Knox College the week before.[25]

Rockne continued to soft-soap the Hawkeyes with flattering public
comments. "We have a wholesome respect for Iowa's team and Coach
Jones after their Knox game, and we anticipate a mighty hard fight,"
he told reporters.

Jones wouldn't take the bait. "Beating Knox didn't spell anything," Jones answered. "Against Notre Dame Iowa must play vastly better, both offensively and defensively, or we will be annihilated. Until I see how the men behave tomorrow I won't know whether I have a real football team."[26]

Howard Jones was never given to provocative statements under any circumstances, and he had more pressing issues on his mind anyway. His team was depleted by injuries, and though with thirty-four regulars his squad was roughly the same size as Notre Dame's team, it was common for a home team to suit up a much larger squad than the visitors. That very week, Jones had called for more students to try out for the team, and practice had been bolstered by fifteen new candidates.[27] They stepped onto the practice field at the most daunting time of the season, with "all records being broken for the length of the practice and the fierceness of the scrimmages."[28] That Howard Jones wanted to win just as much as Rockne did was evident not just in the rough practice work but in the fact he too had sent scouts to spy on the opposing team earlier in the season.[29]

Friday night marked the big pep rally on campus, to be followed by a student mixer in the school gymnasium. The Iowa marching band began playing outside the Natural Science Auditorium at 6:45. Stirring marches led the students, players, and coaches into the hall. The auditorium was a large lecture and performance theater within the larger Beaux-Arts structure housing it, a building that would be renamed McBride Hall in 1934.

The room featured a tall, rounded proscenium arch with plastered decorative elements above the stage, and a curved backdrop with a half-dozen niches built into the shell. Balcony seating hung over the floor seats on all three sides facing the stage. It was from these overhead galleries that the representatives of the professional colleges shouted yells back and forth, pitting medical students against engineers in bouts of organized cheering to determine which had the most "pep."

Professor Edward H. Lauer, chairman of the evening's event and later Iowa's athletic director, spoke first. "We are going to meet a team tomorrow that occupies a peculiar place on our schedule. In the past years, we have met conference teams, we have done things to them and they have done things to us. Then we ended by pouring our spite out on Ames," he said, referring to cross-state rival Iowa Agricultural College, now known as Iowa State. "This year we elected Notre Dame to take Ames' place!"

A procession of speakers followed Lauer. The first up was Bill Kelly, captain of the 1920 team, who had returned to Iowa to coach the freshmen. Avoiding any boastful or disparaging remarks, Kelly instead paid homage to the fans, stating that Iowa would have "9,000 rooters to Notre Dame's 100" and that the home crowd "ought to sway the results of the game."[30] Among those pulling for Notre Dame would be three carloads of students who drove all the way from South Bend.[31]

After the Hawkeyes finished speaking, Eddie Anderson was asked to represent the Notre Dame squad. He confidently predicted victory, but hoped that Iowa would "win the Big Ten" so that "everybody would know who was the Western champion." He closed by stating that "Notre Dame men never brag, but we expect to be on top tomorrow."

The last of the speakers was Major Ray C. Hill, who, in addition to being one of Jones's assistants, was a war veteran and former West Point player. He praised his boss, saying that Coach Jones was "able to give us as good a team as anybody in America."

Lauer wrapped up the meeting with remarks about "the fairness of play which characterized both teams," asserting, "it was always the best team that won" such contests.[32]

Following the singing of the Iowa school hymn, "Old Gold," the crowd dispersed for the gymnasium, or wherever the evening's destinations might be. There were just a few hours of calm left now before the storm would follow on the gridiron. While the pregame fun went on, both coaches expected their players, unlike their fans, to forgo excessive late-night activities so they could get sufficient rest before the game.

The sun rose at 6:10 A.M. the following morning, struggling to force its sunshine through the cloudy gray sky. It was October 8, 1921—a historic day for football. Seven hundred miles to the east, Pittsburgh was hosting West Virginia, and station KDKA in the Steel City was making that match the first college game ever aired on radio.[33] Fans in Iowa City had no such convenience; they would have to go to Iowa Field or wait for news of the outcome.

The Notre Dame players were brimming with confidence in their hotel that morning, if not displaying downright cockiness. Tackle Arthur "Hector" Garvey flashed three fingers to his quarterback, Chet Grant, symbolizing the three-touchdown margin by which he expected his team to win that afternoon.[34] The team clearly expected to handle the Hawkeyes with little trouble, and with Army the only remaining challenge on the schedule, a victory in Iowa would leave them free to dream of a Rose Bowl invitation at season's end. In a few hours, the first obstacle would be overcome and they could head back to South Bend with that postseason goal in sight.

The stadium slowly came to life as the morning passed into midday. Gates were unlocked, ticket booths opened, and when the preparations were complete the spectators began to enter the stadium. Resplendent in gold and black skullcaps, carrying canes as always, the Howling 300 came en masse to take their usual seats near midfield.[35]

The day remained cool and dark as game time approached, with a strong wind blowing from the south onto Iowa Field.[36] The stadium was modest by the mammoth standards to be set just two years later with the opening of the Rose Bowl in Pasadena and of the Coliseum in Los Angeles. Still, the facility had recently been renovated and expanded, with a hint of the grandeur of those larger structures to be found in the concrete and limestone arches spanning the Washington Street entrance at the east side of the field. A crowd of more than eight thousand fans had turned out, and many had arrived by the interurban line that served the stadium via tracks running along the bridge above that new entrance.[37]

Whether they had traveled by trolley, train, or Model T, all fans shared one thing above all else: everyone eagerly anticipated this matchup. The hype before the game promoted not only the virtues of the two teams, but also the two men leading them into battle. The Ivy League pioneer, with one undefeated coaching season on his résumé, was squaring off against the trailblazing upstart from South Bend, who had racked up two clean slates while reinventing how the game was played.

Rockne felt good enough about his team's prospects that he dispensed with any pep talk before the game.[38] Instead, he simply moved among his players in the locker room, quietly conferring with them one by one. By 2:30 in the afternoon they were ready. Rockne's Notre Dame team streamed out onto the field, followed a few moments later by the Iowa squad.[39] Kickoff was less than fifteen minutes away.[40]

Rockne liked to set a physiological trap before each game by using his team's warm-up as a precision display of pigskin power. While Iowa tossed around three footballs, the Irish used twenty. Notre Dame's uniforms were crisp and new, while Iowa's looked ragtag and baggy. The Iowa players couldn't help feeling like a "bunch of hicks" going against such a well-drilled machine.

Jones had anticipated the situation and had avoided any hint of pressure or desperation when he addressed the team before the game. He spoke simply and directly. "We are going to learn a great deal of football today," is all he said. There was no rah-rah speech nor plea to "win one for old 'Gold.'" As a result, the players were loose when they took the field, and, though awed by Notre Dame's appearance, they were not intimidated by it.[41]

If Jones was intimidated, he was not letting on. He believed that the successful coach must never reveal his worries to the team. As he put it, "You must always appear cool, regardless of how you are burning inside, for if you show your nerves to your men they may borrow your worries—and there goes the old ball game."[42]

The only hint of nervousness Jones displayed was the string of unfiltered cigarettes he smoked before the game.[43] Tobacco was Rockne's salve of choice as well, though he was content simply to chew on an unlit cigar. Both men might be justified in feeling a few extra butterflies in their stomachs, as a football game was perhaps a more nerve-wracking experience for coaches in those days. The rules limited interaction with the players on the field during the contest. Other than his halftime speech and time-outs, a coach had almost no opportunity to offer direct instruction to his team. Implementing strategy was left more in the players' hands than it is today.

Once warm-ups were completed, the two coaches parted, joining their teams on the sidelines to make way for the captains to move out onto the field to meet with the game's four officials for the coin flip. The refs were easy to spot in white shirts, pants, and bow ties, but the uniforms of the two sides were less distinctive. The black shirts of Iowa were nearly identical to the dark blue jerseys of their opponents, save for the horizontal stripes along the Hawkeyes' long sleeves.[44] It might have seemed a minor detail at that moment, but the similarity would have a major impact later in the game.

The Hawkeyes won the coin toss. They would get the ball first and defend the south goal. The two teams moved toward midfield to spread out into their kick coverage formations. The Notre Dame squad was spaced along the 40-yard line, flanking Hector Garvey on either side of the ball. He paced back toward his own goal, spinning to face toward his teammate, kneeling to hold the pigskin ready for him. Upon the official's signal, Garvey began running toward the ball. His kick would begin the first play of the first game of an epic rivalry.[45]

5

When Worlds Collide

Give that fellow Jones two good tackles and he'll win nine out of every ten games he plays.

—Anonymous contemporary, date unknown

All eyes followed the flight of the ball as Garvey's kick spun down toward Iowa's captain, Aubrey Devine, at the 20-yard line. Devine mishandled the ball, but managed to gather it in and start upfield, only to slam right into the onrushing Notre Dame defenders, managing just five yards for his trouble.[1]

A few moments later, the two teams faced off at the line of scrimmage. Hunk Anderson was really keyed up for the challenge, and could hardly control the rage within him to show who was the toughest lineman on the field. "Look at all this raw meat!" Anderson growled at Duke Slater as the Iowa star set up across the line from him.

Their much-anticipated duel had been a major subtext of newspaper columns for days before the game. Rockne knew all about Slater's ability and had coached his team extensively on how to combat the big lineman. Someone, perhaps Coach Jones himself, had taken advantage of Slater's reputation to gain a psychological advantage over Notre Dame. A pair of Slater's oversized shoes had been left in one of the lockers in the visitors' dressing room, leaving the Irish wondering if they were facing a team of giants. Now gamesmanship was over and the battle was under way. Amid the fray, Anderson and Slater faced off in single combat, fought in a zone largely apart from the other twenty players on the field.

Iowa found success in running the ball early in the game. With Anderson so caught up in his personal challenge with Slater, Gordon Locke went unstopped. That success couldn't be sustained, however, and with Iowa stalled, Aubrey Devine punted the ball. Both teams proceeded to trade possessions, with neither side making much headway. The Hawkeyes finally got something going when they put the ball into play from their own forty-three. Locke was able to punch through the line again, following Slater's lead to pick up yardage.

The big Iowa tackle was getting under Anderson's skin. Hunk had turned the game into a personal vendetta, ignoring team play to focus all his attention on the man across from him. Slater's response employed the finesse of a Viking berserker raiding the Irish coastline. He would simply grab Hunk by the back of his jersey, lift him up, and push him aside with one arm before plowing forward to sweep aside the defensive secondary. When Slater finally tired of Anderson's targeting him instead of the ball carrier, he snapped. "Why don't you go after Locke instead of me?" he barked. "He has the ball!"

Hunk shot back, "Rock told me to pour it on you!"

With that, Slater turned to his quarterback. "Big day today, Aub," he called back to Devine. "Right through here, Aub."[2]

Devine kept the ball this time and ripped off thirty yards. With Locke punching through the line and Devine racing around it, the Hawkeyes made steady progress toward the goal, until just one foot remained before the end stripe. It was fourth down, with the two lines facing off inches from the goal line.[3]

The Notre Dame players had never seen a trap play before, and they weren't ready for it when it was called.[4] Locke took one step to his right and then bolted back to take the ball and charge between the left tackle and guard. Glenn Devine moved to block the Notre Dame tackle out, while Slater angled to force the guard in. For once, the block on Anderson was missed, and he was left free to plug the hole. Locke swerved just enough to avoid a head-on collision, and caromed off to fall just over the goal line.[5]

After Aubrey Devine's kick, the score stood at 7–0 in favor of the Hawkeyes. Jones's side had drawn first blood, but the Irish weren't fazed. There was a long way to go.

Aubrey Devine's next big play came on defense. He intercepted a pass deep in Iowa territory, thwarting an Irish drive that had crossed midfield. Again the home side moved the ball, but after the drive sputtered at the Notre Dame 35-yard line, Iowa faced another fourth-down decision.[6]

The Hawkeyes lined up as if to go for it. Then, as the Iowa center stooped down to ready the ball, the backfield players shifted into punt formation, but Devine intended to try a drop-kick field goal instead of playing it safe with a punt that would net just eighteen yards after a touchback.[7] The defense responded by tightening up to challenge the kick as Devine readied himself to accept the ball. Both sides charged as the ball was snapped. They hurled themselves forward, their bodies smashing together like knights in medieval combat, before collapsing into a jumbled heap. Devine raised the pigskin, and then let it drop. As it bounced off the grass, his leg whipped upward and launched the ball in a slow, lazy arc. It fell through the uprights and triggered a raucous celebration.[8]

Rockne paced back and forth, looking up at the scoreboard, and studying the tally. Only three times before since Rockne became head coach had a team scored more than ten points on Notre Dame in an entire game. Iowa had ten on the board at that very moment, and it was still just the first quarter. That unsettling fact at last caused a hint of unease to flicker along the Irish sideline.

Of course, there was no need to panic. Rockne's usual confidence returned as his boys began to move steadily down the field after the kickoff. The Notre Dame team marched to Iowa's 25-yard line and lined up there as the second quarter began. John Mohardt zipped the ball to Eddie Anderson, who was wrestled down at the 5-yard line. After a couple of unsuccessful stabs at the line, quarterback Chet Grant decided to run a "tricky" play. It was supposed to be a pass to Eddie Anderson off a fake split buck. Grant faked handoffs to the halfback, then the fullback, but the trio collided while executing the feint. Instead of just keeping the ball and running in the final yard, Grant tried to finish the play as called. In the chaos of the botched play, Grant lost control of the ball and it slid off his fingers just as he tossed it toward Anderson in the end zone.[9] Locke intercepted and ran it back to the 38-

yard line. Poor execution had doomed Notre Dame's first real threat at the last possible moment.

Iowa's subsequent possession failed to deliver results, so Notre Dame quickly got the ball back. Possession continued to shift back and forth until Iowa fumbled on Notre Dame's 35-yard line. After a few short gains, Mohardt heaved the ball down the field to Roger Kiley, who raced in for the score. After the conversion, the scoreboard read Iowa 10, Notre Dame 7. Now it was time for Howard Jones to fidget on the sideline.

The two sides wrestled back and forth the rest of the quarter, with Notre Dame moving the ball but failing to score. The first-half clock expired just as a Notre Dame drive sputtered on Iowa's 25-yard line, another frustrating possession that gained yardage but yielded no points.[10]

The two teams withdrew to huddle with their coaches, leaving the field for the Iowa band to march out for its halftime show.[11] Jones was no orator, but Rockne's forte was delivering the halftime speech. He was renowned for using just the right approach to motivate his team. Exaggerations or even outright falsehoods were permissible sins when employed for the greater good. This time, however, neither acting nor invention was required—Rockne was clearly upset and not holding back.

"You guys should be penalized for abusing the ball," he snorted.[12] Rockne often warned his players against becoming too infatuated with glowing press clippings, and he was convinced they'd fallen into the malaise of underestimating the Hawkeyes.

His worries included more than just his team's lukewarm effort: tactics were another concern. He needed to figure out a way to handle Duke Slater. "He's a hell of a body blocker," Anderson told his coach, " . . . you couldn't play him outside nor inside." Slater was too big and too quick, Hunk went on. "Duke repeatedly swept me out of the way by body-blocking me from the side."

It was decided that Anderson would line up directly across from Slater in the second half, in the hope that Hunk could stay on his feet and watch out for side blocks coming his way.[13]

On the offensive side of the ball, Rockne called for more passing.[14] Sure that his adjustments would result in better execution, he was confident that his Irish could easily make up the three points they were down. There was no doubt in his mind that his boys were "ready to roll."

He wouldn't share that confidence with his team, of course. In a pickle like this one, he often resorted to sarcasm more than to strategy to sting his team into action. "Let's go, girls," was his standard insult.[15]

As the teams returned to the field, they found that the moody gray sky was growing darker. The blue-clad Catholics were the first to enjoy possession after halftime, but they could do little with the ball. Both sides just continued to joust back and forth, until Gordon Locke came up injured. It appeared that the loss of the powerful fullback might shift the balance of power toward Notre Dame, but after the Hawkeyes took a time-out, he was able to return. Whatever advantage might have been lost in his absence was quickly reversed.[16] With equilibrium restored, the stalemate continued.

Later in the third quarter, Rockne began making substitutions, pulling Mohardt in favor of Thomas Lieb (who later became another Olympic medalist, winning a bronze in discus throw at the 1924 Summer Games in Paris).[17] Still Notre Dame made little progress.

Finally, the Iowa team was pinned down deep in its own territory, and, after a punt by Aubrey Devine, Notre Dame took over at the Iowa 25-yard line. The pressure was now all on Iowa.

The Hawkeyes rose to the challenge, blunting two meager offensive attempts. Then Notre Dame found success when Coughlin roared down to the 13-yard line. Two short gains later, the quarter ended, with Notre Dame seven yards away from taking the lead.

Though the Irish had failed to score, they had moved the ball in the third quarter, which buoyed their spirits. Now, as the last stanza began, the goal line was just a few yards away. Rockne was looking to grab the lead. It was third down, but it came at the time of the game in which he always seemed to hold the advantage. It looked to be the crucial turning point when his opponents always crumbled.

Yet all that momentum quickly dissipated. A fake went awry, and Coughlin was tackled for a four-yard loss. Faced with a fourth-down decision, Rockne opted to go for the lead instead of a tie. Mohardt, back in the game, zipped the ball, but the pass only gained three yards, and Notre Dame's efforts came to naught once more.

It was a huge play, but there was still almost a whole quarter to go, and since field position favored the Irish, Jones employed a defensive strategy. Facing the prospect of running a play from his own 5-yard line, with a determined foe clawing its way back into the game, Jones felt it better not to risk a turnover so close to the goal. Aubrey Devine booted the ball right back on the next snap, a common ploy in those days to catch the defense off guard and prevent a long runback off a fourth-down punt. The stratagem paid off, with Notre Dame taking over some forty-three yards from the end zone.

Notre Dame could manage just two yards on the next three plays, so Mohardt lined up to drop-kick a field goal to tie the game. Yanking the snap out of the air, he dropped the ball squarely, and kicked it cleanly. The ball spiraled toward its target, but fell harmlessly short of the cross-bar; again the home side had dodged a bullet.

Starting over from their own 20-yard line, the Hawkeyes found Notre Dame unwilling to yield. One play, then two, and finally the third amounted to only five yards, and Iowa was obliged to give up posses-sion again. As usual, Aubrey Devine handled the kicking duties, and Mohardt returned it to midfield.

Mixing passes and runs with equal effect, Notre Dame moved to Iowa's 20-yard line. Then progress slowed. Handing off twice to Paul Castner produced only three yards. On the next play, Mohardt flung the ball, but again disaster struck. Mohardt never saw Lester Belding, or perhaps mistook the black jersey for blue in the fading light. In any case, the ball fell right into Belding's arms.

It was first down now for Iowa at their own 13-yard line. Aubrey Devine and Locke carried three times for exactly ten yards, and the down marker flipped back to first. The next two efforts yielded only a few yards, so again the Hawkeyes played it conservatively. Third down saw Devine deploy the "quick kick" again, and when Notre Dame put the ball in play it was from the Irish 40-yard line.

Locke came up injured a second time, and went out. After a few modest gains, and some penalties, Notre Dame again went to the air. This time it was August Desch doing the passing, but the result was the same. Belding snatched it back at his own 43-yard line.

Rockne's men were down, but still not out. There was fight left in them, and more importantly they still had time. A few moments later, Iowa had to kick it back. Aubrey Devine's punt was blocked, and the scramble for the ball left Notre Dame with a first down at Iowa's 23-yard line. This was it. The outcome of the game was about to be decided.

Notre Dame gained a few yards on the ground before passing to Kiley on Iowa's 7-yard line. It was first and goal. Suddenly, Notre Dame started going backward again. An offside penalty and tackles for losses moved the ball backward fifteen yards. Then Notre Dame's passing miscues struck again. Aubrey Devine intercepted, and the ball turned over on Iowa's 10-yard line.

Devine was stuffed on the first play, and then ran for twelve yards on the next two carries to earn a first down. Time was running out, but Rockne was still not done. After the defense stuffed three straight running plays, the Hawkeyes were obliged to punt. As Aubrey Devine's boot soared down the field, Slater exploded off the line and chased down Grant at midfield.[18]

Rockne sent in Frank Thomas to replace Chet Grant for a trick play that was a desperate chance to salvage the game. Mohardt took the ball, faked a reverse to the other halfback, and then dropped back to pass. Paul Castner streaked down the field, and hauled in Mohardt's toss at Iowa's 25-yard line.[19]

Now only Glenn Devine stood between Castner and six points. Devine dove toward the turf, desperately stretching to stop the galloping Hibernian. He was just able to grab Castner's ankle and with one hand wrestle him to the ground.[20] That was it—the game was over. Howard Jones had led his team to victory over the best team in the country, and he had used just twelve players to do the job.[21]

It was a bitter pill for Rockne to swallow. The statistics favored the visitors. Notre Dame had twenty-one first downs to Iowa's fourteen. They outgained the Hawkeyes 398 yards to 245. The passing edge was even more dramatic, with fifteen of twenty-two Catholic heaves completed to just one successful pass play out of six tried by Iowa.[22] Yet in the one stat that mattered most, Notre Dame had come up short.

The writers of the University of Notre Dame Football Review for 1921 could not bring themselves to accept the result. They referred to every metric save for the final tally when they opined that their players "reserve the right to know they were the better team" despite the numbers on the scoreboard.[23]

Rockne was nothing if not a fair sportsman, however, and he offered no excuses for losing. Meeting Jones at midfield, Rockne simply said, "Con-

200 4/5   Iowa 10 Notre Dame 7   AH   Photo Kent

Gordon Locke crashes toward the goal while Duke Slater, visible without a helmet at the bottom of the pile, leads interference. Iowa's upset victory in 1921 marked the first time Knute Rockne faced a team coached by Howard Jones. The win shocked college football and ended Notre Dame's long unbeaten streak. (Image courtesy of the University of Iowa.)

gratulations." Thinking of a rematch, he added, "But Howard, you've got to give me another chance some time."

Jones's reply was characteristically brief and to the point: "You name it."[24] Rockne's opportunity would come a few years later.

For the present, Rockne could only praise the victor. "I'd like to see a lot more of that fellow," he said of Jones. "He's got some tricky maneuvers."[25]

The scene inside Notre Dame's dressing room could only be likened to a funeral. Several players wept openly.[26]

Rockne shed no tears, but inside he was seething. He "went into a rage," so deep that he had to cool off by walking around the field with a friend.[27] The team would feel his wrath on the practice field soon enough, but Rockne knew that the time for that would come later. His main concern at that moment was healing damaged egos and restoring confidence for the games to come.

Eventually, Rockne would take the blame. He always expected more of himself than he did of his players. He internalized every defeat, calling any failure a "coaching loss."[28] "There are no alibis," he told his team.[29]

For the moment, though, he tried to fashion some sort of lesson from his team's misadventure. "This defeat will do us some good and may teach something to our followers, who think we can't be beaten," he said.

Rockne wasted no time in acting on lessons learned. He immediately ordered green jerseys as an alternative uniform color to ensure there'd be no repeat of the confusion that led to the disastrous turnovers against the Hawkeyes.[30] Thus began a tradition of special "green jersey games" throughout Notre Dame's history, born of a defeat at the hands of Howard Jones's Iowa eleven.

While Rockne was thinking green, the people of Iowa City were painting their town red. Joyous crowds milled around the downtown area celebrating the victory. On the corner of Clinton and Washington, fans piled up old barrel staves and scraps of wood to fuel a roaring bonfire that would burn for an hour. Someone found a discarded piano, and it too was tossed in and consumed.[31]

Not surprisingly, the train ride back home was less merry for the Notre Dame team. It was a somber, embarrassed group that arrived for the stopover in Chicago. As they passed between stations, the dejected coach and his team split into small groups to avoid detection as the losing Notre Dame team.[32]

Rockne still felt like hiding a few hours later as the train drew close to South Bend. He was overcome with a sense of failure, but his admirers would have no part in self-pity. A thousand students had trekked the three miles from campus to greet the team, and they cheered as if the Ramblers were conquering heroes. The crowd surged forward as the team detrained, demanding that Rockne speak. Genuinely touched by the outpouring, with tears welling in his eyes as he searched for something to say, he reassured his fans. "As long as you want me, I'll be here," he said.[33]

The scene was made famous in the 1940 film, "Knute Rockne, All-American." In that iconic performance, Pat O'Brien plays Rockne returning from a heartbreaking loss to an unnamed foe. Although Howard Jones himself appears later in the film as a fellow football coach, the movie does not reveal that Jones was the man who bested Rockne that day. As usual, it was Rockne who ultimately basked in the glory, even in defeat.

In the direct aftermath of the loss, however, Rockne was not concerned with his legacy. He was thinking ahead to the season's upcoming games. "We're starting all over this week," he told reporters as his team got back to work.

The coach drove his troops mercilessly, as his "wrath continued through a week of hard practices."[34] The payoff came when Notre Dame shut out Purdue 33–0 the following Saturday. Week five saw Nebraska head out to South Bend for the first time. Rockne's troops battled to a 6–0 victory over the Cornhuskers at Cartier Field. Two weeks later came the annual showdown against Army. The Cadets were shelled 28–0 at West Point's Cullum Field.

Just three days after Army came Rutgers in a game at the Polo Grounds. The Notre Dame team stayed in the New York area between those two games, working out at the Deal Golf and Country Club in New Jersey the day before the second game.[35] Rockne had agreed to schedule two games in such a short span because the Rutgers game would bring his team to New York City for the first time.[36] The Polo Grounds, with its capacity of thirty-eight thousand, was the largest stadium to host the Irish up to that time and represented a stage that was just too big for the Irish mentor to pass up.[37]

On paper, Rutgers didn't seem like the kind of team that would cause Rockne to worry. Evidence that the Scarlet Knights were overmatched was apparent in news reports from New York that speculated on just how hard Rockne's wrecking ball would swing through the home team.[38] In the end, Rutgers proved less of an obstacle than Army had; Notre Dame won 48–0.

After spending so much time away from home, Rockne decided to treat his team to a night in the Big Apple while they were on the East Coast. Alumnus Joe Bryne Sr., who ran insurance and travel agency businesses in Newark,[39] was an old classmate of Rockne's and "had a substantial bankroll from which the bands were easily removed." Since Bryne's vice president, Danny Sullivan, had also attended Notre Dame and "knew his way around Broadway,"[40] the team had no trouble securing tickets to a show.

The show's star was Will Rogers, the folksy cowboy comedian known as "Oklahoma's Favorite Son." Born William Penn Adair Rogers on the Dog Iron Ranch in Oolagah, Indian Territory (in what is now Oklahoma),

to parents of part Cherokee descent, Rogers parleyed his ranching background and horsemanship into a show business career, first as a circus
performer, and then as a vaudeville entertainer. He built his act around
the roping tricks he had learned in his boyhood on the ranch. Rogers's
talents came to the attention of Florenz Ziegfeld, a major Broadway
impresario who specialized in flamboyant spectacles featuring major
vaudeville stars like W. C. Fields, backed by a bevy of scantily clad show-
girls. In 1915, Rogers began appearing in Ziegfeld's "Midnight Frolic" in
the top-floor nightclub of his New Amsterdam Theatre, a move that had
catapulted Rogers into the big time.[41]

Three years later, Rogers left Ziegfeld's show for Hollywood and began making pictures for Sam Goldwyn. After starring in four movies in
1921, he returned to the stage early in November, opening a new show at
the Shubert-Crescent Theater for a rival producer.[42] It was to that showcase on Flatbush Avenue in Brooklyn that Rockne brought his team.[43]

Word that the Notre Dame squad would be in the house quickly
spread as the entourage arrived at the theater. As the show got under
way, Rogers ad-libbed a few words about Notre Dame, then tossed his
lasso out over the audience and circled Rockne's bald head. He pulled
the Notre Dame coach up to the stage, drawing Rockne into the show.
It was the beginning of a lasting friendship between the two men.[44]

Howard Jones enjoyed no such show business shenanigans that year,
but he did finish the 1921 season with an unblemished record, bringing
the Big Ten Championship to Iowa for the first time in more than twenty
years.

An invitation to play the University of California at the Rose Bowl
followed, but the conference leadership had ruled against the participation of any Big Ten team in such a game even before the season started.
The Iowa Board of Athletics likewise stood against such participation.[45]
Despite further consideration of the matter, the offer was refused.

Notre Dame's rebound after losing to the Hawkeyes had reignited
the team's postseason prospects. Despite the loss to Iowa, many felt
Rockne's team was still the best in the East, and there was talk about
a Rose Bowl bid after all. Another prospect was a game against Centre College of Danville, Kentucky, to be played either at Soldier Field in
Chicago[46] or in San Diego. Centre was in demand for postseason slots
after it defeated Harvard during the season—yet another sign that the

Ivy League was losing its grip on football power. Both opportunities were scuttled, though, when charges arose that some of Rockne's players had participated in semipro games. The scandal added a sour note to an otherwise successful season.[47] When everything was sorted out, Centre played Arizona State on December 26 in San Diego, and the Bears faced Washington and Jefferson College in the Rose Bowl on New Year's Day.

Even after his team had played its last game of the season, Rockne continued to make headlines amid rumors that other schools were after him, a familiar refrain for many years to come. This time the whispers held that he was headed back to Chicago, to coach Northwestern.[48] After days of speculation, the *New York Times* reported that Rockne would stay at Notre Dame after all.[49] There were places he wanted to go, but he could get there without leaving South Bend.

How They Played the Game

For when the One Great Scorer comes to mark against your name,

He writes—not that you won or lost—but how you played the Game.

—Grantland Rice, 1908

Howard Jones was on top of the college football world in 1922. The Hawkeyes repeated as Big Ten champions, recording another 7–0 record and pushing Jones's winning streak to seventeen games. Another Rose Bowl invitation was forthcoming, this time to face USC, but again the offer was declined. The *New York Times* reported that Howard Jones had issued a statement explaining that his players would "have to be away from school two weeks" if they were to participate.[1]

Despite the fact that Jones had beaten Rockne the year before, that his Iowa team had a better record on the field the past two seasons, and that as many All-American selections were coming out of Iowa City as out of South Bend, Rockne continued to outshine Jones—and, indeed, every coach in the country. Notre Dame enjoyed continued success, of course, just not quite the same perfection Jones brought to Iowa. A scoreless tie in the Army game of November 11, 1922, was the lone blemish interrupting Notre Dame's string of mostly lopsided victories.

Despite falling short of victory against Army, Rockne gave his charges another opportunity to enjoy New York City's nightlife after the game against the Cadets. This time the team gave their own show as they traveled through Times Square atop a double-decker bus. Jim Crowley used the upper level as his platform to give a mock campaign speech. He vowed to repeal Prohibition should his candidacy succeed, amusing the milling crowd along the sidewalk with the youthful exuberance of his facetious oration.[2] The squad took in the Ziegfeld Follies later that night, which Will Rogers had rejoined in June 1922 upon reuniting with promoter Florenz Ziegfeld.[3]

Three weeks later, Rockne and his troops headed toward their season-ending showdown with Nebraska. His team suffered a hard-fought 14–6 loss to the Cornhuskers in that game and finished the 1922 season with an 8–1–1 record. The team may not have been considered the nation's best, but they were still winners.

Rockne's growing celebrity was built not just on his many victories but also on the cachet of his links with luminaries like Will Rogers. Rockne's charisma was tailor-made to draw attention, but his popularity also rested on more tangible qualities than his personality. Rockne had done more than win games; he had "advanced the mystique of the Notre Dame football program through creation of brand equity." The three main ingredients of that "brand equity" were a winning tradition, brand awareness, and the perception of quality in Notre Dame football.[4] Yet there was more to it than just that brand equity.

It is difficult to underestimate the importance of coaching the most successful football team of any Catholic university in America. Rockne's association with Notre Dame put him in a unique position denied other coaches: despite his own Lutheran faith, Rockne's position as Notre Dame's coach made him the unofficial representative of all the nation's Catholics, and the standard-bearer for their cause, and his on-field success earned him a legion of devout followers. In a way, Catholic Americans perceived him as a latter-day Robin Hood, stealing the glory of the gridiron from the rich Eastern Protestants who had hoarded it for decades, to share it with the "huddled masses" of Catholic immigrants across the land. Rockne echoed this idea, if not in a specifically religious context, when he stated, "Western supremacy in football is a triumph of the middle class over the rich."[5] Rockne confirmed public hopes that the religious and class divisions of the day could be overcome. Catholics might still be barred from swanky private clubs, but they could get a fair shot on the football field, and Rockne made the most of those opportunities. When Rockne and his Fighting Irish bested the likes of Princeton or Army, even a fan of Marquette or Boston College could enjoy a degree of solidarity with fellow Catholics at Notre Dame.

Rockne's story was tailor-made for the times and perfect for the emerging middle class. Film and radio were in their infancy as mediums of art and commerce when Rockne took over as Notre Dame's head coach, but by the mid-twenties they were quickly becoming polished tools for the packaging of stars. Heroes and villains glowed more intensely on giant movie screens and praise resonated more strongly when transmitted by booming voices on the radio. The cult of celebrity was emerging for the first time, driven by the power of the new technologies of mass communication. Rockne, himself an immigrant, became a symbol of assimilation and success at a time when a multitude of foreigners were struggling to fit into American society and achieve the American Dream.

Rockne enjoyed a stream of positive publicity befitting a Hollywood movie star. He also worked actively to craft his public image. Rockne's genius lay not just on the football field but also in the fledgling realm of public relations. He was a marketing savant in an era when the ideal of the honorable yet humble gentleman was being challenged by a new generation of brash self-promoters. Rockne was so forward-thinking that he would even come to realize the potential of television at a time it was little more than a laboratory experiment.[6]

Fitzgerald's 1925 novel *The Great Gatsby* fictionalized the era's real-life conflict between the new wave and the old. The difference between Rockne and Jones echoed, in some ways, the struggle of new money versus old depicted in *Gatsby*. However, while Gatsby found the affections of Daisy Buchanan beyond his reach, Rockne found the American public very ready to embrace his advances. His almost uncanny ability to shape his public image was facilitated through three avenues of promotion—from within Notre Dame, through fawning sports reporters, and through his association with Christy Walsh.

Rockne took steps to control his image as early as his second year as head coach. In 1919, he appointed Notre Dame student Archie Ward as his team's unpaid publicity director in exchange for free tuition, plus room and board.[7] While Ward would go on to a long career in the sports department of the *Chicago Tribune*,[8] his legacy would carry on in South Bend: Rockne kept a student press agent on hand throughout the rest of his tenure at Notre Dame.

With cronies like Ward in the press corps, Rockne enjoyed generally positive coverage, and he was able to charm most other journalists he met along the way. More often than not, newspapermen were receptive to whatever stories he offered. They recognized the star quality they instinctively knew would sell papers.

Perhaps the most famous of these writers was Grantland Rice. One of the most influential sports reporters of his day, Rice had played football at Vanderbilt before becoming a syndicated columnist.[9] As a former athlete himself, Rice felt it was his duty to magnify the virtues of the glorious champion, not expose an athlete's flaws. His florid, hyperbolic writing style was designed to build sports figures into modern-day titans and support his contention that the "postwar period gave the game the greatest collection of stars that sport has ever known."[10]

Grantland Rice met Rockne in 1920, when the writer was covering Notre Dame's annual game with Army, part of a series that would become another vehicle fostering the Rockne mythos.[11] The two men quickly became friends, sparking a long-lasting and mutually beneficial relationship. They grew so close that they would often share "Tennessee milk," a Prohibition-era libation heavy on the Jack Daniel's white dog whiskey, at Rice's New York apartment when Rockne was in town.[12]

The third leg of Rockne's publicity triad was Christy Walsh. A lawyer-turned-sportswriter, Walsh is generally regarded as the first sports agent. In 1921, Walsh convinced Yankee baseball slugger Babe Ruth that he could make a lot more money with a little better management. Walsh proved his worth, not just to Ruth but to many other major sports figures of the day as well, inventing the job of sports agent in the process. He cut product endorsement deals, arranged speaking engagements, negotiated book contracts, and found a myriad of other revenue streams for his clients. Trading on his clients' fame, he arranged for articles credited to them to be penned by ghostwriters hired for the purpose, including celebrated writers like Damon Runyon, Gene Fowler, and Ford Frick.[13] Walsh made sure his stars appeared together both in public and in advertising promotions, reflecting glory off one another to blaze more brightly together as a constellation than they could shine individually.

The growing myth-making power of the media could push the heroic ideal but in the wrong hands also could serve a darker purpose, rekindling old prejudices and promoting doctrines of exclusion. In 1915, D. W. Griffith's film spectacle *The Birth of a Nation* helped fuel the rebirth of the Ku Klux Klan, decades after the original Klan had disbanded toward the end of the Reconstruction Era in the South. The Invisible Empire rose from the ashes in Stone Mountain, Georgia, the same year that the film debuted. While this "second Klan" still harbored hatred for African Americans, its influence would have failed to spread much past the borders of the Old Confederacy without a broader appeal than fear of black ascendancy. The new Klan found that appeal by targeting Catholic and Jewish immigrants, along with homegrown groups such as the Mormons, claiming to be defending the purity of the American ideal as defined by the Klansmen themselves.[14]

The Klan capitalized on a growing anxiety about the future of the country in the postwar era, an unease fueled by fears of foreign influence on the nation. A general suspicion of all immigrants grew in re-

Appearances by the Ku Klux Klan on city streets across Indiana were not an uncommon sight in the early 1920s. Here three Klansmen in white robes mill around Valparaiso, c. 1923. (Image courtesy of Steven R. Shook.)

sponse to the expansive ideology of Communist Russia and to a series of bombings blamed on foreign-born agitators. In September 1918, Marxists were suspected of planting a bomb that killed four people at the Federal Building in Chicago. In the spring of 1919, Italian anarchists known as Galleanists sent several deadly mail bombs, including those in June that were detonated nearly simultaneously in eight American cities. On September 16, 1920, in an eerie foreshadowing of the 1993 and 2001 attacks on the World Trade Center, a horse-drawn bomb set off in Manhattan's financial district of Manhattan killed thirty-eight people and injured hundreds more.

There was perhaps no other place in America where the new Klan's message of foreign influence came to resonate as strongly as it did in Indiana, despite the state's history and demographics, which worked against acceptance of the traditional Klan appeal. The state had been a stalwart bastion of the Republican antislavery crusade during the Civil War. Also, compared with their numbers in the Southern states, few blacks lived in Indiana in the early twenties. For these reasons, antiblack rhetoric failed to touch a nerve with any real sense of urgency there. Few Catholics lived in Indiana either, except in the northern areas around Notre Dame, but the university was a tangible symbol of that faith—and such symbols of "the other" drew the Klan's attention.

The national leaders of the new Klan were looking to expand the group's influence in the Midwest. To this end, they sent emissary Joe Huffington up from Texas, and in 1920, Huffington identified David Curtis Stephenson of Evansville, Indiana, as a logical prospect to recruit locally for the KKK. Stephenson had a reputation in the area as the consummate salesman, and he already had experience peddling memberships in a local social club for veterans. The Vendome Hotel in downtown Evansville was Stephenson's home base, and it was there that Klansman Joe Huffington had found the dapper salesman seated in the lobby, reading his newspaper and enjoying a fat cigar. At first, Stephenson was uninterested in Huffington's sales pitch, but he grew more intrigued as the conversation progressed, convinced not by passion for the cause but by the potential of the marketplace. Huffington explained that the KKK was open to "any white, male, native-born gentile citizen of the United States of America who owes no allegiance . . . to any foreign government, nation, institution, sect, or ruler." That would include just about every adult Protestant male in Indiana, and since Stephenson would keep 40 percent of all membership dues, he needed little convincing once he had calculated the potential profit in his head.

Fraternal organizations like the Masons, Elks, and Woodmen were growing in popularity at the time, and Stephenson set out to rebrand the Klan in the image of those respected groups. After all, Huffington had assured him, the new Klan was "not out to lynch Negroes."[15] Huffington was less interested in racial purity than raw power, and, in his mind, if the Klan was going to be the way to get it, the group's appeal must be as wide as possible.

Stephenson worked to transform public perception of the Klan in Indiana from a rabble of hate-mongering Dixie rednecks into a benevolent order of upstanding citizens working to preserve the American way of life. Beatings and lynchings were a thing of the past; Stephenson replaced them with festive picnics and Klan donations to local churches. By Independence Day of 1923, he had been so successful that he was to be rewarded with a promotion to the rank of grand dragon, overseeing "the entire northern realm."

The celebration of his elevation was planned for Malfalfa Park in Kokomo, Indiana. It was billed as a tristate rally, but it was open to all, and legions showed up from as far away as California and Florida. As thousands traveled there by train or car, Stephenson flew comfortably above the traffic. Winging his way toward Kokomo in a bright yellow biplane, he gazed down from the back seat toward the hopelessly jammed road below. Hundreds of abandoned cars littering the route made further motoring impossible. A stream of humanity trudged along on foot, tracing an undulating line toward the rally, like ants marching off to the horizon. They waved at the plane buzzing overhead, cheering the registration markings on the wing—EVANSVILLE KKK No. 1. Stephenson must have felt his prediction of two hundred thousand attendees had been vindicated.[16] Drawing such a crowd was quite a feat considering Kokomo was a city of only thirty-eight thousand at the time.[17]

The rally was an all-day affair featuring bands, speeches, and refreshments for the crowd. A huge American flag suspended between two giant trees provided a colorful backdrop for the stage, where Imperial Wizard Hiram Evans, the grand poobah of the Klan back in Atlanta, would bestow the honor on Stephenson. To the watching crowd, the two men represented a united front, but in reality they hated each other more than the "mongrels" they feared were corrupting America. The promotion was only being offered to Stephenson as an olive branch to mollify the ambitious Hoosier and to ensure that the membership dues Stephenson generated kept flowing to headquarters.[18]

The two men put aside their differences long enough to show solidarity onstage and to watch the Klan parade that followed Stephenson's two-hour speech. The rows of white-robed Klansmen passing in review embodied the growth of the organization in Indiana. Every week, two thousand more men were added to the rolls.[19] Eventually, the Klan would boast a membership of between one-fourth and one-third of all white males in Indiana.[20]

Stephenson, like Jones, must have felt on top of his world at that moment, though his realm was a decidedly darker one. The Klan honcho had built a broad base of influence and power while amassing a fortune of over $3,000,000. He lived luxuriously in his Indianapolis mansion and enjoyed relaxing outings on his lavish $75,000 yacht.[21] Stephenson recognized that the election coming up in 1924 was an opportunity to test his power and to leverage his war chest toward winning even more influence. He knew that if he backed the right horse he might extend his reach past the governor's mansion, perhaps all the way to the White House.

The administration at Notre Dame hadn't expressed much official concern about the Klan up to this point, at least on record. The university authorities quietly monitored Klan activities but took the stance that formal statements would just lend publicity to the group. There was little urgency to make such statements, since the campus had remained largely free of Klan harassment. That could always change, but until it did, life went on as usual.

Rockne's biggest concern regarding Klan activities naturally revolved around football. His team had gone deep into KKK country to play Georgia Tech in 1922. Instead of addressing religious tensions on that trip, Rockne had sought to motivate his team by reading them a telegram from his "sick" young son Billy begging them to win the game. In truth, the boy had been perfectly healthy, but the ruse had worked beautifully: Notre Dame prevailed, 13–3. The 1923 schedule offered no concerns about the Klan: Georgia Tech would come to South Bend that year.

The 1923 season began with a bang in South Bend, as Notre Dame walloped Kalamazoo College 74–0. It soon became clear that Rockne was developing another winning team, building further prestige with every victory. Aiding that success was a promising crop of new players that was coming up through his system. Four of them were talented backfielders whom Rockne had dismissed as "a combination of average players" their freshman year.[22] He was either being coy or for once had really misjudged his material when he made that comment, for they soon would become the most famous backfield in the history of football.

The foursome of Harry Stuhldreher, Don Miller, Jim Crowley, and Elmer Layden made their starting debut together in the third game of the season, against Army, on October 13, 1923. This was the fifth season the two schools had played each other since Rockne had managed to restore the academy to the schedule in 1919.

Every game, all the way back to the two schools' very first meeting in 1913, had been played at West Point. The crowds had grown too large for the stadium there, and Rockne, always mindful of marketing opportunities, lobbied to have the game moved. New York City, where the Irish had beaten Rutgers back in 1921, was where the action was. Either Yankee Stadium or the Polo Grounds were the obvious choices for the game, but both were booked for the World Series matchup between the Yankees and Giants. The other option was Ebbets Field in Brooklyn, home of baseball's Brooklyn Dodgers. It was fitting that the football game would be played in a baseball stadium, since the annual Army–Notre Dame game had risen to nearly the same height of popularity as the Fall Classic. Only a handful of other major sporting events, like Triple Crown horse races or major heavyweight title bouts, drew the same interest as the World Series and, now, Notre Dame's annual game with Army.

Notre Dame won the game 13–0 before a capacity crowd of twenty-eight thousand. It was the first time Notre Dame had played before a packed house, although the crowd was slightly smaller than that attending the game three years before in the larger Polo Grounds.[23] The victory extended Rockne's undefeated record against the Cadets as either a player or head coach, with only 1922's tie to blemish his otherwise perfect record against them.

Rockne would only suffer one loss in 1923, a 14–7 defeat in November to Nebraska in Lincoln. Notre Dame had played another successful, if not perfect, season. In six years at the helm, Rockne had yet to choke on the sour taste of even one losing campaign.

Over at Iowa, Howard Jones likewise maintained a successful record, although 1923's results were not quite up to the standards of the previous two years. His Hawkeyes won five games and dropped three, all to Big Ten opponents.

In November, it was announced that Howard Jones had written a book, *How to Coach and Play Football*,[24] which revealed the details of the "Jones system." In it, the coach diagrammed plays, discussed training methods, and laid out the philosophy that had made Iowa a winner. However, Jones's foray into publishing was eclipsed by bigger news: the 1923 season was his last at Iowa.

Jones's resignation came less than two months after the close of the season. Hawkeye fans were in shock. Just the day before the announcement, the local Rotary Club had hosted Jones and honored his team. The festivities had included a rendition of "For He's a Jolly Good Fellow," with lyrics tailored to suit the occasion.[25]

Many reasons were offered to explain his decision to leave. Some claimed that he opposed Iowa's move to combine the athletic and physical education departments. Others claimed that his wife was behind it: she just didn't like living in Iowa.[26] Jones himself later wrote that he felt he had done all he could in Iowa City.[27] His official statement at the time read, "Because of certain conditions which arose, I found it necessary to accept a position where service of less than 11 months would be required, and where climatic conditions would be more desirable."[28] This hardly made sense in light of the fact that his new job at Trinity College, in Durham, North Carolina, would encompass the same duties he had performed in Iowa, while adding the job of baseball coach to his numerous responsibilities. The press was at a loss to explain Jones's action, claiming an inability to "dope it out" in the slang of the day. More money, one writer suggested, was the real reason.[29]

The truth was never revealed, although some people seemed in the know. T. E. Jones (no relation), athletic director at Wisconsin, dismissed a rumor that Howard Jones was angry about being pressured to schedule a game with the Badgers. "I know the reason he resigned," T. E. Jones claimed, "but I do not feel that is my place to give it any publicity."[30]

The fact is that Leah Jones had left Howard. It was true that she never really liked living in Iowa, but her home life was more probably the reason for that dissatisfaction than the community around her. The end came with a cold and indifferent finality. Art Cohn, a columnist with the *Oakland Tribune,* revealed the story many years later, after Jones's death.

> He was a young football coach. And every inch a gentleman. And madly in love with his beautiful wife. He adored her. But one night he came home and she wasn't there. Nothing was left but a curt note. She had gone away. Forever.
>
> [Jones] was never the same again. He was the kind who took those things hard. He couldn't understand why she had hurt him so. But he said nothing. He could never burden anyone with his troubles. Everything just welled up inside. He moved to another town and got another job and tried to forget.
>
> He had changed by now. He spoke very little and smiled even less. He was too choked up inside. And the irony of it was that fame had begun to touch him. He became the highest salaried coach in America, the head of his profession. His name became as well known as a movie star's.[31]

The old Howard Jones faded away the night he read his wife's cold farewell. A new man, the stern, craggy-faced, jug-eared "Marine drill sergeant," would slowly take his place.[32] The aftermath of lost love and long-felt pain forged this new version of Howard Jones. The moniker had not yet been bestowed on him, but he adopted the persona of "the Headman" the very day he found himself alone.

7

Here Come the Irish

Cheer, cheer for old Notre Dame,

Wake up the echoes cheering her name,

Send a volley cheer on high,

Shake down the thunder from the sky,

What though the odds be great or small,

Old Notre Dame will win over all,

While her loyal sons are marching

Onward to victory.

—Rev. Michael Shea and John F. Shea, 1905

Notre Dame was not the first Catholic university in America, nor was it the biggest. By 1924, however, it would cement its reputation as the standard-bearer of Catholic pride nationwide, well before academic excellence caught up with its athletic prowess. It was becoming America's Team long before the Dallas Cowboys coined that term decades later.

Despite the school's gridiron success, despite Rockne's unequaled reputation and the rabid loyalty of his fans, there was one thing that Notre Dame lacked, one advantage the school did not enjoy: Notre Dame did not have a first-class football stadium in which to play home games. This was a reality that Rockne was determined to change as soon as possible.

Cartier Field was a rather modest arena in 1924, more like the primitive facilities of the 1890s than the giant stadiums rising across the country. Like other schools that opted to enlarge their old stadiums rather than build new ones, Notre Dame had expanded Cartier Field over the years, but it would never hold more than twenty-seven thousand fans.[1]

The facility at Trinity College, where Howard Jones would toil in 1924, was even smaller. Hanes Field was a modest facility used by Trinity's baseball team, as well as the minor-league Durham Bulls in the spring and summer months. It could not accommodate a crowd of ten thousand; its capacity had been increased to eight thousand the year before only by augmenting the existing seating with temporary bleachers.[2]

Perhaps these realities caused Jones to have second thoughts about his decision to leave Iowa. He had not given up on Leah either, and although he had put his home up for sale at the end of October, he tried one last time to save his marriage.[3] The *New York Times* reported on January 29, 1924, that Jones had decided to stay at Iowa and was trying to get out of the deal with Trinity.

One month later, he slipped quietly out of town.[4] He was following Leah, who was reported to be in Denver to "reap the benefit of the western climate, for her health's sake."[5] It was no use: she would not return to him, and Howard Jones was not going back to Iowa.

Hawkeye fans had not forgotten how Jones had raised Iowa football to an equal footing with any school in the country. They refused to let him go without a proper send-off. On February 21, the Rotary Club hosted a luncheon and presented him with an engraved Hamilton pocket watch to show their appreciation.[6]

A month later, at halftime during the Iowa-Illinois basketball game, grateful Iowa students and alumni gave him a "huge" loving cup. The applause was described as "prolonged," and Jones was "visibly affected by the demonstration."[7] It was one of a handful of times in Jones's life when his emotions reached the surface for all to see. It must have been a low point for the man. In two short years, Jones had fallen from the top of his game to what one newspaper called a "minor league berth."[8]

Rockne and Jones appeared to be heading in different directions, both professionally and personally. However, the rumor mill still linked the two, at least tangentially. In March 1924, the *New York Times* marked a visit by Rockne to Iowa City to meet with the university's athletic board with the headline, "Rockne Has Conference."[9] Bonnie Rockne dismissed the talk of her husband replacing Jones at Iowa as "a joke," though Rockne himself reminded newsmen that his contract at Notre

Dame would run out in June 1925.[10] The speculation officially ended a few months later. On January 15, 1924, the *Daily Illini* carried the news that Iowa University alumni favored Burt Ingwersen, an assistant at Illinois, to become the new head football coach.[11] As for Rockne, his dalliances with other schools had paid off. He was staying at Notre Dame, and fear of losing him drove Notre Dame to sign him to a new ten-year contract.[12]

Rockne, unlike Jones, enjoyed tranquility at home, but he would soon face other conflicts at his doorstep. The Klan was on the move, expanding its range and its membership rolls. D. C. Stephenson's personal power was growing too, and he was looking to turn the KKK's rising membership into votes and to use those votes to influence Indiana's politicians. The former Democratic candidate for office was now courting the Republicans, who dominated Indiana politics. It would prove to be a truly unholy alliance.

Stephenson was determined to deliver the "Klan vote" at the primary election scheduled for early May 1924 and become a kingmaker in the process. Newspaper ads and reminders in the Klan's own publication,

David Curtis Stephenson, shown here c. 1922, led the Ku Klux Klan in Indiana and helped orchestrate the group's clash with Notre Dame's students in South Bend in 1924.

the *Fiery Cross,* helped push his slate of candidates. Stephenson's office mailed out more than six hundred thousand letters to voters in Indianapolis and dropped voting lists on every Indiana doorstep the night before the election. In the run-up to the vote, Stephenson sent out door-to-door canvassers to poll registered voters. They found only one area where their message was poorly received—South Bend.[13] It was time for Stephenson to confront this pocket of resistance and take the crusade into the very heart of Catholic life in Indiana.

A South Bend rally was set for just a few days after the election.[14] It was scheduled for Saturday, May 17, 1924, at Island Park, near the St. Joseph River. The venue was just a short distance from Notre Dame's campus, and concern grew among the student body as the date approached. The election had demonstrated the Klan's political muscle, and now the White Knights were coming to town. The possibility of violence suddenly seemed very real.

Meetings were held in town to warn everyone of the looming threat. Students took reports back to campus and spread the word.[15] When the day came for Klansmen to start arriving in South Bend, the students of Notre Dame were ready.

Visiting Klansmen expected the same warm welcome they had experienced throughout Indiana, but things were different in South Bend. Roving gangs of students sowed confusion and rushed the Klansmen, harassing the visitors and stealing their white robes. By 11:30 that morning, the only white hoods seen on the streets of South Bend were those worn by the Notre Damers, who donned them as war trophies in a mock parade that mimicked the promised Klan procession, which never materialized.

As their courage grew, the students gathered around the Klan's downtown headquarters at the intersection of Michigan and Wayne. The cross of electric lights "burning" in the third-floor window drew the students like a bonfire beckoning them to a pep rally. Gathering potatoes from the outdoor displays in front of the first-floor grocery store, they began to hurl the suitably Gaelic missiles toward the glowing red bulbs behind the glass. Notre Dame quarterback Harry Stuhldreher, one of Rockne's promising backfield foursome, expertly dispatched the last glowing light.

Finally the students, about one hundred strong, decided to rush the Klan's headquarters. The mob was turned back by a pistol-wielding

Klansman at the top of the stairs inside the building. Incredibly, despite the anarchy that had raged all day, no one was seriously hurt.

Stephenson arrived amidst the chaos, just as a light rain started to fall on the city. He confronted South Bend police chief Laurence Lane, railing to him about the rampaging Notre Dame students. Lane, himself a Catholic, was no doubt struggling to balance the responsibilities of his job with an inner sympathy toward others of his faith. Most officers of the local sheriff's department, however, were Protestant, a fact Stephenson no doubt knew and planned to exploit in the aftermath of the day's events. In the meantime, he played the role of outraged victim to the hilt.

The Notre Dame students had regrouped on the Jefferson Street Bridge, a strategic location, to stop passing vehicles and subject them to vigorous "inspection." The hunt for any remaining Klan members was in full swing, and the students were determined to root out anyone who fit the description. At least one motorist had to be saved from the students' ire by the intervention of the police.

Stephenson demanded action to protect his men and bring the "hooligans" to justice. Lane was getting pressure from all sides: earlier, Notre Dame's president, Father Matthew Walsh, had sought an audience with him. Father J. Hugh O'Donnell, the university's prefect of discipline, and Father George Holderith were sent to speak with the police chief, but they were told nothing beyond the news that the Klan's parade permit for later in the day had been pulled.

Stephenson confronted the chief of police and sparred with local reporters, but he could do little else. He and the diminishing Klan rabble were virtually trapped within Island Park, surrounded by mounted policemen deployed around the perimeter. Any lingering resolve rapidly melted in the rain, which turned into a deluge as evening approached. Forced to formally cancel the parade, Stephenson issued a face-saving announcement intended to hide the fact his permit had already been pulled. The rally was over. While the downpour had swept away the combatants, it had not extinguished the hostility. The beaten Klansmen vowed to have their revenge. Sunday passed peacefully, but on balance the weekend had been a disaster for everyone involved. Most of the Klansmen had no taste for violence and were shocked by the donnybrook. Those who could do so had quickly skipped town at the first sign of trouble. Stephenson was furious. He was obliged to race out of town himself, leaving in humiliation to speed toward a prearranged show-down with Evans in Indianapolis.

Father Walsh and his administration were bewildered. They strug-gled to understand why the police chief had disregarded every warn-ing. Both the city and county law enforcement agencies had egg on their faces. They felt embarrassed and, to the townspeople, looked incompe-tent. County Deputy Sheriff John Cully took action, deputizing thirty townsmen to reinforce his beleaguered force. Cully, himself a known Klansman, ensured that all the new "special deputies" were also mem-bers of the Invisible Empire.[16]

By Monday, the calm of Sunday's respite had given way to further tension. That night, a dozen South Bend police waited near the Klan's headquarters, hiding in the darkness to avoid detection. It was around 9:00 P.M., the usual time the group's weekly meetings wrapped up. Deputy Cully, anticipating trouble, also decided to keep watch so his force would be ready if it came to pass.

The downtown streets remained unnaturally quiet after Saturday's ruckus. The stillness continued, even with police on hand and even after a new cross of electric lights was raised in the third-floor window of the Klan's headquarters, where the previous cross had been destroyed just two days before. Then the calm was broken by the sound of footsteps echoing in the night. As the noise grew closer and louder, a mob of shad-owy figures emerged from the darkness. Five hundred students were on the march, descending on the intersection of Michigan and Wayne.

Chief Lane was determined to avoid the loss of control he'd suf-fered last time. His men understood his expectations as they watched the Klan building. Their bodies tensed as Lane reacted to the arrival of the student mob by quietly cautioning his men to watch for his signal. Fists tightened and nightsticks were raised. Meanwhile the Klansmen had filed out of the building to quietly flank the entrance, apparently reinforced by some of Cully's "special deputies." None of the students advancing on the Klan's doorstep noticed the lawmen, and they didn't seem to regard the Klansmen as a threat. The Notre Damers simply went about their business without concern. They launched another fusillade of pilfered potatoes toward the hated third-floor window. That's when all hell broke loose.

"All right boys," Chief Lane bellowed, "let's show them who's run-ning this town!" Upon their leader's command, the cops waded into the rear of the student phalanx, thrusting and swinging their clubs as they pressed forward. The Klansmen then sprang into action from the front, launching rocks and bottles into the students before directly engaging the mass of fighting bodies. It was chaos. Rocks and bottles careened back and forth. Fists were swinging and shots rang out.

Chief Lane's show of force quickly spun completely out of control. Policemen were fighting with the students, the students were fighting with both cops and Klansmen, and, save for the makeshift white armbands worn by the Klan members, it wasn't always possible to tell who was who. Police grappling to arrest Klansmen were challenged by demands that they grant immunity to Cully's "special deputies."

Chief Lane forced his way out of the mess, dashed the two blocks back to headquarters, and placed phone calls to plead for help from the nearby Mishawaka police and local railroad detectives. Then he dialed one more number. He needed Father Walsh's help, too.

The bulk of the students retreated to the courthouse, located just three blocks from Klan headquarters. When Walsh arrived there, he found them sprawled across the lawn, some moaning and doubled over, others bloody and in shock. There hadn't been time for Chief Lane to pass details on to him, but Walsh quickly sized up the situation. It was time to act.

Walsh scrambled up the monument in the plaza, and balanced himself on the old Civil War cannon mounted atop the base. At first it was tough to be heard, but Walsh shouted over the noise and confusion. "Whatever challenge may have been offered tonight," he called out, "whatever insult may have been offered to your religion, you can show your loyalty to Notre Dame and South Bend by ignoring all threats."

The students were not ready to turn the other cheek, not in the wake of such an ambush. Not even if the head of their school urged them to do so. Not if there was an ounce of fight left in them. But Walsh persisted, asking them not to sink to the Klan's level of settling disputes with violence. He pleaded with them, ending with an appeal "to show your respect for South Bend and the authority of the city by dispersing."

As he spoke, the fight slowly drained out of even the hottest heads in the crowd. Discretion was deemed the better part of valor, and the students chose to live and fight another day. Tonight there were wounds to heal and tired bodies to rest. The students desperately needed sleep. The Notre Dame boys offered a halfhearted salute to Walsh, then slowly started shuffling off, away from the fracas and back toward their homes.

Walsh remained atop his perch, waiting until all his charges were safely on their way. Chief Lane, watching from his car a short distance away, locked eyes with Walsh, shifted the car into gear, and slowly drove off into the night.[17]

Divisions only deepened in the days after the battle. Inside the Klan, Evans used the incident to go after Stephenson, although both men publicly blamed the students for the violence and used it as confirmation of the stereotype of rowdy Irishmen. The people of South Bend, even prominent Catholics within the community, also blamed Notre Dame. Only Walsh refused to divide his own house, hoping to avoid dissension that would only add to the damage from the affair. Instead, he called on the one man on campus who could work miracles to bring them all together.

The task Walsh gave Rockne was simple: use his extraordinary speaking skills to get everyone back on the same page, a page that Father Walsh intended to write. The entire student body was called to Washington Hall to hear that message. Naturally, Rockne employed the language of the gridiron to sway his audience.

"Follow the signals of the quarterback," he advised the students. "Father Walsh is your quarterback, and you are the great Notre Dame team." It was Rockne's standard locker room fare. "Follow the signals . . . and when you do, you will be in the right." No team of his was ever more enthusiastic. The cheer that followed shook the room.

Although Walsh kept a close eye on the campus in the following weeks, stepping up security and requiring his students to sign "no rioting" pledges, the real battle shifted from the streets to the newsroom. The writers of the *Fiery Cross,* the Klan newspaper, did their worst, printing lurid accounts of Irish hooligans rampaging out of control. Newspapers across the country picked up the story and splashed provocative headlines across their pages.[18] There was outrage in the press, but perhaps in some quarters there was also a measure of quiet admiration. At least some Catholics may have been happy that someone had gone nose to nose for them. Ironically, throughout the entire affair, Rockne was still a Lutheran, not a Catholic, and his University of Notre Dame team was not yet, officially, the Fighting Irish.

Four Horsemen, Seven Mules, and One Gloomy Gus

I looked, and behold, a white horse, and he who sat on it had a
bow; and a crown was given to him, and he went out conquering
and to conquer.

—The Apostle John, *Book of Revelation,* First Century AD

It was almost halfway into the decade, and America was on a
roll. By 1924, bad times seemed like fading memories, and most people
were too busy chasing the good life to dwell on the past in any case. Opportunities abounded and it seemed the future would surely be even
better. With good times rolling along, nothing seemed too outlandish,
too big, or too improbable.

The price of a new Model T Ford Runabout had dropped from $500
in 1919 to an amazingly low $265 in 1924.[1] By June of that year, to-
tal production of all Model T types had reached 10 million.[2] Brands
like Chrysler, Kleenex, Wheaties, and IBM would debut in 1924, soon
to become household names, and products that hadn't even existed a
generation before were flying off the shelves.[3] Telephones, record players, radios, and cameras had gone from novelties to necessities. Racy
automobiles and ever-faster airplanes had become playthings for the
rich. All that buying and selling kicked off a rise in the stock market
toward the end of the year that seemed like it would last forever.[4]

The business of illegal booze was thriving too, and men with more
shady ethics than Henry Ford were making a killing off Prohibition.
Bootleggers were running wild in Chicago. Al Capone had become the

73

number two man in the Torrio Gang, and he was busy waging war against his rivals, the North Side Gang ruled by Irish gangster Dean O'Banion. Their feud came to a head in May 1924, when O'Banion learned that one of his illicit breweries was about to be raided. He tricked Torrio into buying the place just before the law swept in,[5] an affront that escalated the conflict from uneasy tension to all-out war.

Despite the increasingly modern tone of daily life, the allure of antiquity still managed to captivate the public. Tutankhamun was proving that a man in tattered rags could still become a fashion icon. British archaeologist Howard Carter toured the United States throughout 1924, giving lectures on King Tut's tomb, which he and George Herbert had discovered two years before in the Valley of the Kings. The golden treasures they had unearthed sparked a craze for exotic motifs that influenced fashion, design, and even architecture.[6] Sid Grauman's Egyptian Theater in Hollywood was a product of that inspiration. The opulent palace was a fitting showplace for cinematic dreams of distant lands.

Studio pressmen and actors' agents crafted idealized images of the stars bringing romantic roles to life. Newspapers and fan magazines trumpeted lavish tales of the glamor of Hollywood. It was never too early to begin promoting a performer's career. Since 1922, the Western Association of Motion Picture Advertisers had heralded the promise of a baker's dozen of young starlets, predicting their future stardom. Crowning them as "WAMPAS Babies," the association feted its thirteen picks at its annual WAMPAS Frolic and Ball, which had been moved up the coast to San Francisco in 1924 from its usual Hollywood venue because of a Los Angeles ordinance prohibiting dancing past 1:00 A.M.[7] Although only a few of those chosen actually went on to enjoy the predicted stardom, one young beauty among the 1924 WAMPUS Babies would fulfill that promise in spades. Her name was Clara Bow.[8]

The sporting world celebrated its big names too. Jack Dempsey reigned as the heavyweight boxing champion, Walter Hagen was the biggest name in golf, and Babe Ruth relished the chance to defend the New York Yankees' first World Series title. It was an Olympic year too, and over the summer Paris hosted the best in amateur competition between the athletes of forty-four national teams. As a former track runner, Rockne followed news reports from the Olympics with interest, but football remained his primary focus during the summer. He was slated to teach his style of coaching for three weeks at a clinic in Los Angeles.[9]

Summer football camps had become a nearly annual ritual for Rockne. Sharing the finer points of the game with other coaches was a good way to make extra money while advancing his already sterling reputation as a master of his profession. This was his first time in Los Angeles, and Rockne brought his wife Bonnie, their three children, and the maid west with him.

It was a typically hot summer day on July 7 when his train arrived at Union Pacific's First Street Station in East Los Angeles, located up an embankment overlooking the dry bed of the Los Angeles River. The palm trees and hilly scrub brush of the Pacific Coast formed quite a change in scenery from the Midwest's rural woodlands, peppered with lakes and streams. Rockne had spent the previous three weeks in Superior, Wisconsin, running a basketball camp, a post that demonstrated his versatility in teaching athletics.[10]

Rockne had come to Los Angeles at the behest of officials from the University of Southern California. They had invited him via telegram the previous December, offering him seven hundred dollars for three weeks' work.[11] The strong Notre Dame alumni presence in the City of the Angels no doubt cemented Rockne's already easy decision. Notre Dame graduates in Los Angeles welcomed him with an informal "stag dinner" at the Ambassador Hotel, held three days after his arrival.[12]

Before he could enjoy their hospitality, however, Rockne had to negotiate the infamous L.A. traffic, already getting congested by 1924. The convoy of sedans shuttling Rockne and his family from the station had a run-in with a road crew, a streetcar, and other motorists on the First Street Bridge. The incident provided comic relief in the *Los Angeles Times* the following day. The vehicle transporting Rockne had pulled to the side of the road to avoid being hit by the streetcar, the story recounted, whereupon the "repair boss forward passed a dainty bunch of anathema." The burly road worker was "stopped when Rockne came to the rescue," the story went on. "In a booming voice that would have knocked over the County Courthouse," Rockne told him to "dry up."[13] The man behind the wheel suffering the insults of the angry gang boss was USC's head coach, Elmer "Gloomy Gus" Henderson.

Henderson held the best winning percentage of any head coach in the history of Trojan football, a record unmatched to this day.[14] He was called "Gloomy Gus" not because of a sour disposition but because of his penchant for praising the opposition while bemoaning the weaknesses of his own team before every game. The technique was familiar to Rockne but not really perfected at Notre Dame until Lou Holtz arrived in 1986. It was *Los Angeles Times* sportswriter Paul Lowry who gave Henderson the nickname in his column; soon after Henderson's arrival in 1919, Lowry noted that his pessimism resembled that of Gloomy Gus, a popular cartoon strip character of the day, saddling him with the nickname forever.[15]

Henderson opened the school the week before Rockne's arrival, overseeing instruction for the fifty high school and college coaches in attendance. Rockne would now take over, with Henderson serving as his assistant. The buzz surrounding Rockne's presence fueled rumors that a game might be scheduled between the two schools, but it was not to be; both teams had already set their schedules for the upcoming season. Sportswriter Braven Dyer left open the possibility of a match in 1925 or some time after that.[16] His vague remarks suggested that talks were going on behind the scenes, but nothing concrete ever came of them.

Rockne's stay in Los Angeles was an early but important step toward cementing relations between Notre Dame and USC. His visit was a big success for both sides. The people at USC liked what they saw of him. In a letter dated October 1, 1924, the head of USC's Physical Education Department stated that Rockne's "course in football coaching was very well received," praising the films, or "football reels," he showed at the school and saluting Rockne's instruction as a "splendid piece of work."[17] Knute and his family were just as happy with the experience and became enchanted with Southern California. "I do not know of any trip, which I have ever made," Rockne wrote to his hosts, "where I enjoyed myself more than I did in your country."[18] Three weeks in the Southern California sunshine had definitely agreed with the Rockne clan.

Rockne's return to South Bend left him about a month to prepare for the opening of fall camp. Prospects for his team seemed bright. With that promising backfield foursome heading into their senior year, the offense looked to be potent. Notre Dame had outscored its opposition 275–37 the year before and suffered only the one touchdown loss to

Knute Rockne conducts a USC coaching clinic in the Los Angeles Coliseum during the summer of 1924. This experience, along with his visit to Pasadena at the end of that same 1924 season, sold the Rockne clan on Southern California. (Image courtesy of Notre Dame Archives.)

Nebraska. The schedule looked favorable too. After playing in Lincoln the year before, it was the Cornhuskers' turn to travel for their annual match with Notre Dame, meeting in South Bend in 1924.

The early season results suggested that Rockne's positive outlook was more than just optimistic talk. Notre Dame began the year with two easy wins. Meeting Lombard and Wabash in South Bend, Notre Dame dispatched both effortlessly, 40–0 and 34–0, respectively. In both matches, Rockne employed his "shock troops," a tactic the coach would use throughout the season.[19] The shock troops were second-string but still capable players who opened the game and softened up the opposition before the first team was brought in, fresh and chomping at the bit, to wallop the other side.[20]

The first two games of the season had proven so easy that they were little more than extensions of training camp. Rockne was hoping that they would help build confidence and hone teamwork as the Irish headed into the third game of the year, against Army. That contest was one of the two major games against powerhouse foes that Rockne scheduled each year. The Western powerhouse was Nebraska, while Army provided the big Eastern challenge on the docket.

The game against the Cadets would return Rockne to the biggest venue his teams had ever visited. Seating in the Polo Grounds had been expanded to accommodate the magical number of sixty thousand fans.[21] The stadium was available this time because the Giants had already lost the World Series to the Washington Senators the week before. On October 18, spectators in the Big Apple would be thinking about the gridiron rather than the baseball diamond. The match would also be the first game between the two teams to be broadcast on radio. It was so big that not just one station but two, WEAF and WJZ, carried the game.

In 1924, Army boasted a fine team that included a talented transfer from Penn State, halfback "Light Horse" Harry Wilson, yet Notre Dame was still a six-to-five favorite. The sixty-six players Rockne spread out across the field for the pregame warm-ups constituted an unusually large traveling squad and represented an intimidating display of football power that oddsmakers estimated would carry the day.

All the hoopla drew a legion of big names to the game. The stands were filled with celebrities, and the press box was jammed with high-profile sportswriters. Among the luminaries enjoying the game were Jimmy Walker, New York City's flamboyant Irish Catholic mayor (an outspoken critic of the Ku Klux Klan), and actor John Barrymore. The scribes included future author and screenwriter Gene Fowler, then working for the *New York Mirror;* Paul Gallico, syndicated columnist for New York's *Daily News;* former *South Bend Tribune* reporter Ring Lardner; and Brooklyn-born Heywood Broun, writing for the *New York World.*[22] Despite the renown of those authors, their accounts of the match would soon be forgotten, eclipsed by the words of one man, Grantland Rice, whose work that day would chisel a lasting epithet that reimagined Rockne's stars as supernatural avengers, an epithet that over time would become enshrined as a part of Irish lore.

Notre Dame prevailed that afternoon, 13–7. The team stayed the night in New York City, and Rockne decided to celebrate with another visit to see Will Rogers, who was again starring in the Ziegfeld Follies at the New Amsterdam Theatre. This theatre, an Art Nouveau showplace on West 42nd Street in Manhattan, had been New York's biggest stage venue when it opened in 1903.[23] Its narrow brick façade towered ten stories above the ornate arched and columned entrance at street level, jutting above the adjacent shops and restaurants like a finger pointing skyward. Inside, the décor featured rich wood paneling, intricately carved and gilded detail upon the curved fronts of the multiple box-seat sections, and two sets of balconies suspended above the expanse of floor seats angling up from the stage.[24]

The Irish players were packed together in the front rows of the floor seating. Rogers wore a blue college sweater with ND in large letters sewn on the front as he strutted out to begin the show. Upon seeing their colors, the boys sent up an ovation that shook the theater. Marilyn Miller, a former Ziegfeld star, poked her head out from offstage, and asked, "What's going on out there?"[25]

"I don't know," Rogers shot back. "Unless they're cheering my North Dakota sweater!"

Afterward, the team returned to their lodgings at the Belmont Hotel. Morning newspapers had already been delivered to the hotel lobby newsstand, and Notre Dame pressman George Strickler noticed the headlines from the game in the early editions. The words of Grantland Rice leaped from the page, overshadowing more prosaic accounts of the game. "Outlined against a blue-grey October sky, the Four Horsemen rode again. In dramatic lore they are known as Famine, Pestilence, Destruction, and Death. These are only aliases. Their real names are Stuhldreher, Miller, Crowley and Layden. They formed the crest of the South Bend cyclone before which another fighting Army team was swept over the precipice at the Polo Grounds yesterday afternoon, as 55,000 spectators peered down on the bewildering panorama spread on the green plain below."[26]

The piece was a mishmash of improbable vistas and mixed metaphors, with biblical overtones added in for good measure, but it fit the crazy spirit of the times and captured the imagination of sports fans everywhere. It also inspired Strickler to set up the kind of publicity stunt usually reserved for movie stars or politicians. Even Rockne was unsure about the idea, but Strickler prevailed. The young publicity man wired his father back in South Bend to make arrangements. Upon the team's return to practice Monday, the four backfielders posed on saddle horses from the South Bend Riding Academy.[27] A photographer named Christman snapped the iconic portrait of the Four Horsemen

This shot of Notre Dame's 1924 backfield quartet as the Four Horsemen of the Apocalypse became perhaps the most famous photograph in college football history. The Horsemen's success culminated in Notre Dame's January 1925 win over Stanford in its only Rose Bowl appearance. The team's exploits countered negative propaganda by the Ku Klux Klan, which had dogged the school throughout 1924. (Image courtesy of Notre Dame Archives.)

upon their noble steeds. The image captured the foursome gazing stoically at the camera, each wearing a warm-up jacket and leather helmet, with a football cradled in one arm. Within days, the photo appeared on sports pages across the country.

Ironically, the whole Four Horsemen theme had been unwittingly inspired by Strickler's own words. At halftime in the game against Army, he had compared the backfield quartet to imagery inspired by the 1921 silent film *The Four Horsemen of the Apocalypse*, starring Rudolph Valentino, comments that had prompted Rice to run with the biblical allegory.[28]

Notre Dame won the game, but Stuhldreher, Miller, Crowley, and Layden gained something more. Their exploits at the Polo Grounds, praised in Rice's lyrical words and frozen in time with the help of Christman's photograph, launched them from superstar status to immortality. Of all the players who had worn Notre Dame's blue and gold, only Gipp had reached such a lofty plateau before them.

As good as the Four Horsemen were, though, they would have been nothing without the linemen opening holes for them to gallop through. Somehow, in the aftermath of the naming of the Four Horsemen, those largely unheralded linemen came to be dubbed the Seven Mules, a nickname that fit both the equine theme of the Four Horsemen and the workmanlike efforts of the linemen. The rock-solid appeal of the linemen's nickname contrasted well with the theatrical showiness of the epithet given their better-known stablemates.

Howard Jones, unlike Rockne, was neither making headlines nor mentoring legends. He was virtually in exile. Trinity College had dropped football for more than two decades, reviving the sport only a few years before Jones's arrival.[29] Jones found neither great talent to work with at Trinity nor stirring victories to be won. The college's schedule featured mostly intrastate battles against the likes of North Carolina, North Carolina State, Guilford, Elon, Wake Forest, and Davidson. When Jones took his team into Virginia to play Richmond, the crowd numbered only eighteen hundred.[30] Wofford of South Carolina was the only out-of-state foe hosted at Hanes Field. This was not the sort of schedule that spawned titanic battles or inspired biblical allusions. Trinity's 4–5 record was Jones's first losing season since his second year at Iowa, and only the second losing season he'd ever had.

Meanwhile, Notre Dame continued on its roll. The win over Army was followed by a 12–0 victory over Princeton in New Jersey. Then Notre Dame raced past Georgia Tech and Wisconsin. The team snapped the losing streak against Nebraska in similar style, beating them 34–6 on Cartier Field. The only other close game was a 13–6 win over Northwestern in Chicago, notable as Rockne's first contest at Soldier Field. The final game against Carnegie Tech was deadlocked at halftime, but Struhldreher's passing decimated the Tartans in the second half, and Notre Dame ran away from the engineers 40–19.[31] With that, the third unblemished season of Rockne's career was complete.

With the 1924 season over, one question remained in the minds of football fanatics: who should meet on New Year's Day in Pasadena? It was a question with an obvious answer, but the answer brought problems that were not so easily resolved.

Go West, Young Man

From what they've said about Hollywood, one would imagine that it is filled with hop joints, wild women, and all that sort of thing. I wish it were. It's the deadest, dullest, hole in the world.

—Charlie Chaplin, 1922

The official date recorded for the founding of the City of Los Angeles is September 4, 1781, when forty-four settlers gathered at the San Gabriel Mission to set out for the site chosen for the new settlement. These *pobladores* (townsfolk) reflected the ongoing diversity of Los Angeles's population, being described in contemporary documents as composed of *peninsulares* (settlers born in Spain), *criollos* (settlers of Spanish descent born in New Spain), *mestizos* (persons of mixed Spanish and Native American descent), *negroes* (persons of full African ancestry), *indios* (American Indians), and *mulatos* (persons of mixed Spanish and African descent). By some accounts, the new town was called El Pueblo de Nuestra Señora Reina de Los Angeles sobre el Río de Porciuncula (the Town of Our Lady Queen of the Angels on the River Porciuncula), although historians disagree as to the exact name.[1] Whatever its original name, by the time California became part of the United States in 1850, the city was known simply as Los Angeles, or sometimes, in a nod to its pious origins, as the City of the Angels.

In 1925, Los Angeles was still considered a rather quaint, unsophisticated hamlet, considerably less refined than even its northern rival, San Francisco, let alone older cities like Chicago and New York. Writer H. L. Mencken eventually gave the city the derisive nickname Double

Dubuque, an allusion to the number of Midwesterners who had moved there since 1890 and fairly accurate—until further demographic shifts reshaped the city decades later.[2] Even the city's skyline symbolized the area's modest stature. In other cities, even San Francisco, skyscrapers were rising well over 400 feet, but in Los Angeles, the fear of earthquakes limited buildings to 150 feet until the new downtown City Hall was completed in 1928.[3]

In 1924, Los Angeles was hardly the image of today's urban sprawl. Much of the region was ranch and farmland, from Santa Barbara to San Clemente, with Los Angeles smack dab in the middle. Even its famous movie colony had only been established in Los Angeles for about a decade, after moving west from the New York area to take advantage of California's year-round sunshine and varied terrain, which offered perfect movie locations.[4]

Los Angeles was, however, a growing city. From just over 100,000 residents in 1900, its population had ballooned to almost six times that number by 1920, making it one of the ten most populous cities in the country, the first on the West Coast to reach that distinction. By 1930, it made the list of America's top five most populous cities, with more than 1 million residents, having added the largest number of new Angelenos in the city's history.[5]

Although it was bigger than some cities with professional teams, Los Angeles had no major-league sports franchises. It had no big-time pro basketball team; the National Basketball Association hadn't yet been formed at the time. Two "Los Angeles" pro football teams would arrive in 1926, one in the NFL and the other in the first AFL, but they were traveling teams, meaning that they played no games on the West Coast.

Many of the things that modern Angelenos take for granted about their city today didn't even exist in 1925. There were no freeways and little smog, and back then the iconic Hollywood sign spelled out "Hollywoodland." In typical showbiz style, the Hollywood sign on the hill today is nothing but a stage name, originally built not to salute the movie biz at all but rather as a crass promotion to advertise a real estate development by that name. Those extra four letters were only dropped and the sign repurposed to promote the surrounding community in 1949, when the Parks Department of the City of Los Angeles took over maintenance of the aging structures.[6]

What Los Angeles did have in 1924 was suburbs. In fact, Los Angeles was derided as "forty suburbs in search of a city," likely a bastardization of the description of the city as "nineteen suburbs in search of a metropolis" in Aldous Huxley's book *Americana*. One of those suburbs, Pasadena, was located just eleven miles northeast of downtown Los Angeles, in the shadow of the San Gabriel Mountains. Like many of those "forty suburbs," it was both a part of and distinct from the sprawling area around it. Today Pasadena boasts palatial homes and world-class art museums and proudly claims many famous sons, including Brooklyn and Los Angeles Dodger Jackie Robinson. Despite these impressive credentials, Pasadena's greatest claim to fame is as host to the Tournament of Roses, held every New Year's Day.

Those festivities culminate, of course, in the Rose Bowl Game after the parade. Until 1934, it was the only major annual postseason football game in the country. Apart from a very few exceptions, such as the Bacardi Bowl held intermittently in Havana, Cuba, between 1907 and 1936 and occasional one-off games like the Fort Worth Classic of 1920, the Rose Bowl Game was without peer. It wasn't until well into the Great Depression, when the Orange Bowl and Sugar Bowl games began, that real alternatives to the "Granddaddy of Them All" were available.

New Year's football games in Pasadena were played at Tournament Park until the growing crowds drove the decision to build a grand stadium nestled among the surrounding hills in a dry gulch known as the Arroyo Seco.[7] The stadium was built in a horseshoe configuration, with an open south end. Today that section is enclosed and features the words "Rose Bowl" in script letters below a three-dimensional, neon-accented rose stem.[8]

The first football game held in the new venue was a regular-season contest in October 1922 when USC lost to California's Golden Bears 12–0. The Bears declined the invitation to play in the first Rose Bowl game held in the new stadium the following January, so USC stood in as the Western representative.[9] On New Year's Day, 1923, the Trojans evened their record there by beating Penn State 14–3. The following year, Navy tied Washington 14–14. As the 1924 season closed, speculation began as to which two teams should be selected for the third game in the new stadium.

Tournament of Roses officials made tentative approaches to the two teams they judged best suited for the contest. Stanford, coached by Pop Warner in his first year at Palo Alto, was the obvious Western representative. The Stanford team—then known as Cardinals before they became the Indians and ultimately, decades later, the singular Cardinal—were Pacific Coast Conference champs, and boasted a 7–0–1 record. They had tied with their archrival, California, in the last game of the season in an impressive come-from-behind fashion at Berkeley.[10] Notre Dame was clearly the best team in the East, and, on November 25, the *Los Angeles Times* printed an Associated Press announcement that Stanford and Notre Dame would indeed meet on New Year's Day.[11] However, the story warned that the pairing was unofficial. Stanford balked, objecting that Notre Dame had a dubious academic record, and, if truth be told, was beneath its dignity.[12]

The next day, the same paper printed a second Associated Press report implying that Notre Dame was the party holding up the decision and that a suitable opponent was still being sought. Despite some talk of the Haskell Indians standing in for Stanford, the only serious alternative if Stanford fell through was the University of Southern California.[13]

The not-so-subtle prejudice against Notre Dame irked Rockne. With fond memories of his summer school stint clearly still in his mind, he privately preferred the Trojans and quietly made his choice known to the Tournament of Roses president, W. F. Creller.[14] In public, however, he diplomatically announced, "Any team the Coast officials may pick to meet Notre Dame will be suitable to us."[15] In the end, the Cardinals agreed to face Notre Dame. The offer of a more generous percentage of gate receipts proved a strong inducement in persuading the Stanford officials to drop their objections.[16]

Rockne took in stride Stanford's final acceptance of his team. In fact, it was decided to promote the Irish with a barnstorming pregame tour worthy of heavyweight Apollo Creed in the Oscar-winning film *Rocky.* Departing on December 20, they headed for Chicago before tracing a circuitous route along the Illinois Central line bound for New Orleans. From there, they continued on the Southern Pacific's Sunset Limited, traveling through Houston to a final stop in Tucson for a last practice.[17]

Rolling into Southern California at 7:30 A.M. on New Year's Eve day, the three Pullman cars of the Domer entourage were transferred from the main line to the local Pacific Electric. The railcars were then shuttled to the Maryland Hotel in Pasadena, where the tracks of the "Big Red Cars" passed directly in front of the teams' accommodations.[18] The players, however, were delivered to their lodgings in style in a fleet of new automobiles.[19]

A similar roundabout route was planned for the return trip, this time with the Irish heading north to San Francisco before turning east toward Salt Lake City and on to Denver, through Lincoln and on to South Bend by way of Chicago.[20] The entire journey would take the Notre Dame squad on the road for a total of seventeen days.

Along the way they would act as goodwill ambassadors to America, a role keenly understood by their coach and promoted by Notre Dame's prefect of religion, Father John O'Hara. O'Hara had sold Notre Dame's president, Matthew Walsh, on the idea of using the wholesome image of the school's young athletes to counter the negative propaganda of the Ku Klux Klan. Although administration officials were initially reluctant, they eventually approved the idea and came to regard the opportunity to generate positive publicity as "almost providential."[21]

The entourage for the trip totaled almost sixty, including thirty-three players, Coach Rockne and his assistant Tom Lieb, Father O'Hara as team chaplain, and the squad's student manager, Leo Sutliffe. A handful of Rockne's fellow coaches were also on board, including Rockne's protégé Edward "Skip" Madigan, who joined up in Tucson. As head coach of the St. Mary's Gaels, Madigan provided valuable scouting tips on Stanford's tendencies. Angus McDonald, the comptroller and vice president of the Southern Pacific Railroad as well as a Notre Dame alum and former Irish quarterback, brought along his own party in his private railcar. Managing the logistics was the railroad's representative, C. E. Darkus, who was described as "busier than the celebrated one-armed paperhanger" by the *Los Angeles Times*.[22]

A thousand cheering fans awaited the train as it pulled into Southern Pacific's Central Station in downtown Los Angeles.[23] Many rooters had been in town for just twelve hours, arriving on the Golden State Limited at 7:30 the night before. Whisked directly to the local Knights of Columbus hall for a pep rally, they had practiced yells for the big game, determined to provide the most spirited of welcomes. Like most Rose Bowl visitors, they planned side trips during their stay, including a tour of the city and a junket to Catalina Island.[24] As the team stepped down onto the platform, however, the fans were focused squarely on football.

The welcome proved as warm and enthusiastic as envisioned. Shouting and cheering greeted Rockne and his charges from the moment they arrived. The Ancient Order of Hibernians of Los Angeles bestowed a "massive silver football" upon the team as ten photographers recorded the gleaming gesture of support. It was all speechmaking and handshakes before Rockne and his crew waded through the crowd and out of the station to the street, where they piled into the waiting autos. Then it was off to the Maryland Hotel, where the players would stay in "luxurious bungalows."[25]

One booster who could not make the trip was Albert R. Erskine, president of the Studebaker Corporation. Studebaker was the other pride of South Bend. It was a car company that in its wagon-making days had been the biggest manufacturer of wheeled vehicles in the world.[26] Erskine had been too busy to go with the team, but he had seen the team off back in South Bend and promised to follow the game by wire reports. It was Erskine who had arranged for the autos to take the team to the hotel. The cars included a Studebaker Big Six sedan for the coach, just like the one given to Rockne back home by Notre Dame alumni and faculty, and a string of Duplex Phaetons for the players' use while in Los Angeles.[27]

Their entourage made only one stop en route from the station to the hotel: at St. Andrew's Church in Pasadena, home to one of the oldest parishes in the area,[28] where the players took communion under the spiritual guidance of Father O'Hara.[29]

Stanford's Cardinals had arrived three days before Notre Dame, to considerably less fanfare. Their preparations were detailed in the *Los Angeles Times* before the game, in an article written by Walter Ekersall, one of the game officials, whose full-time job was reporting for the *Chicago Tribune*. He looked forward to "a great game," asserting, "the known ability of the two coaches is enough to predict a struggle of the most open variety."[30]

The two coaches shared more than just a love of football. They were both clients of Christy Walsh, and the three of them posed together for a publicity shot on the Rose Bowl field before the game. Warner and

Rockne show a sense of unease in the photo, betraying the building tension before the game. Walsh seems more relaxed and confident, looking right into the camera while the attention of the two coaches is directed elsewhere.[31] Perhaps Walsh could afford to relax, since he would come out the winner whatever the outcome of the game.

The battle that followed proved to be a contest of speed and wits against power and strength. Though Stanford boasted one of the best players in the country, fullback Ernie Nevers, he failed to cross the goal line even a single time. It was a heroic performance—Nevers was nursing two broken ankles—but though he ran well, he also threw an interception for a touchdown that gave Notre Dame a 14–3 lead after they had been trailing by a field goal early in the game. Madigan's scouting and Rockne's subsequent preparations for Stanford's pass plays had paid off. The Irish defensive backfield was ready for Nevers's tosses.[32] In all, Notre Dame scored twenty-one points off Stanford turnovers.

The Cardinals' last chance to make a game of it evaporated when Notre Dame stopped Nevers just inches from a touchdown on fourth down late in the game. Walter Eckersall raised his hands to signal a score, but referee Ed Thorp overruled him, turning the ball over to Notre Dame. The luck of the Irish had held. Newspaper photos of Eckersall holding his hands skyward and reports of Nevers claiming "It was past the goal line" stirred up controversy after the game, but no touchdown was allowed during it.

Stanford had racked up considerable yardage throughout the contest. Stanford outgained Notre Dame, much as Rockne's team had won the statistical battle against Iowa back in 1921.[33] The tone of the *Notre Dame Scholastic* was different this time, however. The writers saluted not the team that gained the most yards, but rather the one that scored the most points. Notre Dame had prevailed by a score of 27–10, after all. Anyway, it was the team's faith, the writer argued, that had really won the day. They had prayed, he wrote, and "their prayers were answered."[34]

The fans back in South Bend had gathered in pool halls, bowling alleys, and wherever a radio could be found to hear the play-by-play. Others had followed the progress of the game via a Grid-o-Graph, a device resembling a scoreboard upon which a white light representing the position of the ball was moved along a gridiron laid out on the face of the board. Grid-o-Graph units were often installed in public places around the country for big games such as this. They were complex devices, with the names of all the players flanking the center section that represented the field, and the score and the time remaining shown along the top.[35]

The campus in South Bend went wild upon hearing the final score. Although many Notre Dame students had gone home for the holidays, those hardy souls still in town braved blizzard conditions to conduct "parades [and] impromptu demonstrations in public places" and generally to enjoy "great hilarity."[36] It was a great moment for the entire community. All of Rockne's hard work and past successes at Notre Dame had built to this day. The win had cemented the school's reputation at the top in college football, and praise began showering on the coach and his team like rose petals falling on a victorious Roman legion.

Many players were too exhausted to enjoy the evening's postgame celebration in Pasadena, but Rockne pressed the flesh on their behalf. Notre Dame fans swamped the Maryland Hotel late into the night.[37] With the Rose Bowl win, Rockne clearly had surpassed all comparison to his colleagues, including both Pop Warner and Howard Jones.

The next day was spent touring Hollywood and its famous studios, where the team met screen stars like Douglas MacLean and Colleen Moore. One stop offered the opportunity for Rockne to pose with film star Rudolph Valentino; Valentino's 1921 film, *The Four Horsemen of the Apocalypse,* had been the ultimate source of Grantland Rice's widely adopted name for Notre Dame's backfield—the Four Horsemen—in 1924. Later, a lunch hosted by Christy Walsh featured remarks by both coaches, and a salute to the stars of the game. Walsh made sure that sportswriters from around the country were in attendance.[38] That night, further festivities were held in the team's honor, also at the Biltmore Hotel.[39]

On Saturday, January 3, Rockne saw the players off on their long trip back to South Bend. Notre Dame students were due back in class on January 9, but the coach and his family planned to stay on in Los Angeles for a few days.[40] A bit more vacation time in the warmth of Southern California seemed like a fair reward for a great season. Plus, Rockne still had a few official functions to attend. There was also one other piece of business. People at USC were eager to speak with him. The need for such a conversation went back to December, when Stanford finally agreed to appear in the Rose Bowl.

When the Rose Bowl bid fell through, the Trojans arranged to play the University of Missouri on Christmas Day.[41] The Los Angeles Christmas Festival was one of those one-off, postseason affairs that came along from time to time. The game was played on December 25, 1924, in the Coliseum, with USC prevailing 20–7.

Besides the fact that it was the only such game ever played, it was unique in one other respect. It was the last time USC would wear blue uniforms. For whatever reason, Coach Henderson had sent his boys out twice before in azure togs and won both games. Playing a superstitious hunch, he picked that shade again as a good luck charm for the winter matchup.[42]

Despite the victory and Henderson's winning total of nearly 90 percent at USC, the administration had been under pressure from anxious alumni dissatisfied with the status quo. The Trojans had beaten Cal only once in six tries during Henderson's tenure and had lost the last five straight. If USC were to challenge the powers on the coast, it would have to prevail over the Bears. Perhaps worse, relations between USC and both Cal and Stanford had been severed, a conflict sparked by recriminations over ineligible players.[43] Though officials denied it, rumors swirled that the two Bay Area schools had demanded Henderson's removal as the price of setting things right.[44] Whatever the specific reasons, the Trojans had decided that Henderson must go.

While speculation raged as to who might be the new coach, the administration decided to try a desperate "Hail Mary." They were going after Rockne. Everyone knew he had always listened to other job offers in the past. Cornell had come knocking in 1919 and Colgate and Northwestern in 1921. There had been talk of him going to Carnegie Tech in 1923, and, of course, it was no secret that Iowa had reached out to Rockne when Jones left the Hawkeyes. The University of Wisconsin had made inquiries just a few weeks before the Rose Bowl game.[45] Now it was the Trojans' turn to court the flirtatious pigskin mentor. Sometime before Rockne left Pasadena, possibly at Christy Walsh's event at the Biltmore on January 2, officials quietly approached Rockne about replacing Henderson.[46] As it turned out, the wily Norwegian was indeed receptive to the Trojans' entreaties. He had developed good relations with the staff at USC during his teaching stint there the summer before, and his wife was captivated by the region's warm weather and wide-open possibilities.[47]

The talks also covered the possibility of scheduling a game between USC and Notre Dame. According to Gwynn Wilson, graduate manager of athletics at USC, Rockne carried a proposal for such a game when he left Los Angeles for Mexico to play the ponies in Tijuana before heading home.[48] While this claim may have been only a cover story for the ongoing job discussions, since it seems odd to discuss scheduling a team when you're trying to lure away its coach, USC might have considered the prospect of scheduling a game with Notre Dame a consolation prize should the Trojans fail to hire Rockne.

Rockne was still committed to a long-term contract back in South Bend, but given USC's willingness to buy out Henderson's remaining salary of $14,500 and pay him a $2,500 bonus for "excellent work," the Trojans may also have been prepared to recompense Notre Dame for releasing Rockne.[49] Of course, at $10,000 per annum for the next nine years of his contract, the price would have been steep. Whether because of naïveté at USC or misleading assurances from Rockne that the good fathers at Notre Dame would readily let him go, existing contractual issues did not derail the conversation.

Rockne's true intentions remain unclear. On the one hand, it is possible that he never really had any intention of taking the job. He had used every previous outside offer to win leverage at Notre Dame, either to boost his power in struggles with the administration or to gain pay raises, and perhaps he was just calling the same play one more time in his talks with USC. On the other hand, there were tensions between Rockne and some officials at Notre Dame. The public perception of Rockne marching in lockstep with Notre Dame's leaders as fellow crusaders for the Catholic Church was not always accurate. At least since 1922, Rockne had battled for power against Notre Dame's Faculty Board of Control of Athletics. The winter of 1925 was no different, as Rockne resisted moves by President Walsh to place more academically oriented faculty in positions of influence. These men, such as Rev. Thomas Irving, were firmly opposed to the coach's growing autonomy.[50]

However serious Rockne was about USC, though, he was not willing to commit to a move without assurances that two conditions would be met. The first was that Henderson would be well taken care of—a trivial matter, since that was USC's desire as well. The second was that Rockne be given time to discuss the offer with the powers at Notre Dame before any word of the negotiations leaked out. Keeping a lid on their conversations proved problematic, however.

After relaxing in Mexico, Rockne headed back north through Los Angeles. He planned to follow the same route his team had traveled before him, which would take him through San Francisco. Newspaper reports on January 14 placed two USC officials, Vice President Harold Stonier and Comptroller Warren Bovard, in the Bay Area to present Rockne with a more formal job offer before he left California.[51]

The whole affair began to unravel from that moment on. One day after departing San Francisco, when reporters confronted him about the rumors that were spreading like wildfire, Rockne denied ever talking to USC.[52] Two days after that, as he passed through the Windy City, Rockne told the *Chicago Tribune* that he would "stick to Notre Dame."[53] Apparently, that was news to the folks in Los Angeles: that same day, Bovard wired Rockne that USC would meet all the conditions he had asked for.[54] Throughout the ongoing intrigue, no job had formally opened at USC. Elmer Henderson was still officially the Trojans' head football coach. The sword did not fall on him until 10:00 A.M. on January 15, when Trojan officials discreetly met with Henderson off-campus, in the office of prominent alum Lee Phillips, in the Pacific Mutual Building near Pershing Square. Bovard had visited Henderson at home late the night before to work out details,[55] and Henderson's resignation was finally announced by USC late on January 15.[56]

The powers at Notre Dame were not amused by stories of their head football coach caught up in another intrigue. President Walsh decided to play pressure defense, reminding Rockne that he was under contract and that if necessary Notre Dame was prepared to use legal action to keep him there.[57] The strain left Rockne, in his own words, "sweating blood."[58] By January 19, any possibility of Rockne leaving for USC ended when Stonier named Willis O. "Bill" Hunter as USC's "temporary" head of athletics, a position that Rockne would have filled had he come west. The story in the *Chicago Tribune* claimed that a wire from Rockne to USC declining the offer had precipitated Stonier's action.[59]

Neither USC nor Rockne got what they wanted out of the incident.

The Trojans hadn't signed the replacement they had hoped for when they forced Henderson out. Rockne had failed to handle the process deftly enough to obtain his release from Notre Dame, assuming his interest in the job was genuine. If his flirtation with USC had been just a ploy, it hadn't improved Rockne's leverage at Notre Dame. In fact, the coach had lost face in the aftermath, and the Faculty Board had asserted its power over him. The only winners, perhaps, were President Walsh and his administration at Notre Dame, but their victory came at the cost of bad publicity and a further straining of their relations with the head football coach.

Despite the fact that they'd been left standing at the altar, the Trojans still had a shot to salvage something out of the mess. There was still the matter of adding Notre Dame to their schedule, an offer Rockne had told reporters in Chicago that he would raise with the Faculty Board. Of course, he also had stated that approval of such an arrangement was unlikely, since it would involve so much travel for the players.[60]

The Rose Bowl trip had been a double-edged sword for Notre Dame in that regard. Such an absence was justifiable as a one-time exception, but the Faculty Board, fearing that too much football publicity might send the wrong message, moved to prevent such postseason activity in the future. Shortly thereafter, the board banned all postseason appearances, a prohibition that would remain in effect until 1969.[61] Notre Dame's desire to reduce such lengthy travel by its team, together with the embarrassment generated by rumors of USC's offer to Rockne, quickly torpedoed the proposal for a game with the Trojans.

Meanwhile, in Los Angeles, speculation over Henderson's replacement was rampant. The earliest suggestion was Harry Stuhldreher, the Notre Dame quarterback, who hadn't even graduated yet.[62] More serious suggestions included Skip Madigan of St. Mary's College, whose Gaels had whipped Southern California in the Coliseum back in November, when they stood in for Stanford at the last minute; John Wilce of Ohio State[63]; Gill Dobie of Cornell[64]; and Frank Cavanaugh of Boston College. Rockne suggested William Spaulding of Minnesota, who would eventually wind up not at USC but across town at UCLA.[65]

Rockne recommended one other candidate, a coach he had faced only once but who had so impressed him that he recommended him to USC. Like Rockne, this coach had recently signed a contract at another school, though in this case it was with a small, unheralded university in North Carolina instead of a major football power. Prying him away from that post wouldn't be as much trouble as chasing Rockne had been. The coach that Rockne recommended was a former Ohioan with an Ivy League pedigree. His name was Howard Harding Jones.

10

A New Man in Charge

Heroing is one of the shortest-lived professions there is.
—Will Rogers, 1925

While the unpleasant task of replacing a football coach can sometimes become a rather messy affair, the carnage falls far short of the typical transition of power among criminal gangs. Replacing a mob boss almost always gets vicious and bloody. In 1925, during the turf wars of the Prohibition Era gangs, it was the Chicago way.

The night of January 24, 1925, was a typically cold winter evening in the Windy City. Frigid air drifted in off Lake Michigan, and though it hadn't snowed in almost two weeks, the low would hit twenty-three degrees that night.[1] Johnny Torrio, Al Capone's boss and the man in charge on the south side of Chicago, had gone out shopping with his wife, Anne, but with their errands complete, it was time to settle in for the evening.

It was dusk when driver Robert Barton parked Torrio's big Lincoln Town Car in front of the gangster's expensive Clyde Avenue apartment. The couple gathered their things and headed toward the entrance, where Anne held the door open for her husband as he juggled the stack of boxes in his arms. At that moment, Torrio must have seemed more like a henpecked spouse than the powerful mob boss he really was.[2]

Suddenly the drudgery of domestic routine erupted into moments of terror. Two men jumped out of a blue Caddy, guns blazing, unleashing a fusillade into the Lincoln that riddled the passenger compartment and shattered the window glass. With the driver dispatched, they advanced on Torrio. He hit the ground as several rounds pierced his torso and right arm, before a bullet slammed directly into his groin.

"Bugs" Moran, the new head of the North Side Gang, leaned over the prone Torrio to press the barrel of his pistol against the wounded mobster's temple. There was nothing but an impotent click of metal on metal when he pulled the trigger—he was out of ammo. Moran scrambled back to the waiting getaway car as his cohorts shouted for him to beat it before the cops showed up. Torrio's wife frantically dragged her husband into their home as the assassins sped off into the night.[3]

Incredibly, Torrio survived the assault, but his long recuperation triggered a reevaluation of his priorities. He had been facing prison time even before the assassins struck, and the prospect of a stint in the big house, combined with his brush with death, was too much. He wanted out.

"Al," he told Capone, his right-hand man, as his henchman leaned over his hospital bed, "it's all yours." The handover meant that Capone would now run the outfit's brothels, breweries, and gambling joints. "It's Europe for me," Torrio mused.[4] By the end of 1925, he would be back in his native Italy.[5]

Fortunately for Elmer Henderson, his removal as coach of the USC football team did not require the same kind of bloodshed. It did enflame passions in Los Angeles, however. Henderson was lauded in the press as the man whose arrival "immediately lifted the institution out of the doormat class which it had occupied during the years immediately preceding."[6]

Yet the same author wrote glowingly a short time later about Henderson's replacement, Howard Jones. He was "the kind of a man who will build up at U.S.C. a battling eleven that will uphold its honor," the author wrote, " . . . and, even more important, Jones strikes us as being an individual who will have the confidence and the respect of not only his team and student body but of the representatives of the rival schools as well."[7] While the reporter's words hinted at USC's ongoing conflict with the Bay Area schools, the thoughts of Trojan alumni were less about sportsmanship and more about results. They simply hoped Jones would deliver the long-sought victory over Cal when competition with the Golden Bears resumed.[8]

If it had been up to the student body, Howard Jones might never have come west. The annual ceremony on the Trojan campus to award varsity monograms to the football players was highlighted by a five-minute standing ovation for Henderson. It was his last official act as head coach, and when the ceremony was over the "Gloomy Gus" era at USC came to a close.[9]

Years later, Al Wesson, the first sports information director at USC, reflected on the shake-up of the Trojan coaching staff. "Under Henderson," Wesson remarked, "USC had outgrown its old association with and rivalry with Pomona, Oxy, Whittier and L.A. High," seeking instead to join the Pacific Coast Conference, which was dominated by Cal and Stanford. USC had finally been admitted in 1922, but Henderson quickly rubbed people the wrong way. "Gus was a forceful character, a bit blunt, and none too diplomatic," he explained. Delving into USC's break with the two schools in 1924 and its subsequent ouster from the PCC, Wesson remarked, "For a variety of reasons, probably none of them worth a damn, Cal and Stanford resented Henderson." They seemed to think "he wanted to run the Pacific Coast Conference before we ever got into it."[10] Considering this intercollegiate acrimony and the pressure from USC alumni for a win over Cal, the decision to replace Henderson was inevitable.

The news that Howard Jones had been hired to replace Henderson broke on February 4, 1925, trumpeted by the *Los Angeles Times* with the headline, "Iowa Gridiron Mentor Succeeds Henderson."[11] The formal announcement came at the Los Angeles Athletic Club, where the thirty-nine-year-old Jones was introduced.[12] He had quietly slipped into town three days before, and was staying at the home of one of his former Hawkeye players, Harold Van Metre, while he met with the Trojan officials.[13]

People back in North Carolina were shocked: Jones was locked into a five-year contract. Reports from Durham labeled the stories of Jones's departure for USC "erroneous," but the reality was otherwise.[14] Only formalities remained before Jones would obtain his release and sign with USC.

Jones would enjoy considerably higher pay than the $6,000 per year Henderson had received at USC. His $10,000 annual salary would put him on par with Rockne at Notre Dame and rank him among the highest-paid coaches in the nation.[15] In addition, he retained a limited share in the Excello Mill, his father's paper business, soon to be consolidated under family ownership.[16] In years to come, he would, aided by Christy

Walsh, profit from a second book on football, numerous product endorsements, and even film appearances.[17] With a comfortable salary and new opportunities opening in Los Angeles, money would not be a concern. In any case, as a gentleman of means, it was not his way to appear to chase a dollar as Rockne might sometimes seem to do, leaving Jones less vulnerable to rumors that he would leave his current coaching post for one at another school.

Since Jones had to finish the baseball season at Duke, he would not be able to permanently relocate to Los Angeles until spring practice in March 1925. Moreover, rumors held that he had requested to live in Los Angeles only during the season. One newspaper column in the *Los Angeles Times* stated that while Jones's plans were "indefinite," he had taken "a wild fancy to Southern California during the course of his stay" and was "considering growing up with the country."[18] Los Angeles would soon take a wild fancy to him, and both would quickly grow up together.

Just as Jones was finishing his term in North Carolina, President Calvin Coolidge was beginning a new political term in the White House. Coolidge had ascended to the Oval Office when Warren Harding died in office in 1923, and now, in March 1925, was sworn in for a second time, after winning election in his own right the previous November. The same election that had confirmed the status quo in the White House had brought change to the governor's mansion in Indiana, bringing in Governor Edward L. Jackson, a native Hoosier. Sworn in as Indiana's thirty-second governor on January 12, 1925, the day Rockne left San Francisco to return home after the Rose Bowl, Jackson was an accomplished lawyer, a war hero, the sitting secretary of state of Indiana— and an active and "unabashed" member of the Ku Klux Klan.[19]

The Klan was at the height of its power in 1925. That summer, a massive parade of Klansmen would file down Pennsylvania Avenue in Washington, D.C.[20] The group continued to grow in Indiana even as the rift intensified between Imperial Wizard Evans and his grand dragon, Dwight Stephenson. The conflict between them prompted Evans to order Stephenson removed from office within a year of the big Kokomo rally back in 1923, but it hadn't really affected Klan activities in the state. Stephenson simply declared independence from the national organization, and most Klansmen in Indiana ignored Evans's decree.[21]

Stephenson had continued to focus the Klan's activities in Indiana on politics. He had backed Jackson for governor through the primary and the general election in November. Stephenson had been in charge of Jackson's inaugural ceremony and celebration at the Indianapolis Athletic Club, and remained a trusted advisor to the new governor. But Stephenson had bigger dreams, hoping to become the power behind the governor's chair no matter who was in office. Stephenson had a taste for money, for the power that riches could bring, and for the women that both would attract. At the moment, he had set his sights on one special lady, a young woman named Madge Oberholtzer.

Oberholtzer was an attractive twenty-eight-year-old employee of the Indiana Department of Public Instruction. Stephenson had met her in the wake of the Klan's sweeping electoral success, at the glittering inaugural ball held at the Indianapolis Athletic Club. The two had been seated opposite each other at dinner, and although each had arrived with an escort, they quickly formed a mutual attraction.[22] Stephenson eventually asked Madge to dance. As they joined the couples paired up on the dance floor, she was unaware that she was waltzing into a nightmare.

Stephenson was not interested in the kind of woman who'd throw herself at him.[23] He enjoyed a challenge, if not the sick thrill of stalking helpless victims. For two months he wooed her, taking her on quiet dates, involving her in political errands, and stroking her ego by suggesting she write a textbook he was planning for the Indiana schools. She was happy, and why not? Stephenson was handsome, powerful, rich, and well educated; he dressed impeccably and seemed like a perfect gentleman. So far, everything had been on the up-and-up, but by mid-March, Stephenson was ready to make his move.

Madge returned home late in the evening of March 15 to word that Stephenson's secretary had called. Madge's mother, who had taken the message, said Stephenson needed to see her right away regarding important business before he left for Chicago. Madge returned the call and told her mother that she was going to Stephenson's house, then bid her good night as she waited for the driver to pick her up.

When she arrived at Stephenson's estate she found him drunk, surly, and surrounded by armed bodyguards. It was shocking to see him in this state after hearing so many speeches in which he'd railed against the evils of alcohol. When she suggested she should leave, he growled, "You're staying with me." She struggled, but Stephenson's goons quickly cut off her desperate efforts to escape. They grabbed her and forced whiskey down her throat until she nearly passed out.

Shuffled outside by Stephenson's henchmen, she was thrown into a car, rushed to Union Station, and hustled onto his private railcar. In the sleeping berth, he tore off her clothes. His teeth bit down deeply into her flesh, drawing blood that trickled down her naked body. Then he raped her brutally. This was not the first time he had meted out such abuse: his appetites were as sick as Jack the Ripper's, if not as lethal, but his power and influence had made it easy to intimidate victims into remaining silent. Except for Hiram Evans's spies, no one outside his inner circle knew the true depths of his depravity.

Stephenson knew better than to take Madge across the state line and violate federal law. He ordered his men to get her off the train in Hammond, Indiana, before they crossed into Illinois. They all went to the Indiana Hotel, where the couple was registered as man and wife under assumed names. Madge was tossed into the same bed with her tormentor, and the two were left alone in the darkness, in a hotel room that to her might was well have been a prison cell.

Stephenson quickly passed out. His snoring drowned out Madge's whimpering as she crept out of bed and fumbled around the room. Then she found it. The pistol he carried would be her deliverance, if only she could bring herself to pull the trigger. Her hands trembled as she raised the weapon toward the rumpled mass of body and bed sheets, but she could not face the scandal that would ruin her parents. So she turned the gun on herself, pressing the barrel against her head. Just then Stephenson stirred, and her instinctive reaction was to slide the gun back into his pants, where she had found it. She then set herself to make it through the night, disgusted with his beastliness and her own weakness. She finally succumbed to the need for sleep, but the hours that followed would build her courage and strengthen her resolve.

The next day she found her opportunity. She tricked her captors into allowing a quick shopping trip for the makeup and supplies she'd need to freshen up. With the attention of Stephenson's bodyguard distracted just enough, she used the money she'd been given for sundries to buy mercury bichloride, a corrosive and poisonous disinfectant. Back in the hotel room, she downed as many of the tablets as she could before the mercury bichloride took effect. She collapsed, convulsively vomiting blood on the cold bathroom floor. Suddenly, Stephenson's sick fun was not so amusing. He was in a state of near-panic.

Inquiries began back in Indianapolis when Madge's parents grew alarmed at her disappearance. Three days after she left, her parents went to a detective agency. Upon returning home, they discovered her in bed, near death. Stephenson's men had smuggled her back home while her parents were out.

Madge lived just long enough to supply a notarized statement detailing her ordeal. Two weeks later, Stephenson was arrested.[24] The downfall of the Klan in Indiana was at hand. Stephenson had spoken out in support of Prohibition and defended the "virtue" of American women from the predations of dark-skinned and menacing immigrants. Now that the public knew that he had been the predator, the rank and file within the Klan quickly became disillusioned. The scandal broke Stephenson's power, led to his conviction and incarceration for second-degree murder, brought down his political allies, and devastated the Klan, crippling it in Indiana and precipitating a rapid nationwide decline.[25]

Just as the Klansmen of Indiana lost faith, Rockne was strengthening his. A lifelong Lutheran, he'd had to stand aside when his wife, his family, and his players went to Mass. While not a devout man, Rockne admired the expressions of faith and the sense of community the Catholic Church brought to life at Notre Dame.[26] He was beginning to reconsider his beliefs. The religious context into which Father John O'Hara placed Notre Dame's triumphant season and Rose Bowl victory may also have influenced Rockne. With O'Hara presenting the team's success as a vindication of Notre Dame's fight against the prejudice of the Ku Klux Klan,[27] it was not surprising that Rockne was considering becoming a Catholic himself.

Rockne expressed interest in joining the church just as Oberholtzer was suffering her ordeal. He would begin his religious instruction in South Bend as she lay dying in Indianapolis. On April 18, Oberholtzer was laid to rest. She had found her peace at last. Rockne still sought his.

The coming months would be long, hot, and full of scandalous headlines. More gangsters would die in Chicago. Stephenson would pressure his political cronies for help while Evans consolidated control of the Klan, even as its power began to wane.

For Howard Jones in Los Angeles, the spring was a time of hope as practice opened at his new university, but the promise of new opportunities was followed by a summer of despair. On July 28, Jones's wife finally filed for divorce,[28] charging him with "extreme and repeated acts of cruelty."[29] Jones's obsession with his first love, football, had come at a price. It had cost him the love of his wife.

"The Game Is On"

What Bonnie wanted from Rock, she usually got.

—Anonymous, date unknown

Howard Jones had been brought to Los Angeles precisely to replicate the success Rockne had achieved in South Bend. Colleges across America had grown enamored with the idea that a football program could finance campus expansion, and the University of Southern California was no different. The school had been growing since Rufus von KleinSmid had become president there in 1921, and the men in charge hoped they could follow Rockne's example even if they could not have the coach himself. In 1903, USC had enrolled barely three hundred students, and though by 1925 the student body had risen to about five thousand, von KleinSmid was thinking well beyond those that figure.[1] Shortly after arriving from the University of Arizona, he had set a goal of $10 million for the university's new fund-raising campaign.[2]

To finance the expansion he planned, von KleinSmid had severed the school's relationship with the Methodist Church and sought to replace its financial support by courting the real estate developers and oil barons who were the business powers of Southern California.[3] He also wanted to boost the revenue stream from ticket sales for football games in the Coliseum, which had diminished without Stanford and Cal on the schedule. Howard Jones was hired to restore order to the football program and fill those seats in the stadium.

As fall practice got under way in 1925 Howard Jones resumed molding his team, a process he had begun back in April, before the summer

Brice Taylor overcame racism and physical challenges to become the Trojans' first All-American selection in 1925. (Courtesy of the University of Southern California.)

break, when he had greeted sixty of Henderson's players.[4] This group gave Jones plenty of material to work with. Jeff Cravath, a future Trojan head coach, and Brice Taylor, one of Jones's African American standouts, bolstered the line. The backfield featured Mort Kaer and Morley Drury, the latter destined to become "the Noblest Trojan of Them All." The end position was in the capable hands of Hobbs Adams, Morris Badgro, and Jones's very own Knute—Knute Stark, in this case.[5]

Jones had decided he needed to evaluate his players further under game conditions before wading into the toughest part of the season's schedule, so that spring he had taken the unusual step of seeking two last-minute contests, to be played on the same day to start the season. The doubleheader was played on September 26, 1925. Cal Tech and Whittier invaded the Coliseum, only to be slaughtered by a combined score of 106–0.

It would have been understandable for Jones to become distracted during such lopsided games, given what else was occurring in his life. The same day as the doubleheader, Denver judge George F. Dunklee granted Leah Jones a preliminary decree of divorce in Colorado. Jones was awarded custody of his son Clark for ten months of every year, an arrangement not at all unusual at the time. A property and alimony settlement was made out of court.[6] He began his tenure at USC, officially and legally, as a "single father," which was *very* unusual for a prominent man of the community in 1925.

Private woes were not mirrored in Jones's professional life, however. Overpowering victories continued as the season progressed. The Trojans won nine of their first ten games of the season, outscoring their opponents 404–38. Jones was developing an impressive offensive machine, not at all bad for a coach often dismissed as a pale imitation of his contemporaries. His team was just as impressive at practice during the week as it was during games on Saturday afternoons. Teet Carle, athletic news director at USC in 1925, was a frequent visitor to scrimmages at Bovard Field. He took note of Jones's brand of power football and coined a new nickname for the team. One afternoon, he and his assistant, student John Parsons, watched the offensive line as it swept forward ahead of the advancing ball carrier. Moving as one unstoppable unit, they bulldozed everything in their path. Awestruck, Parsons turned to Carle and blurted out his impression of their precision and power. "They look like a bunch of wild cattle," he said, "just like a thundering herd."

Carle decided to use the new moniker in all future press releases.[7] As the team stampeded through the schedule, the nickname stuck, lasting throughout Jones's tenure at USC. The Trojans had become, unofficially, the Thundering Herd. Like Rockne's Four Horsemen, this nickname for Jones's ground-churning machine was linked to a film released that very year, a Western based on a Zane Grey novel, entitled *The Thundering Herd.*[8]

Like Jones, Rockne enjoyed lopsided wins at the start of the season, although Notre Dame's schedule did not include any doubleheaders. Baylor, Lombard, and Beloit fell by a combined tally of 129–3. His team stumbled badly, however, when it faced Army in the fourth game of the year, losing 27–0, the worst drubbing Notre Dame had ever suffered at the hands of the Cadets—or any other team for that matter.

Rockne's squad finished October having won five games out of six. The first week of November saw the team struggle through a 0–0 tie with Penn State before bashing Carnegie Tech 26–0. While the big season finale against Nebraska was just two weeks away, Notre Dame had a date with Northwestern first. Rockne had a more personal, and perhaps more important, date before either of those games, however: he was to be baptized into the Roman Catholic Church.[9]

Rockne's decision to convert was deeply intertwined with football. He had been impressed with his players' devotion when they arose early on game-days to attend Mass.[10] Sitting in the back of the little Catholic church across from Grand Central Station when the team was in New York, he would quietly observe their worship.[11] Being left out of something so much a part of his boys' spiritual lives left a void in the old Lutheran's soul that compelled him to act. The overall climate of Catholicism on campus also influenced him, and as he and the school seemed to meld into one, it was only natural that he took the final step. Rockne decided to convert in March, and received religious instruction from a former player, Rev. Vincent Mooney.[12] By November he was ready.

Rockne's baptism into the Catholic Church was scheduled for November 20, 1925.[13] The ceremony would take place at Notre Dame's Log Chapel, a quiet spot surrounded by pine trees, yet located just a short distance from the heart of the Notre Dame campus. This chapel was perfect for such intimate services. Father Stephen Badin had built the original back in 1832. Father Sorin had lived there when he founded Notre Dame a decade later. The original structure was destroyed by fire in 1856, but fifty years later the university erected a replica.[14] For Rockne it would be a place of transformation: he would enter a Lutheran and emerge a Catholic.

Though Rockne was close to his players, and their faith had inspired him, they were not present for the ceremony. His wife Bonnie, Rockne's two sponsors, and "Scotty" (as he called Father Mooney) were the only witnesses. However, Rockne did bring along his irreverent sense of humor. Noticing that only one candle had been lit for him, he commented, "It looks to me, Scotty, like you're pretty tight with the wax."

Mooney heard Rockne's first confession right after the baptism. The next morning saw his first public expression of his new religious life when he joined one of his sons, Knute Jr., at the Communion rail of St. Edwards Hall, part of the grade school that existed at Notre Dame in those days. "Daddy, go back," his son implored him as they both strode up to the rail. "This is for Catholics." Upon learning that his father had been quietly received into the Catholic Church the night before, the young boy beamed with delight. "I'll offer my Communion for you, Daddy," he said through the broad smile spreading across his face.

There was, of course, one more ritual ahead that day, something that the public could witness: Notre Dame's home game against the North-western Wildcats. The Irish players knew their coach had become a Catholic, but the news failed to inspire them, at least initially. The Irish were trailing 10–0 at halftime, and inside the locker room, the players prepared for a humdinger of an eruption from Rockne. Instead, he saun-tered in, apparently unconcerned about the dismal first half. "Good af-ternoon, Ladies," he began. "So this is the Fighting Irish I've heard so much about. Well, when you go out there in the second half and get the beating you deserve, I won't share it with you. I will no longer be your coach." He turned toward his assistant. "You take 'em, Hunk." With that, he turned and walked right back out. He had just joined the church, but now he was abandoning his team.

Rockne remained in the stands for the first eight minutes of the sec-ond half. It was long enough for his troops to rally, and take a 13–10 lead, which they held to win the game.[15] As usual, his gambit had paid off, and all was forgiven when the final whistle sounded.

There was just one game remaining, the annual showdown with Ne-braska, scheduled for Thanksgiving Day. This and the game against Army were always the biggest two dates of Notre Dame's year. This season, the Nebraska game would prove to be the biggest game of the year for USC too.

The Trojans had been trying to set up a game with Rockne since 1923.[16] A game had almost been arranged for the 1925 Rose Bowl, but Notre Dame had faced Stanford instead. The Trojans were rebuffed when they had pitched the idea again right after the Rose Bowl, de-spite pleas for an Irish-Trojan match from Notre Dame alumni in Los Angeles. Rockne was the stumbling block.

When USC's Harold Stonier had sent Rockne off in January with a proposal for games starting the following year, Rockne had publicly promised to discuss the idea with Notre Dame's Faculty Board, al-though he had warned that "he didn't think the proposition would be acceptable, due to the necessitated long absence of the players from their studies."[17] By the fall of 1925, Notre Dame's administration had banned postseason games as requiring excessive travel,[18] and there was little room on the 1926 schedule in any event. That fact was reinforced just three days after Rockne's baptism, when Rockne announced seven of the ten games he had scheduled for the following season. Only the Quantico Marines had been added, to replace one team dropped from the 1925 slate.[19]

In an article published in the *Chicago Daily Tribune* on November 25, however, Walter Eckersall revived rumors of a USC–Notre Dame match in 1926, suggesting that Rockne might look favorably on such a game.[20] It's likely he wrote the report because he got wind of the fact that the Trojans were pressing Rockne one more time. There was certainly plenty of motivation for them to try. Though the Trojans had been reinstated into the PCC for 1925, there had been few of the big games that von KleinSmid wanted during the rift. Feeding on the likes of Pomona-Pitzer might bolster the win/lose record, but it didn't do much for ticket sales. Besides, Howard Jones was not the kind of man to be content with easy mismatches. He wanted a challenge. He wanted to play Notre Dame. In fact, everyone at Southern California wanted a big game to cap future Trojan football schedules, and there was no bigger prize to snare than Notre Dame.[21] Before Gwynn Wilson, USC's graduate manager of athletics, set the 1926 schedule, therefore, he spoke with Jones about trying one last time to snare the Irish.[22]

Wilson began thinking about how to win that prize. He'd heard about the escalating tensions between the fans of Nebraska and Notre Dame, as demonstrations of anti-Catholic sentiment in the stands at Lincoln grew more objectionable with each trip the Irish made to the Cornhuskers' home ground. He knew that momentum was building in South Bend to drop the Cornhuskers from Notre Dame's schedule, and he realized that this growing animosity presented USC with a chance to overcome the obstacles that had foiled all previous attempts to schedule Notre Dame.

Wilson was driving toward the USC campus on his way to work when it all came together.[23] It was Monday, November 23, 1925; Thanksgiving was just four days away. He would have to sell Stonier on his idea, but if things worked out, arranging the match would be quite a coup for the ambitious young man. The more he considered it, the more sense it seemed to make. What if USC could replace Nebraska on Notre Dame's schedule?

Wilson went straight to Stonier's office, located in the same Bovard Hall where Henderson had said his goodbyes a few months before, to pitch his idea. Wilson, twenty-eight years old, had been a Trojan for eight years, first as captain of the track team and student body president, then as the Athletic Department's graduate manager. He was rail thin, with a long, narrow face topped by loose, wavy hair trimmed short on the sides, a popular style for men at the time. Like most men of the day, even factory workers, he wore a coat and tie to work, though Wilson favored bow ties over the necktie that adorned Stonier's starched white collar. While Stonier was only seven years older than Wilson, he was already considered one of the nation's finest educators in the field of business and finance.[24] His bearing was more formal and polished than Wilson's, as befit his status, and the touch of gray at the temples added a fatherly air to his characteristically kind and gentle expression.[25] Stonier listened attentively to Wilson's pitch. He was interested but skeptical: after all, every previous attempt had been met with rejection. "Go on," he urged Wilson, doubtful but still curious as to what Wilson had in mind.

Wilson related the rumors that acrimony between the fans of Notre Dame and Nebraska might provoke a break between the two schools. If so, he argued, the timing might be perfect for USC to renew its offer.[26] Notre Dame would want a challenging contest to fill the gap in its schedule, and Wilson also believed that Notre Dame would find a long-term series, like the one it had maintained with Nebraska since 1916, more attractive than a simple home and home proposition for a couple of games. Notre Dame would no doubt be looking to find another annual opponent to replace the Cornhuskers if they parted ways.

"Well, it would be a series," Wilson said. "Each year we alternate. We could offer them a $20,000 guarantee here if they would match it there, and I'm sure they will." Wilson's enthusiasm was so infectious that failure hardly seemed a possibility.

Stonier thought it over for a moment before asking "Why don't you go talk to Rockne about it?"

"Well, he's in Lincoln, they're playing Nebraska Thanksgiving Day."

"Catch a train," Stonier replied.

"I'll have to make some arrangements, and reservations," Wilson protested.

"I mean today."

Wilson hesitated, and then reminded Stonier that he was a newly-wed. "I'd really like to go, Hal, but I kind of hate to leave my wife. We've only been married a short time. . . ."

"Today," Stonier interrupted. "Take her with you."[27]

Three days later, Wilson found himself standing in the lobby of the Lincoln Hotel. It had been a hectic trip. He and his wife had rushed to pack and then struggled to deal with the crowds at the Santa Fe Railroad's La Grande Station, before riding the California Limited to make a connection in Kansas City to reach Lincoln the night before the game.[28] Now it was game day, and Wilson was face to face with the Notre Dame coach.

"What are you doing here?" Rockne asked him.

"I'd like to talk to you about a game," was Wilson's reply.

"Well, I can't talk to you now," Rockne protested, gesturing toward the chaotic scene around them. "But I'll get you a reservation on the team train back to Chicago. We'll talk about it on the way home. In the meantime, I'll get you a couple of tickets to this ball game."

Unfortunately for Rockne, the game wound up being a disaster. It had been a cold, snowy, miserable day, and the Cornhuskers won, going away 17–0.[29] Worse yet, the Fighting Irish and their fans had been the targets of more offensive abuse from Nebraska's home crowd. The greatest offense was a halftime show mocking the Four Horsemen as "bricklayers," a slur reflecting a common portrayal of Catholics as fit for nothing beyond menial labor.[30] Perhaps worst of all, the rude display had left the clergy of Notre Dame determined to end football relations with Nebraska, a move Rockne could not accept. He regarded Nebraska as having the best talent in the country every year. The Cornhuskers had just walloped Notre Dame,[31] and Rockne would be damned if he was going to turn tail and run.

Faced with Rockne's state of mind, Wilson definitely had his work cut out for him. He must have been questioning his own judgment on the way to Chicago. Not only did he have to deal with Rockne's sour disposition but the train ride itself became an uncomfortable experience. The Wilsons were berthed among the Notre Dame squad, and Marion Wilson, Gwynn's recent bride, had to listen to the banter of the young athletes in all its unsavory glory. Her tender ears would recover more quickly, of course, if her husband's mission ended in success.

Rockne was not in a receptive mood, however. His effortless avoidance of the topic, executed with all the agility of a halfback dodging tacklers on an open field run, did not bode well for USC's chances. Whenever Wilson tried to broach his request for a match, Rockne changed the subject, steering the conversation away from the upcoming season and back toward the problems he'd faced during the season just ended. Rockne skirted the issue clear through breakfast and into lunch. Finally, Wilson moved to outflank his elusive target. He suggested they leave their wives behind and adjourn to the observation car, where they could speak in private.

As the two stood on the open platform at the rear of the train, facing the miles of track rapidly disappearing into the distance as they sped toward Chicago, Wilson tried again. Rockne continued to talk about anything other than Wilson's proposal. Finally, Wilson pressed him for an answer. "Wilson, I'm going to say no, and I'll tell you why," Rock said. It was something Wilson didn't want to hear. "You know what they're calling my team in South Bend, all over the country as a matter of fact?" Rockne was practically growling. "Rockne's Ramblers," he grumbled. "And I don't like it!"

The coach was clearly concerned about pressure from within his own administration. With Father Walsh using the Faculty Board to counter Rockne's influence, the last thing Rockne needed was another battle over scheduling. "We're going to play at home more. I'm pretty sure I can get a game with the Western Conference," he said, referring to the open date that losing Nebraska would create.

Rockne also hoped he might soon win approval to build the new stadium on campus he had sought for so long, a stadium big enough to host the huge crowds that Cartier Field could not accommodate. With a new facility, he could win support for the kind of scheduling Wilson was proposing. Without it, even some home games would have to be played on the road, at places like Chicago's Soldier Field. "Maybe in a couple of years, but not next year," Rockne lamented, shutting the door on Wilson's offer.[32]

By this time the train had almost reached Chicago. There was precious little of Illinois left now before the train reached Inglewood Station outside the city, where the two men would part ways. The Notre Damers would go on to South Bend, while Wilson would stay on in Chicago to attend the Big Ten meetings that were coming up in a few days.[33] He hoped to snare an opponent for USC there if the Notre Dame gambit didn't pan out, and by now that looked like the best he could hope for.

Wilson said his goodbyes to Rockne and headed back to his wife. Marion was surprised to hear that the coach had turned him down. She had been chatting with Rockne's wife, Bonnie, while the men had been discussing Wilson's offer, and Bonnie had mentioned the rude treatment Notre Dame fans had suffered in Lincoln. It was clear to Marion that Bonnie had really enjoyed the Rose Bowl trip, and that both Knute and his wife would enjoy returning to Los Angeles for another game. Explaining all this to her husband, she urged him to give it another shot. "Why not try again, Gwynn?" she prodded him.

"There's no way I could go back and knock on his door and start begging," he replied. Yet as Wilson stared in silence at the door to Rockne's private compartment, he began second-guessing himself, wondering if he had overlooked some avenue for persuading Rockne to give USC a try. The Wilsons watched the landscape whizzing by in silent resignation, lost in the distant chugging of the locomotive and the rhythmic cadence of the wheels, clicking as they bumped along the rails below them. There was nothing left to say. Wilson's mission had failed.

A few uneasy minutes passed, and then the door to Rockne's compartment slowly opened. The coach emerged, his fingers nervously twirling an unlit cigar as he moved down the aisle. He stopped once or twice along the way, speaking with his players, then continued on. Finally, he reached Wilson and sat down, trying to suppress a sheepish grin. "Gwynn, maybe you'd better tell me about that game again," he said. Rockne listened more carefully this time to the details of Wilson's proposal. "I'll call you in the morning," he said after Wilson wrapped up his pitch.

The next morning, Wilson sat nervously in his hotel room, eyeing the phone and periodically checking the clock like an expectant father. It was nine o'clock, and so far there had been no word; Wilson's fingernails were chewed almost to the quick. Finally, the metallic clanking of the phone's bell broke the awkward silence. Wilson anxiously picked up the receiver from its cradle. Rockne was on the other end.

"Gwynn, the game is on," Knute told him.[34] It was all Wilson needed to hear.

12

The Plastic Age

Today, they're sensible and end up with better health.
But we had more fun.
—Clara Bow, 1951

Clara Bow worked the gearshift lever, slamming the gas pedal down to pick up speed. Everything was a matching shade of red—her open-top Kissel roadster, chewing up Sunset Boulevard; the mass of curly hair blowing wildly atop her head; even the pack of chow dogs in the backseat, barking madly at the pedestrians walking along the sidewalk. The people of Los Angeles had grown accustomed to the sight of the red-headed terror dashing about town, as the once-naïve WAMPUS Baby blossomed into a full-fledged movie star. By the spring of 1926 the transition was complete, and Bow was living life with the same energy and passion she brought to the silver screen. It really didn't matter whether she was headed for the studio or off to score another case of hooch from her favorite bootlegger. Where she was driving today was less important than where her career was headed tomorrow.

The Plastic Age, released late in 1925, had been Bow's first big hit for producer Bud Schulberg at Preferred Pictures. The success of the film had not prevented Schulberg's studio from bankruptcy, and he soon joined with Adolph Zukor at Paramount Pictures. Schulberg brought Bow with him, and the fiery actress had risen to thirty-eighth place among the Galaxy of Stars of her new employer by April 1926—but she was still destined for much greater heights.[1] *The Plastic Age* was based on a novel of the same name written by Brown University professor

Percy Marks, who mined the "flaming youth in rebellion" among his students for source material. Bow played a high-spirited girl who lures the athletic hero into staying out late to drink and dance instead of going to class or football practice. It was a typical campus drama of the day, depicting college life in all its ivy-covered glory. It was prophetic, too, because within a few months, Bow would become infatuated with young college athletes in real life.

Bow begin shooting her next film, *Mantrap,* that same month.[2] It was directed by Victor Fleming, who would later direct both *Gone with the Wind* and *The Wizard of Oz*. Fleming became Bow's mentor and confidant; he even became a lover, one of a string of paramours who would include Gary Cooper, Gilbert Roland, and, it was said, even Dracula himself, Bela Lugosi.[3] Under Fleming's tutelage, Bow used *Mantrap* as the vehicle propelling her rise from up-and-coming young actress to the biggest star in Hollywood.

As it happened, Bow was not the only one in Los Angeles starting a new romance that spring. Howard Jones had also found a new lover. Jane Dean Ridley was an attractive divorcée of twenty-eight, some twelve years younger than Howard. She was of medium build, five feet four inches tall, with fair, clear skin, brown eyes, and light brown hair. She had an oval face, with a straight nose above her rounded chin. Jane was not, perhaps, quite the vivacious flapper that Bow was, but she too led an exciting life typical of the day's "modern woman."

Jane had been born Florence Jane Dean on September 8, 1897, in Tipton, Iowa, about twenty-five miles from the Iowa City campus where Howard Jones would arrive two decades later. Her family later moved to Los Angeles, and in 1917 Jane traveled throughout Asia on the U.S. Army Transport *Warren* with her brother, William Dean, an army officer stationed in the Philippines.[4] One year after that boat trip, William died in the influenza pandemic raging across America.[5]

In 1919, Jane witnessed a firebombing in her neighborhood, as she and her fiancé, George Ridley, were returning by car after a trip to Texas. The victims were horribly burned, and Jane helped the police attend to the injured in the chaos of the attack.[6] The investigation into the scandalous crime climaxed when the chief suspect, a high-ranking engineer with the Board of Public Utilities, leaped to his death from the eleventh floor of the Hall of Records in downtown Los Angeles.[7] On May 29,

1920, less than a year after the horrific firebombing, a justice of the peace in Bakersfield, California, married the couple, and Jane became Mrs. George Ridley.[8] By 1926, the marriage had ended without children.

Jane had seen Howard Jones play against her brother William when he was on the football team at West Point. News reports stated that Howard and Jane had met back in October 1925, at the beach house of Dr. Harold Van Metre, but they offered no further details of their courtship.[9] In any event, Jane became Mrs. Howard Jones on March 31, 1926, during the Easter recess at USC. That a newspaper column described the union as having "surprised many of his friends" was perhaps not unexpected; the Headman, quiet and reserved, was unlikely to offer many confidences about his dating habits.[10]

The nuptials took place less than a week after Judge Dunklee, back in Denver, granted Howard and his first wife, Leah Clark, their final decree of divorce. Howard and Jane married just two days after Leah married Richard B. Porter in Chicago.[11] The ceremony uniting Howard and Jane was held at the home of the bride's mother in Lankershim, as North Hollywood was known at the time. The residence was described as "beautifully decorated" with orange blossoms, roses, tulips, and foliage. Only a small circle of friends and family attended the modest ceremony: Jane's parents, Harold Van Metre as Howard's best man, Mrs. Van Metre as Jane's matron of honor, Bill Hunter, and the young flower girl, Helen Clark. The bride wore an "exquisite creation of pink crepe de chine trimmed with handmade Chinese lace" and carried "an arm shower of lilies of the valley and maidenhair ferns." There was no report that any of Howard's family attended.[12]

The happiness of the day offered no hints at the time, but Howard Jones's new bride and Clara Bow would later have darker things in common. Both would eventually struggle with mental illness, and both would spend years of living apart from their husbands. Both would be institutionalized, with Jane spending the last decades of her life under psychiatric care, but for the moment, in spring 1926, Jane was a happy newlywed and Bow still a high-spirited, independent woman living life to the fullest.

Howard Jones had no doubt timed his wedding and honeymoon to facilitate a return before spring practice opened in mid-April. Understanding Howard's obsession with football was part of being his wife, an adjustment Jane would have to make after living with an oilman in her first marriage.

Upon returning to campus, Jones began to prep his team for the coming fall. As he watched his players on Bovard Field, the pool of talent he observed was good enough that Jones spoke positively about the coming season to the beat writer of the *Los Angeles Times,* Braven Dyer, after working with his troops in camp. One of the standouts he mentioned was Don Williams, a sophomore from Santa Ana. "Don Williams is the best quarterback prospect I have had since the days of Aubrey Devine," Jones told the scribe. Williams had been a standout on the freshman team in 1924 and had been judged promising during the previous spring's practice, but he had been ineligible for the 1925 season. Jones had spotted other talented players too, observing to Dyer that "Williams had plenty of strenuous competition in Morton Kaer, Howard Elliot, and one or two others."[13]

Morley Drury, Manuel Laraneta, and Bert Heiser were expected to join Williams in the starting backfield. The foursome was regarded as even more talented on the defensive side of the ball. The ends were Morris Badgro, Allen Behrendt, Gene Dorsey, and Charley Boren, a converted halfback being returned to his original position.

The best player on the line, Brice Taylor, was excluded from spring practice because of eligibility issues.[14] Jack Fox, a freshman looking toward his first varsity season, was filling in for him during camp.[15] Jeff Cravath, coming from Santa Ana like Williams, was the team captain. He and Hobbs Adams brought experience up-front that, without Taylor, was in short supply.

Another lineman of note was Marion Morrison, a sophomore coming up from the Spartans. Morrison had been born in Winterset, Iowa, in 1907, but had moved to Southern Calfornia with his family seven years later, eventually settling in Glendale, a small community near Los Angeles. Morrison became a football player like his father before him, and in 1924 his Glendale club won the state championship, after losing to Long Beach by one touchdown in the title game the year before. Morrison had hoped to attend the Naval Academy, but when the appointment never materialized and USC offered a football scholarship, he became a Trojan instead.[16] Morrison would not play much in 1926; in truth, he never did make much impact on the team as a player, mak-

Trojan lineman Marion Morrison poses in a practice jersey, c. 1926. Though he made little impact on the Thundering Herd, he would win worldwide fame as John Wayne after leaving USC. (Courtesy of the University of Southern California.)

ing his mark only after leaving school. Like Frederick Slater back in Iowa, Morrison always went by the nickname Duke. He would retain the nickname, but in a few years he would exchange his identity as a football player for a new role, becoming the movie star John Wayne.

Jones was optimistic about the season, but was also wary of the competition on the schedule. "We ought to have a better team than last year," he predicted. "I look for California, Stanford and Notre Dame to give us our toughest battles and we'll see no pink tea with any of our other opponents."[17]

It was certain that Rockne was serving no tea in South Bend. He was still working to get back to the championship form of the Four Horsemen team. The 1925 season had hardly been a failure, but the team had lost badly to both Army and Nebraska. When the expectations were as high as they were at Notre Dame, just good was not good enough. As it turned out, the start of the 1926 season exceeded expectations. Notre Dame's first game was a 77–0 blowout over Beloit, and in its first eight games Notre Dame gave up only 7 points while scoring 197.

The Trojans' start was nearly as impressive. They beat Whittier 74–0 and Santa Clara 42–0 in the first two games, and ran up 187 points to their opponents' 13 through their first five games. The most satisfying win for Trojan fans was the 27–0 thumping of California's Golden Bears. Their first victory over the dreaded Bears since 1915 showed that hiring Howard Jones had already paid off.[18]

However, Jones fell short of a Bay Area sweep when the Trojans stumbled in the Coliseum the next weekend; they fell to Stanford by a single point, 13–12, having missed both opportunities to complete extra points. Morley Drury had been injured in the win over California the week before, but despite lacking their best player, the Trojans barely missed a chance to beat the Cardinals. With the ball deep in Stanford territory near the end of the game, a pass went awry and the Cardinals intercepted, sealing their victory over the Trojans.[19]

The Trojans soon got the steamroller fired up again, rumbling over their next three opponents by the combined tally of 106–13. The Thundering Herd was back, stampeding toward the final showdown against Notre Dame.

Meanwhile, the run-up to the Notre Dame–USC game didn't go as smoothly for Rockne as it had for Jones. The final game before heading out to Los Angeles was against Carnegie Tech, at Forbes Field in Pittsburgh, the home of the National League Pirates. No one thought the Tartans stood much of a chance, least of all Rockne, so the coach decided to take the game off. He wanted to attend the Army-Navy game in Chicago instead, to be on hand with Tad Jones and Pop Warner to finalize their All-American selections for 1926. Warner sent a message through Christy Walsh warning Rockne not to underestimate Carnegie, but Rockne wouldn't listen. The promise of extra publicity, extra cash, and a suite at the LaSalle Hotel in Chicago for both Knute and Bonnie was simply too seductive for Rockne to turn down. Besides, Rockne believed that Assistant Coach Hunk Anderson could handle the team. Rockne had skipped the Indiana game to scout Army, and Pop Warner would be missing his game on the same day that Rockne would skip the game against Carnegie Tech, so why worry? Rockne was so convinced that his system was superior that he felt the specific parts and pieces didn't really matter once everyone was properly trained.

His complacence turned out to be an embarrassing mistake. Hunk Anderson was well trained all right, perhaps too much so. He proved reluctant to contravene Rockne's dictates and failed to make needed adjustments.[20] Anderson was slow to react when Notre Dame's "shock troops," the second-stringers sent in to wear down the opposing team before the starters came in, fell behind the Tartans. The score was 13–0 at halftime, and the final two quarters of play just made things worse. The newswires glowed red-hot after the game as the shocking result raced across the country: Carnegie Tech 19, Notre Dame 0.

The loss dashed Notre Dame's title hopes. Irish fans were stunned, Rockne was humbled, and the team was in a funk. There was only one thing to do: regroup, and win the remaining game on the schedule, a game that would have to fill in for the postseason contests from which they were now barred. Rockne gave his players personal motivation by reminding them, "We can redeem ourselves."[21] The truth went unspoken, but was widely understood. Rockne and his team knew that the blame for the Carnegie debacle was as much on his shoulders as anyone's, and that any redemption would be his alone.

13

The Greatest Game I Ever Saw

I read all my life of Notre Dame whose scholastic standing is
one touchdown and a field goal higher than any other modern
educational hindrance.
—Will Rogers, 1926

It seemed almost like the circus had come to town. A big crowd
had gathered on the Southern Pacific platform to greet the famous visitors from the East, and now that the Notre Dame team had arrived, the
ruckus was growing even louder. The brass lungs of a calliope began
pumping out a hearty rendition of "When Irish Eyes Are Smiling" into
the cool night air, heightening the sideshow aura of the festivities. It
was almost 9:00 P.M. in Tucson, and although it was cooling off, the
day had been much warmer. December was usually Arizona's cool-
est month, but an unseasonable heat wave was baking the state. The
railcars were not air-conditioned, making the trip across the desert hot
and uncomfortable. Rockne and his players were relieved to leave the
train at last and stretch their legs, but this was no time to relax. That
would come later, at the Santa Rita Hotel. At the moment, everyone
wanted a piece of the Irish.

"We're just out to hold the score down, that's all," Rockne shouted
over the screeching of the calliope. Reporters had come out from L.A.
to query the Notre Dame mentor before taking on the Trojans, and the
wily coach was happy to feed them whatever fit his pregame agenda.
Kickoff was less than forty-eight hours away, and he was not about to
tip his hand.

"If we could have ended the season about a week ago we'd have been all right," he continued, bemoaning the condition of his team after a long, hard season. "We're just taking a chance. I don't know how the boys will hold up, but they'll try."[1]

It was true that some of his better players were out and others banged up. The best prospects at tackle and fullback hadn't played all year, so Rockne's lament wasn't all applesauce. Still, he always stockpiled talent, so his grumblings were usually filtered through a fine strainer of skepticism. Rockne's complaints that his "crack" quarterback couldn't play were a real dose of the blarney.[2] He publicly claimed that his team was "no great championship football team,"[3] but he knew better.

The Ramblers had received a similar hero's welcome at every stop along the way to Los Angeles.[4] While in Tucson, the team would follow the same routine that had worked for Rockne two years before. After two final practice sessions, slated for the next day, the team would enjoy a banquet at the Tucson Country Club Thursday night.[5] Then they'd board the Golden State Limited for California early Friday morning.[6]

As the Irish squad traveled west, Howard Jones was busy finalizing their upcoming reception in the Coliseum. He prepared for Notre Dame in Los Angeles the same way he had when facing the Irish in Iowa back in 1921. There was no fooling around—not that there ever was on the Headman's watch. Jones had driven the Herd relentlessly, and the team had looked sharp in its last drills. Aubrey Devine had played a key role. His scouting reports helped ready the Freshman Spartans for their role mimicking the Irish formations in practice.

A small group of onlookers watched the Trojans' preparations. Among them was the Headman's brother, Tad Jones, and he was impressed. "Howard certainly has a speedy bunch," Tad commented, then added "It should be a great game."

Local papers leaned toward USC. Braven Dyer of the *Los Angeles Times* was so impressed that he wrote, "If Knute Rockne's Notre Dame gridders defeat U.S.C. at the Coliseum Saturday afternoon the South Bend boys will have to step high, wide and handsome."[7]

The showdown of the two titans, each beaten only once so far in the season, was turning out to be every bit the blockbuster they had hoped for when the two schools inked the deal the year before. It was the first time an Eastern school had ventured west of the Rockies for a regular season game, and a crowd of one hundred thousand was anticipated, according to the *Notre Dame Scholastic*.[8] While that number may have been a bit of an exaggeration for a stadium that only seated about seventy-eight thousand, it did indicate the high demand for tickets that the game had generated.

Both teams had plenty to motivate them besides the anticipation of playing before such a huge turnout. One writer in the *Notre Dame Scholastic* reported that the Irish were "somewhat enraged after their Carnegie setback and it's a lead pipe cinch that Southern California will get plenty of punishment before the issue is settled one way or another."[9] As for the Trojans, they were eager to show up the San Francisco bookies favoring Notre Dame at 3 to 1 odds. The honor of the entire West Coast was at stake: local journalist Paul Lowry predicted that a USC win over Notre Dame "would put the locals ace high in the esteem of Eastern gridiron critics."[10]

Howard Jones's main concern was to prevent overconfidence in his team. In light of Notre Dame's loss to Carnegie Tech the week before and the Trojans' recent landslide victory over Montana, sportswriter Bill Henry of the *Times* speculated that the Trojan coach would have "extra work now to convince his boys that they haven't got the Notre Dame game all tied up in a paper sack."[11] Rockne's pessimistic public assessment of his own team's chances no doubt added to the danger that the Trojans might misjudge their foe.

Despite the early odds favoring Notre Dame, most well-known coaches called the game even, while the few who were bold enough to pick a side favored USC. Bill Spaulding of the Southern Branch (now UCLA) predicted that "the Trojans will cop the game because the Notre Dame team is all played out," a popular theme echoed by Rockne himself. Tad Jones was more cautious in his predictions, calling the game a toss-up. "As the line goes, so goes the game," he opined, putting the outcome squarely on the shoulders of each team's forward wall.[12]

The matchup was one the biggest ever in Southern California, perhaps outshining even the Rose Bowl game played the previous January. All seventy-six thousand tickets were accounted for by mid-November.[13] For those unable to secure a seat in the stadium, the game was to be carried locally on radio station KHJ, with Bill Henry of the *Los Angeles Times* calling the action.[14]

The game was also homecoming for USC. Not just one, but two banquets were held the night before the game. The official homecoming dinner was held at the Shrine Auditorium, where one thousand guests listened to the Jones brothers and Knute Rockne deliver remarks. The other dinner was hosted by Christy Walsh at the Biltmore in honor of his three "writers," Pop Warner, Tad Jones, and Knute Rockne.[15]

It was raining as the banquets got under way, and there was speculation that the gloomy weather might persist through Saturday afternoon's kickoff. The skies soon cleared, however, and game day conditions were fair, with no moisture to slow down the footing or contribute to turnovers.[16]

Rockne and his players, thirty-five strong, arrived at the game in a fleet of Studebakers, as they had at the Rose Bowl stay in 1925. The cars were provided by Paul G. Hoffman's dealership on Figueroa, located down the street from the USC campus. The vehicles had also carried the gridders from the train station to the Ambassador Hotel the day before.[17]

The route took them down Wilshire Boulevard toward Vermont, before turning right toward Exposition Park. Finally the Coliseum came into view. It was one of the biggest stadiums any of them had ever seen. The design of the massive concrete structure echoed the glory of ancient Rome. Laid out as an elongated oval, the stadium had a cavernous interior in which the field was surrounded by a regulation-sized running track. The huge expanse between the field and the perimeter walls left spectators somewhat removed from the action, particularly at the peristyle end with its iconic colonnade, since the field was shifted toward the other end. The grass was somewhat chewed up after a season of football and the recent rain, but the footing was still firm if not cosmetically pristine. Everything was ready for the game.

The stadium was still new, having opened just three years before. While work had not yet begun to increase its capacity to 100,000 for the Olympic Games that were still six years away, the stadium could already accommodate the 80,000-plus spectators that would fill the stands.

The festivities began an hour before kickoff with a parade through the Coliseum of decorative floats sponsored by Trojan fraternities and sororities. The floats featured designs "burlesquing the Irish, their pugnacity and other characteristics."[18] Presumably this lampooning was in better taste than the antics of the Cornhuskers the year before, since no complaints were lodged after the game. Then again, Rockne had never really complained about Nebraska either, although other Notre Dame supporters had found the atmosphere there unacceptable. If Knute had gotten his way, Notre Dame might still have been hosting the Cornhuskers in South Bend that very day.

Rockne hadn't gotten his way. He was here instead, on the Coliseum floor, soaking up the grandeur. It was not the biggest football crowd he'd ever seen; that honor belonged to his fellow spectators at Soldier Field the week before, for the Army-Navy game. However, the current crowd was the biggest crowd ever to see him lead a team into battle. It must have been exhilarating.

Rockne had one last bit of showmanship planned before getting to the serious business of football. The coach had brought his very own WAMPUS Baby, Sally O'Neil, to the game. She was an attractive young Catholic girl from Bayonne, New Jersey, and a rising starlet for Metro-Goldwyn-Mayer. Her brother had played for Notre Dame, but today she was the team's mascot. It was a popular practice to officially designate a celebrity to be on hand as a lucky charm for big games, and Rockne was taking no chances when it came to ensuring good fortune.[19]

O'Neil was petite, standing only five feet two inches tall, and at eighteen years old was younger than many of the players on the field. Newsreel cameras rolled and cameras snapped off publicity shots as she stood by Rockne, smiling and autographing footballs. The two celebrities offered a marked contrast in styles. O'Neil was the perfect twenties starlet, with cropped, curly brown hair peeping from the cloche hat pulled down coyly over her eyes, full lips painted bright red, and a stylish outfit that included a boldly patterned jacket with a wide collar, immaculate white gloves, and matching shoes. Rockne's worn, fatherly face seemed in tune with his drab attire. A news photo captured her with an arm gently wrapped around the shoulders of Rockne's oldest boy, William, as she posed with father and son. She was the only one smiling. The two Nordic males displayed their best game faces, mimicking the stony gravity of the peristyle arches visible in the background.[20]

The pageantry of the day extended into the stands. The Trojan student section deployed massive "card stunts," well-practiced displays in which the students, divided into groups, held aloft colorful printed

Usually it was the Trojans who enjoyed the support of the Hollywood crowd, but at times Rockne also hobnobbed with movie stars. Here the coach and his son William pose with actress Sally O'Neil on the Coliseum floor before the kickoff in Notre Dame's debut against USC in 1926. (Corbis Images.)

placards that together formed large visual designs. Card stunts had been around since about 1908, but a Trojan yell leader by the name of Lindley Bothwell had taken them to a new level in 1922 when he created the first animated ones.[21] This time the Trojans were pulling out all the stops. When the rooters flipped their cards, a huge Trojan horse appeared, rearing up on its hind legs, with its tail swishing back and forth at the command of the yell leaders stationed below the crowd.[22]

Rockne and Jones, meeting on the field below the crowd, nervously exchanged pleasantries as their teams warmed up. The visitors wore their traditional dark blue, while the home club wore cardinal. Notre Dame's jerseys were plain, solid colors while the Trojan uniforms were accented on the chest and long sleeves with wide black "friction stripes." This detail was a common feature of the era, consisting of strips of leather or Snugtex belting sewn onto the jerseys. The appliqués were designed to help players hang on to the ball.[23] Rockne had provided Notre Dame with distinctive new pants of a golden silk that shimmered in the bright California sunlight and were reputed to be "several pounds lighter than the canvas variety" worn by the home team.[24] Both squads wore more or less identical leather helmets, with domed crowns above heavy padded flaps over the ears. The helmets had no face guards; such protection wouldn't be adopted for another three decades.[25]

Kickoff was scheduled for 2:00 P.M. USC won the coin toss and chose to start on defense. Brice Taylor did the honors for the Trojans, sailing the ball over the goal line. In a portent of kicking woes to come, the Trojans were offside, and on the re-kick Notre Dame returned the ball out to the thirty-three. With the ice broken, the game could get under way in earnest.

Early jitters continued, however, as Notre Dame put the ball in play. This time the Irish committed the error, jumping offside. The Irish quickly settled down and started moving the ball, only to have their drive stopped moments later. They punted back to USC, and from there the two teams sparred back and forth throughout the first quarter without landing any heavy blows.

Yardage came in halting spurts, until progress would stall. The two strong defenses caused possession to shift rapidly between the two sides, with "quick kicks" on third down ensuring field position in the conservative strategy of the day. The officials got the biggest workout in the first stanza, calling a total of eight penalties for eighty yards. After fifteen minutes of play, the game remained deadlocked in a scoreless tie.

Notre Dame drew first blood in the second period. Short gains near midfield preceded a dash of twenty-seven yards to USC's fifteen. Deft ball faking by Irish quarterback Charlie Riley fooled the Trojans, and fullback Harry O'Boyle scampered through the line until hauled down from behind by Trojan Morton Kaer. On the next play Riley hid the ball behind his back and took off around the end to race in for the score. The point after touchdown capped the seventy-five-yard drive, and pushed the lead to seven points.[26] For the first time in five and a half quarters of football between the two coaches, Howard Jones found himself trailing.

The Trojans responded a short time later with a long drive of their own. Kaer dashed twenty-seven yards to take the ball into Notre Dame's side of the field; then, two plays later, flung the ball to Allen Behrendt at the thirteen. He charged toward the goal but was stopped just short; Kaer punched it in on the next play. Brice Taylor dropped back to kick the extra point, but the ball was batted down. Notre Dame still led 7–6.[27] The half ended with that same tally showing on the scoreboard.

The second half began much as the opening of the game had, with costly penalties and missed opportunities. Kaer tossed a forty-yard strike to Morris Badgro at the Notre Dame 21-yard line, but another offside flag negated the pickup. Moments later, another Kaer pass was intercepted.

The Trojans soon got their chance when a punt was blocked and Jeff Cravath fell on the ball at the Trojan 43-yard line. A couple of short runs moved the ball ten yards, to end the quarter with USC in Notre Dame territory and driving. There were just fifteen minutes left to play, with Notre Dame leading by a single point.

Rockne was forced to call a time-out when the Trojans' Don Williams, who had come in for Kaer in the third quarter, ran for another ten yards on the first play of the final period. After the break, the Trojans kept hammering through the line, and had reached the 18-yard line when Rockne stopped the clock again. His efforts to stem the tide failed. The Herd kept driving down to the 9-yard line before they stalled and Jones was forced to take his own time-out. This time it paid off. When the ball was put back into play Williams smashed through left tackle for a touchdown. USC led 12–7.

This time it was Morley Drury's turn to attempt the kick. The ball flew off his toe low, but cleared the defenders' outstretched hands this time. Then it hit the crossbar with a thud, and caromed back toward the turf. The Trojans had scored twice, and both times they'd botched the conversion attempts.

Howard Jones was a conservative man and a conservative coach. He would play it safe the rest of the way. With a chance to extend the lead with a forty-three-yard field goal late in the game, Jones pulled Williams when he saw him lining up to try the placekick. The Trojans punted out of bounds instead and gave the ball to Notre Dame at the Irish 17-yard line.[28] It was standard strategy and a move that even Rockne defended in the postmortem discussion.[29] However, his defense would not prevent debate among press and fans that went on for weeks.

Rockne, unlike the Headman, *was* a gambler. With only a few minutes left, the Trojans fumbled, and Rockne saw his chance to roll the

Notre Dame's John "Butch" Neimiec catches a pass while USC's Morton Kaer closes in on the tackle during the teams' 1926 game in Los Angeles. (Image courtesy of Notre Dame Archives.)

dice. He pulled Charley Riley for Art Parisien, the "crack" quarterback who was supposedly too banged up to play. Notre Dame fans knew Parisien was one of the sharpest passers on the team, but, looking at the diminutive back running on to the field, everyone else must have wondered what Rockne was thinking.

Parisien was probably the smallest guy on the field, weighing no more than 148 pounds "soaking wet."[30] Few in the stands knew he was the team's best passer. A natural lefty, Parisien could throw with either hand if he had to. The little man promptly completed a thirty-five-yard pass. Now Notre Dame was on USC's 20-yard line. Then two running plays lost three yards. It was third and thirteen. Notre Dame had to get a touchdown, since a field goal would leave the Irish two points short.

Parisien took the snap and rolled to his left. The Trojan defenders swarmed toward him, but lost track of John "Butch" Niemic coming off the line. He was wide open. Parisien dropped the ball right into his hands and he went untouched for the score. Cravath blocked the kick for point and the score remained 13–12.

Rockne pulled Parisien on the ensuing kickoff. His replacement, Vincent McNally, sealed the game with an interception a short time later.[31] It had been a hard-fought win for Notre Dame and a heartbreaking loss for USC.

In the Trojan locker room, the mood was understandably downcast. As Jones walked among his players, checking on injuries and praising their efforts, a figure appeared in the doorway. It was Rockne. The Notre Dame coach sought out Jones and the two warmly shook hands.

"When you beat this guy, you've got to play smart football," Jones said as he greeted Rockne. "Congratulations, Knute."

Rockne smiled back. "Thanks, it was the greatest game I ever saw. Your team played a great and a clean game of ball, Howard, and there's no disgrace in their losing." Thinking back to 1921, he quipped, "That makes it even between us."[32]

The day was not quite finished for Rockne and his team. There was a dance at the Ambassador Hotel, and another event at the Shrine Auditorium, the "Stage and Screen Theatrical Ball," a benefit for the Hebrew Sheltering Home for the Aged.[33] The Irish were feted by a crowd of more than five thousand, including movie stars Wallace Beery and Joan Crawford.[34]

The Victory Dance at the Ambassador Hotel hosted both the winning team and their vanquished foes, along with both coaches. The fact that the two teams mixed after the game, especially after such a bitterly fought contest, demonstrated the respectful nature of their new rivalry. After all, there was no real reason for them to be foes. There was no state pride at issue, or conference championship at stake, just the spirit of competition that had brought them together in the first place.

That spirit extended to the coaches. When he left, Rockne bid his rival a warm farewell. "See you in Chicago," he said.[35]

What's All This Fuss about a Football Game?

On behalf of Troy, whose soil we tread, am I come to seek thy mighty aid, to make it one with mine.

—Euripides, *The Trojan Women*, 415 B.C.

The question was simple and direct, just like the fiery redhead who was asking it. "Teet, what's all this fuss about a football game?" Clara Bow demanded to know.[1]

Unlike some others in Hollywood, Bow's questions seldom masked any artifice or guile, nor offered any hint of sarcasm. She simply aimed to satisfy her curiosity. She had sought out one of the few people around her she could trust not to mock her ignorance, the publicity man the studio had assigned to her. His name was Teet Carle.

It was the fall of 1927 when she started wondering about football. By then Clara Bow had become the hottest thing in Hollywood. In January, her biggest picture yet, *It*, had been released to rave reviews. The film was a smash romantic comedy based on the novel of the same name by author Elinor Glyn. The movie helped define the spirit of the age. A title card at the beginning of the movie used a quote from Glyn to define "it" as "that quality possessed by some which draws all others with its magnetic force."[2] "It" was youth, vitality, and sex appeal all rolled into one. Clara Bow had all of those things in spades. Any girl could become a flapper, but only Clara Bow became "the It Girl."

Actress Clara Bow, shown here c. 1927, was among the legion of Hollywood celebrities who became USC football fans. (Photo by Eugene Robert Richee for Paramount Pictures.)

Despite her fame, Bow never treated stagehands and studio crafts-men as if they were beneath her. The crew loved her for her down-to-earth, working-class simplicity. She was "one of the boys," privy to their scuttlebutt and lunchtime conversations. So when she heard them talking about the Thundering Herd, she wondered what the hubbub was all about.

Teet Carle had gone from being the publicity man for USC to work-ing in the publicity department for Paramount Pictures. Part of his job was keeping movie stars happy, seeing to their needs, and if possible, steering them clear of trouble. Sometimes the job meant satisfying sim-ple curiosity. In the case of Clara Bow, that was a big part of the job. Despite her fame, she was still incredibly uneducated and unsophis-ticated about virtually all aspects of life outside a movie studio or the boudoir. Carle, himself a graduate of Southern California, responded to the young star's curiosity by purchasing tickets to the upcoming game against the Cal Bears so she could find out for herself.[3]

It was going to be a big game, giving USC a shot at the conference title and a chance to win two in a row over the men from Berkeley. So far, only a 13–13 tie against Stanford had marred the Trojan's record, while the Bears were unbeaten and untied. It was going to be another packed house in the Coliseum.[4]

Bow had the habit of getting herself into all sorts of escapades, and the studio dared not let her loose in public without a chaperone. Carle and another studio man, Cal grad Barney Hutchinson, escorted her to the game. They were seated near the tunnel leading up from the locker room, where she could get a good view of the players as they trotted out onto the field. All it took was one look at the handsome young athletes in their cardinal uniforms and she was smitten.

"Where've these boys been all my life?" she asked Carle.[5]

Carle sensed trouble brewing. These were just college boys, he reminded her.

"How old d'ya think I am?" the twenty-two-year-old Bow chided him in turn.

The Herd trampled the Bears 13–0 that afternoon, and, as usual, Drury had been the star of the game.[6] Still, in true "It" Girl fashion, Bow wasn't content to just watch the team play. She had to meet the Herders. "How d'ya get in touch with these boys?" she asked Teet.

Carle was certain trouble lay ahead, but it would do no good to hold back now. She'd find out one way or another, he reasoned, and there was no telling how much trouble she might get into along the way if she tracked them down on her own. So he told her that most of the guys were in the Sigma Chi fraternity.

"Ya mean Morley Drury is . . . " she began.

"Yes, Clara," Teet cut her off. "Morley Drury is a member of Sigma Chi."

A few hours later, Drury's memorable afternoon in the Coliseum would be followed by a night on the town that he would never forget. The adventure began when the phone rang at the fraternity house. Still sore and battered from the game, Drury asked a pledge to answer the call for him. A few minutes later, the pledge came looking for the Trojan star. "Morley, I don't know what to do, sir," he complained. "Some lady who says she's Clara Bow wants to speak with you."

The Thundering Herd had plenty of Hollywood fans, and it wasn't unusual for movie people to call on the Trojans. Director John Ford was there at the very moment the phone rang, but Clara Bow? No, Drury was sure that a call from the "It" Girl was too good to be true. Sure that his frat brothers were pranking him, he started to brush off the caller.

"I ain't kiddin'," said the voice at the other end of the phone. Her distinctive Brooklyn accent would have been a dead giveaway to anyone familiar with her voice, but in the era of silent films, it failed to confirm her identity. "I wanna meet ya!" she insisted. Despite misgivings, Drury gave in and told her the address on West 36th Street. "Give me fifteen minutes," she replied. "I'll honk the horn."

A short time later, Bow roared up fraternity row in her roadster. The boys of Sigma Chi were stunned. "Bring a fella for Tui," Bow instructed Drury, who had come out to the curb to see for himself. She gestured to the friend seated next to her, Tui Lorraine, so Drury fetched teammate Tom Dorsey, and they all sped off into the moonlit night.

Bow raced around Los Angeles for hours, chattering like a magpie. It was a good thing too. Drury was so starstruck he could hardly speak. He couldn't believe his luck. These weren't two sorority sisters. They were movie stars! After a stop at a Hollywood speakeasy where the girls drank alcohol but the guys, always fearful of the wrath of Howard Jones, stuck with Cokes, the foursome made their way back to Sigma Chi. It had been a crazy, impossible night, something that could happen only in Los Angeles.

Inside the house, the frat brothers swamped Drury and his pal, pumping them for details. "Relax," he said, "You didn't miss a thing." It was true. The lurid versions of the night's events that arose years later far exceeded the reality of the encounter.

That improbable night was the beginning of Bow's lifelong love affair with the Trojans, but her infatuation with the team was more about camaraderie than romance. She would become a regular fixture at home games and host postgame parties at her Beverly Hills home. The Herd, including the injured Marion Morrison, who was inactive for the 1927 season but who still roomed with teammate Lowry McCaslin, would spend Sundays like no other team in college football. Bow's Panatrope record player provided the music. Her German chef cooked the food. Movie actresses like Tui Lorraine, Lina Basquette, and Joan Crawford supplied the Hollywood glamor.

Bow enjoyed the freedom such gatherings afforded. She was free to be herself with the young Trojans, as she was with the stagehands on the studio lot. She could dance with them, flirt, and have a good time without worrying about her image, or guessing what angle the boys might play to take advantage of her, as so many in Hollywood had done before. Her time with them brought back fond memories of her tomboy days back on the streets of Brooklyn. They were all just young people having fun together.[7]

The Trojans gained another new fan that fall, although it would be some years before she would be old enough to attend their games or join their parties. On November 9, 1927, Jane Jones presented her husband Howard with his second child, a seven-pound, eight-ounce girl whom they named Carolyn. It was a good thing she came along when she did: the Trojans were scheduled to play Colorado two days later, and if the timing had been different, Howard probably would have missed her birth.

The coverage of Carolyn's birth in the *Los Angeles Times* demonstrated local preoccupation with the Trojans' upcoming game against Notre Dame. The writer announcing the event noted thankfully that Howard was "expected to recover in time to personally lead the Trojans back to Chicago for the Notre Dame game."[8] He needn't have worried. Although Howard Jones loved his daughter dearly, his mind would always veer back to football when the need arose. Three days after Carolyn's birth, Colorado fell to USC 46–7, and the week after that, the Trojans overpowered Washington State 27–0. As for the Notre Dame game, USC's preparations continued to the very last moment before the team boarded the train for Chicago. Even en route, Jones would subject his team to rigorous "skull sessions," in which the players would review Irish formations and diagram plays gleaned from scouting reports that Aubrey Devine had drawn from not just one, but three of Notre Dame's games that season.[9]

This would be the first time the Trojans ever ventured east of the Rockies for a game, and since USC hadn't left the state for a game since 1925, many of the players were looking forward to their first trip outside California. The contest with Notre Dame would have to stand in for a postseason game, because the Trojans were in a feud with the Tournament of Roses Committee. No matter how good the Trojans proved to be, they would not be playing in Pasadena come January. Warren Bovard blamed Leslie B. Henry, chairman of Pasadena's Football Committee, citing the "childish and long-standing antagonistic attitude of Henry toward S.C." Gwynn Wilson, speaking for Bovard,

This cartoon ran in the *Los Angeles Examiner* before the 1927 game between USC and Notre Dame. The artist, Al Zinnen, went on to become an animator for Disney Studios. (Courtesy of Los Angeles Library.)

stated that USC would not accept a Rose Bowl invitation "as long as Henry is connected with the football committee."

The whole dispute swirled around the perception that Henry would "crucify the Trojans if it was the last thing he ever did."[10] The Trojans had been insulted by comments Henry had made in a speech over at UCLA, allegedly denouncing the lax entrance and eligibility requirements of the "Big Three" of the Pacific Coast Conference, which included USC. Neither repeated discussions with the Tournament of Roses Committee nor denials by Henry that he had actually made the remarks in question would satisfy Bovard. So the trek to the Midwest would have to be the Trojans' reward for a successful season of football.

Jones was planning on a traveling squad of about thirty-three.[11] Los Angeles was planning on sending them off in style. The whole town was behind the team, and an entire week of special events was planned in the run-up to Saturday's game. Bandstatter's Hollywood Montmartre, a dapper European eatery that catered to the movie crowd before Chasen's or the Brown Derby came on the scene, was planning a Cardinal and Gold night for Friday. Its special menu for the day would feature items named for USC players, such as "Drury ginger ale" and a "Hibbs deluxe sandwich."[12]

The big send-off began on the USC campus at 9:30 Tuesday morning. Fans were excused from classes, and a huge pep rally was held at Bovard Auditorium, featuring film of Notre Dame's game with Army followed by students performing "Father Time and Football," a series of skits illustrating the history of the game and its rise on the Pacific Coast.[13] Capping the dramatizations was the appearance of a Trojan figure, in full regalia, astride a magnificent horse that had been owned by Rudolph Valentino before the actor's tragic death the year before. The meeting wrapped up with the usual cheerleading and "throwing of serpentine"—the traditional hurling of streamers that would remain a part of college football until well into the 1960s.[14]

In the afternoon, students gathered on campus and at 3:30 set off in a colorful column from University Avenue just as the Trojan War Flag was raised above Bovard Tower, signifying the university's determination to upend the Irish and avenge the previous year's narrow defeat.[15] The noisy procession wound its way through the downtown district, lead by a squad of police cars and flanked by motorcycle officers. The vehicles, including the three buses carrying the Trojan band, were festooned with all manner of streamers and banners. The parade, said to be a mile long in total, headed to the train station downtown, where five thousand fans waited to see the team off.

The crowd began gathering at Central Station an hour before the scheduled departure time of 5:00 P.M. The station, a long, ornate building on the corner of Central and Fifth, had a large lobby area lit by tall windows facing the street and rows of chandeliers hanging from the coffered wood ceiling. It was packed with fans by the time the team arrived. For forty-five minutes the uproar reverberated through the waiting area, as the crowd reached a "state of temporary insanity." The Trojan band provided musical accompaniment as the yell leaders led the students in raucous cheers. The entire affair was called "the greatest thing in the way of a rally this University ever has done."[16]

Finally the team climbed aboard. The Southern Pacific train was a Trojan Special, operating on a Golden State Limited schedule of sixty-four hours to Chicago, including four half-hour stops each day to stretch legs and toss a football around. Described as "super-deluxe," the train had a barber shop, maid service, "shower baths," and "all other means of comfort and convenience the company can give." In all, 110 people made the trip, including players, staff, and fans.[17]

When the time came to depart, a warning boomed from the station's loudspeakers, alerting the crowd that the train was ready to leave. The fans spilled onto the tracks, surrounding the end car with a mass of humanity. They cheered and waved to the players, who had gathered on the open observation platform facing the crowd.[18] The conductor checked to make sure all was clear and then gave the highball sign to the locomotive crew at the head of the train to get under way. This prompted engineer B. J. Hubbard to begin twisting knobs and throwing levers on the locomotive's backhead, like the Wizard of Oz fiddling behind the curtain. He squeezed the spring-loaded handle of the Johnson bar and pushed it forward, setting the delivery of steam to the pistons to produce maximum torque, opened the cylinder cocks, and then blew the whistle to signal a final warning that the train was about to move. As he slowly pulled the throttle lever toward him, the great steel beast lurched forward. As Hubbard expertly worked the controls to bring the complex system of boilers, valves, and piping to maximum efficiency, the locomotive slowly picked up speed until the train cleared the station and finally disappeared from view. The two-thousand-mile run to Chicago had begun.

Howard Jones had led teams to Chicago several times before, although never a Trojan team and never to Soldier Field. Rockne had coached in the giant stadium once before, during the championship season of 1924. The Irish had been the visitors then, with forty-five thousand spectators on hand to see them play Northwestern.[19] This time, Notre Dame would be the home team, and the spectators at Soldier Field would number well over one hundred thousand. As the crowds for big games grew too large for Cartier Field, Chicago had become Notre Dame's alternate home city for its premier matchups. This game would be the first in a string of blockbuster contests that would help Rockne raise the funds to build a fitting home stadium in South Bend.

In 1927, Chicago was the second-biggest city in the United States and a center for manufacturing, meatpacking, and transportation. Like Notre Dame, the city owed its name to the presence of French explorers, who found the region inhabited by Algonquian peoples when they ventured there in the seventeenth century. The Algonquians called the land *shikaakwa,* or "stinky onion," for the plants growing along the river there, and the French corrupted the name into *Chicago*.[20] The city that arose along the Chicago River grew rapidly, attracting people from all over the world, including, in time, the Rockne family from Norway. By 1927, the onions were long gone, and the strongest smell wafting across Chicago was the scent of illicit booze from illegal breweries and gin mills, mixed with the stench of the dirty money and corruption it generated.

Chicago was a huge sports town. For college football, it was home to the University of Chicago Maroons, coached by Amos Alonzo Stagg, with the Northwestern Wildcats in nearby Evanston. The pro teams of the NFL Bears and the Chicago Cardinals also called it home, as did baseball's Chicago Cubs and White Sox. Boxing was big there as well, and the city hosted many heavyweight title bouts. The 1927 Notre Dame-USC game was going to be its biggest sporting event yet.

Rockne had begun prepping his squad in earnest after returning to South Bend from the November 19 game with Drake. He had just five days to get ready, though it was said that Rockne had pointed his team "toward Howard Jones and his Trojans for a good many weeks." Rockne, of course, gave his usual pessimistic assessment of his team's condition, but in fairness this late in the season every team had its share of nicks and bruises. He offered a more favorable assessment of the Trojans, telling newsmen, "I think Jones has a better team this year than last." Rockne did add a rider, however. "You want to remember that USC will be playing under a cold weather handicap in Chicago next Saturday and that will mean a lot for Notre Dame." The weather, it seemed, might just be Rock's secret weapon. "If it snows, so much the better," he smirked.[21]

Of course, Howard had planned for any contingency. One of his assistants, Cliff Herd, had purchased long underwear for everyone on the team before leaving Los Angeles. The players' physical condition was not so easily addressed. The Trojans were every bit as banged up as Rockne's squad. Both Morley Drury and "Racehorse" Russ Saunders had recently spent two nights in Good Samaritan Hospital to rest. Fullback Harry Edelson was also mending, though it was hoped he would be able to play.[22] The worst blow was the state of the Trojans' best quarterback, Don Williams, who not only was nursing a serious kidney injury[23] but also had suffered three fractured vertebrae against Washington State.[24] He had to be left behind, forcing Jones to shuffle his starting lineup.

The Trojans' trip to Chicago was almost as memorable as the game itself. "Bridge hound" Howard Jones, Bill Hunter, Cliff Herd, and Gordon Campbell, once he came aboard, formed a card-playing foursome at every opportunity. Backup quarterback Rockwell "Rocky" Kemp amused his teammates with "the loudest pair of pajamas ever discovered outside of Hollywood's most exclusive motion-picture circles." Not to be outdone, teammate George Templeton donned his long johns after dinner on the first night and liked them so well he decided to go sans outerwear for the rest of the evening.

Gordon Campbell and his wife were scheduled to join the train in Hutchinson, Kansas. The engineer planned to slow the train as it neared the station and stop just long enough to take on the new passengers. It turned out to be a fortunate change to the normal schedule.

Gwynn Wilson had moved up to the cab to avoid last-minute requests for tickets, and Howard Jones had ordered Wilson to take *Los Angeles Times* sportswriter Braven Dyer with him, to spare the coach from answering "darn fool questions" about the outcome of the upcoming game. While the cab was cramped by the addition of Wilson and Dyer to engineer Hubbard and his fireman, having four sets of eyes up front would soon prove advantageous.

As they approached Hutchinson, the men in the cab spotted a dark silhouette blocking the tracks. As the locomotive's headlight revealed more detail, it quickly became apparent that a car had stalled, with two people still inside. Hubbard threw back the throttle and quickly engaged the brakes. Frantically working to stop the train, he pulled at the cord above him to blast a shrill, desperate warning from the locomotive's whistle. The engine squealed to a stop as the terrified driver and his wife scrambled out of their motionless vehicle. When the iron horse finally halted, just six feet separated tons of hardened steel and superheated steam from disaster. If not for the need to pick up Campbell and his wife, the train would have sped through the town and plowed right into the stranded automobile.

With catastrophe averted, the trip continued apace. Thanksgiving Day was spent rolling through Kansas. The scenery was described as "nothing to rave about," but since most of the players had never been east of Arizona, they found plenty to look at anyway, even if was "only a bunch of farm houses which are deserted because their owners have pulled up and left for California."

Coach Jones granted his players a reprieve from their normally strict training diet and ordered them a Thanksgiving meal that was served in the dining car at noon: turkey, cranberry sauce, and all the usual trimmings, with pumpkin pie for dessert. The feast was reported to have been "disposed of in scandalous fashion" by both players and coaches.

Afterward, players and officials expressed their thanks aloud for the good things in their lives. Cliff Herd, said to have one of the biggest appetites on board, declared that he was thankful to have had plenty to eat. Jeff Cravath, now one of Jones's assistants, was thankful for being in love. Bill Hunter expressed thanks that Cravath had taken his place as the Headman's bridge partner. Gwynn Wilson gave thanks for his two-week-old baby boy back home. Even though Howard Jones was notorious for his steadfast unwillingness to delegate his duties (particularly when it came to coaching the linemen), he expressed his thanks for all his assistant coaches. No doubt his staff would have confided that they were grateful for the opportunity to work under the Headman. Henry Monahan, traveling with the team as the representative of the Southern Pacific Railroad, rather prosaically expressed his thanks that there had been no delays in Hutchinson and the train was still running on time.[25]

Aubrey Devine came on board when the train reached Kansas City.[26] Coach Jones immediately sequestered himself with his scout to glean whatever last-minute nuggets his spy could provide. The team had completed several workouts along the way, at Tucson and in several towns in Kansas, and Jones surely wanted to integrate Devine's final observations into his plans for their last practice session, slated for Stagg Field in Chicago.

Jones's obsession with detail finally drove him to distraction just miles from their destination. It was Thursday night, and Howard was sleeping soundly in his berth when he was overcome with a vision: Notre Dame was pummeling the Trojans 32–20 at halftime. He began storming around the car, enraged that the game had slipped so far out of his control. After awakening, he realized it had all been nothing but a bad dream.[27]

The Trojans arrived at Chicago's Englewood Station, near State Street and 63rd, at around 9:30 on Friday morning. They were greeted by a welcoming committee that included local business and civic leaders, the mayors of both Chicago and Los Angeles, the commissioner of the Big

Ten, the governor of Illinois, and the vice president of the United States.[28] Chicago alderman George Maypole led the committee. It had been Maypole's resolution back in September that had thrown open the city's hospitality to the visitors from the West Coast. In flowery civic style, it began, "Whereas, this game is comparable in the public interest it commands to the Army-Navy game which was played in Chicago last fall, . . ." and went on to explain that, "under the contract between the University of Notre Dame and the University of Southern California, this game was to be played on the athletic field of the University of Notre Dame." The document then extended the "appreciation of the people of Chicago of their action in transferring a game of such great interest to our city."[29]

The Trojans left their hosts and headed directly for Stagg Field and that final workout. Afterward they retired to their lodgings at the Windermere Hotel on 56th and Cornell.[30]

Rockne didn't even leave South Bend until after the Trojans had arrived in Chicago. His practices back home had centered on stopping Drury, with tackling drills taking up the better part of an hour during the last full workout before the game on Thursday. After a short practice in the morning, the Irish left South Bend around 6:00 on Friday night.[31]

Friday evening offered one last chance for the coaches, their respective teams, sportswriters, and various hangers-on to relax before the contest. Once again, two banquets preceded the game. One, held at the Windermere Hotel, was sponsored by the alumni of USC.[32] Since Howard Jones refused to allow his charges another break in training, their dinners were served in another part of the hotel, away from the fancier fare enjoyed by those in the banquet room.[33] After speeches by Jones, Bill Hunter, Warren Bovard, and Trojan captain Morley Drury, the Rev. H. V. Griffin, acting as toastmaster, led the cheers for the assembled group. The room thundered with the chant of "All the world is sad and Drury, all the world is sad and Drury," mimicking the lyrics of an old minstrel tune, "Old Folks at Home," better known as "Swanee River."[34]

The other gathering, Christy Walsh's annual All-American banquet, was a somewhat more commercial affair, held the same night at the Palmer House. Walsh brought along some of his most famous stars. Photos of the head table that night show Pop Warner, Babe Ruth, and Knute Rockne on one flank and Lou Gehrig, Howard Jones, and his brother Tad Jones on the other. The Yankee stars wore football jerseys, with a

Many sports greats attended the banquet held the night before the 1927 Chicago game between USC and Notre Dame. Shown here, from left, are Pop Warner, Babe Ruth, Knute Rockne, Christy Walsh, Lou Gehrig, Howard Jones, and his brother, Tad Jones. (Image courtesy of USC Digital Library.)

large *ND* emblazoned on Ruth's chest and an equally bold *SC* printed on Gehrig's. Photos of the sluggers were provided to newspapers nationwide via Walsh's news service and reprinted across the country.[35] The two baseball titans performed a football skit for the entertainment of the one hundred sportswriters, coaches (including Rockne's predecessor, Jess Harper), and members of the public.[36] Afterward, the four coaches answered questions from the audience. Warren Brown of the *Chicago Herald-Examiner* was the master of ceremonies throughout the evening, with the proceedings broadcast over radio station WJJD.[37]

Chicago, and perhaps the whole country, was in the grip of football fever. At the request of Mayor Thompson, the Loop was awash in the colors of the two schools, plus the red, white, and blue of the American flags displayed throughout the downtown area.[38] Special trains and exclusive tour packages had lured fans to Chicago from all over the Midwest.[39] The society pages of newspapers across America listed who was attending the game. On this last weekend in November, Chicago would be putting on the Ritz, and Soldier Field was going to host the biggest bash in America.

15

See You in Chicago

Wait a minute, wait a minute, you ain't heard nothin' yet!

—Al Jolson, *The Jazz Singer*, 1927

Soldier Field, like the Coliseum in Los Angeles, was a massive municipal stadium built in the style of the ancients. The Chicago architectural firm of Holabird and Roche had reinterpreted classical motifs in their winning bid for the project's design competition in 1919, but the style was influenced more by Rome's Parthenon than by the home of that empire's gladiators.[1] Construction began in 1922, along a north/south axis in Municipal Grant Park, between Lake Shore Drive and Lake Michigan. In true Chicago style the original $2.5 million bond issue proved inadequate, and rising costs required an additional $3 million to be raised in 1924. By 1928, the city would have spent a total of $8.5 million on the facility.[2]

Seating was arrayed in a U-shaped configuration, with great columned structures rising above the stands on the two long sides. These colonnades had tetrastyle temples on each end with double rows of thirty-two Doric pillars spaced between them. A third, even grander pantheon spanned the open end, far away from the edge of the north end zone. The gridiron below the seating areas was surrounded by a running track, also like the Coliseum in Los Angeles, but the larger footprint of the stadium gave the arena an even more cavernous feel than its West Coast counterpart.

Even this impressive structure, however, could not accommodate the influx of fans descending on it to watch the 1927 football game between

Notre Dame and USC. The needed preparations had taken weeks, requiring substantial effort and expense. Hundreds of telegraph wires
were installed in the press section to meet the demand for news coverage,
and dozens of microphones were added to link the site of the game with
radio stations in NBC's Orange Network.[3] Special accommodations had
also been added to handle the spectators swarming to the stadium. Box
seats were constructed between the pillars of the colonnades above the
permanent stands, and additional temporary seating was erected elsewhere to meet the unprecedented demand for tickets. Plans to handle
the overflow crowd, drafted in the weeks before the game, were about
to go into action. The extra policemen, ushers, and concession vendors
added for the game were going to have their hands full.

Preparations had not been confined just to Chicago, for interest in
the game spanned the country. In Los Angeles, home of the Trojans,
preparations were especially lavish. The radio station KHJ had installed
loudspeakers atop its Vine Street studios, where Dean Cromwell and
the USC band would be on hand to add a rooftop rooting section for local fans. The city's May Company department store had likewise rigged
speakers on its new garage structure on Ninth and Hill to broadcast Jack
Keogh's play-by-play to the street outside.[4] Even the Coliseum would
be part of the frenzy. The Los Angeles stadium would open its gates
early and pipe in coverage from Chicago over the PA system before the
UCLA game with Drake, offering fans five hours of continuous college
football action.[5] Within USC itself, students wishing to remain on campus could follow the action in Chicago from Bovard Auditorium, where
a Grid-O-Graph machine stood ready to provide them with up-to-date
reports of the game's progress. Harold Grayson's orchestra would add
live pregame and halftime entertainment.

All the tickets to the game itself had been snatched up a month before, including the forty-two hundred sent to the Trojans, but it was said
that a quarter million could have been sold if capacity had been that
large. The demand for tickets had been so great that Rockne's duties as
athletic director nearly overwhelmed his coaching responsibilities in the
days leading up to the game. At one point, no fewer than seven simul-
taneous long-distance callers seeking tickets jammed the phone lines to
Rockne's campus office. Rockne became so frustrated with the distrac-
tions that when a newsman asked him how his club looked, the Irish
chieftain snapped, "I haven't had time to ask the assistant coaches!"

Finally, though, everything was in place. Chicago, Soldier Field, and both teams were ready. Game day brought a grey, misty haze that clung to the stadium's majestic colonnades. Rain had been considered a possibility, but by halftime the sun would fold back the blanket of rolling clouds hovering overhead, pushing up the temperature in Chicago to just eight degrees short of the day's high in Los Angeles.[6] Wet weather before Saturday had affected conditions, however. Even though the field had been covered during the recent rain, the turf was slick at kickoff.[7] The canvas and straw covering the field had served to tamp down the grass, and though it was not soggy, the footing had become treacherously slippery.[8]

None of the tickets sold—and in many cases resold for a handsome profit—went unused. Fans began pouring into the arena when the gates opened two hours before the start, and continued filing in until moments before kickoff.[9] The throng encircling the field formed a sea of humanity unprecedented in the history of college football. It was a spectacle beyond the wildest dreams of both coaches just a few years earlier.

Among the multitude were a constellation of dignitaries, many of whom had already greeted the teams on their arrival in Chicago: U.S. Vice President Charles Dawes; Governors Len Small of Illinois and Clement Young of California; Mayors William "Big Bill" Thompson of Chicago and George Cryer of Los Angeles; Robert Mc-Cormick, owner of the *Chicago Tribune*; and Edward L. Doheny, oil baron and the president of the USC Alumni Association, who was also one of the few prominent Irish Catholics there to be rooting for the Trojans.[10] Another notable in the crowd was mobster Al Capone, who enjoyed being seen at such events. He had prime seats for himself and his entourage, as did many other members of the city's underworld, who, according

Mobster Al Capone made a show of being on the scene at all the happening places and big events in Chicago, including the 1927 game at Soldier Field between the Trojans and the Fighting Irish. (FBI photo)

to the *Chicago Tribune*, had "called off their shootings until after the game." The "big shot hoodlums" were said to have behaved "just like perfect gentlemen."[11]

Christy Walsh was determined to wring every possible ounce of publicity out of the game, so he brought two of baseball's most famous baseball sluggers to town. Appearing on the field in heavy overcoats, their interest in the proceedings seemed lukewarm as they stood before the crowd. Nevertheless, Babe Ruth and Lou Gehrig performed their duties with the requisite showmanship. As the stadium's loudspeakers boomed the announcement that Ruth and Gehrig were in the house, they bowed in response to the ovation the fans gave them. The "Sultan of Swat" tipped his ivy cap and "Larrupin' Lou" lifted his fedora in thanks, and then, when the cheering had subsided enough for them to be heard, they both made a few remarks through the field telephone.[12]

It was almost 1:30, and kickoff was just minutes away. With the final preambles completed, the Trojans' captain Morley Drury met Notre Dame's captain John Smith at midfield. As the visitor, Drury had the honor of calling the coin flip. The token landed in favor of the Irish, and Smith elected to defend the south goal. Drury chose to start the game on defense.[13] He kicked off moments later, and drove the ball deep into Notre Dame's side, where halfback John Elder caught the ball and returned it to the 40-yard line.[14] The second game between Notre Dame and USC was under way.

The Trojans stopped Notre Dame on their first possession, and a poor punt gave the ball back to Drury and his mates on the Irish 40-yard line. Drury hammered at the line, making two short gains before slipping off tackle and racing down to the 11-yard line. On third down, Drury heaved a pass to Russ Saunders, who sprinted into the end zone. Drury's toe was again called on to kick the ball for the extra point. The snap was bobbled slightly, and Saunders set it down sideways in his haste to avoid the oncoming defenders.[15] The ball barely made it off the ground, and it was easily blocked by Irish right end Charles "Chile" Walsh.[16] The Trojans had scored three touchdowns in two years against Notre Dame, and not one point after conversion had been completed. It was a bad omen.

The Trojans stopped Notre Dame on their next possession, but the defense was offside so the Irish kept the ball. When the Trojans finally stopped the drive and got the ball back, it was at their own 5-yard line. Instead of risking disaster, they kicked it out to midfield on second down. Charles Riley slipped while fielding the ball, a miscue foreshadowing the sloppy footing that would bedevil both teams all day.

Notre Dame made steady gains until Riley tossed the ball to a streaking Ray "Bucky" Dahman, who hauled the long pass in and dashed to even the score. Saunders had slipped trying to keep up with the Irish receiver, and was nowhere near the play. Dahman continued the scoring by kicking the extra point, and Notre Dame led 7–6.

Just ten minutes had ticked off the clock. It appeared at that moment that Howard Jones's nightmare of a wild game might prove prophetic. Instead, both teams settled into a mostly fruitless struggle the rest of the half, with Drury's few open field opportunities thwarted by the slippery footing that sent him to the turf untouched by Irish defenders.

USC had an opportunity in the third quarter, when Drury ran a punt back to Notre Dame's 24-yard line, but the luck of the Irish came through just when Rockne needed it most. Drury slipped on second down. Then his third down toss would create a firestorm of controversy that would rage long after the game was over.

Drury snagged the hike from center and faded back to pass. He drew a bead on Lowry McCaslin dashing down the field, and let it go toward the open Trojan end. At the last moment Riley went high in the air to steal the ball almost out of McCaslin's hands. As his feet touched down at his own 3-yard line, Riley turned, tucked the ball under his arm, and took several steps while moving toward his own goal.

Three Trojans closed in, with Saunders smashing into him "much as a switch engine would smash into any object less adamant."[17] The ball flew out like a cannonball, hitting just short of the goal, where two Trojans gave chase to the bouncing pigskin. McCaslin fell on it, and the jubilant Trojans shouted "Touchdown, touchdown!" Umpire John Schommer disagreed, explaining that a touchdown was impossible by rule, since the ball had been recovered over the end line. The Trojans then demanded a safety, but again their pleas went unheeded.

Schommer stepped over to the spot where he ruled the collision had taken place and marked the spot with his foot. He called out "Either safety or a touchback depending on possession and control," and called the two captains and the field judge, "Pinkie" Griffith, into a conference.

Riley's back was turned to Schommer when he grabbed the ball, and the umpire was fifteen yards away in any case, so he had to rely on the one man with a view of the play, field judge Griffith.

"Not possession or control," Griffith decisively responded. Schommer whistled the play a touchback and Notre Dame took over on their own 20-yard line, per the rules of the day. A chorus of boos rained down from the stands, even though the house favored the Irish, but to no avail.[18] The ruling would stand. The rest of the quarter wound down with no further scoring.

With fifteen minutes to play there was still just one point separating the combatants. Notre Dame had the ball as the period began, and was on the move. Flanagan tore through the line, with only Drury between him and the goal. The Trojan safety chased him down and made the tackle as the Irishman crossed midfield. The drive petered out at the Trojan 35-yard line, but Notre Dame soon got the ball back around midfield. After picking up a first down, the Irish handed the ball right back when Flanagan fumbled after making a good gain, but the Trojans could make nothing of the opportunity.

Again the two sides seesawed back and forth. Trading punts left the Trojans with the ball at their own 20-yard line. Two passes netted only five yards. Kemp tried a pass on third down, but again Dahman picked it off at the thirty. The Irish had to run off six plays before the final gun sounded.[19]

Rockne had again bested Jones by a single point, and again the loss was determined by the Trojans' shortcomings in the kicking game. As the two sides flooded the field and the two coaches congratulated each other, that bitter truth must have stuck in Jones's craw. For a man who stressed fundamentals, such a failure of a basic play was unacceptable.

Both teams left the field in complete exhaustion. The victors celebrated in their locker room under the west stands, exhibiting the style of those accustomed to winning—little boasting but plenty of quiet congratulations. Rockne appeared, made the rounds, shook a few hands, and then headed out for his hotel. As the players began to undress, the team manager handed out tickets for the dinner and dance to follow at the Stevens Hotel. Some reached into the food box to grab a ham sandwich; others gathered, paper cups in hand, as hot coffee was poured.

Notre Dame's trainer had plenty to do. Smith held his hands up to have the tape snipped from his muddy paws. Flanagan lay on the table, getting a rubdown for his wounded legs. There were bruises, scrapes, and sore muscles to attend to, but the trainer's job was always easier when his team won the game.

Licking their wounds under the east stands, the Trojans were just as tired as the Irish and considerably more subdued. It was they who were sad, and truly dreary. Drury approached the Headman, and told him, "I'm sorry coach. We did the best we could." Jones said nothing. He simply smiled and patted his star player warmly on the back.

Despite the bumps and bruises, the pain seemed mostly mental. "Physically," one of Drury's teammates mused, "I don't feel any worse than when I started."

All the players grumbled about the controversial call that they felt had cost them the game. "It was a break that went against us," chimed in one. "It might as well have happened to the other fellow. It was just as tough a break when Drury was loose and slipped in the mud."

Jones tried to squash such talk, though inside he shared their frustration. "What an official rules, stands," he said. He wanted to focus on the positives. "It was a great game. I don't think either team showed any strong superiority."[20]

Rockne used a lighter touch later that night at the Stevens Hotel. After sitting "like a buddha puffing his cigar" through a five-minute introduction that praised his brilliance, Rockne rose from his seat and began to address the twenty-two hundred people in attendance. "I'm glad my wife is here," he began. "Though she wouldn't believe it anyway."

Rockne worked the crowd, as usual. Among the guests were his boss, Rev. Matthew Walsh, and the auxiliary bishop of Chicago, the Rt. Rev. Edward F. Hoban. "Hunk Anderson coaches the team, Tommy Mills does the scouting, and all I have to do," he quipped, "was blow up the ball."

Rockne's words wrapped up a program that had included speeches by the clergy, the mayors of both Los Angeles and Chicago, a few other civic dignitaries who praised both teams, and the man who carried the impact of any outcome with dignity and grace, win or lose—Trojan coach Howard Jones.[21]

There wasn't time for the Trojans to dance the rest of the night away. The schedule barely left room for Howard Jones to address the gathering. The team's train would depart at 10:30 that night, and the players had no desire to hang around town. It was going to be a long, somber trip home.

Although USC had another game left to play, the team showed no interest in football as the Santa Fe special got under way, preferring to read, play cards, and talk about anything other than the gridiron to pass the time. Finally, when they reached Gallup, New Mexico, someone produced a football and the boys set aside their disappointment long enough to at least resume a little horseplay with the pigskin.[22]

Howard Jones never stopped thinking about football. He was smoldering inside the entire way, and even he could sometimes fall short of his own ideal of good sportsmanship. "When I was coaching at Iowa I protected John Schommer when he called a bad one on a blocked punt in the Michigan game," Jones told reporters. "This time I'm not standing behind him, since I feel his decision was an injustice to my players and to the school and alumni whom they represent."[23]

The Trojans returned to Los Angeles sixty hours after leaving Chicago.[24] Their fans had not abandoned them. The team was received outside the city by several busloads of Trojan Knights, who escorted the squad directly to campus. Students packed Bovard Auditorium, ready for the "impromptu rally" that was planned for 10:00 that morning. Catherine Colwell, the student body vice president, opened the event by introducing rally committee chairman Shields Maxwell. Then Harold Stonier gave a brief pep talk in which he praised both teams.[25]

Drury and Jones were the only two combatants who addressed the three thousand in the attendance. Captain Drury spoke first. "Fellow students," he began. "When we left here last week for Chicago I told you that we expected to bring home the bacon. I am compelled to come back and stand before you empty handed. All of us, from the coach to the last sub, feel very badly about our defeat."

Reminding everyone that there was still one game left to play, he added "But we shall go into the game against University of Washington Saturday with undaunted determination to win."[26] Drury paused, as if his remarks had ended, then blurted out "After all is said and done, we feel that we traveled a long distance to be robbed of a victory."

Yell King Paul Elmquist introduced Howard Jones. The Headman was more restrained than Drury, complimenting Rockne's troops instead of complaining about the officials. "Notre Dame has a fine football team," he said. "It played a great game last Saturday. But it is no finer team, nor played any better that Southern California last Saturday. They happened to come out on the long end of the score." Acknowledging the reality of the defeat, he added, "That's the end of that." Then he expressed pride in his players, despite the loss. "Our boys were good sports and took things like men and sportsmen, even if they had heavy hearts."

Afterward, Jones was more willing to critique the controversial call. He reenacted the play as he saw it, while adding his final comments on the matter. "Quote me direct on this," he stated firmly. "Here is the way the play appeared to me. Riley intercepted the pass. He ran three or four steps with it. Then he was tackled by our men. One of our men fell on the ball behind the goal line and out of bounds for a safety." Then he added bitterly, "The safety, if allowed, would have given Southern California two points and won us the game, 8 to 7. There were many in the stands who saw the play the same way." He reinforced his viewpoint by recalling that he "personally talked with some of these spectators after the game, who did not have a shadow of a doubt about the play."

Jones was clearly allowing his frustration to bubble over. Catching himself, he then tried to soften his comments. "But maybe I should not say this. I want everyone to get this straight and understand me. This is no alibi. The game is over. I make no alibis for what goes down as a defeat."[27]

In Los Angeles, talk about the disputed play started well before the team returned home. Films of the game, with slow-motion footage capturing the interception from three different angles, had been rushed to the coast, to be shown nightly at the Shrine Auditorium starting the Monday after the contest. Local high school and university teams were invited to the showings, with a different team saluted as the guest of honor each night.[28]

Opening night did not come off without a hitch. The reels were delayed seventeen hours in transit by a storm in Illinois, and then a union dispute in Los Angeles held up the first showing on Monday night. The union stagehands, organist, and projectionist, and the film cutter assembling the footage, objected to the decidedly nonunion Trojan band playing in the facility before the screening. A replacement projectionist had to be found, and the editing was not complete when the show began two hours late.[29] The rest of the week's showings took place without incident, since the Trojan band didn't appear past the first night.[30] Despite the rough debut, the showings were a smash hit, and MGM showed the newsreel across the country.[31]

The Trojans put their misfortune behind them in time to smack the Washington Huskies 33–13 the following week. The day after that game,

Clara Bow hosted the team at her home on Bedford Drive in Beverly Hills, as she had many times since first laying eyes on them in the Coliseum. The Thundering Herd spent Sunday sweeping her off her feet, literally. It was 4:00 A.M. when they decided to show Clara how they ran interference for Morley Drury on the Trojan's famous sweep plays.

Jesse Hibbs came crashing around end, where the tiny starlet proved no match for the husky Trojan warrior's irresistible charge. Bow was knocked to the ground and tumbled on the lawn. The team was all too willing to help her recover, and, to their relief, X-rays of her sore thumb "showed that no bones were broken," according to the story printed in the *Los Angeles Times* following the impromptu scrimmage.[32]

Bow's often rowdy parties for the Trojans would become infamous in her neighborhood. On one occasion, the police were called out to investigate the ruckus. The Trojans panicked at the sight of the cops, knowing that if Howard Jones ever found out there'd be hell to pay. Bow handled the situation by deploying her Brooklyn-bred street smarts and using her considerable feminine wiles to charm the police. After she had a word with the cops, the players' fears of legal repercussions subsided. All the police asked for was a promise that everyone would keep the noise down and the chance to meet Morley Drury in the flesh.[33]

Notre Dame's team had its own end-of-season celebrations, of course, but they were more formal affairs that lacked the star power of the Thundering Herd's shindigs. The win over USC had ended the season on a high note, encouraging the fans in South Bend to look optimistically toward the future.

Rockne was doing the same, but he was growing impatient with the conditions under which his team had to play. He was tired of being stuck playing home games in Cartier Field, where he was "presenting a first-rate production in third-rate setting."[34] He felt that the Notre Dame administration was not moving fast enough to make the new stadium a reality. To make matters worse, President Walsh had formed three study committees to consider the issue, leaving Rockne out of the key body tasked with developing a plan to finance construction. This upset Rockne sufficiently that, in protest, he submitted his resignation in a letter to Walsh on November 28, just two days after beating USC. Walsh refused to accept the resignation, but the friction was typical of the building acrimony between the factions on campus.[35]

Another big issue that loomed for the coming year was whether Notre Dame would play USC again. Though Gwynn Wilson had envisioned a longer series, the actual contract between the schools had approved only two games. Before Howard Jones left Chicago, Rockne had given him his answer. There would be at least two more games.[36] It was hoped that the next one would be a decisive win, for one side or another, settling all disputes over missed kicks and bad calls.[37]

In broader terms, 1927 was a year for the record books for the entire country. Back in March, Babe Ruth had become the highest-paid player in baseball when he signed a new contract granting him $70,000 per season,[38] while his seasonal record of sixty home runs would stand for more than thirty years. In May, aviator Charles Lindbergh landed in Paris after a flight that made him the first person to successfully fly an airplane solo across the Atlantic Ocean. Paramount's *Wings* further fueled the aviation craze, mixing scenes of World War I air combat with an engrossing love triangle featuring Clara Bow. Her role in that production solidified her position as the biggest female star in Hollywood. Another 1927 film transformed moviemaking more fundamentally. The release of *The Jazz Singer* marked the first major step out of the era of silent films. Actors' dialogue would no longer be read off written "title cards" displayed onscreen. Modern cinema, featuring action synchronized with speech and prerecorded music, had arrived.[39] The change would affect everyone in Hollywood, including a young Trojan fan named Clara Bow.

The year was transformative in domestic and world affairs as well, signaling profound political changes around the globe. In China, the Nanchang uprising at the beginning of August marked the formation of the Communist People's Liberation Army. That same month in Germany, Adolf Hitler, himself six years away from taking power, gave a major speech at a Nazi Party rally in Nuremberg outlining his ideas for National Socialism. In the Soviet Union, Joseph Stalin consolidated power by ousting rival Leon Trotsky from the Soviet Communist Party. In Massachusetts, the August execution for murder of anarchists Sacco and Vanzetti set off riots in cities around the world, including Paris and London, confirming the case as an international cause célèbre. The controversial trial and conviction of the Italian immigrants six years earlier had spawned growing protests around the world, culminating in the 1927 riots to protest their punishment.[40]

Meanwhile, on the home front, the crazy pace of life continued to accelerate into 1928. In politics, Al Smith became the first Catholic to head the ticket for a major American political party when he won the Democratic presidential nomination. Among the celebrities appearing on campaign posters supporting his candidacy were Babe Ruth and Knute Rockne.[41] As always, Chicago chose its leaders in a more violent fashion. Capone was heavily involved in the "Pineapple Primary," an election in the Windy City that was tainted by shootings, bombings, intimidation, and stolen votes.[42]

Technological advances allowed a station in Schenectady, New York, to begin the first regularly scheduled American television broadcasts in May. In films, Disney's production of the animated short *Plane Crazy* marked the first appearance of Mickey and Minnie Mouse, followed in November by *Steamboat Willie,* which featured the little mouse in the first animated "talkie."

Transportation was changing too. Henry Ford had moved on from the venerable Model T in 1927, replacing it with the Model A in 1928. The new design was bigger and more powerful and offered more amenities and more options.[43]

Both Howard Jones and Knute Rockne would also have to retool their machines for 1928. Jones had to find replacements for key players like Morley Drury, but Rockne would face a more daunting job. Only one of his regulars was coming back, and the past two freshman classes had been considered weak. A sportswriter called the prospects for the upcoming season "anything but bright."[44]

Some speculated that it was time for Rockne to dream up a new offense.[45] With the material at hand, he was going to have to pull a rabbit out of his hat if his new team was going to have any chance of living up to the image of the Fighting Irish in 1928.

However, at least one aspect of team life was settled. The school's administration had long objected to the moniker "Fighting Irish" as having negative connotations. Then in 1927, President Walsh relented, officially dropping any objections to the nickname.[46] After years of being known as the Catholics, the Ramblers, the Hoosiers, the Hibernians, and sometimes, derisively, the Bricklayers, the team had a real, official nickname.

16

Win One for the Gipper

Fight On for ol' SC

Our men Fight On to victory

Our Alma Mater dear,

looks up to you

Fight On and win

For ol' SC

Fight On to victory

Fight On!

> —Milo Sweet, with lyrics by Sweet and Glen Grant, 1922

It was the halftime speech to end all halftime speeches, an Oscar-worthy performance delivered a year before Hollywood started handing out those famous gold statuettes. The words flowed like the notes of a master's composition, perfect in tune and tempo, delivered with the deft touch of the virtuoso. It was one part truth, one part fiction, and Rockne hokum through and through. The story has become a part of American folklore, as legendary in sports as Bobby Thompson's "shot heard 'round the world" or the U.S. hockey team's "Miracle On Ice," with an impact so far beyond sports that it became the slogan of political campaigns decades later.

The date was Saturday, November 10, 1928; the place, the Polo Grounds in New York City. Notre Dame had invaded the city to take on Army. A full house of ninety thousand fans filled the stands, many the familiar "subway alumni" who swelled the ranks of Notre Dame supporters. Before the game, political and religious overtones charged the atmosphere in the wake of the 1928 presidential elections, in which Herbert Hoover, the Protestant Republican secretary of commerce, defeated Al Smith, the Catholic Democratic governor of New York. In this context, a win on the football field by Notre Dame would not only restore a bit of luster to South Bend in an otherwise unremarkable season but also bolster Catholic pride after the sting of Smith's defeat. Even the Irish beat cops of the New York Police Department were cheering for Notre Dame over the Cadets from their home state of New York.

In the first half, the battle had been hard-fought but frustrating. Notre Dame had frittered away its best opportunity when a fumble at Army's 2-yard line was recovered in the end zone for a touchback.[1] At halftime, the score was deadlocked in a scoreless tie.

The Notre Dame team facing Army that day was one of Rockne's lesser squads, probably the weakest of his career. The rebuilding job he'd faced coming into the year had proved every bit as challenging as expected, although his team had performed considerably better than Rockne's most pessimistic estimate, given at the end of September, when he had suggested that they'd be lucky to win a single game.[2] The team had won four thus far, against two defeats. The losses had been to Wisconsin and Georgia Tech, the latter one of the best teams in the country.

Rockne was anticipating a tough game against Army, fearing that his talent might not be enough to carry the day. When talent and experience fall short, strategy often proves irrelevant; this left just one option in his bag of coaching tricks: psychology.

Rockne left nothing to chance in that regard. Boxer Jack Dempsey had delivered pregame motivation, sending off the team with a rousing call to "Go out there and beat Army!"[3] Now it was halftime, and since the mercenary brought in to stir up the troops had failed to do the trick in the first half, it was up to Rockne to get the job done.

As the team shuffled into the locker room for the break, there was no hint that anything noteworthy was about to take place. Rockne made the rounds as usual, checking on injuries and, where necessary, soothing bruised egos. Then he moved to the center of room, as always, surrounded by his team, all eyes fixed on him. Magic was about to happen, though no one could have guessed it at that moment.

Rockne began addressing his boys slowly and deliberately. He spoke of other games, similar tight spots, and the man who had done so much to overcome powerful Army teams in the past. Everyone at Notre Dame knew about the late George Gipp, and even those too young to remember him felt the loss. Most had lost someone in their own lives—a father, an uncle, or perhaps a neighbor; in those days, lives were cut short for many reasons. But the Gipper was special—the fallen hero cut down in his prime—and just about everyone could relate to such a tragedy.

Rockne talked of the Gipper—the great young athlete and vibrant football star—recalling his stunning exploits and his swift death, weak and pale in the terrible grip of pneumonia. He painted the picture of the pathetic shadow of vigor that his star had become, then repeated Gipp's whispered plea for posterity. They were the most famous words of his coaching career.

"On his deathbed George Gipp told me that someday, when the time came, he wanted me to ask a Notre Dame team to beat the Army for him," he solemnly recited.[4] That someday, Rockne hoped, had arrived.

It was later said that when Rockne finished, there was not a dry eye left in the room.[5] There was a pause as the players reflected on Rockne's words, an intuitive moment of silence shared by everyone in the room. Then the players suddenly sprang to life. They were electrified, almost enraged, as if filled with the Holy Spirit, even if it was only the Spirit of Notre Dame. The team charged out of the dressing room, ready to launch a crusade.

Yet it was Army who struck first in the second half, taking a 6–0 lead shortly after kickoff. The setback still didn't diminish Notre Dame's fighting spirit, and the Irish evened things up near the end of the quarter. Army blocked the extra point, so the score remained tied, until Rockne reached deep into his reserves to pull one last rabbit out of the leprechaun's hat.

With two minutes to go, Rockne sent in a fleet-footed but lightweight end, Johnny O'Brien, to replace the injured John Chevigny. The fresh and rested O'Brien blasted past the man coverage of exhausted Army defender "Red Christian" Cagle and reeled in a looping pass to dash in for the winning score of 12–6. Forever known as "One Play" O'Brien, the seldom-used reserve had added another chapter to Rockne's gospel of winning football.[6]

O'Brien's contribution to the day's glory was soon forgotten. The halftime pep talk, first reported in an article by Francis Wallace running under the headline "Gipp's Ghost Beat Army," might have suffered the same fate were it not for the 1940 film *Knute Rockne, All-American*, which elevated the story to mythic status. Scholars have challenged the truthfulness of Gipp's deathbed request, and different versions of Gipp's words have circulated. Moreover, it is uncertain if the 1928 Army game was even the first time Rockne used the tale[7]; one former Notre Dame player has claimed that Rockne quoted Gipp's deathbed request much earlier, before Notre Dame played Indiana in 1921.[8] Nonetheless, the legend lives on.

Almost completely forgotten were the games played just after that famous day in Yankee Stadium. The Irish hosted Carnegie Tech at Cartier Field the following week, and a funny thing happened on the way to immortality: the Tartans bashed Notre Dame 27–7. It was the first loss on the Irish home field in twenty-three years. Rockne had two weeks to recover from that debacle and prepare for USC. He was going to need them. He'd already lost more games in 1928 than he had in any season since becoming head coach at Notre Dame.

While the Irish were struggling, the Trojans were getting stronger every week. Howard Jones had reworked his squad beautifully. "Dynamite Don" Williams, so called because he "hits the line like a ton of dynamite and whizzes around end like a runaway engine," had wrestled the quarterback duties away from Russ Saunders, who was moved to fullback. The only question about the "Thunderbolt from Santa Ana" was his durability: there was some doubt about how well his back injury of the previous year had healed.

Williams's understudies were Rocky Kemp, star of the freshman team the year before, and a good-looking kid from Santa Monica named Marshall Duffield. Harry Culver of the *Los Angeles Herald* had praised the young back, saying, "When you see a blond, baby-faced but sturdy gridder hurtling off tackle, tossing perfect spirals or booting the ball with an air of nonchalance, that'll be Duffield."[9]

Lloyd Thomas was one halfback, playing at nearly the same weight as most linemen. The other was Harry Edelson, who'd missed out on the double date with Clara Bow back in 1927 because of injuries.[10] The talent in the backfield, coupled with stalwarts on the line like the team captain, Jesse Hibbs, and newcomer Ward Bond, really put the thunder in Jones's offense. The coach decided to open things up a bit this season, to feature more deception in addition to his usual power game.[11]

The Trojans had run roughshod through their schedule. While they had struggled some with St. Mary's, and stumbled in a scoreless tie on a miserable, sandy field devoid of grass at Cal, they were hitting their stride going into the Notre Dame game, having won their last three contests 78–7, 27–13, and 28–7.

Rockne brought his team out west using the usual route of the Golden State Limited, leaving South Bend on Saturday, November 25. Thirty-five players made the trip this time.[12] They would spend two days in Tucson, as Rockne wanted enough time for them to rest and acclimate themselves to the warmer weather they'd find waiting for them on the coast.

The first day of their desert stop was spent going though two "stiff workouts." Sportswriter Braven Dyer described the team as having "more pepper and enthusiasm than a bunch of school kids on a picnic." Dyer marveled that "they have the spirit of victory burned into their very being day in and day out."[13]

At times Rockne could imprint that spirit with a rather caustic branding iron. A favorite tactic was reminding former high school hotshots that talent was no substitute for effort. "You forgot to show him your newspaper clippings," he'd say when the play didn't go well. "He doesn't know how good you are." Part of his genius was that he always knew who needed a kick in the pants, and who needed a pat on the back, and he always seemed to dispense the proper dose of whatever was required at exactly the right time "to motivate them, relax them, and make them more confident."[14] This ability to connect with his men was facilitated by his "incredible facility for remembering names."[15]

Rockne's easy familiarity with every one of the hundreds of players in his program made each one feel special.[16] Howard Jones, on the other hand, often forgot his players' names. He frequently sent someone into action by simply calling out, "You!" before adding, "Go in at guard."

A special train of Irish rooters caught up with the team in Arizona as the squad was practicing on Wednesday. The fans would spend twelve hours being entertained there before heading off for the coast. The team's workouts always drew big crowds. Rockne invited sportswriters to stop by, and though he claimed that the practice was "secret stuff," he added ironically that since only about five or six thousand spectators would be on hand, they "needn't worry about exposing anything important."

The team was staying through Thanksgiving, to celebrate the holiday and take in Arizona's game with Whittier College.[17] The traditional feast was served at a banquet after the Whittier-Arizona game, attended by both visiting teams.[18] Rockne was the main dinner speaker, but he was preceded by a USC alum, who spoke of the "metamorphosis" he'd seen his school undergo in the decade since he graduated. Rockne predicted that the Trojans were about to undergo another great metamorphosis in the Coliseum. His comments "brought down the house."

The Irish mentor continued the comedy at practice the following morning, but the target of his barbs fell closer to home. Noting a pass that was batted into the air, where it might still be caught, rather than downward where it would be certain to fall incomplete, he admonished the hustling defensive back, "We're not playing volleyball this morning!"[19]

Rockne played quarterback while using the "scrubs" to mimic the Trojan offense. When asked if his old coach Jesse Harper had been scouting the Trojans, he claimed he hadn't scouted them at all, just before his team ran the Trojan plays like "nobody's business." *Los Angeles Times* reporter Braven Dyer mused that if Howard Jones could "get Notre Dame's plays without sending Aubrey Devine all over the country it could save U.S.C. a lot of money."

Notre Dame's biggest problem was not lack of preparation, but lack of depth. Compared with the first team, Rockne's reserves were described as "heavier, but correspondingly slower, both mentally and physically."[20] The problem was exposed in the first two weeks of the season when star fullback "Rip" Collins suffered a broken wrist. His absence was a big factor in the team's losses, but he had since been fitted with a special brace and was back in the lineup.[21]

Rockne always knew when to guard against overconfidence and when to avoid defeatism. When he had better material, he'd claim his team didn't stand a chance, but when he was overmatched, he would talk up his squad. "I have had a lot of fighting football teams during my years at Notre Dame, but I never coached an eleven that has fought harder against insurmountable odds and disheartening obstacles than this 1928 machine," was his pronouncement before leaving Arizona at week's end. The Whittier Poets and the Fighting Irish squads boarded the same train Friday morning for the journey to Los Angeles.[22]

In his usual style and in contrast to Rockne, Howard Jones was saying little before the game and showing even less. Locking the gates to Bovard Field, Jones was conducting his practices away from prying eyes, be they friend or foe. Word had leaked out, however, that Saunders was working at quarterback. Duffield was out with a bad shoulder, and Saunders was an insurance policy to spell Don Williams.

Before practice Jones huddled with his assistants to devise defensive strategies to stop Rockne's attack, but when he emerged from the last workout, Jones announced a change to his starting lineup to help his own offense.[23] Marger Apsit would start at inside halfback. Jones would hold Harry Edelson in reserve, keeping him ready to come in at fullback if Saunders was needed at quarterback.[24]

The odds favored the Trojans by 10 to 8.[25] Everyone around Los Angeles had an opinion, with most of Hollywood backing the Trojans. Clara Bow had no doubts as to which team would win, exclaiming, "Why, Southern California of course. The Trojans are playing on fight this year, not their reputations, so I think Notre Dame is in for a real beating." Lon Chaney agreed, declaring, "The Trojans for my money," as did Buster Keaton, who picked "Howard Jones and the Trojans." There were a few dissenters. Despite time spent partying with the Trojan team, or perhaps because of it, Joan Crawford said, "I like the Irish."[26] With predictions made and bets laid down, all that remained was for the teams to play the game and find out who could gloat and who would have to pay up.

Game day brought typically pleasant conditions for early December in Southern California. Mild sunshine warmed the "firm, fast turf" that offered good footing for the players, unlike the slippery grass in Chicago the year before.[27] Capacity was far below that in Soldier Field, but the game was the third straight sellout in the series.

Eighty thousand people watched the captains, Jesse Hibbs of USC and Fred Miller of Notre Dame, face off at midfield for the coin toss. This time the Trojans won, and elected to receive the kick. Frank Carideo kicked off, but the Trojans could do little with the ball. Neither team seemed able to mount much of a threat early on, but one incident in the first quarter seemed a bad omen for Rockne: Notre Dame's starting center, Tim Moynihan, suffered a broken wrist and had to leave the game.

Irish fortune quickly shifted when Williams turned the ball over at his own 26-yard line. The Irish were frustrated by the Trojans, however, who broke up pass attempts on first and fourth downs and limited the Irish to five yards running in between. The defense of the Irish aerial attack showed that the Headman understood the threat and had learned from past mistakes.

The Trojans drew first blood later in the first quarter when they drove sixty yards after Hibbs blocked a punt. Saunders plowed through a hole "big enough to drive a truck through" on the scoring play and went in untouched by Irish defenders. The crowd's elation quickly turned to disappointment when Hibbs struck the ball low and the point-after kick sailed under the crossbar. Would the Trojans ever make an extra point against Notre Dame?

En route to USC's first national championship, the Trojans race past the Irish during their 1928 match at the Coliseum in Los Angeles. (Image courtesy of the UCLA Library.)

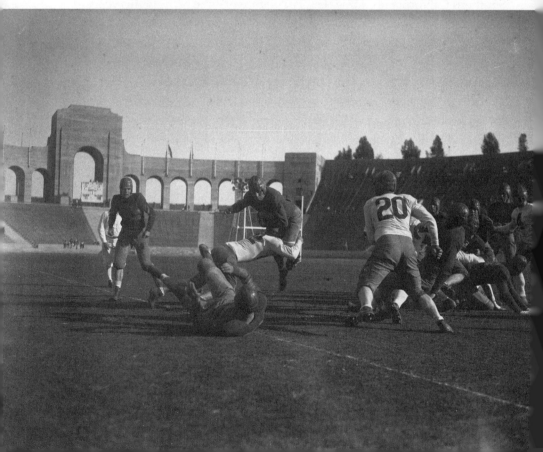

As it turned out, they would, and the question was moot in any case. The Trojans ran away with the rest of the half, scoring twice in quick succession in the second quarter. Williams tossed a touchdown to Apsit, and USC guard Tony Steponovitch intercepted Irish quarterback John Niemiec. Rushing the Irish quarterback, he batted the ball straight up, snatched it out of the air, and rumbled sixteen yards to push the Trojans' lead to 19–0. When Hibbs licked his second successful extra point, the Trojans led 20–0.[28]

Notre Dame played gamely in the second half. They cut the Trojans' lead to 20–7 in the third quarter after Jack Chevigney faked a reverse, and behind great blocking by All-American Fred Miller and sub Frank Leahy, raced fifty-one yards for a touchdown.[29] The teams traded scores in the final stanza, and when the gun sounded the scoreboard showed the Trojans on top 27–14.[30]

Howard Jones had accomplished something that only one other man had been able to do. He had defeated the great Knute Rockne twice. Their personal duel stood even now, at two games apiece, although Notre Dame led the series with USC 2–1. Jones expressed his relief at breaking the one-point barrier that had stymied both coaches for two straight years. "Of course, I'm satisfied to win by any score," Jones told reporters. "I don't believe Notre Dame is as strong as it was last year, but any Rockne team is good, and a constant threat. All of my boys played great football today, and I'm proud of them."[31]

Rockne had little time to congratulate his rival after the game. He had planned to attend USC's homecoming dinner and dance that night, but within an hour of the game's end he had left the Coliseum. His youngest son, Jack, had swallowed a peanut back home, and it was lodged in his lung.[32] In critical condition, the boy desperately needed surgery, and Rockne was whisked to Central Station for the trip back to South Bend.[33]

The win over Notre Dame would be the last of the season for the Trojans. Even though they won the Pacific Coast Conference championship, their feud with Pasadena's Football Committee kept them out of the Rose Bowl and denied them a postseason game.[34] Cal took their place in the January 1929 Rose Bowl, facing Georgia Tech, a pairing that denied football fans the chance to watch the country's two best teams battle for National Champion honors. That Rose Bowl game would be memorable for Cal's "Wrong Way" Roy Riegels, who scooped up a fumble and sprinted toward the wrong goal. His mix-up scored a safety that gave Georgia Tech a one-point victory.[35]

Howard Jones had to be content with the PCC title, his third undefeated season as a head coach, and the National Championship, as judged by the Dickenson System, a rating scheme devised by University of Illinois mathematics professor Frank G. Dickenson. The trophy was awarded to Coach Jones during a rally on campus three days after the Rose Bowl game in January.[36]

"The 1928 Trojan varsity was not the greatest group of individual stars that Howard Jones has coached since coming to Southern California," declared sportswriter Paul Lowry of the *Los Angeles Times* in his summary of the season, "but it was the greatest team."[37]

The Headman penned his own conclusion in the same paper, writing "I want to thank Los Angeles fans for their splendid support this season. I only hope that we can continue to give you good football and that it will continue to prove entertaining to all of you."[38] Although his ghostwriter, Al Wesson, may have been the one to put the words on paper, they no doubt accurately expressed Jones's appreciation. Few coaches had come as far, not even his brother Tad. The Headman had succeeded in elevating the status of USC football. He had helped begin the first real intersectional series in the college game. Finally, his Trojans had beaten the master himself, Knute Rockne, and brought a National Championship to Los Angeles.

Despite all that, the Headman's accomplishments would be overshadowed in history. A pep talk in New York of dubious origins and a blunder in the Rose Bowl of epic proportions would be the memorable stories of the 1928 football season. But for one afternoon, at least, Howard Jones was the biggest name around.

17

Capone's Last Game

There is no cause to worry. The high tide of prosperity will continue.

—Andrew W. Mellon, Secretary of the Treasury, 1929

It was freezing cold in Chicago on Valentine's Day, 1929. It had snowed on and off the previous week, and though flurries had stopped falling, four inches of the white stuff still lay on the ground.[1] Despite the cold, business went on in the Windy City's Lincoln Park neighborhood. Seven men had gathered inside the S-M-C Cartage Company at 2122 North Clark Street, a plain brick building with a fabric awning over the large front window advertising the firm's shipping, packing, and long-distance hauling services. These legitimate activities were just a front for "Bugs" Moran's North Side Gang, which used the location as a transit hub for bootleg liquor.

Johnny May, a former safecracker working as a mechanic for the gang, was servicing one of their trucks inside the unheated garage while his dog, Highball, sat nearby, his leash tethered to the bumper. The German shepherd quietly watched his master tinkering with the vehicle, and kept an eye on the six other men milling around the warehouse. Five of them were mobsters in the gang, but the sixth was Dr. Reinhardt Schwimmer, an optician who hung around the underworld to get his thrills.[2]

Four more men arrived a couple of hours before noon. No one saw them go in, but a short time later, neighbors heard the roar of automatic weapons and the booming sound of shotguns, followed by frantic barking as the shooting stopped. Alarm turned to relief when they saw a pair of uniformed policemen emerge from the structure, leading two other men in civilian clothes at gunpoint to a large Cadillac sedan. The car sped off, but the scene remained eerily quiet.

Things just didn't seem right. Save for the unceasing sound of the dog's wild barking, it was too quiet and much too still. Where were the detectives who should be investigating the scene? The neighbors were suspicious, but what could they do?

Finally, suspicion gave way to action, and a neighboring tenant crossed the street to check things out. Inside he found the frantic dog still on its leash, and seven bodies sprawled on the floor in pools of their own blood.[3] The "cops" had been phonies, killers masquerading as police to lure their victims into complacency. The St. Valentine's Day Massacre, as it came to be known, had just decimated the North Side Gang.

Who were the killers? The usual suspects were questioned, but no one inside the operation ever talked. Innocent witnesses were intimidated, and no arrests were ever made.[4] One of the dying victims was able to whisper an accusation, blaming the shootings on crooked cops.[5] Soon all manner of theories emerged. Some fingered the Purple Gang out of Detroit. Others argued that the massacre was the work of Moran himself, trying to rid himself of troublesome underlings.[6] Time passed, but no clear evidence emerged to point at those responsible.

Capone was the most likely suspect, given that the victims were his rivals. Despite his denials, most people believed that he had ordered the hit. The trouble was, no one could prove it. Capone had an airtight alibi that put him eleven hundred miles away in Florida as the bodies were hitting the floor.[7] Only one thing was certain: no matter who had orchestrated the murders, Capone was now the undisputed boss of all Chicago.

The brutality and scale of the carnage shocked the public. People could no longer look the other way. For the first time, the Feds really stood up and took notice. The incoming U.S. president, Herbert Hoover, led the charge in Washington. "I want that man Capone in jail," he told Treasury Secretary Andrew Mellon.[8]

Capone's days of high living were coming to an end. So were America's, but the good times wouldn't end without a blaze of glory, like the machine-gun fire in Chicago. There were signs of instability, but they went unheeded. Hints of change that would affect every aspect of American life, including college football, were dismissed as the grumblings of pessimistic malcontents.

The first big shock hit in March, when a tremor rocked Wall Street. After years of sustained growth, the market dropped dramatically. As panic began to spread, the banks calmed frantic nerves by announcing continued lending. With liquidity assured, frightened investors slowly came back, and the market recovered.[9]

The financial sector had been saved, and for a time the short-lived panic seemed to be a mere bump in the road. Other economic sectors were less optimistic. Business was slowing. Steel production was down, housing starts (the number of new private houses on which construction had begun) had slowed, and declining auto sales had the executives in Detroit worried.[10] Still the band played on.

A more fundamental upheaval was shaking the movie business. The advent of talking pictures had changed the industry for good, and silent films were falling by the wayside. While some studios continued to release silent versions of their sound movies for a few more years, the handwriting was on the wall. Theaters would have to invest in new infrastructure to show sound films or go out of business. Some theaters, and even some movie studios, would not survive the transition.[11]

It was even worse for actors. Voice tests weeded out the on-screen talent who couldn't adapt. No one wanted a leading man with a thin, squeaky voice or a femme fatale with an unintelligible foreign accent. Clara Bow was so popular she was getting thirty thousand fan letters a month, but even she was threatened by the new technology.[12]

Bow had always been a spitfire on screen, full of brass and self-confidence. Inside she was far less self-assured. She felt uneducated and inadequate, and was terribly self-conscious about her thick Brooklyn accent. Her anxiety about the new sound technology brought out the stammer she'd struggled with since grade school. Furthermore, the need to stay close to the primitive microphones of the day inhibited her naturally kinetic acting style. Her exaggerated pantomime, like that of all the silent movie stars, suddenly seemed overwrought.

Her film studio rushed Bow's first talking picture, *The Wild Party*, into production early in 1929, without giving her any vocal training or making any effort to bolster her self-confidence. While the film's title described the era well enough, it did not match Bow's experience on the set. While Bow was lucky that her director was Dorothy Arzner, one of the few women to helm major productions in that era, there was only so much Arzner could do to ease the star's anxiety. The microphone, still dangling ominously over Bow's head, might as well have been an executioner's axe, ready to slice through her career and send her straight back to Brooklyn.

Bow's finances were no more secure than her acting career. Despite her popularity, she was overworked and grossly underpaid compared to other stars. Her home life was a mess; she had too many hangers-on, including her lecherous father. If she failed to make it in the new talkies she'd have little to show for a decade of stardom. She needed someone to take charge of her money and protect her from the leeches and dead-beats around her—someone to "go in and clean out that mare's nest she lives in," as studio head Bud Schulberg described it. That someone was Daisy DeVoe, a strong-willed studio hairdresser she'd befriended. DeVoe quickly began turning things around. One casualty was Clara's house parties. From now on, the Thundering Herd would have to settle for an annual banquet in their honor.[13]

Despite such retrenchment, Clara Bow did attend the biggest of Hollywood's parties of 1929. The gala, held on May 16, in the Blossom Room of the Roosevelt Hotel,[14] was hosted by the Academy of Motion Picture Arts and Sciences, itself formed only two years earlier, in 1927. The group was handing out awards for the very first time, for outstanding film achievements of 1927 and 1928.

A string of luxury automobiles began delivering the 270 guests, variously bedecked in black tie or chiffon, satin, and diamonds, as the sun was setting on Hollywood Boulevard. Once inside, they were seated at thirty-six tables in the ballroom, arranged amid flowering cherry trees in pots, with Japanese lanterns hanging overhead.[15] The tickets, at $5 each, granted guests the privilege of dancing with Hollywood's elite before sitting down to a fine meal prepared by the hotel's kitchen.[16] The menu featured a first course of consommé celestine, followed by a choice of entrée—either filet of sole au beurre or half broiled chicken on toast—and desserts of ice cream or cake.[17]

The dozen awards were presented after dinner, in a brief ceremony conducted by Douglas Fairbanks, the Academy president.[18] When *Wings,* a 1927 war film in which Bow had starred, was judged best picture among the eligible films released between August 1, 1927, and July 31, 1928, Clara Bow accepted the statuette, not yet nicknamed Oscar, on behalf of the producers.[19] There was no suspense in the announcements; the winners had been revealed months before. But nominees who failed to carry home a golden statue enjoyed the consolation of waxed-candy replicas of the "Award of Honor" at each table.[20]

Bow also remained a winner among moviegoers. After the release of her first talkie, *The Wild Party*, her fan mail increased to forty-five thousand letters per month.[21] Not only had she survived the switch to talkies but her fans loved her more than ever.

Meanwhile, Hollywood continued to reach out to USC, and Clara Bow was not the only one showing interest. As early as 1927, the Motion Picture Academy had begun working with the university to develop some of the world's first film courses, and just three months before he handed out the first Academy awards, Douglas Fairbanks had lectured to a USC class on "photoplay appreciation."[22]

The good looks and youthful appeal of Howard Jones's young football players did not go unnoticed by filmmakers either. College-themed pictures were all the rage in the Roaring Twenties, and in May 1929, members of the Thundering Herd were cast for the Fox Studios production of *Salute*.[23] Fourteen of them, including Captain Nate Barrager, Marshall Duffield, Russell Saunders, and backup linemen Ward Bond, boarded a Union Pacific train bound for Annapolis and the Naval Academy.[24] Also in the group were director John Ford, former Trojan Duke Morrison, and a future cowboy star named Rex Bell,[25] who had been "discovered" while working as a truck driver making a delivery to the studio lot.[26]

The trip was supposed to be a secret, because the players feared it might be considered a violation of the prohibition against "professionalism," but their participation was splashed across the pages of the *Los Angeles Times* the next day. Fox publicity people denied knowledge of the students' involvement, and the USC's president, Von KlienSmid, stated that it was not professionalism because they went as "workers in a picture and not to give a football exhibition for money."[27] In the end no player suffered any problems with eligibility.

Howard Jones was not yet in the movie business, but he was receiving rave reviews for his role as coach. In February, he signed a new contract with USC that ran through spring 1934, the first time the school ever inked a deal for more than three years. The added job security also came with a boost in salary to $12,000 annually.[28]

The Headman also received a vote of confidence from his peers. He was scheduled to become the new president of the Pacific Coast and Rocky Mountain Association of Football Mentors in 1930, having been elected during the association's meeting at the Biltmore Hotel in late December 1928.[29]

Like Rockne, Jones was able to parlay his coaching success into lucrative side jobs. He would be headlining a coaching school in Kansas in early summer,[30] before heading back to Los Angeles in July for another such clinic on his own campus.[31] Around that same time, Jones announced the upcoming release of his second book, *Football for the Fan*, scheduled for September.[32] Cowritten with Trojan public relations man Al Wesson, it was less a coaching manual than an effort to break down the game for neophytes. One section was devoted to answering the questions of celebrity fans, among them Clara Bow, Mary Pickford, Oliver Hardy, Douglas Fairbanks, Gary Cooper, Fay Wray, who would be chased onscreen by King Kong in 1933, and Allen "Farina" Hoskins, the black face of the *Our Gang* series until he outgrew the role in 1931. Bow asked, "What was the better method of kicking off—kicking from a placed ball or the use of a player holding the ball?"[33]

Though Rockne's team had lagged behind Howard Jones's in 1928, the disappointing season had not caused Rockne's stock to crash at Notre Dame. On the contrary, it was Rockne's ongoing success since 1918 and his consequent influence that was causing a building tension at Notre Dame. That success had won Rockne a great deal of autonomy, to the point that the school's administration regarded his clout as a threat to the power structure. President Matthew Walsh had handled the tension between academics and athletics with skill and flexibility. He allowed the coach free rein where he could, yet acted swiftly when necessary, such as the times when Rockne accepted jobs elsewhere while still under contract to Notre Dame. Nevertheless, several administration officials regarded athletics as secondary to academics and insisted that the school's coaches accepted that relationship. Two of those pushing for more control were Father Michael Mulcaire, the university's vice president and head of its athletic board, and Father Vincent Mooney, head of the school's Physical Education Department.[34]

The retirement of President Walsh and his replacement at Notre Dame by Rev. Charles O'Donnell shifted the balance in the struggle over athletics. As a native of Indiana and a graduate of Notre Dame,[35] President O'Donnell understood the school's culture and appreciated its athletic traditions, but he was also in the vanguard of the university's drive for academic excellence.[36] O'Donnell cut the figure of the stereotypical Irish priest—though decidedly more Bing Crosby's Father O'Malley than Ward Bond's Father Lonergan. An intellectual and a poet, O'Donnell's high forehead, fine features, and clear eyes displayed his intelligence and calm demeanor. While he valued sport, he deplored "the almost exclusive eminence of Notre Dame as a place where a football team is turned out."[37] Rockne soon discovered that while O'Donnell might be open to persuasion on some issues, academic eligibility for his players was not one of them.[38] There would be no more George Gipp exceptions under the Golden Dome.

Nevertheless, O'Donnell too had to work within constraints. As much as the new president might want to change things, the fact remained that Notre Dame had committed to building a new stadium and needed money to pay for it. In February, O'Donnell told alumni at a luncheon in New York that the university had budgeted $750,000 for a new on-campus stadium.[39] The new facility would be ready for the 1930 season, but while construction was under way, the football team would play every game away from South Bend. They may have officially become the Fighting Irish back in 1927, but they would truly be Rockne's Ramblers in 1929. How Notre Dame's officials squared that decision with their concern that the players spent too much time away from school was anybody's guess.

Rockne's dream of a proper home stadium for his team was finally coming true, yet rather than celebrating, Rockne felt threatened. In June, O'Donnell had proved his determination to uphold academic standards by refusing to intervene when a promising halfback flunked out and was declared ineligible.[40] Mulcaire and Mooney were even more intransigent, and the friction was proving too much for Rockne. He believed that the university's athletic director should have a say in sports appointments at Notre Dame, yet the school had hired a basketball coach over his objections and rehired him in 1929 without even consulting Rockne. The placement of Mooney's name above Rockne's in the department's organizational chart just added insult to injury.[41]

In response, Rockne once again tendered his resignation in a telegram to O'Donnell dated July 1.[42] Recognizing that Rockne's departure just as construction began on the new stadium might jeopardize the fund-raising efforts that would pay for the work, O'Donnell sought to assuage the coach's wounded feelings instead of calling his bluff. He talked Rockne out of leaving and arranged for Father Mooney to take a sabbatical, thus removing at least one source of Rockne's frustration.[43]

Rockne had tried the same drastic measure back in 1927, resigning when he had quarreled with Rev. Walsh over the need to build a new stadium in the first place.[44] This time the stakes were much higher. Forces were quietly building, not just at Notre Dame but nationwide, to challenge everything the coach stood for. People were looking at football's place in higher education and wondering if there was too much hoopla, too much money, and too many shady deals going on.

Concern about academic irregularities and an overemphasis on winning didn't keep the rosters of assistant coaches at major schools from swelling. In 1928, the Trojans had no fewer than ten assistants, including a kicking specialist brought in from Australia.[45] The 1929 USC yearbook, *El Rodeo*, listed eight, with an additional twenty-two student managers.

Rockne would have to wait until 1930 to lead such a cadre of assistants, although he did have a whopping pool of fifty-one student managers at his disposal.[46] In 1929, Notre Dame listed just four assistants to back up Knute Rockne—but that group included the indispensible Tom Lieb.[47]

Lieb had played football for Rockne, competed at the Olympic Games after graduation, and coached the linemen at Notre Dame for three years. He'd left his alma mater for an assistant job at Wisconsin before returning to South Bend for the 1929 season.[48] Events would soon oblige Rockne to turn over many of his coaching duties to his top assistant, a responsibility that required Lieb to call on all his ability. Fortunately, the talented underling had the experience and intelligence that would one day make him a successful head coach in his own right. Rockne would soon praise his second in command, saying, "A man can afford to be sick with a helper like Tom Lieb around."[49]

Worn down by his frantic work schedule, Rockne was not a well man as the 1929 season got under way. Doctors told him he had phlebitis, an inflammation of a vein caused by blood clots blocking circulation that often caused debilitating symptoms ranging from fatigue and pain to swelling and fever. In some cases, if a clot broke loose and traveled to the heart or lungs, grave illness or death could result.[50] Given the state of medical science in 1929 and the added pressure of Rockne's overwhelming work schedule, doctors were taking no chances. They ordered bed rest for the coach and told him to avoid all stress, including participation in Notre Dame's games. Initially balking at such draconian measures, Rockne bowed to them only after consulting medical textbooks on his own.

Thus began an odd season when Rockne would become a Flying Dutchman of sorts, whose presence was always felt even if he was seldom seen. At some times, he convalesced at his home in South Bend, huddling with a few key players during the week. At others, he visited the locker room in his wheelchair to give dramatic pep talks or reached out to his team via phone when they were on the road. Even though Rockne's doctors demanded he stay in bed, he had a special hearse outfitted to shuttle him to his team's practices, so he could watch the drills. As the news leaked out, rumors spread of his impending demise, a macabre echo of Gipp's last days. The whispers were squelched only by Rockne's vigorous denials and his occasional Lazarus-like appearance on his home field.

A strong tonic for Rockne's woes was the improvement of his team since the disappointment of the 1928 season. The rebuilding year had seasoned green players like quarterback Frank Carideo, halfback Jack Elder, fullback "Moon" Mullins, and linemen John "Boom Boom" Cannon, Frank Leahy, and John Law, the team's captain. Newcomers like halfback Marty Brill, a transfer from Penn, and Joe Savoldi, a beast of a sophomore fullback, added fresh talent to the mix.

Rockne missed Notre Dame's first three games in 1929, but couldn't bear to skip the Carnegie Tech game after two losses to them in recent years; to the dismay of the attending physician, he made his first melodramatic locker room appearance of the year as his team prepared to face the Tartans. Rockne's emotional appeal to "hit 'em, crack 'em, crack 'em, smack 'em!" was just enough to carry the day. Notre Dame won 7–0.[51] Rockne's whispered words, his trembling exhortation to his players to go all out, echoed the last gasp of the decade's excesses. The unbridled frenzy attending college football in the twenties was almost over. Within a single week, upheavals both inside and outside the sport would set off a chain reaction that changed everything.

Within football, the first upheaval occurred just days before Notre Dame faced the Tartans. It was the release of Bulletin Number Twenty-Three by the Carnegie Foundation for the Advancement of Teaching. The bulletin gave a damning report on American collegiate athletics.[52] The foundation had been created in 1905 by Andrew Carnegie, a wealthy industrialist and generous philanthropist, and received a charter by an act of Congress a year later. It had released two previous reports on amateur athletics, the first in 1925.[53] This third report was highly critical of the influence and commercialism of sports, particularly football. The stinging indictment rocked the game to its very core.

The huge success of big-time college football had provoked detractors who decried its brutality and warned against the excesses they felt were at odds with the purity of the college ideal. Almost since the day in 1874 when McGill University popularized rugby in America by traveling from Canada to play Harvard in Massachusetts, the sport had grown, morphing into the gridiron game of football. And as its popularity increased, so too did criticism of America's pigskin obsession. When eighteen young men died playing the game in 1905, opponents of the game nearly killed off football altogether. The sport was saved when President Theodore Roosevelt called together the top Ivy League powers of the era to discuss the situation. Led by men like Walter Camp of Yale, Howard Jones's mentor, the bigwigs heeded Roosevelt's call.[54]

Roosevelt's intervention helped spur a reformation of sorts. The colleges began to adopt new rules to improve safety for players and improve game action that triggered the transformation of a ponderous donnybrook into a faster, more open, more fan-friendly game.[55]

The mania for football that exploded after World War I filled college coffers across the country—but money, like power, corrupts. The academics' complaints of special treatment for players, abuse, and corruption were not without merit. The pressure to field competitive teams did fuel abuses, ranging from the use of paid players or ringers who never went to class to all sorts of skirting of the rules. Scholarships based on athletic ability were not allowed at the time, yet the best athletes always seemed to find a way to pay their tuition, regardless of their academic abilities or their family's financial resources. The critics were determined to stop the shady deals. Rockne and most other leading coaches didn't see it that way. They stressed the value of hard work, the challenge of competition, and the connection of a sound mind to a sound body. Rockne in particular worried about converting football from a "He-man's game to a silk stocking contest."[56]

If the critics had their way, coaches like Rockne might well lose their jobs, since the reformers were demanding the abolition of paid coaching positions and a return to the old volunteer system.[57] The Carnegie Foundation's bulletin named both Notre Dame and USC as examples of schools participating in the scourge of "big time" college football, noting that they were among seven schools paying their coaches $10,000 or more a year.[58]

Bristling at the criticism, Rockne strongly defended the academic integrity of his football program, making public statements to that effect as early as the spring of 1927.[59] In an interview given early in 1929, perhaps seeking to preempt the criticism he knew might be coming, Rockne asserted, "I'm for abolishing all athletic scholarships."[60] Technically, true athletic scholarships did not exist in the NCAA until 1952, but the thrust of Rockne's statement—that a coach should draw his players from the student body as he found it on campus rather than lure the best talent from prep schools far and wide—was notable. Whatever his sincerity about the theory of recruiting for college ball, in practice Rockne persisted in seeking out the best talent he could find. Working with key alumni "who can keep their mouths shut," the coach set about forging an efficient pipeline to channel top players toward South Bend. He kept the effort secret from O'Donnell and his administration, a subterfuge that would eventually land Rockne in hot water.[61]

Howard Jones's position was a bit different. He denied any suggestion of impropriety, stating firmly that he "never solicited a player in my life."[62] This was undoubtedly true. Jones never kept an office on campus and filled his off-season months with golf, fishing, and playing bridge, not scouring high school practice fields.[63] It was the job of his assistants to coordinate the incoming talent, and the administration at Southern California denied any illegal recruiting, admitting only to their alumni reaching out to prospective athletes.

The school strongly objected to any assertion of impropriety. "The inference that members of the athletic department at the University of Southern California went after athletes was without foundation and unfair," asserted administration official Warren Bovard. He pointed out that USC had cooperated fully with Carnegie's representative, Harold W. Bentley, and that the investigator had said that "he had found nothing off-color or out of the way which might reflect on the institution."[64] Bovard neglected to mention that Jones found jobs for his players, as when he sent Morrison and Williams to see Tom Mix in 1926.[65] The rules definitely prohibited such "subsidization," but Jones set up the jobs anyway, just as Rockne found on-campus work for his boys back at Notre Dame.[66]

Just two days after the Carnegie report shook college campuses, a greater crisis ousted athletic critiques from the headlines when the ominous cracks in the nation's financial system fractured into chasms. The stock market had dropped the previous Thursday, before Notre Dame downed Carnegie Tech, but investors had rallied by day's end. There was no rescuing the fallen the second time around. October 28 came to be forever known as Black Monday after the Dow Jones Industrial Average fell 13 percent. As the drop continued on the following day, Black Tuesday, panic ensued. Rumors of suicidal investors jumping out of windows fed the frenzy. It was a bloodbath never seen before on Wall Street, and in the days that followed, stocks continued a mostly steady decline. They wouldn't recover completely until 1954.[67]

The despair spreading in financial circles and the frenzy on Wall Street did not immediately spread to Main Street. Most people weren't worried. The vast majority of Americans were still farmers, laborers, or ordinary workers in other fields, not high-rolling speculators. While the stock market crash was troubling, most people didn't see it as ruinous unless they personally had money in the market. Average folks really didn't feel the pain until banks failed and life savings were lost, or drought set in to ruin farmers' fields, or companies went belly-up, casting their workers into the streets. Those troubles were coming soon enough, but, as of the late fall of 1929, nobody really gave those possibilities much thought.

18

Another Bite of the Onion

The sporting spirit is the spirit of Chicago.

—Lincoln Steffens, 1931

The mountain of debris first appeared on Tuesday, when the students began gathering discarded objects to fuel the giant bonfire. Originally, work had begun at two locations, one within Notre Dame's boundaries, and the other outside them, but then the two piles were combined into a single massive pyre on campus. The mound grew ever higher into the sky as students stacked old crates and pallets by the truckload on the pile of logs, railroad ties, and discarded furniture already in place. They continued to add scraps of wood and boards of every description, and when the peak reached some sixty feet in height,[1] they doused the contents with crude oil to soak until Thursday. It was to be the biggest bonfire, during the biggest week, to celebrate the biggest game Notre Dame had ever played.[2]

The Trojans' visit to Chicago two years before had been a colossal event, yet the crowd was expected to be even bigger this time. Anticipation for the game between the top-ranked Irish and the once-beaten Trojans had soared beyond the level reached two years before, and Notre Dame's students were sparing no effort in expressing support for their team.

The activities began Tuesday night, part of the officially declared "Rockne Day," with a special mass in the Sacred Heart Church, followed by a solemn torchlight parade and more energetic activities, like a cheer competition between residence halls. Everything was planned to lead up to Thursday night, when the marching band would circle the dorms, gathering three thousand students to join with another five thousand supporters from around the town for a massive pep rally and the bonfire.[3] Among the fired-up crowd were New York's mayor, Jimmy Walker, and Senator Arthur R. Robinson of Indiana.[4]

The excitement had been building all season. Notre Dame's first undefeated slate since 1924 was within reach, and if the team managed to defeat the Trojans, it would face only one more real test, the annual clash with Army. Rockne's crew had started slowly in its first four games, overcoming the disruption of the coach's absence to beat Indiana and Navy on the road, before shutting out Wisconsin back at Soldier Field. That 19–0 victory had been the only really strong outing of Notre Dame's first four games, with the Irish beating Carnegie Tech the following week only by dint of Rockne's melodramatic pep talk.

By mid-November, the team was hitting its stride. It recorded stronger wins in its next two games, beating Georgia Tech 26–6 in Atlanta and Drake 19–7 in Chicago. The oddsmakers on the West Coast were impressed, at least enough to make Notre Dame a 2–1 favorite a few days before the game with USC, despite what seemed to be another Howard Jones juggernaut building in Los Angeles early in the year. The Thundering Herd had steamrolled hapless UCLA 76–0, Oregon State 21–7, Washington 48–0, and Occidental 64–0, before narrowly beating Stanford 7–0 on the Farm. The perception of invincibility was shattered when Cal beat the Trojans 15–7 in the Coliseum. Rebounding from that setback, the Herd returned to its dominance one week later, swamping Nevada 66–0 before turning its attention toward Rockne's Ramblers and the trip to Chicago.[5]

Trojan fans sent their team off with the same rousing effort they had shown two years before. Their rally, parade, and train station farewell were very much a repeat of 1927. Howard Jones addressed the students, and then the column of buses and cars made its way up Figueroa. At Sixth, the caravan turned toward Central Station to board the Trojan Special for Chicago.[6]

A bad omen occurred shortly after the team departed. Late Wednesday night, the Trojan war flag hoisted above Bovard Auditorium disappeared, leaving the student groups responsible for raising the flag pointing fingers at each other in the aftermath. The Trojan Squires in charge of the banner protested that they had been given no orders to place a guard, while the Trojan Knights overseeing the Squires responded that they didn't think one was needed. Suspects included Notre Dame alumni in Los Angeles, crosstown vandals from UCLA, and even "students from northern schools."[7]

The only lengthy stop on the Trojans' trek east this time would be in Kansas, although frequent brief respites were planned along the route. The Trojans conducted a workout at McPherson College, a small school located about sixty miles north of Wichita, on a snow-covered field, offering a preview of possible game conditions should the white stuff fall along Lake Michigan. A small pickup game of sorts sprang up in one corner of the field, between teams consisting of assistant coaches and alums, plus one sportswriter and even a movie star who was part of the entourage, Joe. E. Brown.[8] Brown had been a fine baseball player in his youth, catching the attention of scouts for the New York Yankees before he decided to concentrate on his acting career.[9] Brown was typical of the Hollywood crowd with which Howard Jones often rubbed elbows. One year later, the two men would appear together in the motion picture *Maybe It's Love*, with Jones making his acting debut playing a football coach.[10]

Snow was falling throughout Kansas, and the icy whiteness proved an irresistible temptation for the young Angelenos, who had seen more of it in a single day on the trip than they had in all their lives. At Pratt, Kansas, the Herd thundered through the snowbanks, and brought handfuls of the frigid powder back to the train with them. Led by Erny Pinckert, the merry pranksters headed to the coaches' berths in search of unwitting victims. Howard Jones and his assistant Sam Barry, both veterans of the snowy climes of Iowa, proved too savvy for such tricks, but Bill Hunter and Aubrey Devine were caught unawares, opening their compartment door to receive a "white bath" that left them "muttering hoarsely about undergraduate nuts."[11]

Trojan fears of bad weather dissipated as they stepped off the train at the Englewood Station at 8:30 Friday morning. It had rained throughout the week in Chicago, but sunshine greeted the players upon their arrival, and they were confident that the only thunder during play would be provided by their own running game.[12]

The Trojans had found additional relief even before detraining, when Sam Barry's lost lucky rabbit's foot was returned to him by a waiter from the dining car. Barry had been lent the rabbit's foot for good luck on the trip by a teammate of his son at the John Burroughs School back home; apparently its presence had carried the Burroughs team to an un-defeated season. The only condition of the loan was that Barry should return it safely after the trip, and now Barry could keep his word despite his carelessness in losing it.[13]

Once the squad and its gear had been unloaded, the Trojans pro-ceeded to Stagg Field for one last practice before heading to their ho-tel.[14] After practice, they spent the rest of the day lounging around the Windermere Hotel, playing bridge or shooting pool.[15]

That night, local Trojan alumni hosted the team for a dinner. The lineup of speakers featured the president of DePauw University, plus Warren Bovard, the USC's vice president and comptroller, and, of course, Howard Jones. Graduates of Stanford and Cal were invited as well, to foster Golden State solidarity in the hostile foreign territory of Illinois.[16]

The big question under discussion that night revolved around Knute Rockne. No one, neither the Trojans nor the Fighting Irish themselves, knew exactly what role Rockne would play during the game. He had taken two weeks off after the Carnegie game before returning to prac-tice on November 12, but he was still weak and confined to a wheel-chair. Drills were conducted indoors, in the school gymnasium, to keep Rockne out of the cold.[17] Throughout it all, Rockne had insisted he would be in Chicago on Saturday. "I wouldn't miss that game if I had to stay in bed the rest of the winter," he vowed. But would he actually coach or just observe the game? That was the lingering question.

Some people wouldn't buy the line Rockne was selling. "Is that leg trouble of yours on the level or is it merely a publicity stunt?" one fan letter asked.[18] Rockne had become the man who cried wolf. After watch-ing him tell so many tall tales while faking tear-jerking melodrama over the years, skeptics couldn't help reacting with suspicion, even when he truly had a debilitating illness. Only game day would set aside rumor and speculation.

Although the day was hazy, no moisture fell as the hours counted down to kickoff. The throng began arriving early, with the worst seats at the far end, located some six city blocks from midfield, filling up well before the rest of the stadium. Estimates of attendance reached 123,000 people, with the 116,000 paying fans padded by another 7,000 nonpaying spectators, including police, ushers, aides, reporters, and photographers.

The huge crowd demonstrated that the recent Wall Street collapse had not yet slackened demand for tickets to big games. Or perhaps all the tickets had been purchased before Black Monday; after all, the game had been sold out for weeks. Scalpers were getting as much as $30 for tickets with a face value of only $7.[19] Once again, movers and shakers among the nation's elite attended, including Jimmy Walker, the playboy mayor of New York City, who was as strong and devoted a Notre Dame fan as any in South Bend.[20]

Al Capone did not attend this year, however, being otherwise detained. He was still serving a prison sentence on a concealed weapon charge imposed back in May. Cops had pinched Capone in Philadelphia when car trouble on the way to New York, after attending a national "hood's convention" in Atlantic City, prompted a brief stay there while traveling through Pennsylvania. Even if he had been back on his home turf of Chicago, Capone might not have made the game, since law enforcement there, led by Prohibition agent Elliot Ness and his "Untouchables," was really turning up the heat. Capone's ultimate undoing, however, would come not from the work of the police, but from the careful efforts of snooping accountants in the Internal Revenue Service.

Had Capone made the game, he would have seen a Notre Dame team more like the one he had witnessed in 1927, as it was much improved from the weak squad that lost to the Trojans in 1928. The players believed they were the school's best team since the Four Horsemen had stampeded their way to Pasadena, although the current team had developed no single backfield star, or even a consistent group like the Four Horsemen. One week, Jack Elder played the hero; the next, Joe Savoldi, took that role; while a third time, it might be Frank Carideo who stepped to the fore. The offense also differed from that of 1927, featuring relatively few pass attempts and instead relying mostly on a crushing running game. This was unusual for a Rockne team.[21]

Rockne decided to arrive early, and traveled from South Bend by car on Friday.[22] He avoided any public appearance before the game, instead dining with sportswriter Grantland Rice on Friday night.[23] The players came into the Windy City by train on Saturday morning, just hours before the game.[24]

Donning white shirts, the Trojans may have contrasted in color with the Irish, but the two teams displayed equal levels of confidence.[25] When USC quarterback Russell Saunders was told that he would be facing the best Hibernian team since 1924, he responded, "They'd better be."[26] Coach Jones was less brazen. "If Southern California can make two hundred yards against Notre Dame, we stand a great chance of winning the ball game. If we can do as well as we did last year and manufacture over three hundred yards, we will win the game," he predicted.

Aide and chief USC scout Aubrey Devine was more pessimistic. Glumly recalling what he had seen while scouting the Irish, he warned, "If Southern California plays against Notre Dame as it did against California, Notre Dame will win by five or six touchdowns."[27]

The captains for the game were John Law for Notre Dame, a native of Yonkers, New York, and Nate Barrager for USC, a product of San Fernando High in greater Los Angeles.[28] Barrager would go on to become a successful production manager in Hollywood and work with former teammate Duke Morrison in the movie business.[29] The other player on the traveling squad with a future as a studio man was tackle Ward Bond; he would later appear in a string of John Wayne movies and eventually star in the television show *Wagon Train* in the 1950s.[30]

Notre Dame won the toss and elected to receive. Frank Anthony kicked off for the Trojans. Saluted by the roar of well over one hundred thousand souls, he booted the ball to Savoldi at the 22-yard line. Savoldi plowed forward for ten yards, where the charging Trojans mowed him down. The ball was spotted for play, and the Irish prepared for their first play from scrimmage.

Coach Lieb started Notre Dame's "shock troops." Rockne's assistant was in direct control, overseeing implementation of the team's plans, but another presence overshadowed his efforts: Knute Rockne sat directly behind Lieb in a wheelchair, bundled in a heavy overcoat with blankets piled high upon his lap. Old Rock might be weakened, but he was still the field marshal in overall command of his army, and he would have a say in this battle, illness or no.

The Trojans stunned Rockne and the rest of Soldier Field a few moments later. After the Irish were stopped and shanked a punt near midfield, the Trojans wasted no time in capitalizing on the mistake. On the second play, Marshall Duffield dropped back to pass and launched a perfect strike to Marger Apsit, who raced twenty-five yards untouched to score. Duffield failed to score the extra point, so the Herd led 6–0.[31]

Rockne noticed that Bucky O'Connor had allowed the Trojan receiver to slip by him, violating a key point that had been stressed in practice. The coach became incensed when he found out that O'Connor hadn't let on that his swollen eye blurred his vision.[32] Out came O'Connor, and in went Marty Brill.

Notre Dame could do nothing with the ensuing possession. After going back and forth, another bad Irish punt gave USC the ball at the Notre Dame 36-yard line. After two plays, the Trojans' opportunity evaporated when the Irish intercepted a hurried pass at the Notre Dame 32-yard line. Duffield responded a few plays later by leaping high to intercept a pass by Marchie Schwartz, ending the Irish drive at the Trojans' 32-yard line.

After missing on a fifty-yard pass play, the Trojans kicked it back and Notre Dame started a sustained drive. Tom Conley made a sensational catch to move the ball thirty-five yards, down to the Trojan 29-yard line. The next pass was rifled twenty-two yards and connected with Brill at the 7-yard line, and it was first and goal for Notre Dame. On the next play, Schwartz took the snap and handed off to Brill, who smashed into the line and was just two yards short of the goal when the ball came loose. Don Moses recovered, and Notre Dame's chance was gone. Duffield quickly booted the ball back and the Irish had first and ten just thirty yards short of the goal as the first quarter ended.

Controversy returned to Soldier Field in the second quarter. Still trailing 6–0, Notre Dame had the ball deep in Trojan territory. Facing fourth down, the Irish threw a pass to Conley at the goal line, but it bounced off his hands and tumbled into the air. Carideo reeled it in, and an official threw up his hands to signal a score. A heated debate ensued as the officials conferred. The scoreboard at first added six points and then removed them, switching back and forth several times as the argument wore on. Eventually the refs issued their final decree, to a chorus of boos from the partisan crowd. The rules barred a receiver from catching a ball first touched by an eligible teammate, without a defensive player touching it in between, so the pass was ruled incomplete and possession went to USC.[33]

As if aroused by the touchdown that wasn't, the Irish stopped the Trojans cold, and, after a punt, regained the ball around midfield. On first down Carideo called for halfback John Elder to hit Marty Brill with a quick pass over the middle. Elder dropped back, but Brill was nowhere to be found. Elder backpedaled, desperately searching for somewhere to throw the ball, as a gang of Trojan linemen swarmed around the Irish passer. Elder wound up, and launched the ball as far as he could, just to get rid of it. As the ball left his hands three defenders smashed into Elder, knocking him to the ground and into unconsciousness. The roar of the spectators brought Elder back from the black a few seconds later. "What happened?" he asked the teammates who were mobbing him.

"Conley caught the ball and scored," Brill told him.

"Conley!" Elder exclaimed. "What was Tom doing down there? He wasn't supposed to be the receiver!"

"Well," Conley explained, "I was the decoy, remember? I got down on the goal, looked around to see what was happening—and here came the ball!"[34]

The ball had arched fifty-five yards and dropped right into Conley's waiting hands.[35] The passing game that had been withheld for this game precisely to surprise Howard Jones had been unleashed with spectacular, if somewhat unplanned, results.[36]

Carideo missed the kick and the score remained deadlocked at 6–6. When the two sides dashed off the field for the halftime break, the tally was still knotted.[37] It had been a tremendous, evenly played game thus far.

Howard Jones often liked to keep his team on the field at half, rather than head for the locker room.[38] Rockne's preferred to regroup in private. Inside the dressing area, the random cadence of metal cleats clacking on concrete mixed with the soft thuds of discarded leather helmets as the Notre Dame team quickly circled the center of the room. Some players stretched out on benches, others threw blankets on the floor to prepare a soft spot to rest. Trainers worked on battle damage while the team silently waited for the coach to address them—whichever coach that might be.

Tom Lieb was the first to enter when the doors swung open, but all eyes stayed fixed on the entrance. Where was Rockne? Suddenly the doors flew open again, and two student managers held them wide and clear. It was Rockne. He looked pale and drawn, with beads of perspiration glistening on his forehead. The aides maneuvering the wheelchair pushed the ailing coach through the doors and toward a better vantage point at the center of the room, within the circle of players waiting for instruction.

Paul Castner, a former player from the days just prior to the run of the Four Horsemen, began to speak. Castner expressed the emotion that had been bottled up until that moment. He reminded everyone of what Rockne meant to the school and to the team, and of just how much he was risking by being there for them. Eyes glistened and lips trembled throughout the room. It was almost impossible to hold back tears.

On the outside, Rockne seemed a mere shell of his old self, but on the inside he was the same old Rock—always thinking, always planning his next move. The ever-present cigar, rolling nervously between his fingers, hinted at the activity raging inside his head. It was an outward sign that pressure was growing inside him, surely building toward release.

The ailing coach began to stir as Castner finished up. Slowly Rockne struggled to rise, then began to speak. "Go on out there," he whispered. "Go on out there and play 'em off their feet in the first five minutes," he exhorted his boys, his voice rising. "They don't like it!"

With each word Rockne seemed to gather strength, until he was rolling like a runaway freight train, almost shouting at his team. "Play 'em! Play 'em!"

Finally he shifted gears again, fading back into the verge of collapse. "Come on boys," he reminded them, "Rock's watching." As he sank back into the pile of blankets on his wheelchair, the last dry eye remaining in the room began to moisten. Savoldi sobbed. The team was electrified as the players returned to the field.

That halftime speech, Rockne's last great dramatic performance of the season, quickly paid off. Just six minutes into the second half, the Trojans had to punt from their own end zone, and Carideo raced twenty-five yards with the ball before being forced out at the 13-yard line. A few plays later, Savoldi crashed into a solid mass of defenders but pushed through to score. The kick was good and the Irish had forged a 13–6 lead.[39]

Carideo and his mates lined up for the kick and the Irishman of Italian decent swung his toe into the ball, slamming it deep into Trojan territory. The pigskin arched high above the gridiron and fell to Russell Saunders as he stepped back to his own 5-yard line to cradle the ball in his arms. He charged forward, accelerating as he met the mass of blue in the center of the field. His interference blasted the pursuing defenders like a well-tossed ball smashing through wobbly bowling pins, sending bodies flying as Saunders eluded their desperate attempts to stop him.

The crowd roared in response to the thunder of the Herdsman. Hometown fans shouted desperate pleas for someone, anyone, to track down the streaking white comet that was flashing across the gridiron. The visitors went wild, celebrating madly as Saunders tore down the field.

The grass was open and clear at midfield, and Saunders galloped like the famous racehorse Man o' War rumbling toward the finish line. The combined voices of more than 120,000 screaming fans reached a hitherto unknown crescendo, shaking the stadium and drowning out all other sound. Saunders had covered ninety-five yards in a single mad dash to glory, and just a single point again separated the two teams.

The kick for extra point is one of the simplest of all plays in football. It was incredible that it should still present a problem to the Trojans after so many heartbreaks against Notre Dame. Yet just such a failure in the opening stanza of the game had already prevented the Thundering Herd from going for the lead.

This time, Jim Musick would make the attempt. The ball was placed, the snap was good, and Musick's kick cleared the defender's reach. The ball seemed to veer wide, but just barely. As it headed toward the goalpost, it looked like it still might squeak through, but it was inches outside as it passed the upright. The officials crossed their arms frantically: the try had failed. The scoreboard remained at 13–12. Fortunately for the Trojans, there was still a whole quarter left to play.

That one last quarter offered the Trojans just a single chance. They had made a first down at Notre Dame's 28-yard line, but an offside penalty moved the ball back five yards. A third-down pass play was caught, but out of bounds. Just as he had in 1926, Jones elected to punt rather than risk a blocked field goal. The ball soared over the goal line for a touchback, and the Trojan's last opportunity for victory fell impotently into the end zone.[40]

Howard Jones had predicted that two hundred yards of offense might be enough to win. His team managed only one hundred forty-six to Notre Dame's two hundred forty-nine. Still, they left Soldier Field having failed to win by just two missed extra points.[41]

Understandably, Irish fans were thrilled with Notre Dame's victory, no matter how small the margin. They snake-danced through Chicago's downtown Loop, and later that night four thousand of them clamored to join Notre Dame's victory dinner and dance, at which there was room for three-quarters of that number. Howard Jones gave a stirring speech, praising the Notre Dame backfield as "the best set of backs ever seen."[42]

Rockne was too weak to attend the dinner or any other postgame frivolity, and rested to offset the effects of the week's exertion. Despite his withdrawal from activity, a clot in his leg broke loose and narrowly missed catastrophically lodging in his lungs or brain.[43]

Rockne would recover from that brush with death to reach new heights in 1930. The day of his martyrdom had not yet arrived.

19

After a Million Dreams

Whenever there's a big war comin' on, you should rope off a big field . . . and sell tickets.

—Erich Maria Remarque, *All Quiet on the Western Front,* 1930

As the clock struck midnight on December 31, 1929, the old day ended, just as the final moment of every day had slipped into the next since the beginning of time. The party went on, as it had at the last midnight of 1928 the year before, as it always had at the end of every year. The balloons fell, people hugged and kissed and cheered, and the band played on. The Roaring Twenties were over, yet nothing conspicuous had changed. Not yet, anyway.

Calendars were flipped to 1930, but a different date on the wall gave no indication that something special was fading away. No warning was given. No marker was crossed to clearly divide one era from another. No grand announcement signaled that the days of easy money and fast living were coming to an end. Those are details that historians debate after the fact. At the moment, people simply recognized that 1930 had begun, a year like any other.

The annual dose of irrational optimism arrived that New Year's Day as it always did, amid the hoopla and exuberance of celebrating unrealistic hopes and earnest but short-lived resolutions. There seemed little cause to worry, and certainly no reason to panic. The worrisome financial dips of 1929 were widely dismissed as no more than temporary downturns. None of the three previous recessions had lasted more than nineteen months, and no one saw any reason why this time should be any different.[1] No one recognized anything particularly ominous lurking to signal that the recent downturn would be any worse than previous ones had been. No war loomed on the horizon. No deadly disease was rampaging across the nation, as the flu had done a decade before.

Yet in reality, times *were* changing. It was just that Americans hadn't realized how different things were going to be this time around. The new decade would bring disaster, but the depths of the impending economic collapse and the worldwide war that followed it were still years away. Omens of dark times ahead were there if you cared to look, but not even those whose job it was to predict such problems recognized the changes that were under way.

Wall Street was content enough as long as the Federal Reserve kept lending money. Knowing that the government was feeding the money supply calmed financial experts who worried about what might happen if skittish investors hoarded their remaining funds.[2] Economists downplayed problems and issued mostly bright forecasts of speedy recovery. Irving Fisher, a leading financial theorist who had been given the first Ph.D. in economics granted by Yale in 1891, retained his rosy outlook despite the market crash.[3] Right after the plunge he had stated, "The nation is marching along a permanently high plateau of prosperity." Even in early 1930 he persisted in his positive predictions, asserting that the future for stocks was "bright."[4]

Government officials also projected good times ahead. President Herbert Hoover believed that his administration had "reestablished confidence."[5] In December 1929, the Department of Labor issued a New Year's forecast that predicted a "splendid employment year" for 1930. Around the same time, the *Los Angeles Times* quoted William H. Woodin, a director of the Federal Reserve Bank of New York, as confidently stating, "By springtime we shall have forgotten all about the stock market." According to those in the know, there was really no reason to fear a sustained economic downturn.

Most Americans agreed with that assessment. No one thought the stock market woes would last, and everyone fully expected that the economy would soon recover. It had been less than four months since the crash in October, and the effects of those losses had not yet filtered down to the public at large. Even what might seem like real signs of trouble ahead to some could appear like good things to others, at least to those who didn't look beyond the immediate effect on their daily lives.

Falling prices directly benefited ordinary consumers paying less for gas, food, and clothing. Few worried about the investors and operators who were suddenly losing income, or thought about how those reduced revenues would affect others down the line. All people saw was more money in their pockets at the end of the day.

The Rose Bowl Game played on January 1, 1930, demonstrated the continuing appearance of prosperity. It was the first game to sell out in Pasadena since Rockne's visit in 1925,[6] and it generated enough profit that by month's end the Tournament of Roses announced that it planned to fill in the open end of the stadium to increase seating capacity from seventy-eight thousand to one hundred thousand.[7]

The January 1930 Rose Bowl marked the end of the rift that had kept the Trojans out of Pasadena. With relations among the members of the Pacific Coast Conference improving, Howard Jones had pushed for a Rose Bowl bid for his Trojans back in December, and his lobbying had paid off when USC was selected to face the Pittsburgh Panthers.[8]

The Panthers were undefeated, and, besides Notre Dame, the only other Eastern claimant to national honors. However, the Panthers' national hopes ended when the Trojans crushed them 47–14. Among the crowd at Pasadena that day was Will Rogers,[9] watching as Jones won the first of five Rose Bowl victories in the decade, with no defeats, that would earn him a second nickname, "The King of the Rose Bowl."

Many experts had made up their minds about the best team even before the Rose Bowl. Notre Dame's Fighting Irish had been announced as the Dickenson System's National Champions and thus as the winners of the Rissman Trophy back at the end of November, reflecting the practice of the day to ignore postseason results.[10]

Three days after the Rose Bowl game, the Irish added to their trophy case the Albert Russell Erskine Award for the best team in college football. Albert Erskine, president of the Studebaker car company, had endowed the championship trophy, enlisting more than 250 leading sportswriters to rank the best teams. They elected Notre Dame by a wide margin.[11] Even though the Trojans had demolished Pitt, which had been rated above them by both the Dickenson and Erskine selectors, USC finished sixth in both polls.[12] The Erskine Trophy came with a perk beyond the honor of being named the nation's top team. The coach of the winning team was awarded a brand new Studebaker automobile. On January 18, 1930, in Miami, Rockne was awarded the new car for that year, along with a parchment scroll hailing Notre Dame's achievement.[13]

Rockne had arrived in Florida less than a week before receiving the award. His condition had improved, and when he felt good enough to travel he headed to the Sunshine State with Bonnie and their youngest children, son Jack and daughter Mary, to rest and recuperate from the phlebitis that had afflicted Knute since October.[14] Rockne's two older sons were in Kansas City attending the Pembroke School for Boys, but Jack would spend the rest of the winter with his parents in Florida.[15]

Rockne's assistant coaches were also leaving South Bend, and two wouldn't be coming back the next season. Both Tom Lieb and Tommy Mills had accepted head coaching positions in their own right: Lieb at Loyola University, a Catholic college in Los Angeles,[16] and Mills at Georgetown, another Catholic school in Washington, D.C.[17] To replace them, Rockne lured Hunk Anderson back from Saint Louis University, and added graduating lineman Tim Moynihan to round out the staff. That made six assistants, including the two freshman coaches, to oversee the Notre Dame football program, which, including dormitory teams, totaled as many as eight hundred players—fully one-fourth of the school's total enrollment.[18]

The coaching staff at USC remained unchanged, but Jones, like Rockne, was preoccupied with issues of health in the early months of 1930. Howard's father, Thomas Jones, suffered a massive stroke in February, and died while Howard rushed back to Ohio.[19] Howard's mother died just two months later, right before Howard returned to Los Angeles for spring practice.[20] Howard had a big job ahead of him when he got home. Although thirteen lettermen were returning, regular players from 1929 were penciled in at only three positions for the coming season.[21]

Rockne missed most of his team's spring practice.[22] The respite in Florida proved a beneficial tonic. Newspaper photos of him enjoying the sunshine and exercising on a low trapeze bar testified to his renewed vigor. Nevertheless, his recovery was fragile,[23] and he suffered a setback on April 3, when a mild case of bronchitis sent him to St. Francis Hospital in Miami. Just one day later, news reports revealed that his condition was serious enough to send him back to the Mayo Clinic in Rochester, Minnesota, for a "thorough physical examination."[24] On

Sunday, April 6, he boarded a train with Dr. C. J. Barborka, a specialist from the clinic, to head north for the evaluation.[25] Rockne downplayed the implications, saying, "It's not as bad as it seems." His doctor concurred, assuring everyone that the coach would be on the sidelines in the coming season. The patient had five months to fulfill the physician's prediction.

As Rockne was preparing to leave Florida, Scarface Capone was heading there, to Miami. Capone had been released from the Pennsylvania prison where he'd been held for ten months.[26] When he returned to Chicago in mid-March, he was immediately detained by the authorities for questioning, then released again.[27] For Capone, things really had changed: it was clear the law would not be easing up on him.

Late in April, the Chicago police announced the formation of a new "hoodlum squad" and issued a "Public Enemies List" that named both Capone and "Bugs" Moran among the worst of the worst.[28] Two days after his name was splashed across the newspapers, Capone left the country. He and six of his henchmen cleared out of Florida for a "vacation" in Cuba.[29]

Rockne intended to leave the country too, on a summer trip planned as a repeat of sorts of his 1928 Olympic Games excursion. He booked berths on the Cunard liner *Samaria* for the tour.[30] He also canceled all summer coaching schools. Rockne planned to stay in South Bend to facilitate sales of tickets for the trip. He looked forward to the journey that would return him to "the peak of condition required for another arduous football campaign."[31]

That campaign held the potential to be unlike any other in college football since the dark days of 1905. After a decade of exponential growth for the sport, forces were coalescing to challenge the game's prosperity. Despite the aura of business as usual, declining revenues generated by college football would soon threaten its standing, if not its very existence. Ethical concerns expressed by the Carnegie Foundation had already fueled debate in academia about the role of football in American colleges; soon this debate would be echoed in newspapers across the country.

The Carnegie Foundation was not the first group to question the role of sport, and especially football, in academic communities. Criticism had started almost from the first kickoff, and came to the fore twenty years after McGill played Harvard. In 1894, Professors Woodrow Wilson of Princeton and Burt Wilder of Cornell formally debated the topic, "Ought the Game of Foot Ball to Be Encouraged?"[32] In 1898, the Brown Conference Committee Report, a precursor of the Carnegie Foundation's work, sought to prevent college athletics "from interfering with the mental and moral training of the students."[33] The debate would be coming to a head in 1930.

Inspired by Carnegie's latest report, critics determined to carry the day prepared concrete proposals on the issue, such as the one presented to the annual meeting of the Pacific Coast Conference, held in San Francisco in January. That resolution to ban intersectional games would have ended the series between USC and Notre Dame.[34] It was put to a vote and the idea was squashed; afterward the conference heads remained mum, declining comment on the proceedings.[35]

William Wallace Campbell, president of the University of California, undoubtedly would have argued in favor of the motion had illness not kept him away from the gathering. He went public with his personal views in March, penning an article, published in the *San Francisco Argonaut*, decrying the "advancement of football to the detriment of other college athletic activities."[36]

Despite the growing uproar, the promise of money and the popularity of football seemed to stem the tide of change. Calls to reduce the number of games played, to curtail the overemphasis on football created by big, splashy intersectional games, and to eliminate paid coaching positions went unheeded. The reform movement did have an impact, however, and further changes were coming. Hunk Anderson was induced to leave his job as head coach at Saint Louis University when he learned that the new president there planned to "scuttle the sports program."[37] Anderson's departure from Notre Dame after the 1927 season had been engineered by Rockne, who had timed the whole affair to bring Hunk back amid the confusion of changing administrations on his own campus, but Anderson had seen the handwriting on the wall and would have left Saint Louis in any case.[38]

Another school looking to trim football from campus life was the University of Chicago, one of the founding members of the Big Ten. Robert Maynard Hutchins became the school's president in 1929, and he was eager to rid the university of its gridiron heritage. His own succinct statement summed up his views on sports: "When I am minded to take exercise," he said, "I sit down and wait until the mood has passed." It would take another decade, but Hutchins would finally succeed in axing Maroon football in 1939.[39]

Rockne was the leading voice arguing against the reformers, but his illness curtailed his opportunities to publicly respond to the critics. Besides, Rockne had problems of his own within Notre Dame. Father Mulcaire, a reformer who saw the football program as overshadowing the true mission of the university, was now head of the Athletic Board at Notre Dame. He meant to curtail what he saw as Rockne's profligate spending, and limit the coach's autonomy. Mulcaire's position as head of the board gave him the chance to bring political weapons to bear, and he clearly had Rockne in the crosshairs.

Mulcaire and Rockne continually locked horns over issues large and small. Back in December 1929, they had issued conflicting statements to the press regarding possible postseason play, subtly wrestling over which of them had the final say in determining the team's participation.[40] Mulcaire complained to Rockne about the cost of new uniforms, objecting to the $15,400 price tag for the fancy new togs.[41] Likewise, Rockne's request for a protective cover to keep the football field dry before games set off a contentious debate.

"How much would that cost?" Mulcaire grilled Rockne at one of their board meetings.

"Ten thousand dollars," he responded.

"Impossible," Mulcaire shot back. "Our projected football budget is far over the top now. We simply don't have the money."

As the group ran through the pros and cons of the purchase, Mulcaire's faction supported his objection to the proposal. Rockne did what any good field general would do when faced with a blitzing defense. He called an audible, which turned into an end run. He changed the subject, distracting Mulcaire, and the request never reached a vote. Weeks later, Mulcaire was enraged to find the tarp in place and accused Rockne of clear insubordination.

"He deliberately defied the order of the board!" he shouted.

Mulcaire was wrong. The board had issued no order. Rockne's quick thinking had forestalled a vote, and he had quietly bought the tarp out of his slush fund.[42] How long Rockne's shenanigans would go unchecked like that was anybody's guess, but what was certain was that Notre Dame's administration was determined to bring him under control.

What would never change was Rockne's work ethic. Health issues slowed him down in the early months of the year, but 1930 was still filled with plenty of activities outside his coaching duties at Notre Dame. He spent considerable time planning the summer tour of Europe, reviewing ghostwritten articles for *Collier's* magazine (including a series that would become his autobiography), continuing his work for Studebaker, and reviewing construction of the new stadium.[43]

Although work crews had finished grading the stadium site by the end of August 1929,[44] a harsh winter freeze delayed above-ground construction until April 1930.[45] Rockne had been away much of the time the stadium was being erected, but it was still his baby, and the coach would be on hand for the finishing touches before Notre Dame's first game in September.

The current team gave every indication of matching the championship Ramblers that had played all their games on the road the year before. Backfielders Carideo, Savoldi, Schwartz, and Brill returned for the new season, along with end Tom Conley and linemen Al Culver and Bert Metzger. Rockne was infamous for downplaying his own team's talent, but after taking stock of the prospects following spring practice, he was forced to admit the obvious. He confided his real estimation to Curly Lambeau, telling his old friend that the 1930 squad "might be the best team I've ever had here."[46]

20

Divorce and Deception

How Are the Mighty Fallen.

—*Alton Evening Telegraph, 1930*

Notre Dame had recovered from the disappointing season of 1928 in grand style. The Fighting Irish had returned to the pinnacle of the football world, and had done so largely without Rockne, the man who had led the school on the long march to the top in the first place. He was hopeful that he would return to active coaching in 1930, but that issue wouldn't be decided until the fall. It was springtime, and there was plenty of time to consider what lay ahead.

For their part, the Trojans were looking to the past as summer approached. The University of Southern California was turning fifty, and it was time to show off. The school had opened with fifty-five students in 1880.[1] Enrollment had reached seventeen thousand five decades later.[2] The campus had expanded significantly over those years, and the administration had launched a major fund-raising drive to finance further growth. Despite the gloom spreading out from Wall Street, almost a third of USC's targeted amount of $10 million had been pledged by late spring of 1930.[3]

Although USC and Notre Dame were both private schools, there had always been at least as many differences as similarities between them. Notre Dame was older and retained its small size and pious character, while USC had grown along with the city of Los Angeles and shed its overtly religious nature. While Notre Dame remained firmly part of American Catholic life, USC had abandoned its ties to the Methodist Church and become a secular university.[4] Notre Dame was an all-male school, while USC had always been coeducational—the valedictorian of the very first graduating class of three Trojans in 1884 had been a woman, Minnie C. Miltimore.[5]

Although there were plenty of liberal arts students at USC, it was the technical and professional schools that had built perhaps the most outstanding reputation for the university. President von KleinSmid said as much in his remarks at the baccalaureate services held as part of the celebration in May.[6] Rockne tended to sneer at USC's ties to the business world. He once derisively referred to the Thundering Herd as "that Chamber of Commerce team in Los Angeles known as the University of Southern California."[7]

Nothing of a commercial nature seemed quite as intertwined with the city of Los Angeles as the business of making movies, even if the studios were actually located outside the city limits. At times, no other business seemed quite as crass either. "It is not that the morals of persons connected with the moving pictures are necessarily lower than those of persons associated with music, painting or the theater," commented H. L. Mencken and George Jean Nathan in 1922, "it is that, by the nature of the persons connected with moving pictures, the morals, whatever their feebleness, are inevitably and disgustingly vulgar."[8] This view—that movie people were little better than degenerate boozehounds chasing unrepentant harlots—was shared by much of the populace.

The new film courses at USC, which made teachers out of stars like Douglas Fairbanks and Mary Pickford, were among the first steps taken toward building respectability for the profession and raising public perceptions of cinema from lowbrow entertainment to the level of a serious art. The film school at USC would one day become perhaps the best-known of all Trojan studies, but that day was still far off. In 1930, the film community was just beginning to embrace University Park.

Ironically, the most famous Trojan to ever grace the silver screen, then or now, never studied film at USC. As a part of the Thundering Herd, he had attended Clara Bow's parties, where he hobnobbed with famous stars like Joan Crawford and Lina Basquette. However, the idea of being in movies had never entered his mind when he stepped on the USC campus in the fall of 1925.[9] Film courses did not even exist at USC when Duke Morrison was enrolled there, and the law was his chosen course of study anyway.[10] No, Duke entered the movie business by dumb luck.

A referral from Howard Jones brought Morrison to Tom Mix at the Fox Studios at the end of his freshman year. The coach had accommodated a request from the actor for good seats at Trojan home games, asking in return summer jobs for some of his players. Morrison didn't make much of an impression on the famous cowboy star, but Jones's introduction did get Duke a job on the swing gang, moving furniture and props for a sorely needed $35 a week. More important than money, it put him in the right place to be discovered.[11]

Morrison's lucky break came when director Raoul Walsh spotted him toting furniture around the Fox Studios. Walsh was looking for a leading man for his next project, a film titled *The Big Trail*, when Morrison caught his eye. The production was going to be a huge undertaking. Two different English-language versions were planned, one in the standard 35 mm format and the other shot in a new 70 mm wide-screen process, plus multiple foreign language editions using different actors and directors for all but the wide-angle and second-unit shots that could be shared among all variants.[12] The story was a sprawling Western yarn that would require expensive location shoots across five states. The production included a real wagon train with dozens of horses, oxen pulling the wagons, and herds of cattle in tow. A legion of extras filled out the huge vistas, including another ex-Trojan, Ward Bond.[13]

It was not the sort of picture you'd pick to give a newcomer his first starring role, but Walsh was desperate. Tom Mix and Gary Cooper, early choices to play the main character of trapper Breck Coleman, proved unavailable. Many stars from the old silent cowboy films lacked suitable voices for the talkies.[14] So Walsh considered casting an unknown for the role, and began looking for a "personality" instead of an actor.[15]

The tall, handsome Morrison had the looks for the part, but other than a few appearances as an extra or stunt double and one walk-on role in a John Ford film, he had no experience in front of the camera. Still, this was Hollywood, where movie stars were discovered at drugstore lunch counters. After camera, voice, and dialogue tests, Morrison won the part.[16]

One thing about the former Trojan footballer wasn't quite right. In fact, it was completely wrong: his name. He needed one that sounded as sturdy as a cowboy's prized workhorse and as comfortable as a well-worn saddle. Marion Morrison walked off the football field in 1926, but it was John Wayne who stepped into movie history in 1930.

Duke Morrison had been forced out of USC when his scholarship was pulled after the 1927 season, but Gwynn Wilson left willingly, shortly after the cameras started rolling on *The Big Trail*. Wilson had accepted the job as manager of the Summer Olympics that were coming to Los Angeles in 1932.[17] The man who had sold Rockne on the Trojans was about to sell the entire sporting world on Los Angeles.

In a way, the summer of 1930 would prove to be the last calm before the storm of the Great Depression blasted across America. Those last long, hot months were the final days of normalcy before a darkness like that of 1919 set in again.

Even that summer was not entirely trouble free. On June 9, Jack Lingle, a reporter for the *Chicago Tribune,* was murdered in the Windy City at the Illinois Central's Randolph Street station. Father John Reynolds, a Notre Dame man, was among the witnesses. He rushed to the dying reporter to offer comfort and administer last rites before he even knew whether or not the victim was Catholic.[18] It was a shocking crime, a murder that didn't fit the usual profile of mob violence, which almost never targeted civilians that way. When it was revealed that Lingle's real income came from operating as a bagman for Capone, the public began to understand the reasons for the murder and question the whole working of things in Chicago. The fallout from the crime threatened to bring down the mayor and eventually drove the head of detectives from the police commission.[19] It also further raised the heat on organized crime.

The day after the killing, it was reported that Knute Rockne was ready to lead his European tour over the summer.[20] But the trip was not to be; Rockne canceled it five weeks later,[21] after his doctors insisted that he had to have more rest if he was going to be ready to coach in the fall. Rockne's condition must have been more serious than he had admitted back in April, for the cancellation meant losing most of his side income between football seasons, surely a more bitter pill for him to swallow than any tonic his physicians may have prescribed.

Unlike Rockne, Howard Jones fulfilled his off-season coaching duties without incident. It was his turn to be a rambler, as he spent almost his entire summer teaching football on the road. In June, he spent a week at Utah Agricultural College in Logan, followed by a week at Washington State. In July, he followed up with two weeks at Southern Methodist University in Dallas, Texas, before heading back to teach at USC through the first week of August. That left just one month before fall camp opened.[22]

Two weeks after Jones closed his coaching clinic on campus, he learned that the construction firm of Edwards, Wilcox, and Dixon had been hired to enlarge the Coliseum in Los Angeles, in preparation for the upcoming 1932 Olympics. When the improvements were complete, the Coliseum would be able to seat 105,000 fans, double the capacity of the new stadium in South Bend. But while the Irish were just a few weeks from kicking off in their new stadium, the Trojans would have to wait two years before the Coliseum expansion would be completed.

Once the season began, it was obvious that both the Thundering Herd and the Fighting Irish were again among the country's strongest teams. The Trojans opened their schedule by throttling UCLA 52–0, then convincingly beating Oregon State Agricultural College 27–7.

The win over the Beavers came on October 4, just two days after *The Big Trail* opened in Los Angeles.[23] Both the Trojans and their former teammate Duke Morrison—now John Wayne—opened with a splash, but both were about to stumble.[24] The Trojans lost their third game to Washington State 7–6, while *The Big Trail* flopped badly when the film went into nationwide release. The 35 mm format was less flattering to Wayne, since it focused audience attention on his inexperienced acting, whereas the wow factor of the 70 mm format, with its sweeping panoramas, tended to distract from those deficiencies. Yet it was in the smaller format that the movie was most often shown. Only two theaters in the country were equipped to handle the "70 mm Grandeur film" system that was used for the widescreen version; the technology was simply too costly for most theater owners to install during a recession. In the end, the film failed to capture the public's imagination.[25] John Wayne would make two more pictures for Fox, both modestly budgeted, forgettable films. He struggled for nine more years before getting another big break, in John Ford's *Stagecoach,* the role that really made him a star.[26]

Duke's old team would recover more quickly on the football field than Wayne did in the movie theaters. The Herd ran up gaudy numbers in their next six games, piling up scores of 65–0 over Utah State, 41–12 over Stanford, 33–13 over Denver, 74–0 over Cal, 52–0 over Hawaii, and finally 32–0 over Washington.

Meanwhile, the Irish made an equally strong start, knocking off Southern Methodist University 20–14 in their opener before facing Navy one week later. That weekend saw the formal dedication of their new stadium, with a nighttime ceremony held on Friday, October 10, the night before the game. The marching band led a torchlight procession of students and faculty across the campus and into the stadium, where Rockne and other dignitaries made speeches before fireworks lit up the sky. The next day, inspired by these festivities and led by fullback Joe Savoldi, who scored three touchdowns, Notre Dame pummeled the midshipmen 26–2.[27]

"Jumpin' Joe" Savoldi continued to be the wrecking ball smashing through the next four games as Notre Dame ran up a total of 143 points to their opponents' 45. Savoldi was a brute, just under six feet tall and well over two hundred pounds, strong as a horse and as fast as one too. Born Giuseppe Savoldi in 1908 in the little village of Castano Primo, near Milan in the Lombardy region of Italy, Savoldi was all *paisan*.[28] He came to America at the age of thirteen and quickly acclimated to his new country, becoming a standout athlete at Three Oaks High School in Michigan before heading to South Bend.[29] The shock of dark, curly hair atop his head was cut just above the ears and matched the bushy eyebrows shadowing his dark, bright eyes. His handsome face was wide and oblong in shape, and his smile was a wide, toothy grin above a thick, solid jaw. Called "one of the strongest men ever to play football at any university," Savoldi had a compact, solidly muscled physique "only overshadowed by that of his countryman, Primo Carnera," the six foot nine professional heavyweight boxing champion.[30]

Savoldi was a star on Notre Dame's track team as well as the football squad, but it was on the gridiron where he earned his fame. He was the heaviest weapon in Rockne's "Rough Rider" backfield—"the big punch, the one they were all afraid of," as the coach put it.[31] The shock of Savoldi crashing through the line was exceeded only by the even more shocking news of his departure from the team.

The reason for his fall from grace seems almost quaint by today's jaded standards: Savoldi was secretly married. For more than a year, he had been married to a local girl, Audrey Koehler.[32] This might seem like weak material for a scandal at first glance, but this was 1930, and there was more to the story.

Contrary to the usual version of the tale, Notre Dame had no general prohibition against married students.[33] Al Gebert, a backup quarterback at Notre Dame the year before, had been married and suffered no penalty.[34] Jumpin' Joe's problems were more specifically intertwined with Catholic theology and the school's strict adherence to the faith.

Savoldi's first transgression was being a Catholic who had been married by the local justice of the peace instead of a priest.[35] In an era before the Second Vatican Council, such a marriage, sealed outside the church, would have definitely raised eyebrows. But that indiscretion by itself probably could have been forgiven. Savoldi's cardinal sin was ending the union.

Reports of the scandal first surfaced in November, just before the Drake game. A judge in South Bend, assuming the local newshounds already knew the story, casually mentioned that a divorce action filed by someone with the same name as the Notre Dame football star had come up in his court. Rockne approached the reporters, hoping to get them to sit on the story until he had a chance to talk with Savoldi, and perhaps get him to reconsider the action, but to no avail.[36] News of the breakup leaked out, and revealed the secret marriage, cutting off any possibility of further intervention on Savoldi's behalf.

The legal filing was alternately described as an "annulment" or a "divorce," but since the Catholic Church had never sanctified the marriage in the first place, it undoubtedly regarded the end of that marriage as a purely civil matter not eligible for annulment under church law. Although Savoldi confessed his "mistake" in marrying the girl and protested that they had never lived together as man and wife, the die was cast.[37] No remedy of special examinations or makeup classes could save the day this time. Rockne could not repeat the efforts that had worked for Gipp a decade earlier. Savoldi was suspended, leaving the Irish to face Drake with Joe on the sideline. Luckily, it hardly mattered. On a drizzly afternoon in South Bend, Notre Dame won easily, with a score of 28–7.[38] A few days later, Savoldi, faced with quitting the team and leaving the university voluntarily or being expelled, quietly left campus.[39] Rockne saw him off with $1,500 out of his own pocket.[40] It was a sad end to a great run, but not the end of Savoldi's athletic career. He would go on to fame and glory playing in the NFL and grappling in pro wrestling.[41]

Savoldi's departure left a hole in the lineup, but Rockne was hardly bereft of alternatives. Though none were of the same caliber as Savoldi, Larry "Moon" Mullins, Dan Hanley, and Al Howard filled in ably as Notre Dame beat Northwestern 14–0 in Evanston and squeaked by Army 7–6 at Soldier Field.

Rockne's backfield woes were increasing by the time he began prepping his team for the Trojans. Mullins had been injured and was unlikely to be fit for the game.[42] Hanley showed promise but lacked both experience and speed, and while Rockne rated Al Howard as a fine defensive asset, he didn't think he fit well into his offense.[43] With just two days to prepare for the Trojans after the Army game, Rockne would have to think fast.

His usual tales of woe began flowing even before the squad departed from South Bend. "They have a better team than we have right now," Rockne said of the Trojans, adding, "My boys are pretty well battered up." While boarding the train he quipped, "We'll need some luck to win this one, but maybe we'll get it."[44]

Behind the scenes he was determined to make his own luck. He had arranged just one major workout on the way to Los Angeles, the traditional stop in Tucson, and he planned to make the most of it. Meanwhile, Rockne continued his lament, expressing concern about the Trojan offense, which he called "the greatest scoring machine in the history of the school."

With the game just days away, and with Savoldi gone and Mullins definitely ruled out of the game, filling the fullback position was Rockne's biggest problem. Hanley was the next man on the depth chart, and Rockne spent time working him into the offense during the two days of workouts in Tucson. An initial public workout, one dubbed "a sorry sight to behold" by the team's trainer, Scrapiron Young, was held the first day before five thousand spectators.[45] The second day's sessions were kept secret. Closing the gates was an unusual move for Rockne, but suspicions had arisen that signals had been stolen back in 1928, and the Sage of South Bend was taking no chances this time around. That was the story in the newspapers, anyway.[46] In reality, Rockne had other motives.

That final night in Tucson, Rockne's phlebitis returned and hit hard. The coach called his team together for a meeting in the ballroom of the Pioneer Hotel. Sitting in a large chair as the players gathered, Rockne quietly tried to stifle the shooting pains that stabbed at him, but wincing grimaces betrayed his ordeal. Rockne dramatically revealed the ugly state of his red, swollen legs when he asked Scrapiron to dress his bandages. Rockne's doctors had advised him to remain in South Bend and avoid subjecting himself to the stress of coaching his team against the Trojans. Now he asked his trainer a simple question. "Do you think I should continue on?"

Every player in the room answered his inquiry with a resounding cry. They begged him not to abandon them when he was needed most. Rockne arose unsteadily, misty-eyed and smiling, his body still in pain but his spirit seemingly rejuvenated as he responded to their ovation. "Boys," he said, "That was all the answer I needed. Only God himself could keep me from being with you Saturday." Asserting that the show of support had done more for him than all the medical advice of all the doctors in the world, he then went on to review the game plan with his boys, covering every detail, before finishing with a confident prediction of victory. With that, he turned and gingerly made his way out of the room.

Scrapiron smirked to himself as the team cheered wildly. "You poor, unsuspecting, overconfident Trojans," he thought to himself. "Heaven help you."[47]

By the time the Irish rolled into Los Angeles, Rockne had pretty well sold the idea that his team going against the Trojans was like David facing Goliath—without reminding the public how that story had turned out for the giant Philistine. Nearly all the West Coast experts, including Babe Hollingberry of Washington State, Pop Warner of Stanford, Nibs Price of Cal, Bill Spaulding of UCLA, and even Jimmy Phelan of Washington, an old Notre Dame man, favored the Trojans. This time, Tad Jones likewise favored his brother's team,[48] and even Rockne's old protégé Tom Lieb picked USC to win.[49] Sportswriters like former All-

American quarterback Buck Bailey,[50] and even Grantland Rice, also leapt on the Trojan bandwagon.

Though the prediction never appeared in print, *Los Angeles Times* sportswriter Dick Hyland privately told Rice that he expected USC to win by a four-touchdown margin.[51] It was the kind of boast that fit into Knute's narrative perfectly, and Rockne wasted no opportunity in retelling the prediction, as he had before leaving Chicago.

It was homecoming for the Trojans, and they invited their South Bend guests to join them at the annual pregame men's banquet held in the gymnasium of USC's new physical education building.[52] Howard Jones had managed to get in a round of golf with his brother Tad during the day, but by nightfall he had joined his team to listen to what the wily Norseman had to say.

"First of all," Rockne began, "allow me to apologize for bringing such a weak, inferior football team all the way out to Los Angeles for the purpose of competing against the greatest football team ever put together." He then expressed his pessimism. "I realize that the score will be so lopsided that it will not be good for the series," he said. Then, looking forward to when "the sun has taken its descent and the shadows have totally covered the playing floor of the huge Coliseum," he made his request.[53] "When the game is over tomorrow," Rockne pleaded, asking for mercy on behalf of his depleted squad, "I'd like to ask you fine young men of Troy to come over and congratulate my boys on a fine game," adding that "I know you'll do everything you can to hold down the score." Stressing his sense of privilege at sharing the field with such a fine team, he expressed the appreciation his players would feel for a firm handshake and a kind word from the victors after the game. In closing, he looked forward to 1931, when the shoe would be on the other foot. "Thank you," he said, "and when we meet again next year, I hope the odds are kinder to Notre Dame. Bless you, and good fortune."[54]

It was a virtuoso performance, exceeded only by his team's effort in the Coliseum the next day. The Trojans fumbled on their first possession when a low snap bounced off Jim Musick's foot. One play later, Marchie Schwartz, one of the many talents of Jewish descent that Rockne had recruited to his Notre Dame team, hit Carideo for the score. A short time later, Paul "Bucky" O'Connor dashed eighty yards for another score, and the rout was on. When the final gun sounded, the scoreboard read 27–0 in Notre Dame's favor. The Coliseum spectators, among them celebrities like Will Rogers, were stunned.[55]

For the Trojans, the humiliation was devastating and complete. They set foot on Notre Dame territory just three times during the game, and managed only 140 yards in total offense against Notre Dame's 433, while making half the number of their opponents' first downs in the process.[56] Howard Jones sat stoically throughout the debacle, quietly chewing gum or puffing the occasional cigarette, uttering no more than "half a dozen words during the game."[57] The slow burn that smoldered through sixty minutes of football did not prevent the Headman from praising his rival after the game. "Notre Dame showed me the greatest Irish team I have ever seen," he wrote. "The present eleven, to my way of thinking, is the best Knute Rockne ever coached."[58]

Rockne returned the admiration, praising Jones personally. "He is one of the finest sportsmen and coaches I know," Rockne said of him. When asked about this stay in the Southland, Rockne said, "I like to play here. I like your enthusiasm and your fairness."[59]

After the game, Rockne admitted on radio station KHJ that his solution to the fullback problem had been a ruse. Dan Hanley's jersey number was 31, but during practice he had switched uniforms with Bucky O'Connor, the same player who had dashed eighty yards for a touchdown early in the game. O'Connor had worked out at fullback

Bucky O'Connor attacks the Trojan defense while leading the Irish to an upset victory in 1930. (Image courtesy of Notre Dame Archives.)

during spring practice, but he was a bit undersized for the position and had been switched to halfback. Those six weeks in camp had allowed Rockne to plug O'Connor back in at the position when the need arose. The intentionally inept practice in Tucson, coupled with Rockne's verbal sandbagging of the Trojans, set the ambush to perfection. Even Loyola's Tom Lieb had been in on the ploy, deliberately picking the Trojans before the game to feed their overconfidence.[60] It was trickery that was hardly needed. "Notre Dame," Howard Jones said, "was superior in every department of the game."[61]

Rockne, his wife, and his youngest son left Los Angeles with the team on Sunday night. Irish fans gave them a tremendous send-off at the train station, packing the depot to hail the victorious gridders and celebrate their second straight championship. Rockne had been expected to stay on in town for Christy Walsh's All-American football board banquet, but the grueling pace of the season had taken its toll; Rockne felt he "owed it to himself to return immediately." Few in the raucous crowd at the train station were even aware that the Rockne clan were huddled in their compartment, staying out of the spotlight while the team soaked up the glory.[62]

All along the way home, crowds gathered to salute the Irish team. Among them was a group of Navajo Indians in Arizona, who played the Notre Dame Victory March on native drums and horns.[63] In Chicago, thousands jammed the LaSalle Street station when the three special cars of the Golden State Limited pulled into town with the Irish team. After a ticker-tape parade through the downtown Loop, Rockne spoke briefly over WGN radio, the first time he had emerged from his compartment since leaving California. "We thought we had been through some great lines on the football field this year . . . but today had them all beat!" he jested, referring to the mobs that pressed through the police cordon to swamp the vehicles in the procession.[64]

After the whirlwind celebration, which lasted just one hour, it was on to South Bend.[65] A near-riot had broken out back home after the Irish upset over USC on Saturday. A crowd of a thousand students had jammed the downtown area, threatening to storm the local movie theater and generally causing all sorts of mischief. A local bookmaker who had favored the Trojans before the game was rousted by the mob and paraded in shame before the crowd.

Chicago-Dec.10-1930
Notre Dame Returning
From Southern California
Game N.D. — 27
      S.C. — 0

Police were dispatched to deal with the rowdiness, ready to deploy tear gas if necessary. Upon hearing of the commotion, school officials made their way downtown to help restore order. It was the first time since their face-off with the Klan back in 1924 that Notre Dame students had been part of such a melee in South Bend, and the first time anyone could recall such a ruckus after a football game.[66] Excitement still reigned in South Bend when the team arrived a few days later, but the fifteen thousand fans on hand confined themselves to more benign celebrations.[67]

Meanwhile, a more ominous crowd had gathered in New York City just about the time Rockne and his boys were being feted in Chicago. It had begun to form when anxious customers surrounded the Southern Boulevard branch of the Bank of the United States. Word was spreading throughout the Bronx that the bank had refused to sell a depositor's stock. By midday, more than twenty thousand people had arrived and police were called in to restore order. The rumor was false, but that didn't matter. Panic was spreading. Runs started at other branches as the day passed.[68]

The next day, the bank was closed. It never reopened. One of the largest banks in the country had failed, prompting accusations of fraud. The district attorney launched investigations into possible criminal activity. Mayor Walker initiated lawsuits to recover lost city funds.[69] Companies that invested in the bank went belly-up.[70]

The news sent shock waves across the country, causing a general crash of banking stocks. In all, three hundred banks failed nationwide in December 1930.[71] Over the entire year, thirteen hundred had failed, a number twice the average of the previous decade.[72] This was the first such collapse among the big New York banks since the crash of 1929, and the news caused tremors throughout the nation's financial structure.[73] Life savings were evaporating overnight, and at least one devastated investor committed suicide rather than face financial ruin.[74]

The bank failures were the last nails driven into the coffin of prosperity, occurring just as the moribund economy seemed to be stabilizing

Facing page: Chicago celebrates Notre Dame's upset victory over USC in 1930 as the Irish team passes through the city on the way home to South Bend. (Image courtesy of Notre Dame Archives.)

and on the point of recovering its financial health. According to the calendar, the Roaring Twenties had ended the previous January, but any lingering feeling, any enduring spirit of the past era was completely dead and buried by December. There was no going back. The Great Depression had begun.

21

Flying into Destiny

Never regret thy fall,

O Icarus of the fearless flight,

For the greatest tragedy of them all

Is never to feel the burning light.

    —Oscar Wilde, 1881

Memories of heady days were fading like hazy dreams from the distant past. The crash had come little more than a year before, but the trappings of extravagance and glamor were quickly being replaced by soup kitchens and foreclosure notices. Even the rich and famous, it seemed, were feeling the pinch. Groucho Marx was among those singing the blues. "I was a wealthy man on the eighteenth hole of a golf course," he cried. "By the time I got to the club house I was destitute."[1]

Clara Bow had more than just money problems. She was mired in a scandalous court case that threatened her Hollywood stardom. Acrimony between her fiancé, Rex Bell, the truck driver who became a movie star, and Clara's secretary, Daisy DeVoe, had spun out of control toward the end of 1930. Suspicions, misunderstandings, and a ferocious power struggle spawned accusations of embezzlement. The festering animosity erupted into a disastrous public feud that dragged Bow into court. DeVoe's arrest for grand theft launched a countersuit that generated salacious headlines for weeks.

DeVoe lashed out with lurid stories of Bow's drinking, gambling, and paramours, even accusing her of wild sex with the whole Trojan team, a baseless slander that spawned an urban legend.[2] A few of the tales were true; others, exaggerations; but many, like the story of debauchery with the Thundering Herd, were downright fabrications. True or false, De-Voe's accusations spattered ruinous stories across the pages of tabloid newspapers and gossip magazines.

The entire scandal had been unnecessary. There was really no evidence against DeVoe, but District Attorney Burton Fitts, who was totally in the pocket of the studios, brought multiple indictments against her anyway. Fitts was serving Paramount's interests, not justice. Bow had made millions for Paramount producer B. P. Schulberg, but the studio honcho was tired of her offscreen antics. The bad publicity would ultimately give him the excuse he needed to terminate her contract.[3] Bow's days at the studio were numbered.

DeVoe had really done nothing wrong, but others in the crosshairs of the police were not so innocent. Al Capone continued to be target number one. A raid on the Rex Hotel in Chicago, described as a Capone "hangout" where he "sent his henchmen to deal in liquor, gambling and vice," uncovered a trove of records documenting his "illicit dealings." The evidence exposed the complicity of "every branch of government in Cook County and even into the halls of Congress."[4] Treasury agents pored over the seized documents, looking for evidence of Capone's income tax evasion. They hoped to build a case proving that the mobster's lavish lifestyle had been built on unreported income. They vowed to succeed in putting Scarface away, where Eliot Ness and his Untouchables had failed.

Ordinary Americans might not be concerned about fading stardom or the threat of determined lawmen, but they too were watching their hard-earned savings slip away. Between November 1930 and the end of the following January, an additional 875 American banks had failed.[5] Farmers, particularly in the South but later in the Midwest, were facing increasingly hard times. Prices for crops were falling, and drought conditions that had started in the summer of 1930 would persist into 1931, devastating crop yields.[6]

For years, farmers throughout the plains states had stripped millions of acres of native sod, displacing the indigenous landscape to plant wheat. As the drought set in, strong annual winds swept across the barren land, leaving dirt fields where lush farmland had once thrived.[7]

It was the beginning of the Dust Bowl, a phenomenon with long-lasting effects that changed America. The Roaring Twenties were giving way to the Dirty Thirties.[8]

The ill winds of change were not confined to dusty farmland. Squalls of discontent continued to chill the darkening landscape of college football. The Carnegie Foundation was working on another critique of the game, building toward the June release of Bulletin Number 26. Proving that trouble can bring opportunity, the report would hail falling gate revenues as a sign that the "deflation of American football has already begun."[9] A declining economy, the reformers hoped, would hamper the "subsidizing" of athletes.

It was undeniably true that the boom financial years for football had passed. Even mighty Notre Dame had drawn only 42 percent of capacity for its 1930 home games. For Rockne, the cruel irony of the weak financial times was that he had achieved his dream of fielding his team in its own major football stadium just as the expense of that facility had become a dubious investment. Increased overhead meant that although the team still turned a tidy profit for the year, it was no higher than that of the year before, when all games had been played on the road.[10]

Rockne had a more serious and personal problem, though: his health. With his phlebitis controlled but not cured, his physical condition remained worse than the financial state of his football program. The long, difficult season had taxed him, and his doctors warned against the dangers of exhaustion. His friends could see the wear for themselves, noting "the lines of pain around his mouth and eyes" and "a grayish tinge" to his skin.[11] He spent the last two weeks of 1930 in the hospital, traveling to the Mayo Clinic for further care just a week after returning to South Bend after the USC game.[12] Heeding the advice of his doctors to slow down, he backed out of coaching the all-star team of former Notre Dame players that he had promised to lead in a charity game scheduled for December 27 in Los Angeles, one of a trio of such exhibitions planned to benefit the unemployed. Instead, he spent a quiet holiday with his family, who visited him during his hospitalization in Minnesota.[13] Rockne finally left the Mayo Clinic by train on New Year's Eve, slipping quietly out of town in the last hours of 1930.[14]

Rockne still looked forward to the second season playing on his new field, regardless of any worries over money or his own health. He

Knute and his wife, Bonnie Skiles Rockne, c. 1931. The couple met when they were both working summer jobs at a resort in Ohio. (Image courtesy of Notre Dame Archives.)

steadily defended his sport against the criticisms of the reformers and justified the cost of Notre Dame's football program despite the pressure of the failing economy. At the team banquet in January 1931, he expressed the hope that the critics might "keep their hands off college football a little while longer."[15]

Despite repeated denials, rumors that Rockne planned to quit coaching would persist as long as his health remained in question. His thirteen-year record, unequaled by any other coach, left him little else to achieve in his profession. His own ruminations fueled the speculation. Toward the end of the 1930 season, he had wondered aloud if "it was worth it all."[16]

Retirement as head coach would have been understandable for Rockne. His reputation assured financial security for himself and his family. Even if he stepped down as coach, he could have stayed on as Notre Dame's athletic director, guaranteeing a steady income. His work outside the school, including endorsements, coaching clinics, public appearances, broadcasting, training films, and his growing involvement with Studebaker, offered plenty of other opportunities. Still, he insisted that "when autumn comes and the leaves fall off the trees, I'll be on the football field."[17]

Rockne's schedule in the months before spring practice might have seemed daunting for a man just out of medical care, particularly one under orders to slow down, but the coach saw it as just another challenge to overcome. His commitments would keep him on the road for three months, with just enough free time for a handful of days with his family. Driving this frenetic pace was his commitment to Studebaker. Rockne's one great passion, besides his family, had always been football. Not even his conversion to Catholicism in 1925 had engendered the degree of fervent evangelism he'd always expressed for the gridiron game. Then, three years after his baptism, he became a champion for Studebaker, South Bend's hometown automaker, and he'd been proselytizing like a true believer ever since. Not even the fact that modified versions of the company's "Whiskey Six" models were a favorite ride of bootleggers dampened his enthusiasm.[18]

Although he often donated appearances to various worthy causes, Rockne's paying gigs generated substantial income. Studebaker alone was paying him $10,000 per year to give talks to their dealers.[19] With the auto market down 38 percent in 1930, Studebaker executives hoped that Rockne's endorsement could buy enough rah-rah and sis-boom-bah to motivate their dealers for the task of turning around the decline.[20] In preparing his latest round of Studebaker speeches, Rockne employed the same motivational techniques he had used before Notre Dame's big upset of the Trojans a few months earlier. In fact, his standard presentation was a reenactment of the speech that had pushed his troops to gridiron glory.

"I remember very well just before the game in the dressing room everything was quiet," he would tell his audience. "I could hear the band playing in the distance, and gradually the music died away as the band marched off the field. Pretty soon the referee rapped on the door and said we had three minutes to get out on the field."

He would then recall what he told his troops next. "I turned to the team," he would say, as if he was speaking directly to his team in the locker room instead of to auto dealers in a ballroom, "and said, 'Boys, today you are going up against a great football team, how great we don't know, but I don't think they are a bit better than you are.'"

As he continued, he repeated remarks he had made about his players' conditioning before the game, and their knowledge of the game plan. It was the inner condition of his team, he explained, that he could not assess. "It is up to you to go out there and show ninety thousand people just what is in your hearts," he had told his team, and in repeating the words he likewise challenged the salesmen to perform despite difficult economic times.

The rest of the speech repeated his final push to fire up his team that day. "Now if we win the toss we are going to receive the ball," he began, "but if they receive we are going out there and tackle hard and play a good defense. I want you full of pep. Hit them hard and take the heart out of them of them in the first few minutes; . . . and when that ball is in the air, go and get it."

His enthusiasm built as the pace quickened. "When we get that ball that is when we go to work. I want every man to block with everything he has in him and I want every man on the team to dig in his toes, lift those knees high, and when we start driving down the field for the goal line, that is when I want you to go, go, go, go, go, go!"[21]

It sounded suspiciously like the spiel he'd performed for newsreel cameras back in 1928, when he had famously told his team "We're going inside of 'em, we're going outside of 'em, and when we get them on the run, we're going to keep them on the run."[22] It would have been classic Rockne to conflate the two occasions to suit his purposes, or even recycle pep talks, although he advised against that practice for fear of the players catching on to the gag. It didn't really matter. Rockne never let a few facts stand in the way of a good story.

Regardless of exactly what Rockne said when, the results on the field that day in the Coliseum spoke for themselves, and that is what everyone really remembered. With Rockne at the helm, everyone just assumed that he had rallied his troops to victory by a stirring speech before the game, even if the reality was that the Trojans had been overrated. Even USC assistant Cliff Herd had privately recorded that opinion after the game.[23]

Within hours of his return to South Bend on New Year's Day, Rockne left town again to take his show on the road for Studebaker. First he headed east for New York City,[24] spending several days in the Big Apple to pick up the Erskine Trophy and another new car for winning the national championship,[25] to enjoy various banquets and dinners, and to give a speech during the New York Auto Show.[26]

Notre Dame's team banquet briefly brought Rockne home to South Bend in mid-January 1931,[27] but he soon hit the circuit again, heading on to Detroit,[28] then Buffalo,[29] then Boston,[30] and finally Pittsburgh,[31] before heading closer to home for the Chicago Automobile Trade Association meeting at the Sherman Hotel on January 23.[32]

A few days later, he was off again, going south toward Omaha for another auto show.[33] Then it was on to Philadelphia by month's end to pick up a different championship trophy and to mesmerize another group of enraptured Studebaker dealers.[34]

A swing through the Southwest was scheduled for February, with dates in Dallas,[35] El Paso,[36] and Phoenix.[37] While he was in the Valley of the Sun, reporters asked Rockne about football reform. As usual, he took on his critics with a biting response, dismissing football reformers as "Eastern boys who can't take it." Mocking complaints of "overemphasis," the coach said, "You don't hear anybody in the South, Middle West or West raising the question, do you?"[38] Ridiculing Eastern football had become a bit of a recurring theme for him. In Portland, he stated that Eastern football players were getting "softer" and blamed "too much nightlife, automobiling and boozing" for their decline in toughness.[39]

Rockne rode into Los Angeles on the Golden State Limited the following day, February 13, detraining in Alhambra since he would be staying in nearby Pasadena with the family of his old fullback, Moon Mullins.[40] He spent Valentine's Day on the coast, away from Bonnie, an unsurprising occurrence given the nomadic Norseman's near-constant travel.[41] He usually managed to work more than one business interest into a single stop, and this trip would be no different. Paul Lowry of the *Los Angeles Times* reported on February 11 that Rockne, in addition to meetings with Studebaker dealers and other activities, would be visiting Universal Pictures to plan a series of short films about football. His last day in Los Angeles was particularly busy. He found time to visit his old assistant Tom Lieb as the Loyola Lions prepared to open their spring training camp, where he posed for photos and chatted with the players. Braven Dyer of the *Los Angeles Times*, perhaps still sore after falling for the Bucky O'Connor ruse just a few months earlier, reported that Rockne was "still slicing the bologna as generously as ever."[42]

An hour later, Rockne was interviewed on radio station KECA,[43] which would become KABC in 1954. He jokingly dismissed a story that arose out of an "unpleasant row" connected to the charity game he had been forced to miss back in December. The trouble began when E. F. Hutton, a prominent member of the Elks organization that had sponsored the game, demanded an explanation from Rockne for travel expenses submitted for the trip by his Notre Dame All-Star team.[44] The hubbub spurred talk of ill feeling; according to the scuttlebutt, Hutton's insinuations had so soured Rockne on Los Angeles that the affair might jeopardize future games between Notre Dame and USC.[45]

After his radio appearance, Rockne hustled across town to a Studebaker dinner at the Elks Temple, located at the intersection of 6th and Park View Street, overlooking the grounds of what would later be renamed McArthur Park in honor of the famous general.[46] Rockne was a fellow Elk back in South Bend, though he joked "it hasn't helped me any" in resolving the tussle over the charity game the group had sponsored.

The next day Rockne continued on his Studebaker tour. He headed north to the Bay Area for another speech,[47] and made a radio appearance with other coaches on radio station KPO, an event sponsored by the automaker.[48] While in the Bay Area, he also made an appearance at the University of California on behalf of the school's new head coach, his old friend Bill Ingram.[49] He then continued on to the Pacific Northwest before swinging east again.[50]

Rockne was back in Dixie by March 1931. He arrived in Atlanta early in the month, speaking before local Studebaker dealers gathered at the Biltmore Hotel,[51] a landmark structure designed by the same architects who had created the famous Waldorf-Astoria in New York.[52] While in town, he found time to entertain members of the local "Our Gang" Club of Atlanta. The club celebrated the child stars playing "Our Gang," a troupe of precocious children in a popular series of movie shorts that featured their various comedic high jinks. Their young fans in the club were treated to some of the coach's old tales, one being the plight of "poor Fogerty," who was only called into the game to "give his pants to the left halfback."[53]

Finally there was time for a short break from work, and on March 5, Rockne caught an Eastern Airlines Curtis Kingbird plane out of Candler Airfield bound for Miami.[54] His family looked forward to him joining them there for a well-earned rest. Bonnie and their two youngest children, daughter Mary Jean and little son Jack, were staying at a rented vacation home in Coral Gables.[55] Besides the pleasure of rejoining his family, Rockne planned to spend time on the beach, watch Primo Carnera regain his heavyweight crown from Jim O'Malley,[56] and place a few bets on the thoroughbreds at Hialeah.[57]

Of course, his family always had to share Rockne with the public. He agreed to a radio interview with the sports editor of the Associated Press, broadcast from a radio station in Miami. During the interview, he predicted that Miami would someday host a major, season-ending, intersectional football game. Nearly four years later, the first Orange Bowl game kicked off there.[58]

Spring practice was now just a couple of weeks away, but Rockne still had plenty of work to do for Studebaker before the time came to switch gears and focus on football. Just a week after arriving in Florida, he doubled back to Atlanta to hop aboard another aircraft, this time a Lycoming-powered Stinson SM-6000 trimotor, bound for Detroit. From there it was off to Chicago by train, and on to South Bend.[59]

Rockne had completed fourteen events for Studebaker in the first three months of 1931. He signed a new contract with the firm, the biggest one yet, on March 19. The document renewed his tenure with the automaker though April 1932 and promoted him to manager of sales promotion.[60] Studebaker also had plans to launch Rockne Motors, a new line of automobiles, toward the end of the year; the line would bear Rockne's name, and the coach would be its vice president.[61] It was the culmination of his work in the car business, work that went back to speeches made on behalf of rival automaker Graham-Paige in January 1928, four months before he began working for Studebaker.[62]

His first major task in his new position as sales manager for Studebaker was to launch a new program to boost sales. Rockne sent out letters to dealers inviting the cream of the network to "try out" for Studebaker's "All-Star Team."[63] The deadline to respond to the challenge was March 31, 1931, the same day Rockne would leave for the West Coast, where he would answer Hollywood's call.

Before then, Rockne would have one last week in South Bend to attend to football and his job at Notre Dame. Spring practice began on March 23,[64] with just seven days of drills scheduled before the team would break camp to take the first week of April off for Easter.[65] Before leaving town, the coach attended the Managers Banquet in the lay dining hall on campus, where he acknowledged the student managers' contribution to the past season and named the new managers for the coming year.[66]

Rockne's duties for Notre Dame also included attending a Wednesday meeting of the Board of Athletic Control, where he faced another battle with Mulcaire and his fellow reformers. One bone of contention was the intersectional contract with the Trojans. Rockne urged a renewal of the agreement, arguing that the series of games had eclipsed all others on the schedule of the Fighting Irish, save perhaps for Army. He asked that approval be granted, lest they lose the opportunity to extend the rivalry.

Mulcaire and his supporters were dead set against it, however. "The game involves too much travel," Mulcaire protested.

"But we go out there only every other year," Rockne answered. "Anyway, in a few years all teams will be giving up trains for air travel." Relations between the two men had grown cold long before, but Rockne's bold prediction suddenly turned up the heat as Irish tempers flared anew.

"Have you lost your senses?" Mulcaire growled. "We will never allow such a thing!"[67]

Whatever reluctance Rockne had displayed to begin the series with the Trojans back in 1925 had long since disappeared, and he wanted to continue it past 1931. He had been unable to persuade his administration not to break with Nebraska just before the Trojan series started, and now he feared the reformers would prevent him from extending the rivalry with USC. If Mulcaire held firm, the upcoming game might be the last, but the issue was tabled without a vote. As with the purchase of a new tarp, the decision was postponed. The battle would be fought after Rockne returned from the coast.

That Friday, Rockne wrapped up the first week of spring practice and headed downstate to St. Simon the Apostle School in Indianapolis for a banquet honoring the winners of the Indiana high school state basketball championships. Little Washington, Indiana, boasted both the public and Catholic school titles that year—the Washington High School Hatchets and the Washington Catholic Cardinals, respectively. "Big Dave" DeJernett, the six foot three African American star of the

Hatchets squad, had been the first black athlete in the United States to play for an undisputed integrated state basketball championship team.[68] He had done so amid death threats from the Klan, proving that remnants of the once-mighty gang still lingered in Indiana long after the downfall of D. C. Stephenson.[69]

Rockne was the last to speak before the gathering. Afterward, he saluted both squads, shaking each team member's hand in congratulation. DeJernett, uncertain that the Notre Dame coach would want to be seen shaking hands with a man of color, tried to slip by and spare Rockne the indignity. At other banquets, Rockne had frequently told crude jokes stereotyping black football players in the bigoted style of the day.[70] This time, Rockne put DeJernett's fears of a snub to rest by making an exaggerated effort to grasp the hoop star's hand and shake it warmly.[71] Rockne's inconsistency was no different from that practiced by many Americans of the time, who might embrace bigotry in the abstract one moment and then practice inclusion the next, if presented with a black man face to face.

With the weekend behind him, and training camp paused for Easter, Rockne was free to reach for the brass ring out in Los Angeles: a movie offer from Universal Pictures. Rockne's agent Christy Walsh had pitched the deal back in 1930, convincing the studio honchos at Universal to capitalize on Rockne's celebrity and success. The studio offered Rockne a contract for $50,000, worth a full five years of sweat and worry on the practice fields and sidelines of South Bend.[72] Universal planned a college football film and wanted the real-life coach to play the part of the coach in the movie.[73] Rockne had done it before, at least the pep talk scene, when he had stepped onstage one night during a performance of the Broadway musical *Good News.*[74] The stage musical was another college-themed production that later made the jump to the big screen, first in 1930 and again in 1947 with Peter Lawford and June Allyson in the lead roles.[75]

Rockne's bosses at Notre Dame preferred that he pass on Universal's offer, regarding it as yet another distraction sapping time and energy that Rockne should be applying to his duties at the university.[76] Rockne, of course, wouldn't be deterred.

His motivation may have extended past immediate financial gain to a grim determination to give his family long-term security. According to John Kiener, then a student at Notre Dame, Rockne had been given a death sentence. Kiener, who headed Notre Dame's General News Publicity Department as a senior before graduating in 1932, swore that Rockne had confided that his health was much worse than the public knew.[77] Kiener said that the doctors had told Rockne he only had a few years to live. Claiming that the coach had sworn him to secrecy, Kiener remained silent for more than four decades before going public with Rockne's gloomy prognosis.[78]

Even discounting Kiener's assertion, Rockne may have been swayed by the likelihood that his coaching days, if not his life, were numbered. Rumors were rife that 1931 was to be his last year as Notre Dame's head football coach.[79] Leo Ward, a Los Angeles attorney who had steered Adam Walsh toward South Bend back in 1921, said that Rockne "was satisfied in his own mind that coaching was a thing of the past and he was looking for some means to capitalize on his reputation." Ward had become a good friend of Rockne's over the years, and the two were very close in the first months of 1931.[80]

On his last day in South Bend, the coach left a note for his boss, dismissing objections to the movie deal. He argued that the project "might be a chance to put out a picture that might be instructive and educational as regards Notre Dame in every sense of the word."[81] He went on his way, knowing that, at times, forgiveness is more easily obtained than permission.

As usual, Rockne had a full slate of activities lined up for his two-day visit to the West Coast.[82] The Breakfast Club, a fraternal organization in Los Angeles whose first secretary had been Edgar Rice Burroughs, author of the Tarzan novels,[83] planned to host Rockne on his first day in town to induct him as an honorary member.[84] Later that day, he was to speak before the Junior Chamber of Commerce.[85] He also planned to address a local Studebaker group.

Though he frequently traveled by plane, Rockne had failed to book a flight and was planning to make the trip by rail until good fortune crossed his path in the person of Father John Reynolds. The priest had just returned to Notre Dame from Chicago, where he had testified in the case of Alfred "Jake" Lingle, the newsman murdered by the mob during the Pineapple Primary incident. Reynolds and Rockne had been acquaintances since their student days together on the track team. When Rockne bemoaned the time he would lose traveling by rail, Reynolds told Rockne that he also had planned a trip west, and had an airline ticket for the next day from Kansas City to Los Angeles. He gave Rockne his airline ticket, volunteering to go by rail instead. That left Rockne with only the leg to Kansas City to travel by train.

Two hours later, Rockne had reached the Windy City, traveling on the Chicago, South Bend, and South Shore Interurban.[86] There was time enough on the layover to visit his mother Martha,[87] whose birthday had passed on March 6, while he was in Florida.[88] He also dropped by the offices of the *Chicago Tribune* to speak with the sports editor, Arch Ward, before meeting up with Christy Walsh and a friend, playwright Albert C. Fuller, for dinner.[89] They discussed Rockne's movie project; talked about boxer Gene Tunney, who'd retired undefeated in 1928; and shared a few moments of general camaraderie.[90] As the dinner ended and the men parted ways, his friends wished Rockne "soft landings."

"You mean happy landings," he corrected them.[91]

At Union Station, Rockne boarded the Chicago, Burlington, and Quincy Railroad's American Royal, departing at 8:00 P.M. for Kansas City. As Rockne's train rumbled southwest, a trimotor aircraft droned eastward from Los Angeles to Kansas City. The plane, Transcontinental and Western's Fokker F-10A NC 999E, touched down at Kansas City Municipal Airport on Monday evening, just one hour after Rockne's train left Chicago. It was scheduled to depart again at 8:30 the next morning as Flight 5, returning to Los Angeles via Wichita, reversing the route it had just flown. As the ground crew prepped the plane, the mechanics voiced concerns about the airworthiness of the aircraft. E. C. "Red" Long had observed problems with the airframe, noting "panels loose on the wing." He refused to sign the maintenance log, but to no avail. The plane was approved to fly anyway.[92]

Meanwhile Rockne's train pulled into Kansas City Union Station at its scheduled time of 7:00 A.M. The station was an impressive Beaux-Arts structure, with finely crafted joinery; tall, arched windows flanking the main lobby; and ornate chandeliers hanging from the coffered ceilings rising some ninety-five feet above the polished stone floors. Designed by noted architect Jarvis Hunt, Union Station was the third-largest train station in America when it opened in 1914.[93]

Rockne had planned to meet an old friend from his student days, D. M. Nigro, in Kansas City, and to rendezvous with his older sons,

Billy and Knute Jr., who had spent their Easter break in Florida with the family. The boys were headed back to the Pembroke School, but the train was running late.[94] Knute waited for them at the information counter, nervously checking the time and asking for updates as the clock moved toward 8:00. He finally decided to send a wire to Bonnie, writing "LEAVING RIGHT NOW WILL BE AT BILTMORE HOTEL LOVE AND KISSES=KNUTE."[95]

By 8:15 Rockne was really running late, and any further delay might jeopardize his connection at the airport. With a shrug, he bid his friend farewell and expressed disappointment that he had missed his children. "I'll be sure to stop off on my way back to see the boys," he assured Nigro.

With that, he went outside, hailed a cab, and left for the airport. Arriving at 8:20, he paid the seventy-cent cab fare, collected his belongings, and headed for the TWA counter. Rockne checked in just as the train carrying his children pulled into Union Station across town. He had missed them by just minutes.

Rockne was unaware that his flight was also running late. The mail shipment to be loaded on the plane had not arrived, and takeoff had been pushed back to 9:15. Given the delayed mail shipment, together with the rumblings of thunder in the distance that cast doubt on the weather, it was uncertain if the flight would proceed at all.

Finally, the mail arrived. The flight was cleared to go, providing the pilots thought it was safe to do so. The weather was a big factor in their decision. A severe blizzard, one of the worst on record, had just stormed through Missouri, and conditions were still less than ideal. Vestiges of turbulent weather trailing the passing front had created a shifting patchwork of conditions where gusty winds and rain collided with clear air. One moment things looked fine, and the next moment could be sheer terror.

The ceiling over Kansas City was just five hundred feet, and though the airport had received no reports of dangerous conditions west of Wichita, temperatures around other parts of Kansas were hovering well below freezing. Rockne dismissed any doubts about the weather, and cornered Captain Robert Fry to urge the pilot on, virtually "bullying" the airman into going ahead with the takeoff. The coach was impatient to get to the coast, as were his fellow passengers, all successful businessmen who, like Rockne, were used to getting their way.

In all, six passengers waited to board. Besides Rockne, there was H. J. Christen, a wealthy designer of store fixtures anxious to reconcile with his estranged wife back home; John H. Happer, a Wilson Sporting Goods executive from Chicago who was going to Los Angeles to open a branch office; C. A. Robrecht, a West Virginian planning to switch planes in Wichita, about two hundred miles away, to reach his final destination in Texas; Waldo B. Miller, an Aetna Insurance saleman heading home from a meeting on the East Coast; and Spencer Goldthwaite, an advertising man looking forward to visiting his parents in Pasadena.

Rockne's persuasion overruled any objections, and at 9:00 A.M., Captain Fry began preparations for takeoff. Knute was the last passenger to board the plane, choosing a spot among the seven open seats in the cabin. The accommodations were austere but standard for the time. Wood paneling ran below the large windows, extending almost unbroken along the length of the cabin. Exposed portions of the fuselage's tubular framework angled in front of the glass, below simple luggage shelves suspended above the two rows of seats. The plain wicker chairs were padded with the thinnest of leather cushions, but offered no safety belts or restraints of any kind.

The plane had been designed by the American subsidiary of Fokker, the famous Dutch company known for the bright red triplanes flown by the German ace Manfred von Richthofen, the infamous "Red Baron" of World War I. Fokker's F10-A model resembled the later Ford trimotor, except that the Fokker was not an all-metal aircraft, encompassing wood and fabric materials as well.

Its wings consisted of thin layers of plywood glued over a laminated wood framework. Their 71-foot, 2-inch span was mounted high atop the fuselage, forming one uninterrupted surface from wingtip to wingtip. The body of the plane was a slab-sided, lightweight structure consisting of stretched and doped fabric sewn over a welded tubular metal frame that supported the interior cabin and cockpit. The red-and-silver color scheme was accented by the aluminum engine cowls, which gleamed whenever fleeting sunlight caught the edges of the tooled pattern brushed on their surfaces. There were three cowls in all: one mounted on the nose, which jutted out below the flat angles of the cockpit windows, and two slung on pods below the wings. The airline markings signaled TWA's "shotgun marriage" of its two component airlines, combining those of the former Transcontinental Air Transport with the Native American imagery of the former Western Air Express.

With passengers and cargo loaded, doors secured, and final checks completed, pilot Robert Fry and copilot Joshua Mathias started up the three Pratt and Whitney radial engines. The entire airframe rumbled to the cadence of twenty-seven cylinders firing in sequence as the three thundering motors jumped to life. Flaps wiggled and waved as the pilots worked the control surfaces one last time. Chocks were dragged aside to free the aircraft for departure. When all was ready and clearance was granted, Captain Fry moved the throttle forward and the growling of the engines increased to a deafening roar. Coaxing the plane out onto the runway, Fry urged the plane forward. As he guided the craft down six hundred yards of tarmac, it picked up speed and the nose began to rise. At 9:15, the wheels of 999E lifted off the ground and the plane was airborne. One minute later, it disappeared into the darkness that hung low above the Missouri countryside.

Less than an hour later, as the weather turned even darker, a garbled radio message crackled over the plane's radio. It was TWA in Wichita contacting the flight crew.

"I can't talk now," Mathias shot back, "too busy."

"What are you going to do?" Wichita asked.

"I don't know," Mathias answered.

A cold front had smashed into the warm air over the Flint Hills, and TWA 999E was right in the middle of the turbulence. It was rough going, but the plane kept on lumbering along at a little over one hundred miles per hour, well below top speed but within the best range for optimum maneuverability.

"On course and thirty-five miles from the Cassoday beacon," Mathias reported. The navigation aid he mentioned was near Emporia, about ninety miles from Wichita.

"The sun is shining here," said G. A. O'Reilly, the TWA man in Wichita. There was only silence in reply, save for the white noise of crackling static, until the copilot's voice cut through.

"The weather is getting tough," Mathias reported. "We've been forced too low by clouds. We're going to turn around and go back to Kansas City."

Captain Fry banked right, circling around to head northeast. Dense clouds billowed around the plane. Intermittent sleet and snow pummeled the craft, drumming a sickening vibrato on the taut fabric covering of its outer surfaces. The wings, buffeted by swirling winds, began to rock unnaturally.

Mathias again asked about the weather in Wichita. "999E, the ceiling is unlimited," was the response.

The prospect of better weather ahead made the crew reconsider their course. "We will turn around again and try for Wichita," Mathias radioed back.

It was 10:40 A.M. The barometer was dropping rapidly in Wichita. The sun was shining everywhere except for one section of the sky, toward Bazaar, Kansas, some twenty-five miles to the southwest. A black vortex was clearly visible there, hanging in the air before dissolving into the darkness.

"We've headed back but it's getting tighter," Mathias radioed in. "Think we'll come on to Wichita," he said, adding ominously, "It looks pretty bad."

"999E do you think you'll make it?" O'Reilly asked, voicing his concern. "Can you get through?"

Mathias answered nervously, "Don't know yet." The strain of fear and worry choked his words as he repeated his response: "Don't know yet."

Fry and Mathias struggled to control the aircraft. Flying low over the Flint Hills, they scanned past the rain and hail smashing into the windshield. Glimpses of the shiny rails of the Santa Fe route below them helped verify their course. Ice choking the venturi of the airspeed, bank, and turn indicators rendered those instruments useless. They would have to judge speed and attitude by the seat of their pants.

The plane sliced through the turbulence, tossing the passengers violently about the cabin. The aircraft was just two or three hundred feet off the ground, so Fry punched the throttles forward to gain altitude. When he'd reached fifteen hundred feet, he banked left, but the plane nosed into the edge of the funnel cloud. The six passengers in the cabin were smashed together in a crumpled pile as the aircraft dropped into an air pocket. They recovered from the turbulence only to see a terrifying sight outside the window. The left wing was fluttering uncontrollably.

Captain Fry pulled the throttles back in an attempt to dampen the motion, but it was no use. The wingtip continued to flap up to eight inches even after hitting clear air.

People on the ground heard the sound above them and stopped to watch the plane's wild gyrations. Not far away, Robert Blackburn and his son John were feeding their cattle as the crippled airliner flew northwest of their farm. Seward Baker and his sons were about a mile away on the Blackburn Ranch. Other ranchers and farmers around the area noticed something wrong, and searched the sky to pinpoint the trouble.

They saw the plane descending from a cloud, its nose tilted downward as it banked as if to land. The engine roared and the plane climbed to about five hundred feet, then the motors missed again and suddenly oily smoke began trailing behind the aircraft. A loud bang sounded, followed by a thud. Suddenly the left wing sheared off its anchoring and folded over onto the fuselage. The doomed aircraft leveled for a moment, and then fell rightward to begin a death spiral toward the ground. The broken wing of the plane rolled past vertical, flipping end over end as it tumbled toward the ground. Bodies careened violently into the air, falling earthward like rag dolls.

Artist's Conception of Rockne's Fatal Crash!

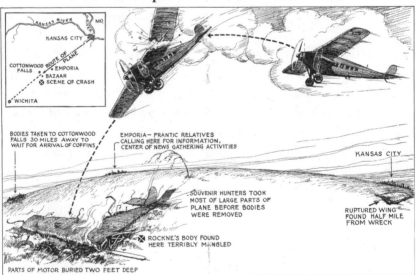

This newspaper diagram of the 1931 plane crash in which Rockne died was reprinted across the nation. (Image courtesy of Notre Dame Archives.)

The plane crashed almost vertically into the wet Kansas soil. Most of the fragile structure smashed into a mass of twisted metal and ragged splinters. The weight of the three engines drove them deep into the damp earth, anchoring the crumpled fuselage, which had piled into a mangled heap. The plane had come to rest just west of Clarence Mc-Cracken's farm, at a spot about three miles southwest of Bazaar, where the ominous dark funnel cloud had been seen from the Wichita tower. The severed wing landed about half a mile from the main crash site.[96]

Shocked locals quickly sprang into action. They raced in their vehicles, on horseback, or by foot toward the downed plane. Telephones soon began ringing everywhere, alerting the townsfolk that help was desperately needed. Rescuers arrived at a gruesome scene. Three bodies were trapped in the nose of the plane, with the rest strewn far from what remained of the cabin. Rockne was found ten yards away. It was said that his rosary was found nearby.[97]

The tragic news soon reached the office of Jacob Hinden, the Chase County coroner. Soon the word was spreading like wildfire, from Cottonwood Falls to Emporia, on to Kansas City, and then out across the country. By midday, news of the tragedy had reached the East Coast.[98]

Rockne was dead.

22

In the Depths of Despair

It is awfully hard to understand.

—Christy Walsh, April 4, 1931

Howard Jones steered his big Studebaker President effortlessly down US Highway 101. The car was the top of Studebaker's line, a well-appointed sedan with room for seven passengers within its plush mohair interior. It was the perfect car for a man like Jones. It was luxurious and roomy, yet not as stuffy as a Packard nor as showy as a Duesenberg. The 337-cubic-inch straight-eight engine under the long, gleaming hood made it one of the fastest American cars on the market, offering the kind of power and performance a sporting man like Jones could appreciate.[1] Like Rockne, Jones was a loyal customer of the South Bend automaker, and he drove a new model every year.[2]

Hugging the coast, he glanced from time to time toward the waves of the Pacific Ocean crashing along the shoreline of California. The highway followed the water's edge almost the whole way until he hit Oxnard, where the route turned inland toward the final leg home. At different points he would pass Monterey, Big Sur, Morro Bay, San Simeon, Pismo Beach, and Santa Barbara—a pleasant and scenic drive all the way.

Howard was motoring down the California coast at the very moment the plane carrying his good friend Knute Rockne was spinning out of control over the low hills of Kansas. Jones was returning from a conference in Santa Cruz, where he'd met with fellow coaches, among them Pop Warner of Stanford and Bill Ingram of Cal. Warner and Ingram also decided to head south once they heard that Rockne was to be feted at the luncheon planned in Los Angeles, although, like Rockne, they traveled by air. None of the three had any inkling that tragedy had befallen their colleague until they arrived in Southern California.

Newsmen in Los Angeles had been trying to reach Jones at his home since the news broke, seeking a statement on Rockne's death. Informed of the calamity as soon as he got home, Jones found himself sharing his emotions with a reporter over the phone before he had time to sort things out in his mind. It was undoubtedly an uncomfortable experience for someone as guarded as the Headman.

"You're the first person I've spoken to," he confessed. "I've just learned of the accident ten minutes ago, and I'm too shocked to say anything." Fumbling for something meaningful to add, he told the reporter, "He was a great coach, a great sportsman, and a great man." Jones then added that Rockne's death was "an irreparable loss."[3]

"I feel the great grief of the sports world at losing Rockne, one of its greatest figures, but then too, I feel a personal loss, for he was my friend," he said. "I'm afraid we will never be able to replace him."[4]

Jones was pressed on the future of Notre Dame's series with USC. "Although it is impossible to say for certain at this time, I am confident that the relations will be continued as long as the two institutions deem it advisable," he responded. "We have a game scheduled for this year in South Bend, and I believe that the contract will be renewed," he added hopefully.

Memories of the past spilled out to shade his speculation about the future. "We have always enjoyed fine competition, close games, and splendid sportsmanship between the two universities and the two teams, and I see no reason why these cannot continue," he said.[5]

Beneath his stoic veneer, he was feeling pain that was deep and profound. Even a man like Jones, who always fought to mask his emotions, could not always hide them. His distress was obvious even to his four-year-old daughter Carolyn. Decades later, she could still vividly recall the visible sense of loss her father displayed.[6]

Howard Jones was not the only mourner among the Trojans. The school's marching band had also traveled to the Bay Area. When the news reached the ensemble, band director Harold Roberts had them stop in the middle of their performance. Trumpeter Leland Auer then blew out a solitary, mournful rendition of "Taps," as the band members removed their hats in respect.[7]

All of Los Angeles felt the loss deeply. Before the main boxing match at the Olympic Auditorium that night, fans stood silently as the house lights were lowered and a gong sounded ten times in memory of the Irish coach.[8] The Elks Lodge, which only days before had been embroiled in a row with Rockne over charity expenses, also stood in silence for the coach. At 11:00 that night, the "mystic hour" at the lodge, the entire membership rose and remained motionless for a full minute of reflection.[9]

The salute to Rockne planned by the Breakfast Club for the following morning became a memorial event instead. Bruce Baxter, USC chaplain, voiced the tribute as three hundred members and guests bowed their heads in respect. "You have won your last victory," he said of Rockne, "and you have gone to stand in the presence of the Divine Referee." Calling him "our friend,"[10] he proclaimed that "sportsmanship has a deeper meaning because you lived, Knute Rockne, and out at USC we mourn the passing of our most worthy opponent."[11]

Later that day at the Biltmore Hotel, the Junior Chamber of Commerce luncheon likewise was forced to switch a planned salute to a living legend to a requiem for a fallen hero. The ballroom was filled with notables of every stripe—businessmen, sports figures, even movie stars. A large portrait of the fallen grid captain, circled with a wreath of laurel leaves accented in the blue and gold of Notre Dame, hung above the empty chair reserved for Rockne as the guest of honor.

When it came his turn to speak, Howard Jones expressed his grief in his usual direct, unadorned style. "He is dead," he began, almost as if he needed to convince himself of the cold reality. Plunging forward, he went on, "but he inculcated into Notre Dame football a spirit that was hard to lick and it is going to last that way a long time."

A stream of emotion had always flowed inside Jones. Where he differed from most men was that the stream seldom broke through the surface. This was one of those rare occasions when others got a glimpse into his soul. "You might think that I would feel otherwise," he explained, "but it is nearly as hard on me as it is on Notre Dame. It is a great thing to meet a great competitor. It was wonderful to defeat Notre Dame but it was never a disgrace to lose to it under Rockne."

Will Rogers sat in the back rows, listening to those who had known Rockne well. Rogers had also known Rockne, of course, and though he

Comedian and movie star Will
Rogers, shown here c. 1920,
was friends with both Rockne
and Jones.

had not been scheduled to speak that day, he was asked to contribute
to the stream of impassioned eulogies.

"Everybody's going to miss him," Rogers said, "everybody in the
whole country." Ignoring the critics who pointed to Rockne as the embodiment of overemphasis and excess, he testified to the personal connection Rockne had forged with the average citizen, commenting, "I
doubt if any person in America could have passed away and had more
good things said about him than Rockne."

"That passing out back there," he continued, referencing the plane
crash, "was just kind of an encore. We saw him pass out right here."
Recalling the shocking upset of USC that was still fresh in everyone's
mind, he added, "He passed out when he walked off the field at the
Coliseum that day they played USC. It was his last real game. That was
the real end and it was the height of his career."

Then Rogers poked fun at his fellow Angelenos. "Rockne did a great
thing for Southern California," he said. Before the Trojans met Notre
Dame, he explained, locals had developed a case of "swelled head." The
Irish had cured that ill. "We owe a lot to him for beating us, because we

was gettin' mighty cocky and he took it out of us. I must say the sports writers took it great."

Rogers then reversed course, saluting the hometown fans who had respected Rockne while hoping that Howard Jones came out on top. "I doubt if another coach in the country could have walked off that field that day without having the crowd half sore at him," he said. Then he added simply, "They wasn't."

As to the current occasion, Rogers mused, "It's too bad that a great man had to die to give a luncheon club a legitimate reason for meeting." Then he noted more seriously that Rockne's death would have one beneficial effect on football. "It will show there is something in the game outside its commercial value."[12]

Back in South Bend, no one was thinking about Rockne's legacy when they heard the news. They were too overcome with shock. "Nobody can make me believe it," said Marchmont Schwartz, Notre Dame's All-American halfback, sobbing upon hearing the news. "It can't be true." His incredulous sorrow was more than just his personal expression of shock and denial. The words summed up the reaction that rippled across Notre Dame.

Devastated mourners quickly began filling Sacred Heart Church on campus to pray and mourn.[13] Hunk Anderson, Rockne's top assistant, simply stated the obvious: Rockne "was part of Notre Dame." Then he added ruefully, "It can never be the same without him."[14]

Stores began closing in South Bend, as if an unseen order had gone out for them to do so. Office workers started going home early.[15] The mayor quickly ordered flags in town lowered to half-staff in remembrance.[16] Everywhere a shared sense of loss and sorrow; a "ghastly silence," blanketed the city and rendered the townsfolk mute.[17]

Rev. John O'Hara, always one to conjoin football and faith, expressed the love for Rockne that all of Notre Dame shared, while celebrating the symbolic importance his life had represented. "Knute Rockne has had a wider influence in developing the ideals of fair play than any other man of his generation," he stated. Then he added, "He did it under the banner of the mother of God. We may feel that she took care of him in his hours of need."[18]

Rockne's earthly mother in Chicago learned she'd lost her son by calling the *Chicago Tribune* anonymously to verify the incomplete reports that were trickling in. Her first inkling of disaster came when her daughter, also named Martha, called her after hearing a bulletin over WGN radio. Martha had heard only that Knute had been hurt. Louise and Florence, two of Knute's other sisters who lived with their mother, stood by as their mother's call was placed to the *Tribune*'s newsroom. Louise, overhearing that the death was confirmed, fainted in shock.[19]

The story of Rockne's demise was proving to be one of the biggest of the year. His death overshadowed those of hundreds of victims of a massive earthquake that had struck Nicaragua that same day.[20] Afternoon editions of the nation's newspapers rushed to print the dispatches of Rockne's fate that flooded in from the various places that were part of the drama—Miami, Kansas City, Chicago, and South Bend. Newsboys on street corners shouted the sensational front-page headlines. Radio shows cut into regular programming to broadcast grim announcements of Rockne's death. Phone and telegraph lines sprang to life from coast to coast.

President Hoover expressed a dour reaction of shock when a White House aide brought him a note containing the news. With pursed lips and a melancholy tone, he mumbled, "What dreadful, dreadful news."[21]

Thousands of newsmen across America penned a steady stream of accolades and eulogies. Grantland Rice wrote that Rockne possessed "brains, ability, character, and the vital qualities of leadership." He lamented that "there are few in this world who can't be replaced. Knute Rockne is one of the few."[22]

Paul Lowry of the *Los Angeles Times* weighed the impact on the nation by writing, "The death of no other individual save the President probably could have shocked the country more than the tragic passing of Knute K. Rockne." Among coaches, Lowry wrote, "Rock stood supreme." Assessing the individual, he added that "to know the man was to love him."[23]

Arch Ward of the *Chicago Tribune* wrote that his old friend Rockne "took college football out of the ramshackle stands of fifteen years ago into million dollar fields and made it the greatest attraction in sport."[24]

Rockne's old teammate and friend Gus Dorais, then the athletic director at the University of Detroit, took a turn as sportswriter for the Associated Press to contribute his thoughts on the tragedy. His words foreshadowed a curious phenomenon that began that spring and continues to this very day. "Rock is not dead to me," he wrote, "any more than any great man really dies."[25]

Rockne was gone, but the Spirit of Notre Dame would live on.

Valhalla Awaits

I can hardly realize that he has gone.

—Howard Jones, April 1, 1931

Bonnie Rockne was still in Florida, finishing the winter vacation she had spent largely without the company of her husband, save for his brief visit earlier in the month. The two older boys had left for boarding school in Kansas. Her daughter Mary Jeanne and youngest son Jack were staying with her, and she had planned to reunite them with their father when he returned.

On the last day of March, at the same moment her husband was crashing to earth, Bonnie was shopping in town with friends. Mr. and Mrs. Tom O'Neil were very close, and Bonnie had spent a lot of time with the couple in Florida. None of the group had any idea that Rockne's plane had gone down, or that he was dead. A man who knew the O'Neils spotted them walking through the shopping district, and flagged Tom down. The man approached discreetly, to prevent Bonnie overhearing, and explained what had happened in Kansas. It fell to Tom to tell her.

"I've got some serious news for you," he said.

"Is it the plane?" Bonnie asked him. O'Neil confirmed her worst suspicions, and then suggested they go to see his brother.[1]

A small group, including official town greeter George Hussey and old friend Francis Wallace and his wife, rushed over to the vacation house to wait for Bonnie's return. Nothing official had come through, only early news reports. Bonnie tried to remain calm amid the chaos, but she was frozen in denial. "I just don't believe it," she muttered to herself, over and over.

Telegrams *had* arrived, beginning with Knute's tender message from Kansas City. Later, a steady stream of condolences began pouring in. Gus Dorais, Rock's old teammate, was the first to reach out to Bonnie. Other gestures of love and respect followed throughout the day. Phone calls from Notre Dame rang through. Finally, confirmation of the worst came, and Bonnie had to face the truth. "Your daddy has gone away," she told her young son Jackie. "He loved you so."

As rescue workers in Kansas got on with the grim tasks of recovering bodies and sorting out what went wrong, preparations began in Coral Gables for Bonnie's return to South Bend. Everyone helped out, gathering belongings and packing luggage for the trip. As Wallace filled one steamer trunk, labeled with Rockne's initials, he found that one old football wouldn't fit. So Wallace suggested that it be deflated to pack flat. However, Mrs. Rockne couldn't bear the idea of discarding even the breath of the old Rock trapped in that battered pigskin. "Oh no," Bonnie insisted, "Knute blew that up himself."[2]

Bonnie, her two children, their maid, and the O'Neils boarded the Dixie Limited[3] late that evening to begin the dark, mournful journey to Chicago.[4] From there they would travel a few hours more by car to South Bend and a reunion with her two older sons and her late husband's remains.[5]

Bonnie had asked Dr. Nigro to oversee the final disposition of Knute's body in Kansas before its release and shipment by rail to South Bend. Before leaving Florida, she had spoken to Nigro by phone, asking him to take charge, and to chaperone Billy and Knute Jr. on their journey home.[6]

The coroner in Kansas had required a positive identification of the body by someone who knew Rockne well. That morbid duty also fell to Nigro and to Rock's old boss, Jesse Harper, whose ranch was just six miles from the crash site.[7]

Nigro drove to the Pembroke School in Kansas City to take custody of Rockne's older boys. "Your dad has been in an automobile accident," he told them, choosing to break the news to them in stages. "I don't know how badly he's been hurt," he went on. "Not badly, I think."

The boys reacted predictably, tears flowing at the mere suggestion of injury to their beloved father. Nigro's promise to take them to their dad restored their composure, allowing them to leave for Cottonwood Falls with a minimum of fuss.[8] The car carrying Dr. Nigro and the Rockne boys raced across the 143 miles of Kansas prairie at maximum speed. The fire siren screaming atop the vehicle cleared any traffic from their path.

Upon reaching Cottonwood Falls, the driver steered toward 314 Broadway Street, where the McKenzie Furniture and Undertaking Company held the bodies of the crash victims. A small crowd stood quietly outside the shop, solemnly greeting the speeding car as it pulled up. Men stood bareheaded, their hats removed to show respect for the dead lying silently inside.

The scene confused the boys. They expected to arrive at a hospital, not a furniture store. "This is not a hospital," Knute Jr said, turning toward a reporter from a Kansas City newspaper. "Where is the hospital?" he asked.

"Come into the drug store for a few minutes, boys," someone said. It was a friend of Dr. Nigro, who had offered to watch the boys while Nigro went inside the mortuary. The mention of treats at the soda counter sufficed to distract the children while the business with the undertaker went forward. Knute Jr. savored a hot chocolate, while Billy sipped a Coca Cola through a straw.

"Is my father alive?" Billy asked between slurps.

"I don't know," their chaperon answered. "You must ask Dr. Nigro."

It wasn't long before Nigro returned, his face betraying the stress and emotion churning inside him.[9] "Come with me, boys," he said as he led them back to the car parked outside, his arms draped around their little shoulders.[10] Inside the car, Rockne's sons learned what had really happened to their father. Billy choked, fighting back tears. Knute Jr. turned pale, bit his lip, and stared ahead blankly. They took the news, it was said, like "little Norsemen."[11] In truth, there were plenty of tears that night. Norsemen or no, they were just young boys.

Nigro had ordered that Rockne's casket be sealed. The Notre Dame coach had been one of those thrown from the plane, and his crumpled body would have made gruesome viewing. Both his legs had been broken and his skull partially crushed.[12] "We should remember Rockne as he was to us," Nigro told his sons.

Nigro gathered what remained of Rockne's possessions from the undertaker—two battered suitcases torn "almost to shreds," a pair of shoes with the heels sheared off by the crash, and bits of clothing that were "ripped to pieces." Rockne's rosary, which had been found near the body, had been mailed ahead by the local sheriff, who found the prospect of giving it in person to Rockne's sons to be "too heart-breaking."[13]

Nigro and Knute's two sons spent the long, numbing night together inside the drug store. Finally, it was time to begin the two-mile journey to Strong City, Kansas. Rockne's body, along with the remains of fellow crash victim W. B. Miller, was gently lifted onto the waiting Santa Fe train for the scheduled departure of 4:45 A.M.[14]

Three hours later, the funeral train pulled into Kansas City.[15] A hastily assembled delegation from Notre Dame was there. Father Mulcaire, coaching assistants Hunk Anderson and Jack Chevigny, team manager Edward Halpin, and Carl King and Howard Edwards, both close friends of Rockne's from South Bend, had made the trip south.[16] They had twenty minutes to greet Nigro and his cohorts, offer their condolences to Rockne's children, and transfer their luggage to the northbound train.

Billy and Knute Jr. welcomed the chance to escape the morbid confines of their father's death train and enjoy a few moments away from its stifling atmosphere of grief. Outside the station the sun was shining, and the warm air provided a refreshing break. The boys later mingled happily with the small group of Notre Dame friends that had gathered to greet the funeral party inside the waiting room. Though their red and bleary eyes revealed their heartache, Rockne's sons were able to smile at the friends who had traveled to show their respect, and willingly posed for photographs.[17] Yet even during those moments of relief, the boys expressed a sense of confusion. "We don't know what we will do until we see mother," William told his friends. "We may not return to Pembroke. We don't know what will happen about anything now."

Soon it was 8:00, and as the departure time drew close the familiar warning of "all aboard" rang out. Five minutes later, the Santa Fe locomotive began rolling forward and the train was on its way to Chicago. Along the way, it would pass through Missouri and Iowa and curve north through Illinois before arriving in Chicago at 7:45 that evening.[18]

The mood was solemn in the Windy City when the train arrived. Signs of mourning were everywhere. All that day, flags had been flown at half-staff at Soldier Field, Rockne's old stomping grounds across the street from the train station. Rockne had been nearly as beloved in Chicago as in South Bend, and a huge crowd of grieving fans wanted to be on hand to pay their respects when he passed through their city one last time. The crowd numbered in the thousands, jamming Dearborn Station, where Rockne's body would arrive, and spilling out into the street between Dearborn and the nearby La Salle depot, from which his remains would depart for the trip to South Bend.[19]

As the train pulled in to Dearborn Station, the subdued crowd suddenly fell completely silent. Hats were removed and held low in a gesture of respect. The throng watched as the funeral cortege detrained, and gathered around the baggage car that held the bodies of Rockne and Miller.

Fifteen members of the Notre Dame Alumni Club of Chicago forced their way through the crowd and stood by the baggage car, ready to receive the grey metallic box[20] containing Rockne's casket.[21] Hunk Anderson slid open the heavy door and helped the alumni pull the container from the train.[22] As the alumni went about their work, their leader, James Brennan, reached out to place a large arrangement of flowers on top of the cold vessel bearing Rockne's body.[23]

Policemen's flashlights illuminated the way as the group moved forward. The sprawling metal roof above the tracks cast deep shadows across the platform, and even with rows of factory-style lights overhead, the cavernous space inside the train shed was smoky and dark. The blazing fire of newsmen's flashbulbs gave intermittent glimpses of grim faces as the men carried the coffin box to a waiting luggage cart. Save for the sobs of those overcome with grief, the crowd remained silent.

As grieving fans pressed closer to the procession, they blocked the way, slowing progress to a crawl. Once the bearers reached the baggage room, the scene grew even more chaotic, as they struggled to "fight their way" inside through the throng of one thousand souls crammed inside the staging area. Despite the commotion, though, Hunk Anderson never broke his grasp of the pall that held his mentor's body, even though his other hand was brushing away the tears he could not contain. Only with the assistance of the police was the entourage able to make its way through the throng and out to the street. There the box was lifted onto a waiting motor truck and secured for the ride to the La Salle station.

The alumni hopped on the truck as it pulled away, hanging off the side to form a sort of makeshift honor guard. Mourners swarmed in behind the vehicle, filling the street with a solid wave of humanity that moved slowly as a single entity. Many more people lined the sidewalks on either side of Dearborn, drawing close to lay hands on the lumbering bier as it passed them. The procession never moved at more than a walking pace, and even that was achieved only with a vanguard of motorcycle police clearing the path ahead.[24]

Slowly the grim delegation made its way to the La Salle station, where the coach's remains were to be loaded onto the New York Central train scheduled to depart at 9:15 P.M. for South Bend. Movement remained restricted. After wading through the crowd, the funerary shipment was loaded for the final leg of the journey. The mourners watched the train depart, motionless in silent vigil until the last glimpse of the New York Central drumhead slipped into the darkness. Then they, too, left, disappearing into the cold Chicago night.[25]

Less than two hours later, the locomotive pulled its string of railcars into South Bend's Union Station.[26] The Art Deco brick structure was just two years old, and featured a large barrel arch roof over the spacious ticketing and passenger waiting areas inside. Behind the station and across the tracks stood the huge Studebaker auto factory, the lifeblood of South Bend's industrial heart.[27]

Just as they had at every stop along the route, people had gathered at the station, but the reverence of the home crowd exceeded that of the earlier groups. Those not completely silenced by emotion murmured in hushed tones until the announcement came that the train was arriving. Then all talk ceased; everyone's attention focused on the steps leading to the tracks. The loading platform was elevated from the waiting area, and only a select group of officials from the university and the city were allowed there, together with local reporters and their photographers.[28] The tremor of the rumbling train shook the station as it approached, and then it came to a stop with a hissing squeal. Rockne had come home, to the city where his remains would rest for eternity.

Rockne's widow would return to South Bend in a more discreet fashion, on Friday afternoon. The Dixie Limited stopped somewhere outside Chicago so that Bonnie and her party could transfer to a waiting automobile. Traveling by road would allow them to return to South Bend without running the gauntlet of well-meaning but overwhelming crowds seeking to show their support. She didn't want to face the mob scenes that had greeted her late husband's remains. The strain had grown with every mile traveled since leaving Florida, and now she was "near collapse."[29]

That night, a prayer service for Rockne was held at St. Patrick's Church across the river from the Notre Dame campus. Rev. William Maloney struggled through the supplication with a trembling voice, openly sharing his grief with the parishioners.[30]

It was Good Friday, April 3, when Knute's body finally returned to his Tudor-style home on East Wayne Street. A cold, drizzling rain was falling in South Bend. Those closest to him waited to receive the bronze coffin, among them his widow, his family, and a few close friends and former players. His remains would soon be lying in state where the multitude could pay their respects, but first his loved ones wanted time with him, to hold him close in their hearts before sharing their beloved Rock with the grieving public. Later that afternoon, Bonnie planned to go over to Highland cemetery to pick out the spot where Knute would be buried.[31]

Since it was Holy Week, special dispensations would be needed to hold the funeral before Monday. Bishop Noll of the Fort Wayne diocese promptly acquiesced, and the services were set for the next day.

A policeman stands guard outside the Rocknes' South Bend home in early 1931, protecting the family's privacy as they mourn Knute's death in a plane crash. Note the floral tributes on the lawn. (Image courtesy of Karen Hickey.)

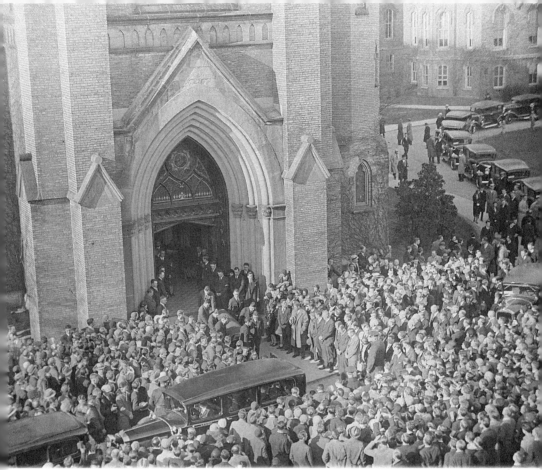

Vast crowds mourn Knute Rockne at his 1931 funeral, held in Notre Dame's Sacred Heart Church. The service was broadcast around the world live via radio and later shown in theaters using newsreel footage. (Image courtesy of Notre Dame Archives.)

It was a fitting choice: Saturday was the traditional day of the week for Rockne's football rituals in the fall.[32]

The sun shone brightly that particular Saturday as the mourners gathered for the service at Sacred Heart Church on the campus of Notre Dame. For days, people had been arriving so they could be there for this moment. Among them were politicians and fellow coaches, business-men and entertainment celebrities like Rock's old friend Will Rogers, and, of course, former players and classmates of Rockne's from the class of 1914. King Haakon of Norway sent his consul from Chicago, Olaf Bernts, to be his representative. Had the capacity allowed it, there would have been tens of thousands on hand, including, perhaps, the whole city of South Bend, but the small chapel held just one thousand. Admission was granted by invitation only. Still, the virtual gallery would number in the millions, for the service was broadcast across the country by the CBS radio network and carried as far away as Rockne's native Norway.

The official pallbearers who carried the bronze coffin into the church shortly before 3:00 P.M. consisted of members of two of Rockne's national championship teams—Conley, Yarr, Carideo, Schwartz, Brill, and Mullins. There was also a host of honorary pallbearers. Among them was a fellow coach, both an adversary and a friend: Howard Harding Jones. Even though his own spring camp had opened in Los Angeles on April 1, Jones had come east to see his friend off into eternity.

The eulogy, that final public summation of Rockne's life, was delivered by Rev. Charles L. McDonald, Notre Dame's president, before the fallen coach was laid to rest at Highland Cemetery. Like Maloney a few days before, McDonald could not fully contain his emotions, despite the heavy burden any clergyman feels to stay strong for his flock. With tearful eyes, he spoke the words that all those present, perhaps even the entire nation, already knew.

"This is not death but immortality."

24

When Autumn Comes

Ain't it a shame he's gone?

—Will Rogers, 1931

Rockne's promise to return to the football field in the fall had been shattered when his plane crashed into the rolling hills of Kansas in the spring. Now, for the first time since 1917, the leading head coach in all of football would not be on the Notre Dame sideline.

Over the years, Rockne's persona had created something of a black hole in the football world—a force so strong that at times it must have seemed as if everything was drawn inexorably toward him. If not all the way back to the days of George Gipp, Rockne had stood preeminent since at least January 1925, when the Four Horsemen had been immortalized by their season-capping Rose Bowl victory over Stanford. Now that the black hole had collapsed, the football universe was in a state of flux, although the impact of Rockne's death would take time to shake out. Nature abhors a vacuum, as the saying goes, and someone was going to step into the limelight as the top coach in the country. As yet, though, no one was sure who that might be.

One thing was certain, however. Howard Jones was not the type of man to dwell on such considerations, or if he did, he would never give any outward indication that such matters crossed his mind. A quiet man of integrity, he was neither boastful nor a self-promoter. Moreover, he was nowhere near as glib and quotable as Rockne had been. Devoted to his principles in an old-fashioned way, almost to the exclusion of all else, he believed that doing the right thing was its own reward.

Of course, all this did not mean that Jones did not feel a burning desire to win. Competition drove him, on and off the football field. More than one colleague learned that lesson the hard way if he missed Jones's lead during a "friendly" game of bridge.[1]

Despite his fierce drive to win, Howard Jones believed that glory and fame were merely the by-products of victory. He did not revel in the acclaim that success engendered. While he might not have been totally indifferent to the perks of celebrity, he wasn't much for flaunting them either. If he spent time with folks like Will Rogers and Harold Lloyd,[2] or in later years like Bob Hope, Bing Crosby,[3] and Fred McMurray,[4] he usually did so in the private setting of a golf course or secluded fishing hole, rather than in the spotlight of public attention.

Jones's dedication to virtue was not boundless, however. While he played strictly by the rules on the field, he was not above bending a few regulations off it if he could not see the justice in strict adherence. Violating the prohibition against providing jobs for his players was such an exception. Many of his boys were from modest backgrounds and couldn't afford college without some sort of help. Ward Bond came from such roots—his father was a lumberyard worker.[5] Marion Morrison had to quit school altogether when his athletic scholarship ended.

Back in Ohio, Jones's family had provided jobs for many working-class families, the kind of families that later sent their sons to play for the Headman. The family paper company even built housing for its workers across the street from the mill.[6] It would have been natural for Howard to consider it his duty to look after his players in the same way his father and grandfather before him had seen to the welfare of their workers.

Despite his cold exterior, Howard Jones was hardly a man without emotion. Still waters run deep, they say, and with Jones, the waters must have flowed very deep indeed. Like a forest stream covered in winter ice, Jones's surface may have appeared frigid and hard, but there were currents stirring underneath. It was just that the ice only rarely thawed enough for others to see those hidden depths.

A sportswriter once called Jones "the Great Stone Face." Yet even that same writer had to acknowledge that "there were a few times he let his emotions go."[7] The death of Knute Rockne was one of those times. Jones was visibly upset at his friend's passing.[8] Yet his practical nature led him to mask his feelings as best he could and get back to work when it was time to do so.

At home, the Headman was more a devoted father than a stern taskmaster. He loved both his children as much as any father could. However, as often happens in the families of great men, Howard's son may have felt the pressure of living in his father's shadow. Clark was not a good athlete—at least, not good enough to participate in college sports—and following in the footsteps of a sports icon must have fostered fears of disappointing his father. Just as his father had during his prep school days, Clark did go out for football at Black-Foxe Military Academy in Hollywood, but Clark was not the natural athlete his father and uncle had been during their days at Exeter.[9] Clark's college success would come in the classroom, and not the ball field.[10]

Howard's daughter Carolyn brought out his softer side. She would inherit his love of music—Nelson Eddy was Howard's favorite singer— and as she grew older, they would play piano duets side by side in their Toluca Lake home. Howard's handwritten notes on sheet music attest to the fact that his attention to detail extended well past the football field.

Carolyn lived a magical childhood. Not only was her father a local hero, but the neighborhood was filled with other celebrities and their families. Carolyn's playmates were the children of movie stars or young stars in their own right, such as members of the same *Our Gang* troupe whose fan club Rockne had entertained in Atlanta. As she grew up, she developed crushes on her father's handsome Trojan players, much as Clara Bow had before her.[11]

Howard's relationship with Carolyn's mother, Jane, was another matter. Writer Art Cohn recalled that, after his divorce from Leah, Jones "missed a home so he married again."[12] Perhaps Howard's second marriage was motivated more by the need to fill the void left by his first wife's departure or the desire to provide a mother for his son, than by the burning romance of true love. Living in an age when gender roles were more rigidly defined than they are today, and coming from a very traditional family, Howard may have found the idea of being a single father uncomfortable. Even today, when popular culture pushes the dictum "follow your heart," decisions about marriage often take such practical considerations into account.

Regardless of his private emotions, Howard Jones may have allowed his focus on football to blur his vision off the field at times, at least as far as his wife was concerned. The collapse of his first marriage may well have been driven at least in part by Jones's obsession with football and his consequent inattention to his young socialite bride. Perhaps his second marriage benefited from the fact that both partners had been married before and brought more patience to the second union—at least during the early days of their relationship. Jones may even have made some effort to change in the wake of his earlier divorce. He could never quit football but, after leaving Trinity, Jones was content to leave the management of an entire athletic department to someone else. This was very evident in the fact that he was seldom seen around campus during the off-season, except when spring practice was under way.[13]

Whatever the exact nature of their relationship, difficult days lay ahead. Within five years, Jane would suffer a mental breakdown so severe that Howard was forced to make the difficult decision to have her

Howard Jones poses, c. 1931, with his second wife, Jane Ridley, son Clark, and daughter Carolyn, as he shows off the new Studebaker he was awarded for one of the four National Championships won at USC. (Image courtesy of Bernadette Vargas.)

committed.[14] This meant that he was once again a single father, in practice if not in fact, the very fate his second marriage may have been designed to prevent. Eventually, his wife was sent far away from Los Angeles, the truth of her condition a closely guarded secret for decades.[15]

In 1931, however, those tragic days were still in the future. As far as anyone around them knew, Jones faced no problems at home. Howard provided Jane with a maid to keep house and a nanny to help look after the children, so her domestic chores must have been minimal.[16] The Jones family appeared to be living a quiet, dignified homelife befitting a successful football coach at a major university.

Despite his lessened workload, Howard spent much of his off-season time away from his wife. Whether or not Jane understood his need to get away, Howard seemed to need quiet and solitude, and would retreat to a favorite spot by a mountain lake to relieve the pent-up stress from his long and grueling football seasons. Even in that setting, his thoughts always came back to football, so the trips must also have served to clear his mind for planning upcoming campaigns. The spring and summer of 1931 were no different, though perhaps his periods away left him time to pause and reflect on life without Rockne.

Much of his quiet time away was spent golfing and fishing. His love of both pastimes may have sprung from the idyllic days of his childhood, when he and his brother would roam the open spaces around his home. He certainly became a fine golfer over the years. He won the low gross score among honorary members with an 82 recorded at the Southern California Newspaperman Association tournament in Ventura in mid-April 1931,[17] and by the end of that summer, his handicap had dropped to 10.[18]

As his attention turned back to football, Jones was determined to avoid a repeat of the only blowout loss he'd suffered at the hands of the Irish. He was equally determined to stop the single-point defeats the Trojans had endured because of their poor placekicking. A kicking competition wrapped up spring camp when the session concluded in late April. Every year, the winner of the contest would receive the Herbert Preston-Paul perpetual trophy, though the award had not guaranteed the Trojans placekicking success in past seasons.[19]

Once practice concluded, Jones could at least try to get his mind off football for a while. He and his wife spent actually some time together in May. They were guests of honor at a dinner dance held at the Normandie Hotel in Los Angeles by alumni of the USC College of Pharmacy.[20] Since Mother's Day was the following Sunday, Mrs. Jones must have enjoyed a rare week as the sole focus of her husband's attention.

Their togetherness ended a couple of weeks later, however, as Howard headed out on the road again. While the rest of USC's athletic honchos were in Portland for the spring meeting of the Pacific Coast Conference, Jones was in Laramie, Wyoming, on a fishing trip. From there, he traveled to Denver for a coaching school.[21] Considering Denver's proximity to the home of his ex-wife, his visit also may have facilitated compliance with the terms of the court-ordered custody of his son.[22]

By mid-June, Howard was back in Los Angeles, and back on campus at USC. Another Trojan coaching school was opening in late June, with the football section scheduled to begin in mid-July.[23] As always, it would end only a few weeks before fall camp opened.

The prospects for the season looked good—pundits once again predicted that the Trojans would wear the PCC crown.[24] Jones downplayed the prediction. "I don't think you'll find the Trojans falling for any advance banquets," he said, perhaps thinking of Rockne's pregame dinner address to his team the previous season.[25]

Knute Rockne had been on his way to discuss his possible involvement in a movie project for Universal Studios when he died in the fatal crash in Kansas in the spring. Although Rockne's death required major changes to plot and script, Universal hadn't given up plans for a film about college football, and by late July, the studio began production on *The Spirit of Notre Dame*. Howard Jones was invited by the studio's head of production, Carl Laemmle Jr., to a luncheon featuring Notre Dame's Four Horsemen; the film's star, Lew Ayres; and the other members of the cast.[26] It must have been a bittersweet moment for Jones, as he helped memorialize his dead colleague for a third time in just four months.

Jones had other business to attend to before the beginning of practice rolled around in September. In August, he had movie work of his own to complete, shooting a series of instructional films based on *Football for the Fan,* Jones's second book on the sport, which he had written with Trojan pressman Al Wesson.[27] Jones's forty-sixth birthday came around just as the Tec-Art Studios production wrapped up, so the producers presented Jones with a huge birthday cake shaped like the Los Angeles

Coliseum.[28] The celebration ended just a few days before the start of fall camp. Later, Jones would also return to the studio lot for work in a feature film, doubling for Richard Arlen in Paramount's production of *Touchdown.*[29]

As camp began, though, Jones turned his attention to the coming season. He was planning a revamped offense for 1931. Changes included a new shift, with the linemen arranged two deep before they moved into their final positions, and new plays that featured more passing. Some of the moves had been planned the year before, specifically with Notre Dame in mind, but injuries to key players had caused Jones to delay implementing the moves. Now it was time for the Headman to put his ideas—worked out with poker chips standing in for his players—to the test.[30]

The problems facing Notre Dame during the off-season of 1931 were more fundamental than those facing Jones at USC. With Rock gone, who would coach the Fighting Irish going forward? The suggestions being thrown out in the wake of Rockne's demise ranged from recalling Jesse Harper from his farm,[31] to luring Tom Lieb away from Loyola, to snatching Jimmy Phelan from his post coaching the Washington Huskies, to convincing Skip Madigan to leave St. Mary's.[32]

In the end, no one would be named head coach. For the time being, at least, that title was retired. Instead, Notre Dame named Hunk Anderson senior coach and appointed Jack Chevigny as assistant, holding the title of junior coach.[33]

Jesse Harper *was* brought back as athletic director, in a move designed both to ensure continuity and to provide more oversight of the football program. The administration was determined to prevent anyone else from exercising the level of autonomy that Rockne had managed to carve out for himself.

Anderson got off to a rough start. By July, he was in the hospital, undergoing an appendectomy while already suffering from meningitis.[34] It took two weeks for him to recover. At least Anderson was more optimistic about his team's prospects than Jones had been of the Trojans'. Upon his release from the hospital, Hunk predicted, "We're going to have a better line, I think." He had made the most of his convalescence, explaining that "I've had a lot of time to think of some football and I believe I got a swell play all rigged up."[35]

Both Irish and Trojan coaches proved clairvoyant. The first week of the season at least seemed to confirm their views. Notre Dame rolled over Indiana 25–0 in South Bend while the Thundering Herd sputtered in the Coliseum, losing to St. Mary's Gaels 13–7. The Trojans lost lineman Johnny Baker in the third period against the Gaels,[36] hurting their offense, according to Coach Jones. They lost any remaining dignity after the game, when visiting fans of the Gaels stormed the field and tore down the goalposts, carting them back to St. Mary's campus in the Moraga Valley as a souvenir of their stunning upset.[37]

As part of the activities at the Trojan-Gael game, fans were invited to contribute to a Knute Rockne memorial fund. Envelopes were handed to each person entering the Coliseum, so their donations could be deposited on the way out in special receptacles placed near the exits.

"For five years Notre Dame under Knute Rockne and Southern California under Howard Jones have been two of the nation's greatest football rivals," stated USC's director of athletics, Bill Hunter, as he announced the appeal. Then he paid tribute to the fallen coach's personal legacy. "Knute Rockne was such a vital part of football that he belongs to the game itself," Hunter proclaimed.[38] Trojan rooters displayed their feelings during the game. The card section spelled out Rockne's name and formed a giant shamrock in the stands.[39]

The Trojans picked themselves up from the disappointment of their season debut to roll through the next six weeks of the campaign. The 6–0 win over Cal was their only victory by a margin less than nineteen points. In all, they outscored their opponents 215–6 during the run. The team benefited greatly from the return of Johnny Baker before the Oregon game in mid-October. His presence gave Jones more options to move players to different positions on the line, allowing him to plug in gaps or shore up flagging play as needed.[40]

Notre Dame was just as impressive, if not more so. The Fighting Irish stomped through all seven of their games without a loss, piling up an overall scoring margin of 201–0. Only a scoreless tie with Northwestern spoiled their otherwise perfect record. Aubrey Devine, Howard Jones's resident Notre Dame scout, returned from watching the Irish play three of their games and stated, "Notre Dame could lick any of those teams with her second string."[41]

It was clear as they rumbled though their schedules that the two teams were heading toward a showdown in South Bend that would determine the success of the season. The hype was building ever higher. Newspaper columnists scrawled their prognostications across the nation's sports pages in the days leading up to kickoff. There was much for them to debate, but the foremost topic, of course, was how Notre Dame would fare without Rockne on the sidelines. The consensus of the scribes' opinions dovetailed with Devine's scouting report. The Fighting Irish would be as strong a foe as ever.

As November 21, the date of the game, approached, Howard Jones repeated his usual routine of imposing extra security amid heightened preparations for Notre Dame. Practices were closed, continuing behind the locked gates of Bovard Field until well past dark.[42] The pressure built so much that the usual precautions devolved into outright paranoia.

Suspicion fell upon one of the Trojan players. He was a third-stringer, unlikely to see action but still privy to team secrets. The rumor began when the player, Bill Hawkins, sat on the sidelines at practice because of an injury sustained the week before. A jest that he was a spy for Notre Dame was overheard, and the farce soon spun out of control. No one could be sure that Hawkins was leaking information, but with the big game looming in just days, assistant coach Gordon Campbell was taking no chances. The stakes were too high to ignore such an accusation.[43]

Hawkins was confronted with the charges just days before the Trojans were scheduled to leave for South Bend. The evidence was circumstantial. His joking comments, and the fact that he remained in touch with some of Tom Lieb's players across town at Loyola, raised questions about his loyalty.[44] Campbell wanted to know if Hawkins was feeding Notre Dame precious information through Rockne's old contact, Lieb.

Hawkins was given just one way to prove his innocence. With little alternative, he agreed to the inquisition that followed, allowing private detectives to ransack his residence, looking for any proof of disloyalty. He was held out of practice, sequestered for the week in a cottage in Topanga Canyon, and left off the traveling squad that would head for South Bend.[45]

None of the thousands of fans at the Southern Pacific's Central Station were aware of the intrigue surrounding the game. Newspapermen were likewise in the dark.[46] Writing from the information they had, they reported that Hawkins's injury was keeping him out of the game and the lineup was being shifted around as a result. Coach Jones had revealed that much, and added that he was experimenting with Johnny Baker at left end to address deficiencies at that position, but the Head-man would not discuss any internal discord.[47]

Even after the team left Los Angeles, no hint got out that Hawkins was being held incommunicado back home. The team halted for its traditional practice stop at Tucson, and the workout was all business.

Coach Jones was still fiddling with his game plan after leaving California, and despite having only a couple of major stops along the way to South Bend, he was using the time available to work on the defensive side of the ball.[48] He was expending every effort to prevent the kind of offensive explosion that the Irish ignited the year before. Jones drilled one single simple idea into his troops: the potent Irish offense meant that just one missed assignment might lead to a touchdown.[49]

Jones spent thirty minutes going over the Irish plays to explain those assignments. He stressed the important role each man played in every situation. "Protect your own sector," he advised, "before lighting out to aid any of your teammates."

Jones considered left halfback Marchmont Schwartz to be Notre Dame's ace, and he ordered his men to guard him "as closely as they would family jewels."[50] Willard "Sonny" Brouse, a Trojan backup quarterback, and assistant coach Aubrey Devine took turns standing in for Schwartz on the Arizona practice field as the second team set up to mimic the Irish offense. The starters lined up across from them, anxious to show the coach they understood his orders and were ready to carry them out.

The two lines crashed together. The collision was violent and swift, the effort tremendous, but something was amiss. The Headman saw a problem with the left end—Johnny Baker was out of position. Jones let Baker have it, but good. Baker could only stand there and take it, because you didn't talk back to the Headman. Inside, the chastised Herdsman was seething—so angry, in fact, that he was within a "whisker of quitting the team right then." Somehow, Baker held his tongue, kept his composure, and remained with the team.

Jones's unusual outburst betrayed the tension in the air. All the Trojan coaches were on edge.[51] There was a lot at stake ahead in South Bend, but despite the stress at least the players seemed to be keeping their spirits up, Baker's frustration notwithstanding. Even the steady rain, drizzling through the full two hours of practice at the next stop in Hutchinson, Kansas, failed to dampen their spirits.[52] Maybe the rain had washed away their worries. Maybe their view was more pragmatic. Perhaps they just considered it good preparation for the conditions they were likely to face in the upcoming game. It was pouring in South Bend.

25

The Game of the Century

The most thrilling contest that any football fan has ever seen.
—*El Rodeo*, Class of 1932

The storm had passed by the time the Trojans reached South Bend, but the dark clouds of troubled times still cast a shadow across the city and the entire nation. The Great Depression was now twenty-five months old, and there was no end in sight. Millions of Americans were out of work, including thousands of factory workers in Indiana. The financial sector was in free fall. Banks continued to fail. After slowly but steadily rebounding from the crisis of 1929, the stock market had started sliding again in early spring 1931, around the time Rockne died.[1]

Industry was struggling nationwide and even mighty General Motors was about to drop its Oakland car brand in response to declining sales, leaving the division's companion marque, Pontiac, to soldier on between Chevrolet and Oldsmobile.[2]

Overseas, a storm of another kind was brewing. All across the globe, plowshares were being beaten into swords. The Empire of Japan had begun seizing territory in Manchuria. In Italy, the Fascists were in power and Il Duce, Benito Mussolini, was ruling the country with an iron fist. Germans were tiring of the decadence of the Weimar Republic and beginning to embrace the hope of change promised by a charismatic politician from Austria named Adolf Hitler. Financial woes added to the discontent and drove calls for change. Money worries were not just an American problem. Financial instability threatened the whole of Europe as major banking houses faced catastrophic bankruptcy.[3] Yet to the average American, those troubles seemed far away. There was already plenty to worry about at home.

At least the weather in the Midwest had improved, if only for the weekend. A steady drizzle had dampened the Trojan practice back in Kansas, but the downpour in South Bend had forced Notre Dame's team to move its final practice sessions indoors.[4]

The rain finally stopped falling Friday night and by Saturday the forecast for the afternoon had turned surprisingly fair.[5] Howard Jones welcomed the favorable weather report. "Football should be played under ideal weather conditions," he said. "It is best for spectators and players that way."

It was a little past dawn on Saturday, November 21, when the skies began to clear in South Bend. It wasn't long before a handful of people began to gather around the stonework cave nestled in a quiet spot on Notre Dame's campus. On fall days like this one, shafts of sunlight would stream down through the thick canopy of foliage above, and when the rays fell softly to caress the ground, they seemed like fingers of the hand of God, reaching down from heaven to touch creation.

Some knelt here to pray, others to add new offerings to the rows of candles arranged along the opening of the rocky void. The flickering glow they cast inside the dark recess stood out brilliantly against the cold gray stones, even as the early morning sun began to warm the campus around it with its radiant embrace. The shimmering candles were reflected in the thin film of water puddled on the ground, left by the storm of the previous day. The deluge had washed away some of the residue of grime and dirt deposited by the factories and mills of South Bend, but the patina of industry always remained. It was part of the fabric of the city.

The Grotto at the University of Notre Dame stood in sharp contrast to the concrete and steel in the city outside the campus. The Grotto had been built in 1896 as a replica of the one in Lourdes, France, where it was said that the Virgin Mary had appeared to a peasant girl in 1858.[6] For three decades, the Catholics of Indiana had sought refuge here to affirm their adherence to the one true, universal faith that would serve them through good times and bad—Notre Dame football. On this day, a few clutched pictures of the man who represented everything that Notre Dame football meant to them. Though he had led them to the Promised Land, he was gone now, and they were left with only their faith and their prayers to sustain them. Many of those prayers were said for their fallen hero, Knute Rockne.

After all, Rockne had nearly single-handedly transformed their passion for football into an almost tangible theology. He had created icons and relics and established dogma and rituals, though Rockne himself held decidedly practical views on such matters, believing that "prayers work best when you have big players."[7] He had most certainly worked miracles, and he had ministered to saints and sinners aplenty, to be sure. He had risen so far that on the gridiron of Notre Dame the Trinity was Rockne the Father, a speedy halfback by the name of Gipp the Son, and the Spirit of Notre Dame the Holy Ghost.

Near the Grotto stood the administration building, topped by the famous golden dome, the most recognizable icon on the campus. Both the priests' spiritual and earthly authority emanated from it. Near the administration building were the twin lakes that inspired the school's formal name, Notre Dame du Lac. Those calm pools of water were also places where flagging spirits could be refreshed in moments of quiet reflection.[8]

Sabbath days like these were observed not on Sundays but on Saturdays in the fall. There had been a Catholic Mass first, as always, but sacraments of another sort would be performed a short time later in the other basilica on the grounds, the football stadium on the other side of campus. Notre Dame stadium was a rather more carnal shrine, where the meek inherited the earth one fistful of dirt and grass at a time.

It was within the walls of this massive cathedral of the gridiron that the game against USC would soon be played. The perimeter of the stadium rose forty-five feet above the surrounding fields and stretched a half-mile in length,[9] to enclose the half-million square feet of sacred ground within.[10] The façade was faced with two million bricks, accented by stone trim that finished off the fifteen thousand cubic yards of reinforced concrete supplied by the Marquette Cement Company. The concrete in turn was supported by four hundred tons of steel, brought by rail in twenty freight car loads from the Olney J. Dean Company in Chicago.[11] Built in the Collegiate Gothic style, the arena stood on the southeast quadrant of the campus, away from the bastion of academic authority under the golden dome.

Despite the hard times, there was still excitement in the air. The Trojans of the University of Southern California had come to town, and the date of November 21, 1931, had been circled on the calendars of both

NOTRE DAME – SO. CALIFORNIA
SOUTH BEND   NOV·21·1931

Rows of parked automobiles surround Notre Dame stadium in the fall of 1931. Inside, the Irish clash with the Trojans for the first time in South Bend. (Image courtesy of Notre Dame Archives.)

teams for almost a year. For Howard Jones and the Trojans, the contest was a matter of revenge, even if Rockne would not be a target of their vendetta. For the Irish, it was the last major obstacle to overcome before they finished the season the following week against Army. Victories in both games would assure Notre Dame its third straight national title.

By 1931, the two universities had become inexorably intertwined. Yet just a few years before, USC might have seemed a rather unlikely school to attain the status of a major rival for Notre Dame. At first glance, others appeared better positioned to challenge the Fighting Irish—Catholic schools such as Marquette or Boston College, for example. In fact, however, Rockne had intentionally avoided scheduling games against other Catholic schools.[12] And while Army, like Notre Dame, stood for something bigger than just learning, as embodied in its creed of "Duty, Honor, Country," its rivalry with Notre Dame began in 1913 almost by happenstance. In Notre Dame's rivalries with both Nebraska and West Point, excellence in football was the glue cementing their bond, but in the former case, religious mockery had dissolved the connection. Then, just when the final link broke with Nebraska, leaving Notre Dame unbound to the Cornhuskers, Howard Jones and his Trojans had stepped in. The new connection faced many obstacles. While the development of efficient rail travel allowed them to overcome the thousands of miles separating South Bend and Los Angeles, more than geographic distance seemed to divide the two schools as they prepared for the sixth installment in their rivalry in 1931. Notre Dame and USC appeared to exist in completely different worlds, with Notre Dame inhabiting the old world of Catholicism, tradition, and rock-solid Midwestern values, and the University of Southern California occupying the new world of change, new horizons, and wide-open Western possibilities.

Although USC, like Notre Dame, had been founded in the spirit of the Lord, the two schools did not share a religious affiliation. The primary founders of USC had been an eclectic trio: Ozro W. Childs, a Methodist horticulturist; John G. Downey, a former California governor who happened to be Irish Catholic; and Isaias W. Hellman, a Jewish banker and philanthropist.[13] By 1931, however, the school seemed more connected to Hollywood than consecrated by a spirit of holiness, especially with its students consorting with the likes of Douglas Fairbanks and Clara Bow. Notre Dame, in contrast, had stayed closer to its Catholic roots.

In sum, none of the factors usually present in the forging of great rivalries seemed to be at work here. It had been the confluence of circumstance, rather than some grand scheme or obvious connection, that had drawn Notre Dame and USC together. Mutual excellence in football then sustained that link.

Despite the teachings of the Catholic clergy at Notre Dame, at times fans of the school's football team may have strayed a bit from their mentors' lofty principles when considering how to welcome these unlikely rivals from Los Angeles. If pressed to list their sins, the faithful in the Grotto might have confessed to abandoning the Golden Rule, for they had probably prayed for the Irish to dispatch the heathens from the West like the Philistine horde in the time of David. Of course, Notre Dame bore little resemblance to David, the humble shepherd boy—in fact, it could be argued that the school had itself become a

Goliath—but no matter, there was still God's work to be done, and the Irish were in no mood to turn the other cheek.

The University of Notre Dame was still the undisputed king of football in 1931, even without Rockne. The congregation had any number of reasons to expect a Notre Dame victory later that day. The team was well prepared, experienced, supremely confident, and entering the contest without a single loss in their last twenty-six games. By game day, the bookies in Chicago were favoring Notre Dame by odds of 10 to 6.[14] Even Howard's brother, Tad Jones, saw fit to make Notre Dame a solid favorite in his syndicated newspaper column.[15]

Though the visiting team was generally in pretty good shape, at least one Trojan star was nursing nagging problems. Quarterback Gaius Shaver, the so-called "Covina Colt," was limping around with infected toes, though he was expected to play on Saturday.[16]

A national radio audience of ten million, including those listening to Los Angeles radio stations KHJ, KNX, and KECA, were tuning in to learn how Notre Dame would fare without "Old Rock" at the helm.[17] The absence of Rockne and his replacement by Hunk Anderson was the one wild card—but it seemed that even Rockne's death was working to Notre Dame's advantage. The team now played not just for their school, the church, and themselves, but also to honor their martyred head coach.

Rockne's ghost practically haunted the stadium. The game program featured prominent reminders of his legacy. Glowing epithets by renowned sportswriters of the day were printed alongside ads for Auburn automobiles and Luxor Completion Powder. A two-page tribute, complete with a large photo of the late coach surrounded by a thick black border, appeared among the pages of team rosters and season stats. Another page reprinted pictures from Rockne's life and from his funeral, with each image again bordered in black. An artist's rendering of the planned Rockne Memorial Field House accompanied an extensive report on the facility, which was set to cost nearly as much as the stadium had. Individual notices added personal expressions of grief. The handwritten exhortation to "Win this one for Rock" by loyal fan Thorpe Goodrich echoed the supposed deathbed request to "Win one for the Gipper" spoken back in 1928. There were even advertisements for various books on Rockne, including two different biographies. His widow, Bonnie Rockne, had edited one of them.

Rockne consults with his protégé and eventual successor, Heartley "Hunk" Anderson, c. 1930. (Image courtesy of the New York Public Library.)

Even outside the stadium one could hardly avoid Rockne's shadow. While GM was dropping its Oakland line, news buzzed around town about the new Rockne automobile to be built by Studebaker, albeit with production planned for the Detroit plant as soon as it could be made ready.[18] This was the car line of which Knute would have become vice president had his life not been cut short.

Rockne still cast a shadow over Howard Jones too, at least for the present. Still, Rockne was dead, the world was moving on, and things were going to be different. Jones would never beat Rockne again in any case. That was impossible.

Two months after Rockne's death, despite the misgivings of Rev. Michael Mulcaire, the contract between USC and Notre Dame had been quietly extended for another two years, but there was no guarantee the series would be renewed after that.[19] By contrast, the Irish had inked a five-year agreement with Carnegie Tech around the same time.[20] The problem wasn't just that Rockne was gone or that the economy had crashed. The national mood was changing. The future was uncertain.

Rockne's death brought other changes to South Bend. While the true believers venerated him, his relationship with the administration of

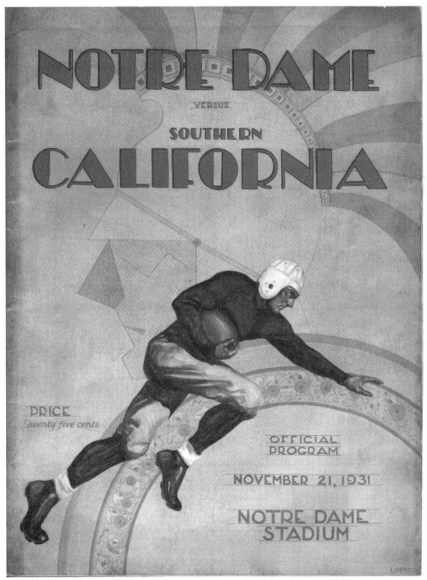

Game program for the 1931 Notre Dame–USC match, the first of their contests held at the new stadium in South Bend instead of at Soldier Field in Chicago. (Author's collection.)

Notre Dame had not always been ideal. Rockne had been a dynamic advocate of college football; his death left no one as influential to counterbalance the forces building against the sport. The financial pressure that a ruined economy placed on running a major football program and criticism from local academics who resented Notre Dame's reputation as a "football factory" distracted from the school's primary mission. Even before Rockne's demise, he had been battling administration efforts to counteract a perceived "overemphasis" on football by more stringent enforcement of scholastic eligibility standards.[21] Relations between Rockne and the administration had at times grown so strained that the coach had actually quit back in 1929 over the expulsion of a talented halfback.[22] His resignation had not been accepted, but the incident demonstrated the school's determination to restore the balance between academics and sports.

When Heartley "Hunk" Anderson was selected to replace Rockne, he was handed a new mandate with a new set of restrictions, including a smaller budget, reduced funding for recruiting, and cuts in the number of scholarships offered. Whereas Rockne had controlled thirty-nine "unilateral" scholarships—slots he could award at his own discretion—Anderson was allowed only twenty. Anderson did retain control of various other grants, most supporting jobs for players (both on and off campus during the scholastic year plus a network to provide summer work), but he lacked Rockne's finesse, and soon this valuable pipeline would wither away.

The bottom line was that times really were changing at Notre Dame. Athletic Director Jesse Harper explained the situation to Anderson at the outset. "I am under orders to tighten the drum," he told Anderson at their very first meeting after Rockne's death.

Mulcaire was even more blunt. "Rockne ran things pretty much the way he wanted," the fiery Irishman warned Anderson. "Now the priests are going to run things around here."

The expenses associated with transporting a large football retinue across the country did not escape the bean counters' scrutiny either. It took money, and lots of it, to pay for a weeklong train trip across the country, with stops along the way to stretch stiff legs and hold practice before the game. Profits for the 1930 season had been about the same as for 1929, but they had come mainly from big dates on the road. The new stadium had driven costs way up, and home attendance was only

42 percent of capacity at the new facility. School administrators worried about what the future might hold in such bad economic times.

The idea of replacing USC with another school closer to home must have been tempting for the likes of Mulcaire. He hadn't wanted to renew the series anyway, and would certainly have been interested in finding out if the team could generate as much cash with fewer expenses by reducing travel costs. Mulcaire certainly didn't favor sending the team off on any new long-distance forays. That reluctance was evident when Rockne's 1925 offer to bring the Irish to Oregon State never materialized, even though Harper was keeping a date open for the match on the 1933 schedule.[23]

The movement at Notre Dame to reduce football's drain on the coffers and return the school to what many saw as its primary purpose of providing a proper Catholic education also entailed undercutting the veneration of the jocks on campus. Reformers wanted to sweep away the wild bacchanalia of big games like the Trojan rivalry, making them as obsolete as the Oakland motorcar and the raccoon coat. If they succeeded, they would end not only the nation's premier intersectional football series but also an entire era of glamor and spectacle.

All of these forces made the current year's Notre Dame-USC game even more important. Howard Jones could not know how often his team might play Notre Dame in the future, but he did have it in his power to beat the Irish today. The last time the Trojans had traveled to play the Irish, the two teams had met in Chicago for the game; Notre Dame's old stadium in South Bend had simply been too small to hold those throngs clamoring to watch the spectacle. Now the Trojans would be playing in the brand-new facility on Notre Dame's campus. While the crowd on hand would be half the size of the throng at Soldier Field, the game would be played on Irish turf this time, on the holy ground of Our Lady rather than in some mercenary venue filled with the bootleggers and floozies of Chicago.

As the game began, it soon became clear that some things hadn't changed much, even without Rockne. Throughout the first half, the Trojans stumbled and bumbled, while Notre Dame played solid football. Perhaps the Lord had been listening to the prayers of those in the Grotto. If so, His will was being done on the football field.

Things didn't improve much for USC until well into the third quarter. With just a few minutes left, the boys from Los Angeles still found themselves on the short end of a 14–0 score.[24] Now was the time to "fight like Trojans," if Howard's team was to live up to the tradition of the ancient warriors whose name had replaced such earlier and more placid nicknames for the team as Methodists, Wesleyans, and Cards.[25] As it turned out, it was at that precise moment, when things looked hopeless for Howard Jones's squad, that the fighting really began in earnest.

As Trojan fullback Jim Musick smashed forward, he rammed the ball toward the left side of the line, crashing into a wave of dark blue that knocked him to the ground. Almost simultaneously, one Irish defender dragged Musick down; a second, Steve Banas, slammed his knee into Musick's face; and a third landed on the helpless Trojan running back as he lay sprawled upon the ground. It had been a "bang bang" play, but that was of little consolation. Emerging from the pile of Irish defenders smothering him, Musick seemed ready for a fight. "They can't win playing that kind of football!" the fullback screamed, not so much at the Notre Dame defense but at anyone who was listening. Picking himself up off the hard turf sixty yards from the Notre Dame end zone, Musick headed toward the Trojan sideline, his nose broken and bleeding.

Of the fifty-five thousand people in the stadium, or indeed of anyone within a hundred miles of South Bend, Musick may have been the only one questioning Notre Dame's chances. Even his teammates might not have agreed with him, at least until that moment. Howard Jones, who always practiced an economy of words that bordered on the miserly, was unlikely to have expressed an opinion. To himself, however, the Headman probably would have acknowledged that the Irish had everything going for them. USC was trailing Notre Dame, the game was winding down, and Jones's chance to beat the Irish—perhaps his last chance—was slipping through his fingers. And to cap it all, one of his best players was going berserk. To the Headman, losing control was the one thing worse than losing a game, and yet he could do nothing except stand on the sideline and watch his team unravel.

That indignity had been forced on Jones all afternoon. Even when they weren't struggling, the Trojans had been busy squandering the few chances they had earned. Earlier in the game, they had nearly reached the goal line only to come up empty, and it was Musick himself who had fumbled the ball at the 1-yard line.

Musick, a twenty-one-year-old senior, had grown up about fifty miles south of Los Angeles in Santa Ana, California. Santa Ana was the

biggest town in Orange County and had beaten out Anaheim as the
county seat when the area split off from Los Angeles County in 1889.
But though Orange County would later be transformed by millions of
transplants, it was predominantly rural in 1931, containing little more
than a few scattered communities separated by acres of citrus and wal-
nut groves. In short, Musick was a small-town boy.

Most of the Trojans hailed from the region around Los Angeles. Fourteen came from the city itself, and others from surrounding communities like Hollywood, Long Beach, and Compton. You could count the
number of those plucked from other states, including Texas and Iowa,
on the fingers of one hand.

Though he was one of those Californians, Musick was more than just
sunshine on the football field. He packed 195 pounds of muscle on his
five-foot-ten-inch frame, and *El Rodeo,* USC's yearbook, called him "one
of the most terrific line plungers seen on the coast in a long time."[26] This
was his last crack at beating Notre Dame, something the Trojans had
managed only once in five tries.

The morning of the game, Musick might have joked that the weather
had improved to facilitate his first and last foray into the normally colder
climes of northern Indiana. With the rain pouring down the day before,
everyone had anticipated lousy weather for the game, but the rain had
stopped and a tarp covering the field had sheltered the grass from the
storm's worst effects. Now the day was warm and clear and perfect for
football. Only the Irish performance had been as cold and disagreeable
as expected. Musick knew that injuries were a part of football. Moreover,
in the days of leather helmets without protective face guards, it wasn't
unusual for a player's face to take a lot of punishment. In fact, Trojan
players a few years later would call one of their more banged-up teammates "Hamburger Puss" for that very reason.[27] Still, something about
this last play had infuriated Musick, causing him to pour his frustration
into his response. And now he was out, simmering on the sidelines.

Yet the play seemed to affect Muscik's teammates as much as it had
the wounded fullback. As Musick staggered off the field, something
changed, something unseen that no one ever seemed able to explain.
Like all the shifting fortunes of sports, all the maddening vagaries of
wins and losses, only the outcome remains undisputed.

Howard Jones, as always focused on practicalities, was probably too
busy to notice the subtle shift in momentum. He had to decide how to

deal with the loss of his starting fullback. The rule book would not let Musick return until the fourth quarter, even if his injuries were patched up enough to make it possible. Once a substitute took his place, a player could not be returned to the field in the same period, a restriction that soon would cause Hunk Anderson much grief. Jones scanned the reserves drawn up along the sideline, considered his options, and made his choice. "Mohler!" he barked. "Get in there!"

Orv Mohler, a 163-pound backup quarterback, strapped on his helmet and ran onto the field. He would replace not Musick but the 180-pound Gaius Shaver, who, despite his infected toes, had started the game at quarterback. Now Shaver shifted to Musick's fullback slot. It was a move that would be unheard of in the modern game, but in 1931 did not even raise an eyebrow.

Before World War II, football offenses were designed very differently than they are today. The standard offensive set was something known as the "single wing." In that scheme, it was not just the quarterback who handled the ball; it might be hiked to anyone in the backfield, who then might hand it off, run with it, or throw it, depending on the play. All backs lined up well behind the line to receive a long snap, as they do in the "Shotgun" and "Wildcat" formations developed in more recent times.

Offensive ideas began changing in the 1940s, as coaches struggled to compensate for the departure of so many young men to war. With the best athletes often in combat instead of college and coaches seeking to make the best use of players with more limited talent, players began to specialize. Coaches revised the T formation, drew the quarterback up close under center to receive the snap, and limited passing to the quarterback position. Depending on the play, the other backs were restricted to simple blocking or to grabbing the handoff and running with the ball, or to catching a pass.

In 1931, though, those changes were still a decade away. Between the wars, coaches across the country developed the single wing to suit their individual outlooks on the game. For the most part, those offensive systems would be named after their inventors. The one for which the nickname *single wing* was originally coined was the *Pop Warner system*, and it spawned a legion of imitators. After Warner moved on to Stanford, his scheme was relabeled *double wing*.

Notre Dame employed something called the *Rockne box,* which differed from Warner's system in that the line was balanced, meaning equal numbers of players lined up on both sides of the center, both ends were split out from the line, and the wingback, who was positioned outside the end in the single wing, was brought in tight. The philosophical approach was different too. Deception was the key rather than power as in Warner's offense.

A big part of that deception was the *Rockne shift,* in which the four backs lined up initially in a full-house T formation, where the fullback stood behind the quarterback with the halfbacks to each side. At the last second, they shifted into a quadrangle alignment on one side or the other of the backfield. This took place right before the snap, leaving little time for the defense to react. When opposing coaches cried foul, the NCAA instituted new rules requiring the offense to set in place for a full second before the snap, a restriction existing to this day. In 1931, even after the rules had changed, the shift pioneered by Rockne and inherited by Anderson was still a potent method of keeping defenses off-balance.

Howard Jones's system was closer to Pop Warner's than Notre Dame's in that Jones stressed power over misdirection, but where Warner used a fixed seven-man line, Jones preferred to shift his forward wall before the snap. As he himself put it, "My own system differs from both those formations in that all my linemen shift—except the center." Jones's unusual system of starting with a formation two rows deep of four men each and then moving the linemen to their actual positions just before the snap, came to be called the *birdcage shift.*[28] That shift would often move the players into an unbalanced alignment, with two tackles positioned on one side of the ball.

With a different quarterback, Mohler, replacing Shaver in the backfield, the Trojans would present a new look, but it was the linemen Jones was counting on to sweep away the hitherto unyielding Irish defense. That defense, a force so powerful that it had allowed only twelve points all year, was stocked with Anderson's own muscular kids, many the kind of hard-nosed young men from blue-collar families that Notre Dame always seemed to have in abundance. Three of them were All-Americans: left halfback Marchie Schwartz, center Tom Yarr, and tackle Joe Kurth. Schwartz and Yarr had been among Rockne's pallbearers, and Yarr was also one of the team captains. This was a tough group that would battle for every inch and end each play with the kind of violent tackling that had broken Musick's nose.

Notre Dame had suited up eighty-one players, while the visitors were limited to forty-five. The Irish drew from a much wider base as well, with young men from eighteen different states. Schwartz was from Mississippi, Yarr from the state of Washington, and Kurth was one of four kids on the team from California. Only eight of the Irish players were from the team's home state of Indiana.

The three All-Americans were holdovers from the previous season, and Anderson had them playing at the same high clip, while working in new players who seemed to fit right in. Only the 0–0 score in an early-season game against Northwestern, played on a muddy field, had interrupted the Irish string of lopsided victories, which included a 63–0 thrashing of Drake one week later.

This was the foe the Trojans faced as Mohler joined his teammates in the huddle. The rules of the day prohibited Mohler from bringing a play with him, as he was not allowed to speak for one snap of the ball. Coach Jones was also barred from signaling plays from the sidelines. Play selection was up to those on the field, so two weeks of preparation were about to be tested. If he had done his job well, the Trojans would be ready.

The vanguard of the Trojan attack would be the inner core of the line, consisting of center Stan Williamson, a Scottish-Irish lad and one of the team captains; and guards Johnny Baker, an All-American, and Lawrence Stevens, a sophomore later to become another All-American. Baker was the kid who had almost quit back in Arizona, after being in Howard Jones's doghouse for much of the season. On the flanks were tackles Ernie Smith and Raymond Brown, both tipping the scales at more than two hundred pounds.

With the line leading the way, the dull spear of the Trojan offense was suddenly pounded into a sharp edge, and Howard's boys finally began to forge an effective attack. If the line was the anvil, the backfield was the hammer, and it was Shaver and Mohler who created the sparks. As they alternated carries, with end Ray Sparling providing a change of pace by running reverse plays from his left end position, the Trojans drove deep into Notre Dame territory. The Irish resolve stiffened, and USC found itself faced with fourth down and six at the Irish 10-yard line.

Mohler called a new play that Jones had installed during the week between games. Tom Mallory, saddled with a nagging sore throat, took the snap from center and faded back to pass, but he rushed the throw and fumbled the ball. Notre Dame pounced on the loose pigskin on their 19-yard line and again the scoring threat fizzled.

The Trojans shuffled back to defense, frustrated and running out of time. If Notre Dame continued to move the ball as they had for most of the game, it would be over for the visitors. Yet the Trojans, whether inspired by Musick's misfortune or some other unknown force, rose to the occasion again, stopping the Irish cold. Schwartz was forced to punt the ball to Mohler, and his runback left USC in good position at the Notre Dame 49-yard line. Helped by an interference call, the Trojans marched down the field until time ran out in the third quarter.

As the fourth period began, Notre Dame still enjoyed their two-touchdown lead. There were just fifteen minutes left to play, a span thought insufficient to overcome such a lead—at least in the days before "Slinging" Sammy Baugh revolutionized the passing game five years later at Texas Christian University.[29]

It would take a miracle now for Jones to raise his team from the dead, but at least he could begin the task with something less than the supernatural. Again facing a fourth-down play, the Trojans needed just one foot of turf for a first down this time, although the ball was wedged up against the sideline, having been placed—per the rules of the time—at the very spot the ball carrier last went down. In this case, the play would be run only one yard from the edge of the field, a position in which USC had found itself more than once that afternoon.[30] With so little room for his linemen along the sideline, Jones's unbalanced alignment had proved to be a real advantage.

Mohler leaned into the huddle. Ten pairs of eyes stared back at him, each revealing a mix of anxiety and determination. No one spoke. They all knew they had to succeed in the play if they were to retain any hope of victory. Thinking of what the Headman would want him to run, Mohler stared back, then coolly called his own number. It was to be power, straight up the middle.

The Trojans snaked a serpentine route from the huddle to the line, a ploy Jones used to disguise the intent of the offense for as long as possible. The home crowd recognized that this was the first time since early in the game that their foe posed a real threat. All fifty thousand rose as one to fortify their own team's stiffening resolve, with a mix of Hail Marys and vigorous genuflection no doubt thrown in for good measure.

There were no signals called in Jones's offense, as plays unfolded strictly on the basis of timing.[31] When the count clicked off in his head, the center snapped the ball back and Mohler snagged it with both hands. He charged toward the middle of the line. Both sides converged, like a rugby scrum. A pile of cardinal and blue heaped together, one side pushing forward with every ounce of strength, the other resisting with all its might. As the whistle blew, the officials raced in to sort out the pile stacked on a spot close to where the play had begun.[32]

Everything hinged on the placement of the ball. Both coaches looked on anxiously, but for Howard Jones the anxiety was intense. Four years earlier, the referee had misjudged a safety and called it a touchback, turning a narrow victory into a crushing defeat. Even the official in question, John Schommer, admitted making an error after viewing the game film. So Jones's faith in officials was shaky at best.

As the players were extricated from the pile, the officials indicated the point of forward progress, but decided that there was not sufficient margin one way or another to make the call by eye. They would have to measure. As they brought in the stick and placed it down, the crowd that had roared so loudly first fell silent and then groaned, save for a small contingent of Trojan fans who had made the trek east. The tip of the ball peeked just past the marker. Mohler had made the first down by two inches.[33]

Given new life, the Trojans wasted no time in blasting forward again. Mohler handed off to Sparling, who sprinted from his left end position to take the ball to the 1-yard line. Next it was Shaver. The fullback plowed up the middle to fall just ten inches short of the goal. On the third try, they went back to Shaver, who beat the Irish defense to the corner to break the scoring drought.

Placekicking was Johnny Baker's other job, so it fell to him to line up with Mohler for the point after try. Orv accepted the snap cleanly, placed it down, and the kick left Baker's foot straight and true, but Irish lineman Joe Kurth reached up and deflected the ball. It was just enough to send it careening harmlessly off target. The score remained 14–6.

After the kickoff, the Trojans held again, forcing Notre Dame to punt the ball back. The once-stout Irish defense now seemed incapable of stopping the Trojan onslaught, as their ground attack moved the ball steadily down the field. Then a pass to Gordon Clark was broken up at the 29-yard line, but as the pigskin hit the turf, so did penalty flags. The collision was ruled pass interference. To the dismay of the hometown fans, the ball was spotted at the point of the foul, and the Trojans set up shop deep in Notre Dame territory.

Mohler made a great run on the next play, sidestepping Irish defenders before being brought down at the 10-yard line. On the last play of the drive, Mohler deftly pitched the ball to Shaver, who raced toward the end stripe and squeezed in as tacklers smashed him at the goal line. Baker's kick was good this time and the Trojans trailed 14–13.

That single point left Jones with that sickening feeling some call déjà vu. Three times in games against the Irish, Howard Jones had gazed at the final scoreboard to see this exact margin, and each time faulty placekicking had been to blame. At that moment, when divine intervention seemed the only way to avoid a frustrating repeat of past near-misses, Jones must have wondered if more regular church attendance would have been a wise insurance policy, even for a man with doubts about the Almighty.

More probably, though, a man of Jones's character and temperament would have held that the Lord helps those who help themselves, and the Trojans had eight minutes left to do just that. They got off to a good start when Baker's kickoff sailed into the end zone, and Notre Dame was forced to start at their own 20-yard line. The Irish stalled yet again, and Mohler returned Schwartz's punt to the Notre Dame 39-yard line, but a few plays later, another good chance slipped through Trojan fingers. A bad snap was fumbled and Notre Dame end Ed Kosky covered it at the 40-yard line. There were now only five minutes left to play.[34]

The Irish rumbled to midfield, and it looked for all the world as if the Trojan resurrection was doomed. Then Notre Dame's Joe Sheeketski at right halfback and Marchie Schwartz at left netted but four yards on two running plays; a crucial third and six stood between running down the clock or turning the ball back to USC.

As the Irish broke the huddle, a roar began to shake the stadium. This was the time for Notre Dame to smite the Philistines once and for all. The backfield lined up in the familiar formation, with Sheeketski, George Melinkovich, and Schwartz behind quarterback Charles Jaskwhich. The four shifted, forming their box, held an instant till the ball was snapped, and then sprang into action. Schwartz took the ball and heaved it down the field toward the waiting Jaskwhich, but Erny Pinckert was able to step between the Irishman and the ball, almost picking it off as he broke up the play.[35]

This time it was the Irish who had missed their chance. Jones responded by pulling both tackles and returning starters Bob Erskine and Bob Hall to the game. Mohler fielded the punt from Schwartz a few moments later, but he managed to return the kick no farther than his own 27-yard line. The Trojans now had just four minutes left, with seventy-three yards of dirt and grass between them and victory.[36] The prospects for success seemed daunting—but just a few minutes earlier, no impartial observer would have given them any chance at all.

Howard Jones looked out on the field and considered the task ahead of his team. There was still a long way to go to avenge last year's debacle, a revenge that Rockne's death had spoiled even if Jones did score a victory in this game. Perhaps Jones thought of the road he'd gone down to get to this place, at this point in time. He may have revisited key moments in the earlier hours of the game or in the weeklong train trip that had preceded it. He may have asked himself if the two weeks of planning and preparation before that had been enough or reflected on the distraction to his team caused by the suspicion that Bill Hawkins had been spying. He may have even recalled all the big games of years past, clear back to his own playing days at Yale.

It had been eighteen years since Jones's alma mater had dropped Army from its schedule, spawning the series of events leading to this moment, from Notre Dame's shocking upset of the Cadets in 1913 to the battle between Rockne and Jones in Iowa in 1921, Gwynn Wilson's trip to Nebraska in 1925, and the struggles between the Irish and the Trojans since 1926. With his death, Knute Rockne had achieved immortality. Howard Jones might still have been more mortal man than legend, but he was determined to finish the journey he'd always shared with his rival. Jones was neither a particularly religious man nor one prone to dwell on the past, so no doubt any retrospection was brief. Even if he had thought about his old friend Rockne or the road they had traveled so far together, he would have had no way of knowing that the journey down that road would go on even after the day's final gun had sounded.

The Final Quarter

Funny thing, that football.

—Hunk Anderson, 1931

This was the last chance. Howard Jones knew it. His players knew it. The opposition knew it. The whole stadium knew it. If the Trojans were going to do the improbable and achieve the impossible, it was going to be right now or not at all.

Hunk Anderson had hoped it would never get this close. The game was seemingly out of reach at the outset of the final quarter. Then, as the Trojan line began wearing down his starters, Anderson was forced to send in subs to stem the tide.[1] Howard Jones countered by sending Bob Erskine, Bob Hall, and Ford Palmer back in to bolster his offense for the final push. Neither coach's moves yielded results. Notre Dame had given up fourteen points, and the Trojans' first two plays after Jones's substitutions had netted just one yard between them.

Now the Trojans faced a crucial third-down play. Shaver dropped back, wound up, and flung the ball into Notre Dame's side of the field. The pigskin zoomed out ahead of a streaking Ray Sparling, who had made it just a step past Notre Dame's Charles Jaskwhich. Sparling leapt forward and dove to the 40-yard line to gather in the pass, as Jaskwhich rode his back to the hard Irish turf. With that one tremendous effort the Trojans had lopped twenty-three yards off the task at hand and earned themselves another first down.

Despite that big play, the Irish were ready on the next one. Orv Mohler pitched the ball to Shaver coming around the left end, and he was cornered by a wall of blue ten yards behind the line of scrimmage. Quickly reversing his field, he raced the opposite way, managing to turn catastrophe into a modest one-yard gain.[2] Shaver's dancing had staved off disaster, but the clock was ticking and there was still plenty of work to do.

On the next play, Hall raced out from his spot on the line to rumble twenty yards down the field, looking to catch the Irish off guard on a tackle-eligible play. Joe Sheeketski was assigned the coverage, but Hall blew past him. Sheeketski scrambled madly to catch up as Hall passed the Notre Dame 20-yard line. Shaver's pass was on target, but high. Both receiver and defenseman leaped into the air to stab desperately at the ball. Hall was the taller man, and came down with it at the Notre Dame 18-yard line.[3]

The Trojans netted no gain on the next snap, but Notre Dame was offside. Sparling then carried the ball three yards on a reverse play right to the middle of the field. Mohler called one more play, a pass out to the right that slipped just out of Gordon Clark's hands.

It was third and seven at the Notre Dame 10-yard line. There was just a little over one minute left to play. Jones sent dropkick ace Homer Griffith onto the field, but center Stan Williamson, the Trojan captain, waved him off. Howard's boys were going to try a placekick.[4] Despite all the kicking misadventures against the Irish over the years, the Trojans were gambling the game on Orv Mohler's hold and Johnny Baker's toe.

The tension in the stadium spread well beyond South Bend, gripping fans wherever they were as they listened to the frantic call of the radio play-by-play. In Los Angeles, business came to a halt as store clerks jostled with customers in downtown shops to push closer to radios broadcasting the game. The crowd gathered across town at Westlake Park, where loudspeakers had been set up and stands erected to accommodate four thousand fans, breathlessly awaiting the outcome of the attempt.[5] At Jones's Toluca Lake home, his wife Jane and daughter Carolyn sat by the radio, urging the Trojans to finish the job.[6]

All across the country and even beyond its borders, fans had gathered to hear the game. In Nebraska, they were listening to station KOIL.[7] In Butte, Montana, the Oechsil Furniture and Ellis Paint store were the local sponsors of the network broadcast.[8] In Brooklyn, fans could choose between two stations—WABC and WJZ.[9] In Ottawa, Canada, listeners turned to CKAC AM.[10]

Johnny Baker, the hero of the 1931 game who almost quit the Trojan team on the way to South Bend. (Culver Pictures.)

Even Will Rogers, while en route to Japan aboard the Canadian ocean liner *Empress of Russia,* noted the particular interest that a group of Chinese college students were showing in the game. They were unusually agitated because they had put money down on Notre Dame.[11]

Inside the stadium, all eyes were fixed on Baker as he readied himself for the task at hand. He unbuckled the chinstrap of his helmet, tossed the headgear aside, and sought to clear his mind and concentrate solely on the spot where the ball would be placed. He had nearly quit the team back in Arizona and already had suffered one blocked kick in this game, but now he had to set all that aside. Everything hinged not on what had already transpired but on what happened next.

The entire stadium crowd stood as one, gazing toward the end of the field where the outcome of the game would be determined. They watched as Mohler checked with Baker, turned to the center, and gave the signal that all was ready. The ball flew back. Mohler took it, placed it down, and spun the laces toward the goal as Baker stepped forward. His leg swung forward into the ball, the tip of his bulky black high-top shoe striking the ball dead on in the old, straight-on style of the day. All eyes followed the path of the ball as it flew toward the goal posts. Flopping end over end it fell cleanly through the uprights. Baker had done it. The Trojans had done it. The scoreboard read "Notre Dame 14, Visitors 16."

There was just one minute left to play. The stunned crowd stood silent in disbelief, save for one small sliver of the stands where the Trojan fans went berserk. The visitors' sideline was likewise a scene of riotous celebration. Coaches and players alike danced joyously. Helmets, hats, jackets—virtually anything not nailed down—were flung skyward.[12] Even staid Howard Jones went wild. He leaped up, knocked the man sitting next to him off the bench, and dashed about, hugging anyone within arm's reach. Racing onto the field, he kissed the first player he ran into, center Stan Williamson.[13] It was as if he had released an entire lifetime of restraint and decorum all at once and thrown it all out the window.

In the press box, veteran newsmen Braven Dyer of the *Los Angeles Times* and Maxwell Stiles of the *Los Angeles Examiner* had risen "as if on a given signal" as the ball tumbled over the crossbar. They quickly shook hands, and then sat down again to continue pounding on their typewriters.[14] They had deadlines to meet, and the story was not yet finished—the game wasn't over.

Notre Dame returned the kick to the 35-yard line. The first play from scrimmage lost ten yards, and then one final, last-gasp heave was intercepted by right end Gordon Clark. Now the newshounds could file their stories. The final gun had sounded.

As Clark hit the turf, the celebration began. Swarming off the field in jubilation, the Trojans poured into their locker room in a steady stream of near mayhem. They were a dirty, bruised, and tired lot, with more than a few wiping tears from their eyes. The first one to burst through the door was halfback Erny Pinckert, immediately followed by Clark who had smuggled in the game ball under his muddy red jersey. "I knew that they couldn't stop us!" shouted Pinckert. As he slapped fellow halfback Tom Mallory on the shoulder, Pinckert let off pressure built up over two frustrating seasons. "I've waited for two years for this day," he bellowed, "but what revenge!"

Johnny Baker was mobbed, pulled in one direction and then another by his crazed teammates. "It felt great" was all he could blurt out in the melee.

Howard Jones entered the fray exhibiting the effects of the uncontrolled celebration. He was red-faced and sweaty, with a rare grin spreading widely across his craggy face. His hair was wet and disheveled, and both his hat and overcoat were rumpled and all but falling off him. Fighting off the overzealous advance of a joyous alumnus, who lunged forward to give him a bear hug, the Headman set about congratulating his players, one by one, with a warm handshake for each. As usual, the Headman struggled to express his inner feelings, but with Jones, actions always spoke louder than words.

"Honestly, I'm too flabbergasted to say anything," Jones said to reporters, "but I'll tell you that it was the greatest team in the world. I knew I had a ball club," he went on, "but the thing that pleases me was that we gave 'em fourteen points and then came back and licked 'em!"[15]

Graduate manager Arnold Eddy bounded in, wearing a derby—what they called an iron hat in those days. Aubrey Devine snatched it off Eddy's head and, reenacting the game-winning kick, booted the hat high across the locker room.[16] "How's that for a kick, Baker, old boy?" Devine shouted as the headwear took flight.[17] Erny Pinckert grabbed it in midflight and dashed into the showers. Still wearing the derby, and only that, he began to wash off the grime and sweat that sixty minutes of football had caked on his bruised and battered body.[18]

Despite the wild jubilation erupting around him, Howard Jones's thoughts quickly moved on from the chaos. Turning to Jack Rissman, the Chicago clothier who sponsored the trophy for the Dickenson System college football championship, Jones quietly told him, "You're just the man I want to see." For once, something other than football was on the Headman's mind. "Can you direct me to the cemetery where Knute Rockne is buried?"[19]

A short time later, the fleet of Buick automobiles shuttling the team to the train station stopped at Highland Cemetery.[20] As the last light of day was fading into the darkness of Saturday night, they reached the burial grounds on Portage Road, just a bit west of the Notre Dame campus on the other side of the St. Joseph River. The caravan passed through the entrance, veered right as the path split in three directions, then swung left at the first crossroad. The vehicles parked, the entourage emerged from the cars, and Jones led them to a spot among the rows of markers running throughout the expansive grounds. This was the final resting place of Knute Rockne, and Jones had come to pay his last respects: one coach who had just made history honoring another who had become a part of it.

Acting as a makeshift pastor, Jones "conducted impromptu services."[21] For once he found the right words, and "spoke feelingly" about Rockne before laying a wreath on the headstone. He then asked for a moment of silence, after which the group filed quietly back to the waiting cars for the ride to catch the train to Chicago.[22]

Once back in their headquarters at the Stevens Hotel in Chicago, the victorious Trojans and their entourage resumed their celebrations. Even Howard Jones, usually the strict taskmaster, relaxed normal training rules and allowed his charges to indulge, despite the fact that two games remained on the Trojan schedule. After dinner, the team went as a group to the theater, and then returned to their hotel for a midnight supper. A steady stream of well-wishers stopped by, heaping further praise on the conquering heroes as the team savored its last night in the Windy City.[23]

The next morning, the Headman again gave his players some latitude and allowed them to sleep well past their usual wake-up time. After breakfast, manager Eddy Arnold ventured out to Jack Rissman's haberdashery on Michigan Avenue to seek a replacement for his soaked and battered derby.[24] Howard Jones did Eddy one better: he presented derbies to the entire team, who wore them as symbolic crowns in honor of their triumph.

By 11:00 P.M. that Sunday night, the Trojan team was aboard the six-car special section of Santa Fe's Pacific Fast Mail, bound for California.[25] The journey was a three-and-a-half-day victory march across the West. At every whistle-stop and small-town coaling station, crowds would gather to salute the team. Schools let out early, and the kids would call out the names of Shaver, Mohler, and Baker.

Even though Gordon Clark had sealed the game with his last-second interception, he had to resort to more surreptitious means to garner attention. Since blocking backs seldom share the glory of their scoring mates, other means were necessary. At one stop, he met the young fans at the observation platform, tossed each youngster a dime, and instructed them to head forward to the team car and call out his name. His teammates, suspecting trickery, accused Clark of having relatives in the town.[26]

Telegrams of congratulations flew back and forth between adoring fans and the Trojan entourage. Councilman E. Snapper Ingram, who was traveling with the team, cabled ahead to Los Angeles suggesting that a civic reception be held to greet the team's return. Fellow councilman Howard W. Davis relayed the suggestion to City Hall, and a resolution supporting a welcome "worthy of the occasion" passed with a unanimous vote.[27]

Shortly after 5:00 A.M. on Wednesday, November 25, 1931, Santa Fe train number 7 steamed into San Bernardino. The formal welcome planned by the local Trojan Club had to be abandoned after word came that the arrival time had been changed from 6:30. Under the supervision of Santa Fe's agent, F. T. Rice, a small group of railcars was split off from the train to carry the team on into Los Angeles. An hour later, the Trojan special steamed out of town, heading for Los Angeles.[28]

A brief stop in Pasadena allowed those who had stayed behind to join the cortege and savor the triumphant return to the heart of Los Angeles. Among them were the parents of Erny Pinckert, and Howard Jones's wife and young daughter Carolyn. Mrs. Jones bestowed a shower of kisses upon her husband as they met again after a week's separation. Little Carolyn was just as happy to see her famous father again, but was distracted by the new experience of riding on a train.[29]

Almost exactly at 8:00 A.M., the train approached Arcade Station, where the journey had begun eight days before. This time, the ten thousand screaming fans awaiting the Trojans were there to savor a job well done.[30] Someone shouted, "Here they come!" and all eyes turned northward, toward the tracks leading into the station. Bedlam ensued. As the fuming iron horse appeared, dragging behind it the six cars bearing the victorious warriors of Ilium, the Trojan band struck up "Fight On" to serenade the champions. Screaming fans swamped the rails, which were cleared only with difficulty as the engine nosed into the station.[31] The players pressed their faces to the railcar windows, watching with amazement the spectacle unfolding before their eyes. The fans beamed back in adulation, as the depot around them echoed with their thunderous praise.

Helen Johnson, vice president of the USC student body, began the formal greetings even before the team had detrained. Then Asa C. Call, president of the alumni association, added his voice to the acclaim being heaped upon the team.[32]

With Howard Jones and his assistants in the lead, the USC team stepped down onto the loading platform and waded into the sea of humanity lapping against the Trojan special. Just as it did for Moses leading the Israelites out of Egypt, the sea parted and let them through.

Mothers, wives, and girlfriends rushed forward to embrace their men. Erny Pinckert towered over his young bride, Beatrice, who reached her arms around him to plant a passionate kiss upon her All-American husband. "Oh Erny!" she cried, "It was wonderful! The team was wonderful! You were wonderful! Everyone was wonderful!" As she released her grasp, the evidence of her affection was visible to all. A red smear of lipstick stained her handsome husband's face. Pinckert's mother watched from the relative calm of the observation car. "You know," she confessed, "I never wanted Erny to play football. I was afraid he'd get hurt."

Teammate Orv Mohler was mobbed by Bernadine Olsen, an attractive coed wearing his fraternity pin, and half a dozen of his aunts and cousins. Swamping the Trojan quarterback, they fought for the chance to land the next kiss. "Whew, I'd rather buck a line," he muttered once the onslaught was over.[33]

The path outside led though a huge floral welcome arch created by Young's Market Floral Shop and paid for by businesses around the city, including clothiers Silverwoods; Harris and Frank; and Mullen and Bluett; Desmonds, a department store; the Tufts Lyon Company, which sold sporting goods; and Coca-Cola. It was through this corridor that the team was forced to run the gauntlet. No Trojan player was spared the feminine onslaught, and by the time they escaped, they were a battered and disheveled bunch, with tousled hair, ties askew, and red but smiling faces, many bearing the same crimson badge of honor as Orv Mohler. As the coeds forming the gauntlet compared notes on their efforts, one sighed, "I kissed thirty of 'em!" Still, it was the one that got away that was on her mind: "I missed Stan Williamson, darn it!"[34]

Eventually, the entourage emerged from the depot and reached the line of automobiles waiting to carry them downtown. Before they left, however, the team performed a little ceremony of their own. By unanimous vote, the squad had decided to give the game ball to the mother

Facing page: The USC team being mobbed at the train station upon its return home from South Bend, 1931. (Image courtesy of Historic Images.)

of Johnny Baker, the hero who had kicked it through the goalposts to earn the victory. The pigskin was presented to her upon their arrival at the station, and with that pleasant task accomplished, the triumphal celebration could go forward.[35]

A police escort led the team through the streets of Los Angeles.[36] The vehicles, decorated in USC colors, formed a phalanx that was both colorful and boisterous.[37] The strains of "Fight On" echoed through the steel and cement canyons of the city. So too did other songs, such as "The Cardinal and Gold" rising from the buses transporting the Trojan band.[38] The Goodyear blimp leisurely drifted overhead, flying the Trojan war flag as it followed the Trojans home.[39]

The crowd waiting for the team to arrive at City Hall dwarfed the one that had met them at the Arcade Station. Fans occupied every nook and cranny of the grounds and the surrounding sidewalks, and the throng overflowed to cover the pavement of Spring Street as far as the eye could see.[40] Still more fans leaned from the windows of nearby office buildings to watch the proceedings unfolding below.[41] In all, more than fifty thousand Angelenos had flocked to the seat of city government to hear the praises of the Trojan warriors.

A combined police and fire department band stood on the hall's granite steps, playing tunes for the crowd as they waited for the team's arrival.[42] Rows of police guards flanked the path they had cleared for the approaching entourage, which now included the official welcoming committee of one hundred civic leaders.[43] Beyond the police officers swarmed the mob of well-wishers, drawn from every corner of the city.[44] Looming over everyone was the city hall's main tower, which rose thirty stories above those gathered at street level, like a giant obelisk marking the epicenter of the tremendous celebration that was about to begin.

The noise of the crowd grew louder as the string of vehicles drew nearer, turning into cheers as the procession turned onto Spring Street and came into view. Slowly negotiating the milling crowd, the cars paused to drop off the players, coaches, and assorted dignitaries. Again the Trojans had to force their way through their fans, this time to climb the steps and wait for the city fathers following them.

Once the long line of politicians, school administrators, and businessmen had filed up the steps, the oration could begin. Helen Johnson offered Captain Stan Williamson an arrangement of chrysanthemums in the shape of a football, as "a token of appreciation to the team from the students of the university."[45]

Mayor John Porter was the first to formally address the crowd, in a speech also transmitted to radio audiences throughout Southern California listening to local stations KHJ[46] and KMTR.[47]

"I am glad to welcome home the fighting football team of the University of Southern California," he began—but as a huge ovation swallowed his voice and drowned out his words, he had to stay his remarks until the applause had run its course.

"This team did a magnificent thing in winning its victory over the great Notre Dame football squad," he continued. "All of you who listened in on the last quarter of that game probably lost either your heads or your voices." Roaring laughter followed when he added, "I know I lost both!"

The mayor then introduced USC President von KleinSmid. "There is no more depression in Southern California!" the Trojan chief exclaimed. He added further praise in a more serious tone, lauding the team's achievements both on and off the field, while addressing their character as young men. "They are good sports in defeat as well as in victory," he said. "We welcome them here today because they are good fellows.

"Incidentally, these football players have had the best coaching in the United States," von KleinSmid boasted, and went on to acknowledge the leadership of Howard Jones in molding the team and the entire football culture of his university.[48]

Mayor Porter then introduced the Catholic bishop of the Diocese of Los Angeles and San Diego, the Rt. Rev. John J. Cantwell. "We are welcoming the first and the greatest football team in the United States today," Cantwell stated. Apparently an Angeleno first and a Catholic second, at least for this one day, the prelate overlooked the fact that the Trojans had bested the pride of the Roman Church. Although the "brogue that hinted at old Erin" added a decidedly Irish flavor to his address, there was not the slightest trace of bitterness in his voice.[49] "These Trojans have met their Greeks and know no defeat," he declared. "They fought an honorable and noble game."

Finally, it was time for Howard Jones to speak. Words did not always roll easily off the Headman's tongue, but when he spoke from the heart, substance usually superseded style.

"When we left here," he said, "I told the crowd at the station that our team was going to South Bend, and that the boys would play football. They went to South Bend," he said, "and defeated the greatest football team in the United States!" Relishing the accomplishment, he added, "that is, the greatest up to that time." The roar of approval again echoed down Spring Street and blared from radio speakers all across the Southland.

"All kinds of credit should go to Baker," he said of the young man he had almost driven from the team before the game. "But it was not Baker alone." It was not in Jones's nature to highlight one man's glory alone. He was a team man all the way. "Eleven men put the ball in a position so that Baker could kick the goal," he reminded his audience.

Everyone loves a winner, and as the Headman turned the dais back to Mayor Porter, he was not just a winner but also a champion. He was on top of his world, or at least his city and his profession. With Rockne gone and Pop Warner subjugated, Jones could easily claim the mantle of the top coach in the game. No one would enjoy the same success in Los Angeles until well past Jones's era, when John McKay returned the Trojans to the top of the heap in 1962.

Politicians, educators, priests, and the coach had all had their say. Now it was time to hear from those who had played the game. Captain Stan Williamson spoke for the players. His words were few and to the point. "I want to thank the city for the wonderful reception. The football team appreciates it."

With the speeches over, Mayor Porter presented gifts to Coach Jones and the team. Everyone received a small table lamp, with the base shaped like a football and the shade in the form of a football helmet in cardinal and gold.

At last it was time for the formal parade to begin. Again the coaches and players pushed through the crowd, toward the twenty Packard automobiles waiting to carry them to the campus.

A string of vehicles had lined up to form the caravan. First were the buses carrying Harold Roberts and his Trojan band. Next came the figure of a Trojan warrior in an open-top automobile, a "stalwart of the student body, clad in glittering cardboard armor." Behind them rode Howard Jones, then his coaches, and finally the players. In addition, an estimated five thousand people trailed the team in cars traveling three abreast as they moved slowly through the city streets.[50]

As this massive parade snaked through downtown Los Angeles to celebrate USC's 1931 victory over Notre Dame, it drew a third of the city's residents out of their homes and businesses to salute their home team. (Image from author's collection.)

Their route took them up Spring Street to Eighth, back down Broadway to Fifth, and then over to Hill for the final leg to campus.[51] Everywhere, the air was thick with showers of confetti fluttering down from open office windows. Streamers falling on the roadway caught on lampposts and storefront canopies, draping like giant spider webs over the buildings of Los Angeles.[52] A chaotic, discordant mix of band music, the blaring horns of cars and buses, and cheering of the crowds thundered through the town as if the San Andreas Fault had opened and meant to swallow the entire city. Yet it was neither nature's rage nor God's wrath that engendered such pandemonium, but overwhelming joy and celebration.

It was a scene never before witnessed in Los Angeles, except, perhaps, for the welcome given Charles Lindbergh after his historic flight across the Atlantic.[53] So great was the triumphal parade for the Trojans that the next day, Bob Ray of the *Los Angeles Times* concluded, "No conquering army of ancient Rome ever received a more tumultuous welcome."[54]

Riding through this historic salute, with the thundering cheers ringing in his ears, and confetti dancing in the air about him, Howard Jones must have felt deeply uncomfortable. The unrestrained emotions whirling around him were totally foreign to his nature. He was in a business that greeted success with fervent public eruptions, but in working for that success, whether on the modest field back at Exeter or before unimaginable crowds in giant arenas like Soldier Field, Jones thought only of winning or losing. It had always been his way to temper both the elation of victory and the bitter disappointment of defeat. Now there was nothing to hold back. He was part of something bigger, something not just for one team or even one school, but for a whole city to celebrate.

Football had grown that far beyond the confines of the gridiron. America had grown too, not so much expanding as coalescing, in a process that brought together the many regions within its borders into a single entity. Howard Jones had been a part of that process in the United States, as his game, football, drew people together with the help of innovations of the age. Born into a world more like that of Twain's Huckleberry Finn—rural, local, and parochial—he now lived in the world of Henry Ford and Cecil B. DeMille, in which technology was spanning regional boundaries to unite the nation. Technology had also replaced the poet as the chronicler of fame. The wonders of Marconi had carried the exploits of his team almost instantly across the nation, while images of the recent game, created courtesy of the genius of the brothers Lumière, would soon be seen by thousands more in movie houses.

Howard Jones might not have been thinking of all the changes he had seen, or even those he had been a part of. But he must surely have thought of the one man beside himself without whom the celebration going on around him would have never happened. It was these two men, after all, who had forged the rivalry of which this game was just one part.

The two men were Howard Jones and Knute Rockne.

27

Aftermath

Tomorrow is the most important thing in life . . . It hopes we've learned something from yesterday.
 —John Wayne, 1971

After the parade wound its way to the USC campus, a huge rally was held at Bovard Auditorium, with three thousand inside and another ten thousand outside unable to gain admittance. Later that day, a luncheon attended by one thousand fans honored the team at the Sala de Oro Salon in the Biltmore Hotel.[1] In the following weeks, local movie theaters showed newsreels of the game, narrated by *Los Angeles Times* reporter Braven Dyer, to packed houses. Proceeds went to the Rockne Memorial Fund.[2]

Although the Trojans were heralded as champions after beating Notre Dame, two games remained on their schedule. Those two opponents offered little opposition, however. Washington fell 44–7 and Georgia was blown out 60–0. Finally, after dispatching Tulane 21–12 in the postseason Rose Bowl game, USC was officially hailed as the nation's best college football team. Together with his players, Howard Jones accepted the trophy—which had been rechristened the Rockne Trophy after that coach's death—in a ceremony on campus January 6, 1932.[3] Ironically, had USC's crosstown rival UCLA not beaten St. Mary's earlier in the year, the Gaels might have taken the honors.

Jones coached another nine years at USC. After another victory over Notre Dame in 1932, the team once again won the national championship. That achievement would mark the fifth straight year in which either Notre Dame or USC was so honored.

Howard's wife Jane soon displayed symptoms of mental illness, and in 1936 she was committed to an institution in Louisiana, where she spent the rest of her life away from her family.[4]

Howard himself died suddenly of a heart attack on July 27, 1941.[5] The tragedy brought great changes to the life of his daughter, Carolyn. The home she knew was sold, its contents were auctioned, and her guardians sent her off to boarding school. The excitement of her father's big games, and the companionship of movie stars were gone forever. As an adult, she became a professional musician and singer, performing in clubs along the East Coast for many years. In time, Carolyn married and had three daughters of her own. Howard's grandchildren and great-grandchildren still live in Southern California.[6]

Howard's son Clark wed in 1948, and worked for the *Los Angeles Times* before becoming a journalism teacher in San Bernardino, California.[7] He died in 1989, having no heirs.[8]

Knute Rockne's widow, Bonnie, never remarried, and spent much of the rest of her life protecting her husband's legacy. In 1940, she returned to Hollywood for the making of *Knute Rockne, All-American,* the iconic film that shapes public perceptions of Rockne to this day. She died in 1956.[9]

None of Knute's children followed their father's path to gridiron acclaim. His oldest son, William, led a troubled life. In 1951, he was shot trying to enter a home in Wichita, Kansas.[10] He recovered, but died nine years later in South Bend.[11] Knute Jr. worked in a munitions factory before being inducted into the Army during World War II.[12] He died in 1988.[13] Knute's youngest son, Jack, served in the Marine Corps during World War II and died in 2008.[14] Knute's daughter, Mary Jean, married and had children of her own. She passed away in Tulsa, Oklahoma, in 1992, three years after her husband.[15]

Two of Knute's twelve grandchildren, John Rockne and Knute Rockne III, did become football coaches.[16] Tragically, another grandson, Mike Rockne, was killed in a shooting rampage at a post office in Edmond, Oklahoma, in 1986. He was working for the postal service, just as his famous grandfather had done back in Chicago.[17]

Hunk Anderson suffered a nervous breakdown in June 1932 and checked into the Mayo Clinic to recover.[18] He was unable to meet the expectations set by his predecessor and resigned before the 1934 season, after Notre Dame had suffered three straight losses to the Trojans.[19] Elmer Layden, one of the legendary Four Horsemen, subsequently returned to his alma mater as coach and athletic director in 1934 and led the first renaissance of Notre Dame football glory, compiling a 47–13–3 record during his tenure there.[20]

Will Rogers became the biggest name in movies during the early 1930s.[21] In 1935, he died in a plane crash, just like his friend Knute Rockne.[22]

Rex Bell checked Clara Bow into the Glendale Sanitarium after she suffered a debilitating bout of nervous exhaustion in May 1931.[23] One month later, she was without a contract and out of pictures. She and Bell married in December, and the couple moved to Nevada.[24] By 1932, Bow had regained enough confidence to return to Hollywood and make two more films before retiring for good. After negotiating a proper salary of $75,000 for each of these films, she was able to leave money worries behind her.[25] Bell later became the lieutenant governor of Nevada.[26] He and Clara had two sons, one of whom attended Notre Dame. She remained a Trojan fan her entire life, however, politely telling her son she just couldn't root for the Irish.[27]

Her marriage would suffer in later years when she once again began exhibiting symptoms of instability. The couple lived apart for many years, although they never divorced. Bow died in her modest home in Culver City, California, in 1965. She was watching a movie on TV at the time that featured one of her old lovers, Gary Cooper.[28]

John Wayne made two more films for Fox before being released from his contract.[29] He then made a string of low-budget Westerns for smaller studios until getting his really big break in John Ford's *Stagecoach* in 1939.[30] He went on to become one of the biggest stars in movie history, often working alongside his old Trojan buddy Ward Bond.

D. C. Stephenson made good on his threats to expose his hold on government in Indiana when his cronies refused to intervene in his court battles. The scandal brought down a host of dirty politicians across the state. Stephenson was released from prison in 1950, but was returned to custody later that year for violating parole. Paroled again in 1956, he violated the terms of his release by staying in Indiana. After moving to

Tennessee, he committed bigamy by marrying without divorcing his previous wife. At the age of seventy, he was arrested for the attempted sexual assault of a sixteen-year-old girl. He died in 1966.[31]

Al Capone was convicted of tax evasion in June 1931. He served time at a federal penitentiary in Atlanta, before being transferred to Alcatraz. He was released from Alcatraz in 1939, but a conviction for contempt of court put him back in prison briefly at Terminal Island in Southern California. He was released again in November of that same year. Having suffered from untreated syphilis for years, Capone's mental state declined drastically during his incarceration.[32] By 1946, doctors estimated his mental capacity to be that of a twelve-year-old.[33] He died in Palm Island, Florida, on January 25, 1947, a few days after suffering a stroke.[34]

The Great Depression continued to hamstring the American economy until huge government spending during World War II sparked industrial activity and put millions of the unemployed into military uniform. The private sector did not really recover until after government control ended in 1946.[35] The year 1933 marked the low ebb of economic woes. Many companies that had managed to survive the initial shock of the Great Depression failed that year. Studebaker, the South Bend automaker, was forced into bankruptcy in 1933, and President Albert Erskine committed suicide the same year. Studebaker did survive, continuing to produce cars in one corporate form or another until 1966.[36]

Despite the gloomy economy during the Great Depression, Notre Dame and USC have continued their football series, with only wartime restrictions forcing a brief suspension between 1942 and 1945. One year after restarting the Trojan series in 1946, Notre Dame and Army ended their annual competition.[37] The Irish have played Navy every year since 1927, but the decline of the military academies as football powers has diminished the impact of that series. Other schools, including Purdue, Boston College, Michigan, Michigan State, Miami, and Stanford, have at times battled Notre Dame in a number of memorable games, but none are annual rivalries.

The Trojans continued heated competition within their conference, most notably with Cal and Stanford, but as UCLA's football program developed, the crosstown duel with the Bruins overtook those older rivalries. It is the only major rivalry between two schools in the same city.

The series between Notre Dame and USC also retains both a unique and unequaled quality. Since the first game in 1926, the two schools have won more national championships, produced more Heisman Trophy winners,[38] and provided more thrilling finishes, unbelievable comebacks, and stunning upsets than any other series. Their rivalry is one of the last remaining traditions begun in the Roaring Twenties, and it remains a vital part of sports and popular American culture to this day.

A Response to Professor Murray Sperber

In 1993, Professor Murray Sperber of Indiana University released his landmark book, *Shake Down the Thunder: The Creation of Notre Dame Football*, which chronicled the rise of Notre Dame football from its earliest days through the tenure of Frank Leahy in the 1950s. Although the origins of the football series with USC was simply a footnote to the book's primary narrative, *Shake Down the Thunder* has been considered the final word on the matter. That is, until now.

Sperber labels as "sentimentalists" anyone giving credence to the story that the wives of Knute Rockne and Gwynn Wilson influenced Rockne in the matter. The tale, he writes in his introduction, "ignores the reality of how the Notre Dame faculty athletic board and coach scheduled games in the 1920s."[1]

Sperber mocks ABC sportscaster Keith Jackson's recounting of the story during a game broadcast as an example of such sentimentality. Jackson, Sperber asserts, "seemed to enjoy the little-woman-behind-the-great-man anecdote because it implies an innocent and charming past to college football—the opposite of reality."[2] The passage fairly drips with cynicism and fully embodies the spirit of Sperber's effort to deconstruct the Rockne mythology.

Sperber notes that Jackson "appears to have based his story of the scheduling of the first Notre Dame–USC game on the reminiscences of longtime Southern California athletic department manager Gwynn Wilson," but goes no further into Wilson's account.[3] In order to consider the matter further, it's important to return to Wilson's original story in more detail.

That story can be distilled into five basic elements. First, earlier attempts by USC to secure a game with Notre Dame had failed. Second, efforts to sign Notre Dame to a game were renewed when the Trojans hired Howard Jones. Third, an opening was created when Notre Dame dropped Nebraska from its 1926 schedule. Fourth, Gwynn Wilson traveled to Lincoln with his wife, Marion, during Thanksgiving week of 1925 to pitch Rockne. Fifth, and finally, the Irish coach relented only after his wife Bonnie, swayed by Marion's warm description of Southern California hospitality, intervened. This is the key part of the story that Sperber discounts as the romantic tale-spinning of "sentimentalists."

Before we look at the evidence in the historical record, let us consider when Wilson first told the story. Was it many years after the fact, in the twilight of Wilson's life, when memories fade, or closer to the actual events?

The earliest recorded account that this author has been able to locate was written by *Los Angeles Times* sportswriter Braven Dyer in his column Sports Parade on November 28, 1942. It should be noted that Dyer covered the Trojans at the time of the events. In addition, aside from the two coaches, all other participants were still very much alive when the story was published and offered no hint of skepticism.

The familiar elements of the tale—Stonier's desire to schedule Notre Dame, the trip to Nebraska, and the conversation between the wives—all appear in that article. Elements of the same basic tale were then repeated in the same newspaper at least five times over the subsequent half-century, and at least twice in the *Daily Trojan*. Moreover, several books, most notably *"The Game Is On"* by Cameron Applegate in 1977, also repeated the story.

In each case, the details are vividly recalled, and the accounts remain remarkably consistent, despite a few minor differences. One discrepancy in the accounts is significant: the amount of money USC guaranteed to Notre Dame regardless of the gate receipts. In the original story, that amount was given as a minimum of $35,000.[4] Later accounts give the figure as $20,000.[5] This is a key detail, as we will see later.

Another variable was the time of Wilson's departure from Los Angeles for the trip to Nebraska. The 1942 account gives that time specifically as noon, while the 1955 account gives it as merely "that night." Further details will show that the earlier time frame must have been correct.

Now, let's go quickly through all five parts of Wilson's story. As this book details in chapter 11, Irish alumni in Los Angeles had pushed for Notre Dame to play a game on the West Coast as early as 1923. These well-documented attempts to arrange a game between the Irish and the Trojans, occurring over a two-year period before Thanksgiving week of 1925, fit perfectly with Wilson's description of USC's earlier efforts to schedule Notre Dame.

The timing of Jones's move to USC is likewise consistent with the story. Jones moved to his new post just eight months before Notre Dame agreed to begin playing the Trojans. In addition, the *Daily Trojan*, USC's school newspaper, reported a specific indication of Jones's role in the matter in its sports page around the time Wilson was heading out to see Rockne. Moreover, in the November 23, 1976, edition of the *Los Angeles Times*, longtime sportswriter John Hall quoted Wilson in a piece entitled "The Creation." "Jones was well aware of what I was up to in 1925," Wilson recalled, "and he was all for it." Again, these facts dovetail neatly with Wilson's earlier description of events.

The timing and impact of Notre Dame dropping Nebraska from its schedule was the third major factor in Wilson's story. The details of the troubled relations between Nebraska and Notre Dame have been well documented in many sources. There is no question that the game played on Thanksgiving Day, 1925, was the final, insufferable indignity for Notre Dame, topping a long list of grievances that had been building in South Bend for years

The key aspect of this break between Notre Dame and Nebraska was that before it occurred, Notre Dame had no room on the schedule for a new opponent. This is reflected in newspaper announcements of Notre Dame's 1926 schedule before the game, such as the one appearing in the *Chicago Tribune* on November 24, 1925. That article, entitled "ND Cards Only One New Foe for 1926," showed the Cornhuskers still listed on Notre Dame's schedule for the following year. It was not until after the game that newsmen reported that relations with the Cornhuskers had been severed.[6] There can be no doubt that this aspect of Wilson's story also fits the known facts.

It is true that only circumstantial evidence exists to confirm the details of Wilson's account of his trip to Nebraska to speak with Rockne. However, the fact that Wilson left Los Angeles just before Thanksgiving to approach Rockne about forming a scheduling agreement *was* known at the time. An article appearing in the *Daily Trojan* on November 25, 1925, "Gwynn Wilson Leaves for East to Secure Games," reported that Wilson had left Los Angeles to see Rockne. Moreover, Walter Ekersall, writing in the *Chicago Tribune* on November 30, 1925, reported Wilson's presence at the Big Ten Conference in Chicago, while several other publications likewise reported Rockne's presence at the Big Ten meeting.

There is no mention, of course, that Marion Wilson went along with her husband, or that the train stopped in Nebraska en route. Nonetheless, a reasonable deduction about Wilson's itinerary can be made simply by looking at the calendar. Since the conference in Chicago did not begin until December 3, Wilson would have had no need to leave California before November 25 (as confirmed by the *Daily Trojan* article) unless he planned another stop along the way. A rail trip from Los Angeles to Chicago took less than three days; if that had been his only destination, Wilson could have enjoyed Thanksgiving at home and still reached Chicago for the coaches' meeting with plenty of time to spare.[7] The original 1942 account leaves us intriguing clues to help establish this itinerary. "Two hours later," Dyer wrote, "the Wilsons were on the train."[8] That meant Wilson must have left on Monday, November 23, if he was to arrive in Nebraska before the game.

Another article, "Rockne Had to Be Sold on the Idea," written by Jerry Crowe and appearing in the *Los Angeles Times* on November 21, 1990, was even more specific about the timing of Wilson's departure. According to Crowe, Wilson "called his wife . . . to meet him at noon at the Santa Fe Station." Timetables of the Santa Fe railroad for November 1925 show trains departing Los Angeles daily at 12:01, fitting that timeline exactly. The California Limited (some accounts have called it the Sunset Limited, but that was a Southern Pacific train, and headed in the wrong direction) arrived in Kansas City at 10:00 A.M. on Wednesday, November 25, leaving plenty of time to catch a northbound train for the final two hundred miles to Lincoln in time to arrive when Wilson said he did.[9]

There is at least one other account to corroborate Wilson's story. Bill Hunter, the athletic director at USC, in an interview with Peter N. Synodia published in the *Daily Trojan* on the anniversary of Rockne's death in 1955, confirmed that Wilson had been sent east with the specific task of engaging Rockne. In "Climate Influenced Rockne's Decision," Hunter confirmed that the desire to play Notre Dame sprang from Harold Stonier's push for a marquee matchup for the Trojan team. In that sense, money did play a big part in the affair, but, as we shall see, there is much more to the story than dollars and cents.

Of course, the key element in Wilson's account is the conversation between the two wives, Bonnie Rockne and Marion Wilson. With no independent account of the Nebraska episode, there is no confirmation of that detail. Until such time as direct evidence is unearthed, there is little one can do but decide if Wilson's account seems believable, and compare it to the alternatives.

Two other accounts besides those of Wilson and Sperber have claimed to explain the origins of the series. Both stories name sportswriters as participants. The first version appeared in an obituary of Mark Kelly, sports editor of the *Los Angeles Examiner* from 1921 to 1936, written by Paul Zimmerman of the *Los Angeles Times*, which ran on December 6, 1952. Recounting the highlights of Kelly's life, Zimmerman wrote, "It was Mark, working with Gwynn Wilson, the graduate manager at SC, who induced the late Knute Rockne to sign for the Notre Dame series."[10] It should be noted that even this account, while silent on the roles of the two wives, acknowledges that Wilson was USC's point man in seeking out Rockne.

The second account named Harry Grayson, a Scripps-Howard newsman with bylines dating back to Rockne's college days, as the instigator. According to Jerry Brondfield's 2009 book, *Rockne: The Coach, the Man, the Legend,* Grayson claimed to have called Jones when the coach was at USC to suggest a matchup with the Irish. Jones, Grayson claimed, balked at the idea of playing Notre Dame. Grayson then called Rockne to pitch the same idea, and when both coaches then claimed no fear of any rival, the two teams were set on a collision course.[11] Don Lechman more recently cited this same source when repeating the story in his 2012 book *Notre Dame vs. USC: The Rivalry.*[12]

In their 1975 book *We Remember Rockne,* John D. McCallum and Paul Castner write that Kelly and Grayson were in cahoots, and worked together to convince Rockne. The book's authors credit the two sportswriters with the whole idea that USC should become a football power, and with bringing Gus Henderson to Los Angeles. None of these stories can withstand scrutiny, and all should be summarily dismissed. First, there is no corroboration beyond the sources already mentioned for the involvement of the sportswriters. Second, the idea that sportswriters would be so influential on scheduling decisions rings hollow. At best, they could only have added a little pressure when the real players involved were reacting to more pertinent forces. Regardless, no agreement for a series could have been forged in the hubbub of 1925 without the loss of Nebraska from Rockne's future schedules.

The later account by McCallum and Castner is the weakest of the three. In *We Remember Rockne,* they write that the break in athletic relations between the Bay Area schools and USC was the catalyst that drove Grayson to phone Rockne. They assert that Grayson "phoned Rockne and persuaded him to start the series the following year, in 1926."[13] The problem with this part of the story is that the feud with the Bay Area schools had been patched up by then. The Trojans played Stanford in 1925 and both Stanford and Cal in 1926. There would have been no need to schedule Notre Dame simply as a stopgap measure during a lingering feud between conference members.

This leaves us with Sperber's claim that financial gain was the motive driving the administration at Notre Dame to sign with USC. Further, Sperber seems to ascribe a minor role, if any, to Knute Rockne in the matter. Sperber builds his entire case on one sentence from a letter Rockne wrote to "a friend" in late 1925. In the introduction to his book, Sperber claims that Rockne wrote, "The Southern California officials came to South Bend and offered the authorities such a fluttering guarantee that they could not turn it down."[14] Without documenting the amount, Sperber then claims that the guarantee for the game must have approached $100,000. On the basis of this one comment by Rockne, and on Sperber's own deduction as to its meaning, he substitutes greed for the story that Marion Wilson and Bonnie Rockne influenced Knute Rockne, a tale that he claims is a myth preferred by "sentimentalists."

The "friend" to whom Rockne wrote the letter Sperber quotes was Paul Schissler, the head football coach at Oregon State. Rockne was responding to Schissler's request to schedule a Thanksgiving game between the two schools in 1926. That request was made *before* Gwynn Wilson approached the Notre Dame coach asking for a game.

Rockne had turned down Schissler once before, on November 19, when he had sent the Oregon coach a brief telegram: "Will have to schedule same teams this year as last year hence cannot accept kind invitation. Looks O.K. for 1927." Ironically, the telegram reiterates that his 1926 schedule was full, confirming again the importance that the impending break with Nebraska would play in enabling a new team to jump on the opportunity.[15]

The letter to Schissler was written just as the news of the contract with USC was being made public. When considered in context of that agreement with USC, the letter takes on different ramifications than a candid note written to "a friend," as Sperber describes it. It was clearly a face-saving gesture by Rockne to explain why he had allowed another school to swoop in and push Oregon State aside in the matter of scheduling. By deflecting the blame toward nameless "officials" of USC and anonymous "authorities" at Notre Dame, Rockne absolves himself of any culpability and cleverly hides his own role in the affair.

Sperber writes that Wilson's story "ignores the reality of how the Notre Dame faculty board and coach scheduled games in the 1920s," yet Sperber may have overlooked that reality himself. Later in his book, Sperber writes, "by 1928, the athletic board had gained full control of scheduling."[16] The Trojans had approached Rockne in 1925, some three years before the date Sperber claims that the board secured that final control.

In addition, Sperber completely ignores how the Trojans scheduled *their* games. There were no mysterious "Southern California officials" to come to South Bend (a city Wilson never visited during the negotiations) to offer a "fluttering" guarantee. Gwynn Wilson was *the* person responsible for scheduling games at USC; only after he left the school did the athletic director take over that duty.[17] To discount Wilson's version of events is to discount the very man responsible for conducting the negotiations on behalf of the Trojans.

What about the money? Certainly a large payday was involved, but just how high was the offer to which Sperber refers? Did USC really offer a $100,000 guarantee? Sperber asserts that "no records exist in the Notre Dame archives of the Southern Cal guarantee." In fact, a record does exist, and is reprinted in this book. The offer was $35,000.[18] That was the exact figure mentioned in that 1942 *Los Angeles Times* ar-

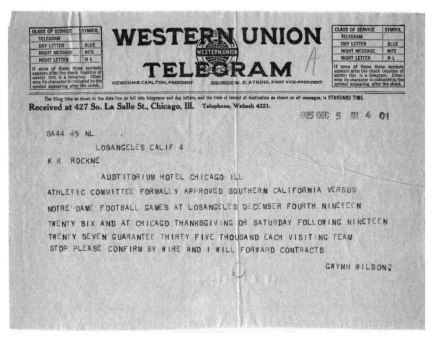

Telegram from Gwynn Wilson of USC to Knute Rockne showing a gate guarantee of $35,000 for the 1926 game between Notre Dame and USC. (Image courtesy of Notre Dame Archives.)

ticle, and within a few hundred dollars of the actual payout for the Nebraska game in 1925.[19]

Even the 1925 Rose Bowl game had paid out only $52,000 to each participant.[20] The idea of an offer approaching $100,000 strains credibility. Furthermore, Sperber records the figure of $75,619 offered as the amount paid to Notre Dame after the 1926 game, noting that it was "its best payday to date."[21] If the guarantee was $100,000, why was the payout almost $25,000 short?

Likewise, the idea that USC officials "came to South Bend" and somehow independently made an offer to Rockne's superiors without the coach's knowledge is simply without foundation. Rockne had too much clout to allow himself to be dictated to by Notre Dame's faculty. In fact, very few college coaches, if any, would have bowed to such faculty interference without a fight. As McCready Huston puts it in his book about Rockne, *Salesman from the Sidelines*, "No coach worth his salt is going to stand any interference by the faculty members of athletic boards with his schedule making." Oddly enough, Sperber quotes this very sentence from Huston and mistakenly attributes it to Rockne.[22] A school's pitch to get Notre Dame on its schedule simply *had* to go through the coach. Without Rockne's support, the proposal was a nonstarter.

As for the question of relations with Nebraska, just what was Rockne's attitude toward dropping them? Again, Sperber himself writes, "Behind the scenes, the N.D. coach tried to reverse the faculty board's decision and continue the Cornhusker series."[23] Does that sound like a man anxious to replace his team's traditional foe with the Trojans? For that matter, why would a faculty board struggling to rein in their independent-minded coach fight "overemphasis" by replacing one high-profile rival with another one that would involve even more travel for their student athletes, requiring more time away from their studies? Adding the Trojans to the schedule of Notre Dame's football team could occur only with a champion supporting the idea, and that champion could only have been Knute Rockne, albeit after a little convincing to overcome his initial reluctance.

Nebraska was the *only* school with a winning record against Rockne. Notre Dame had lost three of its previous four games against Nebraska, and Rockne was not the kind of man to drop a team at such a point in their rivalry. He was not likely to go out a loser if he could help it. Something, or someone, must have caused him to change his mind, and push for the Trojan matchup once it became clear to him that the Nebraska series was over regardless of his own feelings.

In arguing against the traditional story, Sperber points out that "no one on the Notre Dame side of the story, including Bonnie Rockne, ever told the Marion Wilson anecdote during their lifetimes." Of course, no one on the Notre Dame side except Knute and Bonnie Rockne could have had firsthand knowledge of anything that transpired on the team train returning to Chicago. If the couple had kept the details to themselves, there would have been no one in South Bend to discuss the story.

Why would the Rocknes have stayed quiet on the matter? Perhaps they may not have attached the same importance to the incident as the Wilsons did. Perhaps Bonnie needed no prodding by anyone to desire a return to Southern California, and Marion's words had just been icing on the cake. Perhaps Knute preferred not to broadcast a story that could be interpreted as him bowing to his wife's wishes or giving in to her nagging. Wouldn't leaving out his wife's role better fit Sperber's description of Rockne's concept of "Christian manliness"? If so, then keeping certain details quiet to avoid the appearance of being a hen-pecked husband becomes more logical.

While Sperber is correct in writing that no one from Notre Dame present on the train or involved in the decision ever told the story, it is also true that none of those same people gave an alternate version of events, even after people began telling the story in Los Angeles. For that matter, Rockne left the huge 1927 game against the Trojans at Soldier Field out of his autobiography altogether. That silence doesn't mean the game didn't happen.

Bonnie Rockne had plenty of opportunity to refute the story during her lifetime. She made at least two high-profile trips to Los Angeles after Knute's death, where the news media were on hand to cover her travels. The first, in 1931, was in conjunction with the filming of *The Spirit of Notre Dame;* she made the second trip, nine years later, to attend the premiere of *Knute Rockne, All-American.* Although both these visits occurred before the 1942 article mentioning Wilson's account, Bonnie Rockne lived until 1956, long after the story appeared in press accounts, and never publicly objected to it.

It goes without saying that Wilson presented the story as the truth. So did his wife Marion. In a 2008 interview with *Los Angeles Times* writer Bill Plaschke, Gwynn's daughter Joyce Nelson recalled how her father would point at her mother when the game came on television. "That's your game," Gwynn would say to Marion.[24] That view never changed in the Wilson family.

To believe that Gwynn Wilson made up the story, one must also believe that Marion Wilson was in on it, that Bill Hunter was taken in by a hoax. One must believe that someone like Gwynn Wilson, a man renowned for his role in the Olympic Games and for helping to create Santa Anita Park, a trustee at his alma mater with a building named after him on campus, would feel compelled to lie to boost his own ego.

This is the essence of the "little-woman-behind-the-Great-Man an-ecdote."[25] The known facts presented here fit the details Wilson gave perfectly. There is really no credible alternative that can withstand scrutiny. So can we conclude that Marion Wilson and Bonnie Rockne were really responsible for the series?

Gwynn and Marion Wilson pose at the fiftieth anniversary of the first game between Notre Dame and USC, celebrated in 1976. Marion Wilson and Bonnie Rockne played key roles in winning agreement for the proposal that began the series. (Image courtesy of Joyce Nelson.)

When weighing this question, it is helpful to consider an analogy. If a historian was asked to explain what caused the *Titanic* tragedy, the obvious reply would be that the ship hit an iceberg and sank. In contrast, a forensic investigator writing a detailed report would go far beyond that simple explanation, which overlooks myriad factors contributing to the accident and massive loss of life of April 15, 1912.

The investigator might bring in everything from the structural design of the ship's hull and rudder to the decision to provide an insufficient number of lifeboats, the failure to bring the key to the locked storage of the lookout's binoculars, the weather conditions that hampered the crew in spotting icebergs, the fact that warnings of ice in the ship's path were ignored, the speed of travel through the ice field, the decisions made on the bridge once the berg was sighted, and the lack of lifeboat drills before the collision. Could any one of those factors be definitively named as *the* cause of the tragedy? Or did all of them variously contribute to the outcome of events? The real tragedy is that had just one of these circumstances changed, the ship's maiden voyage might have been very different.

So it was with Notre Dame and USC. Had Cornhusker fans behaved differently, bad feeling probably would never have grown between

Nebraska and Notre Dame, and no opening would have appeared on Notre Dame's schedule. Had Gwynn Wilson not heard of the brewing conflict, he might well have stayed in Los Angeles in November 1925, and Oregon State might have been the new team on Notre Dame's 1926 schedule. Had Bonnie Rockne not enjoyed Pasadena so much during her Rose Bowl visit in January 1925, she might not have been as susceptible to persuasion. Had Gwynn Wilson not taken his wife along, she might never have spoken with Mrs. Rockne. Had Marion not used her time alone with Bonnie to promote Southern California, Rockne's wife might have been less inclined to influence her husband. Finally, yes, had USC been located in a smaller city with a more modest stadium, it might not have made financial sense for Notre Dame to bother with a game.

If the decision to begin the series had been only about money, other schools in other places might have been just as profitable, and other series might have started. But the facts are that Gwynn Wilson was there, in the right place at the right time, with just the right sales pitch, and just the right women with him to make history.

Notes

1. The Beginning of the New

1. Laurence Green, *The Era of Wonderful Nonsense: A Casebook of the Twenties* (Indianapolis, IN: Bobbs-Merrill, 1939).

2. Molly Billings, "The Influenza Pandemic of 1918," Human Virology at Stanford, Stanford University, June 1997, modified Feb. 2005, https://virus.stanford.edu/uda/index.html.

3. Warren G. Harding, "Back to Normal: Address before Home Market Club" (speech delivered in Boston, MA, May 14, 1920), in *Rededicating America: Live and Recent Speeches of Warren G. Harding,* ed. Frederick E. Schortemeier (Indianapolis, IN: Bobbs-Merrill, 1920), 223–29.

4. "The 1920s: Sports: Overview," *American Decades,* ed. Judith S. Baughman et al., vol. 3: 1920–1929 (Detroit, MI: Gale, 2001), U.S. History in Context (website), http://ic.galegroup.com/ic/uhic/ReferenceDetailsPage/ReferenceDetailsWindow?displayGroupName=Reference&zid=dff7b5375c7a4d60bb887113f5089ed5&p=UHIC%3AWHIC&action=2&catId=&documentId=GALE%7CCX3468301022&source=Bookmark&u=rosw82806&jsid=fbce7e60f2adff54682edb81cec2c0f6.

5. Gilbert C. Fite and Jim E. Reese, *An Economic History of the United States,* 2nd ed. (New York: Houghton Mifflin, 1959).

6. Murray Sperber, *Shake Down the Thunder: The Creation of Notre Dame Football* (New York: Henry Holt and Co., 1993), 173.

7. "The War in the Yale Bowl," editorial, *New York Times,* Nov. 21, 1914.

8. Grantland Rice, "The Return to Sport," *Country Life,* June 1919, 40, 43.

9. Sperber, *Shake Down the Thunder,* 175, 281.

10. "History of the University: A Place Born of Imagination and Will," University of Notre Dame (website), https://www.nd.edu/about/history/.

11. Michael O'Brien, *Hesburgh: A Biography* (Washington, D.C.: Catholic Univ. of America Press, 1998), 49–51.

12. Ambrose Schindler, interview by the author, Redondo Beach, CA, Sept. 14, 2005.

13. Steven Travers, *The Trojans* (Lanham, MD: Taylor Trade Publishing, 2006), 22.

14. Tom Lewis, "Building All-Americans with Howard Jones," *Street and Smith's Sports Story Magazine,* Oct. 10, 1933, 55.

15. Art Cohn, Cohn-ing Tower (column), *Oakland Tribune,* July 28, 1941.

16. Howard Jones, as told to Norman L. Sper, "Howard Jones' Own Story," *Los Angeles Evening Herald and Express,* July 29–Aug. 2, 1941.

17. Ray Robinson, *Rockne of Notre Dame: The Making of a Football Legend* (New York: Oxford Univ. Press, 1999), 21.

18. Robinson, *Rockne of Notre Dame,* 205.

19. Ibid., 5.

20. Robert Myers, "Simple, Honest, and Deeply Conscientious—That Was Head Coach Howard Jones," *Iowa City Press-Citizen,* July 28, 1941.

21. *The Notre Dame Scholastic* 64, no. 23, Apr. 17, 1931, 719.

2. Prelude to Greatness

1. George C. Crout, "Harding-Jones Paper Company, c. 1955," photograph in the George C. Crout Collection, Midpointe Library System, Middletown, OH, http://www.midpointedigitalarchives.org/cdm/ref/collection/Crout/id/420.

2. H. Jones, in Sper, "Howard Jones' Own Story."

3. Ibid.

4. John Kryk, "Why American Football Added a Fourth Down," *Toronto Sun,* Feb. 2, 2012, http://www.torontosun.com/2012/02/02/college-football-a-different-game-century-ago.

5. David M. Nelson, *The Anatomy of a Game: Football, the Rules, and the Men Who Made the Game* (Cranbury, NJ: Associated Univ. Presses, 1994), 80, 454.

6. "Gossip of the Sports," *Altoona Tribune,* Dec. 17, 1908.

7. See, for example, "Look Out, Harvard!" *New York Sun,* Oct. 30, 1912.

8. "Yale Wants Howard Jones in Football," *New York Times,* Feb. 2, 1913.

9. "Syracuse Coach Goes to Alma Mater," *The Scranton Republican,* Dec. 13, 1908.

10. Bob Barton, "The Perfect Match," Nov. 18, 2009, Yale University Athletics (website), http://www.yalebulldogs.com/sports/m-footbl/2009–10/releases/20091118on3hvw.

11. Kathleen Morgan Drowne and Patrick Huber, *The 1920s* (Westport, CT: Greenwood Press, 2004), 154.

12. "Howard Jones Retires," *Syracuse Herald,* Dec, 17, 1909.

13. "Doc" Jeckyll, Sparks from the Sporting Anvil (column), *Syracuse Herald,* Dec. 20, 1909.

14. "Football Rush Wins Girl," *Los Angeles Times,* July 19, 1911.

15. *Walden's Stationer and Printer* 34, pt. 2, 1911, 42.

16. "Jones to Coach Yale This Year," *Hamilton (OH) Telegraph,* Feb. 23, 1911.

17. Bill Henry, "Coach Jones of S.C. Grid Teams Dies," *Los Angeles Times,* July 28, 1941.

18. "Yale Men Demand Change in System that Brings Defeat to Football Team," *Washington Times,* Nov. 24, 1912.

19. "Yale Discards Army Game," *Arkansas City Daily Traveler,* Jan. 18, 1913.

20. H. Jones, in Sper, "Howard Jones' Own Story."

21. "Notre Dame vs. Army," Nov. 17, 2010, Notre Dame Archive News and Notes, University of Notre Dame Archives (website), http://www.archives.nd.edu/about/news/index.php/2010/nd-vs-army/#.VgyptN2YnDp.

22. "Notre Dame's Open Play Amazes Army," *New York Times,* Nov. 2, 1913.

23. "Walter Camp, Camp's All-America Eleven," *Collier's* 52, no. 14, Dec. 20, 1913, 3.

24. Robinson, *Rockne of Notre Dame,* 50.

25. Ibid., 41–42.

26. H. Jones, in Sper, "Howard Jones' Own Story."

27. Dick Lamb and Bert McGrane, *75 Years with the Fighting Hawkeyes (1889–1964)* (Dubuque, IA: William C. Brown Co., 1964), 58.

28. "Howard Jones, Former Yale Head Coach, Chosen by Board to Succeed Jess Hawley," *Daily Iowan,* Dec. 21, 1915.

29. "Jones's Brother Coach at Yale," *Daily Iowan,* Jan. 30, 1916.

30. H. Jones, in Sper, "Howard Jones' Own Story."

31. "Following the Ball," *Lincoln Daily News,* Nov. 4, 1916.

32. "Iowa Makes Coach Jones Director of Athletics," *Chicago Daily Tribune,* Sept. 16, 1917.

33. Howard Jones, Registration Card, Local Board of Johnson County, Iowa City, Sept. 12, 1918.

34. Robinson, *Rockne of Notre Dame,* 51.

3. Almost Ready to Roar

1. "George Gipp, 'the Gipper': Fast Facts," CMG Worldwide (website), http://www.cmgww.com/football/gipp/facts.htm.

2. Jack Cavanaugh, *The Gipper: George Gipp, Knute Rockne, and the Dramatic Rise of Notre Dame Football* (New York: Skyhorse Publishing, 2010), 64.

3. Photograph of Van Horn Field, digital copy in the collection of the author.

4. Cavanaugh, *The Gipper,* 105–6.

5. Neal Rozendaal, *Duke Slater: Pioneering Black NFL Player and Judge* (Jefferson, NC: McFarland and Co., 2012), 7.

6. *Iowa City Press-Citizen,* qtd. in Mike Finn and Chad Leistikow, *Hawkeye Legends, Lists, and Lore: The Athletic History of the Iowa Hawkeyes* (Champaign, IL: Sports Publishing, 1998), 28.

7. Arch Ward, qtd. in Robinson, *Rockne of Notre Dame,* 76. Arch Ward was a publicity writer for Rockne at the time, but later became the sports editor for the *Chicago Daily Tribune.*

8. Robinson, *Rockne of Notre Dame,* 77.

9. Robert P. Murphy, "The Depression You've Never Heard Of: 1920–1921," *The Freeman* 59, no. 10, Dec. 2009.

10. Robinson, *Rockne of Notre Dame,* 80, 81–82.

11. Robert Burns, qtd. in Sperber, *Shake Down the Thunder,* 107–8.

12. Cavanaugh, *The Gipper,* 136.

13. Michael K. Bohn, *Heroes and Ballyhoo* (Washington, D.C.: Potomac Books, 2009), 141.

14. Robinson, *Rockne of Notre Dame,* 85–87.

15. Moe Aranson, qtd. in Sperber, *Shake Down the Thunder,* 110.

16. Robinson, *Rockne of Notre Dame*, 88.

17. Cavanaugh, *The Gipper*, 184.

4. Heading for a Showdown

1. "300 to Greet Notre Damers," *Daily Iowan*, Oct. 7, 1921.

2. The Chicago, Rock Island, and Pacific Railway System, 1922, digital copy of route map in the collection of the author.

3. "Varsity Gridiron Men of 1921: Daniel Coughlin," *University of Notre Dame Football Review* (sports yearbook), 1921, 13, University of Notre Dame Archives website, http://archives.nd.edu/Football/Football-1921.pdf.

4. DatabaseOlympics.com (online Olympics database), http://www.databaseolympics.com/players/playerpage.htm?ilkid=DESCHAUG01.

5. "Prentiss and Seiling Work at Quarter," *Daily Iowan*, Oct. 5, 1921.

6. "Varsity Gridiron Men of 1921: Earl Walsh," *University of Notre Dame Football Review* (sports yearbook), 1921, 15.

7. Cavanaugh, *The Gipper*, 143.

8. Finn and Leistikow, *Hawkeye Legends, Lists, and Lore*, 77; "Captain 'Eddie' Anderson," *University of Notre Dame Football Review* (sports yearbook), 1921, 9.

9. Francis Wallace, "Turning in the Suits—A Brief Review of the Season," *Notre Dame Scholastic* 15, no. 13, Football Number, 1921, 206–7.

10. "300 to Greet Notre Damers," *Daily Iowan*, Oct. 7, 1921.

11. Reich's Chocolate Shop advertisement, *Daily Iowan*, Oct. 8, 1921.

12. Preston Lockwood, "Greatest Rush to American Universities," *New York Times*, Oct. 16, 1921.

13. "Iowa Is Ready for First Big Game of Year," *Daily Iowan*, Oct. 8, 1921.

14. "Football Men Fight to Hold Jobs on Team," *Daily Iowan*, Oct. 7, 1921.

15. "Iowa Is Ready for First Big Game of Year," *Daily Iowan*, Oct. 8, 1921.

16. Robinson, *Rockne of Notre Dame*, 104.

17. Sperber, *Shake Down the Thunder*, 210, 309.

18. Cavanaugh, *The Gipper*, 278.

19. Sperber, *Shake Down the Thunder*, 125, 141.

20. Ibid., 114.

21. "Record Gathering at Conference Meeting," *Indianapolis News*, Dec. 4, 1920.

22. "Iowa Is Ready for First Big Game of Year," *Daily Iowan*, Oct. 8, 1921.

23. "From Mid-West Grids," *Fort Wayne Sentinel*, Oct. 8, 1921.

24. Chet Grant, qtd. in Sperber, *Shake Down the Thunder*, 117.

25. "Catholics to Come Set to Win Contest," *Iowa City Press-Citizen*, Oct. 5, 1921.

26. "College Football," *Chicago Daily Tribune*, Oct. 8, 1921.

27. "Jones Wants More Players," *Daily Iowan*, Oct. 7, 1921.

28. "Longest and Hardest Drill of the Season," *Iowa City Press-Citizen*, Oct. 6, 1921.

29. "Betting Tightens as Hoosier Team Arrives in Iowa," *South Bend News-Times*, Oct. 8, 1921.

30. "Pep and Spirit Abound at Mass Meeting," *Daily Iowan*, Oct. 8, 1921.

31. "Don't Be Bashful," *Daily Iowan,* Oct. 9, 1921.

32. "Pep and Spirit Abound at Big Mass Meeting," *Daily Iowan,* Oct. 8, 1921.

33. Sam Sciullo Jr., ed., *1991 Pitt Football: University of Pittsburgh Football Media Guide* (Pittsburgh, PA: University of Pittsburgh Sports Information Office, 1991), 116.

34. Chet Grant, "Notre Dame's Boys of 1921: Why They Didn't Go to the Rose Bowl!" *South Bend News Magazine,* c. 1972, PATH-Football Clippings-Iowa, 1921, 19, University of Notre Dame Archives.

35. University of Iowa Alumni Association, Gridiron Glory, 100 + Years of Iowa Football (website), http://www.iowalum.com/magazine/football_history/1920.html.

36. "Notre Dame Works Pass Effectively," *Daily Iowan,* Oct. 9, 1921.

37. "New Old Iowa Field," *The Iowa Alumnus* 19, no. 1, Oct. 1921, 10–11.

38. Grant, "Notre Dame's Boys of 1921," 19.

39. "Notre Dame Works Pass Effectively," *Daily Iowan,* Oct. 9, 1921.

40. Game program, Notre Dame vs. Iowa, Iowa City, Oct. 8, 1921, front cover.

41. Rozendaal, *Duke Slater,* 61.

42. Tom Lewis, "Building All-Americans with Howard Jones," *Sports Story Magazine,* Oct. 1933, 51.

43. Edwin Pope, *Football's Greatest Coaches* (Atlanta, GA: Tupper and Love, 1955), 134.

44. Frederick W. Kent, "Duke Slater Blocking Notre Dame Line, The University of Iowa, Oct. 8, 1921," photograph in the Frederick W. Kent Collection of Photographs, 1866–2000, University Archives, University of Iowa Libraries, http://digital.lib.uiowa.edu/cdm/ref/collection/ictcs/id/5750.

45. "Notre Dame Works Pass Effectively," *Daily Iowan,* Oct. 9, 1921.

5. When Worlds Collide

1. "Notre Dame Works Pass Effectively," *Daily Iowan,* Oct. 9, 1921.

2. Rozendaal, *Duke Slater,* 61–62.

3. "Notre Dame Works Pass Effectively," *Daily Iowan,* Oct. 9, 1921.

4. Emil Klosinski, *Notre Dame, Chicago Bears, and "Hunk": Heartley "Hunk" Anderson as Told to Emil Klosinski* (North Hollywood, CA: Panoply Publications, 2006), 58.

5. Howard Roberts, *The Big Nine: The Story of Football in the Western Conference* (New York: G. P. Putnam's Sons, 1948), 118.

6. "Notre Dame Works Pass Effectively," *Daily Iowan,* Oct. 9, 1921.

7. Roberts, *The Big Nine,* 118.

8. "Close Battle Goes to Iowa by 10–7 Score," *Daily Iowan,* Oct. 9, 1921

9. Jerry Brondfield, *Rockne: The Coach, the Man, the Legend* (Lincoln: Univ. of Nebraska Press, 2009), 101.

10. "Notre Dame Works Pass Effectively," *Daily Iowan,* Oct. 9, 1921.

11. "Band Will Parade between Halves at Notre Dame Game," *Daily Iowan,* Oct. 7, 1921.

12. Robinson, *Rockne of Notre Dame,* 105.

13. Rozendaal, *Duke Slater,* 63.

14. Brondfield, *Rockne,* 100.

15. Robinson, *Rockne of Notre Dame,* 104, 106.

16. "Notre Dame Works Pass Effectively," *Daily Iowan,* Oct. 9, 1921.

17. The International Olympic Committee, "Olympic Games, Paris 1924, Games Results: Discus Throw Men," Official Site of the Olympic Movement, http://m. olympic.org/en/mobile/results-and-medalists/gamesandsportsummary/?sport=325 88&games=1924/1&event=32576a.

18. "Notre Dame Works Pass Effectively," *Daily Iowan,* Oct. 9, 1921.

19. Brondfield, *Rockne,* 101.

20. Grant, "Notre Dame's Boys of 1921," 19.

21. "Close Battle Goes to Iowa by 10–7 Score," *Daily Iowan,* Oct. 9, 1921.

22. "Statistics Give Notre Dame Edge over Iowa," *Daily Iowan,* Oct. 9, 1921.

23. "A Review of the Games: The Hawkeye Encounter," *University of Notre Dame Football Review* (sports yearbook), 1921, 11.

24. John Hall, "The Creation," *Los Angeles Times,* Nov. 23, 1976.

25. Whitney Martin, "Immortal 'Rock' Gone These Many Years, But Feud Lingers On," *Los Angeles Times,* Nov. 25, 1939.

26. Robinson, *Rockne of Notre Dame,* 105.

27. Sperber, *Shake Down the Thunder,* 117

28. Brondfield, *Rockne,* 101.

29. Sperber, *Shake Down the Thunder,* 117.

30. Brondfield, *Rockne,* 100.

31. "Bonfire Is Celebration," *Daily Iowan,* Oct. 9, 1921.

32. Sperber, *Shake Down the Thunder,* 117.

33. Robinson, *Rockne of Notre Dame,* 105.

34. "'Start All Over' Says Rockne as Squad Prepares," *South Bend News-Times,* Oct. 11, 1921.

35. "Gotham Wonders How Bad Irish Will Beat Rutgers," *Indianapolis Star,* Nov. 8, 1921.

36. Westbrook Pegler, "Speed of Indiana Team Bewilders Big Easterners," *Washington Herald,* Nov. 9, 1921.

37. "Polo Grounds Historical Analysis," Baseball Almanac (website), http:// www.baseball-almanac.com/stadium/st_polo.shtml.

38. "Gotham Wonders How Bad Irish Will Beat Rutgers," *Indianapolis Star,* Nov. 8, 1921.

39. "Bryne Company in 70th Year of Business," *Notre Dame Alumnus* 35, no. 2 (Feb.–Mar. 1957): 4.

40. Francis Wallace, *Knute Rockne: The Story of the Greatest Football Coach Who Ever Lived* (Garden City, NY: Doubleday and Co., 1960), 103.

41. Will Rogers, Steven K. Gragert, M. Jane Johansson, *The Papers of Will Rogers,* vol. 3: *From Vaudeville to Broadway, September 1908–August 1915* (Norman: Univ. of Oklahoma Press, 2001), 364.

42. "Will Rogers, Film and Stage Star, Sophie Tucker and Harry Carroll Head Week's Vaudeville Bills," *Brooklyn Daily Eagle,* Nov. 6, 1921.

43. "Montauk Theatre (New Montauk, Col. Sinn's Montauk, Werba's Brooklyn Theater, Crescent Theatre, Triangle Theatre, Billy Minsky Brooklyn Burlesque The-

atre)," Brooklyn, NY, Bayles-Yeager Online Archives of the Performing Arts (website), http://www.performingartsarchive.com/Theatres/Theatres-M/Montauk-Theatre_Brooklyn/Montauk-Theatre_Brooklyn.htm.

44. Wallace, *Knute Rockne,* 103.

45. University of Iowa Athletics, "The 1921 Iowa Hawkeyes," Iowa Hawkeyes (website), http://www.hawkeyesports.com/sports/m-footbl/spec-rel/090512aac.html.

46. Valarie H. Zeigler, "Centre 6–Harvard 0: The Centre Harvard Game of 1921" (research paper, Centre College, Feb. 17, 1976), collection of Grace Doherty Library, Centre College, Danville, KY, http://library.centre.edu/sc/special/C6h0/ziegler.html.

47. "Notre Dame vs. Centre," *Wichita Daily Eagle,* Dec. 9, 1921.

48. Sports Jabs (column), *Iowa City Press-Citizen,* Dec. 8, 1921.

49. "To Stay at Notre Dame," *New York Times,* Dec. 17, 1921.

6. How They Played the Game

1. "Iowa Will Not Accept: Conference Likely to Prevent Game with Southern California," *New York Times,* Oct. 25, 1922.

2. Jim Lefebvre, *Coach for a Nation* (Minneapolis, MN: Great Day Press, 2013), 276.

3. Arthur Frank Wertheim, *Will Rogers at the Ziegfield Follies* (Norman: Univ. of Oklahoma Press, 1992), 12.

4. G. Clayton Stodt and Stephen Dittmore, *Sports Public Relations* (Champaign, IL: Human Kinetics, 2006), 128.

5. Gerald R. Gems, *For Pride, Profit, and Patriarchy* (Latham, MD: Scarecrow Press, 2000), 113.

6. Robinson, *Rockne of Notre Dame,* 135.

7. Stodt and Dittmore, *Sports Public Relations,* 128.

8. Associated Press, "Arch Ward, Tribune Sports Editor, Dies," *Harrisburg (IL) Daily Register,* July 9, 1955.

9. "Grantland Rice, 73, Dies: Famed Sports Columnist," *Brooklyn Daily Eagle,* July 14, 1954.

10. Mark Inabinett, *Grantland Rice and His Heroes: The Sportswriter as Mythmaker in the 1920s* (Knoxville: Univ. of Tennessee Press, 1994), 17.

11. Inabinett, *Grantland Rice and His Heroes,* 88.

12. Ibid., 5.

13. Jonathan Eig, *Luckiest Man: The Life and Death of Lou Gehrig* (New York: Simon and Schuster, 2005), 112.

14. Cecelia Bucki, *The 1930s,* vol. 4 of *Social History of the United States: The 1900s,* ed. Daniel J. Walkowitz and Daniel E. Bender, 10 vols. (Santa Barbara, CA: ABC-CLIO, 2009), 125.

15. Todd Tucker, *Notre Dame vs. the Klan: How the Fighting Irish Defeated the Ku Klux Klan* (Chicago, IL: Loyola Press, 2004), 73–76.

16. Tucker, *Notre Dame vs. the Klan,* 107–8.

17. State of Indiana, "Indiana City/Town Census Counts, 1900 to 2010," Stats Indiana (database), http://www.stats.indiana.edu/population/PopTotals/historic_counts_cities.asp.

18. Leonard J. Moore, *Citizen Klansmen: The Ku Klux Klan in Indiana, 1921–1928* (Chapel Hill: Univ. of North Carolina Press, 1991), 93.

19. Moore, *Citizen Klansmen,* 16–17.

20. Ibid., 7.

21. Tucker, *Notre Dame vs. the Klan,* 110.

22. Robinson, *Rockne of Notre Dame,* 121–24.

23. Ibid., 136–37.

24. "Howard Jones Writes Book on Football," *Davenport Democrat and Leader,* Nov. 12, 1923.

25. "Rotary Club to Host Football Men," *Iowa City Press-Citizen,* Jan. 10, 1924.

26. Finn and Leistikow, *Hawkeye Legends, Lists, and Lore,* 38.

27. H. Jones, in Sper, "Howard Jones' Own Story."

28. "Howard Jones Quits as Iowa Football Coach," *Davenport Democrat and Leader,* Jan. 11, 1924.

29. Billy Evans, "Big Coin Lures Howard Jones to Trinity," *Charleston Daily Mail,* Jan. 27, 1924.

30. "Red Mich, Iowa Grid Coach Wanted Badger Game, Says T. E. Jones," *Wisconsin State Journal,* Jan. 16, 1924.

31. Art Cohn, Cohn-ing Tower (column), *Oakland Tribune,* July 28, 1941.

32. Woody Strode, *Goal Dust: The Warm and Candid Memoirs of a Pioneer Black Athlete and Actor* (Lanham, MD: Madison Books, 1990), 28.

7. Here Come the Irish

1. Raymond Schmidt, *Shaping College Football: The Transformation of an American Sport, 1919–1930* (Syracuse, NY: Syracuse Univ. Press, 2007), 43.

2. "Trinity Working Hard for Game," *The Danville (VA) Bee,* Oct. 11, 1923.

3. Classified ad to sell Jones's house, *Iowa City Press-Citizen,* Oct. 31, 1923.

4. "Howard Jones Leaves City in Quiet Manner," *Iowa City Press-Citizen,* Feb. 26, 1924.

5. Personals, *Iowa City Press-Citizen,* Apr. 4, 1924.

6. "Give Farewell Luncheon for Howard Jones," *Davenport Democrat,* Feb. 21, 1924.

7. "Huge Loving Cup Given Coach Jones by Iowa Friends," *Iowa City Press-Telegram,* Mar. 23, 1924.

8. Billy Evans, "Big Coin Lures Howard Jones to Trinity," *Charleston Daily Mail,* Jan. 27, 1924.

9. "Rockne Has Conference," *New York Times,* Mar. 11, 1924.

10. "Rockne's Wife Calls It a Joke," *Iowa City Press-Citizen,* Mar. 24, 1924.

11. "Iowa Alumni Want Ingwersen to Succeed Jones as Coach," *Daily Illini,* Jan. 15, 1924.

12. Sperber, *Shake Down the Thunder,* 155.

13. Robinson, *Rockne of Notre Dame,* 141–42.

14. Tucker, *Notre Dame vs. the Klan,* 142.

15. Wyn Craig Wade, *The Fiery Cross: The Ku Klux Klan in America* (New York: Oxford Univ. Press, 1998), 115.

16. Tucker, *Notre Dame vs. the Klan,* 152–63.

17. Ibid., 167–72

18. Ibid., 174–76.

8. Four Horsemen, Seven Mules, and One Gloomy Gus

1. R. E. Huston, Ford Production Department, Aug. 3, 1927, available in "Model T Ford Production," Encyclopedia, Model T Ford Club of America (website), http://www.mtfca.com/encyclo/fdprod.htm.

2. Daniel Gross, *Forbes' Greatest Business Stories of All Time* (New York: John Wiley and Sons, 1996), 86.

3. Sheldon Patinkin, *No Legs, No Jokes, No Chance: A History of the American Musical Theater* (Evanston, IL: Northwestern Univ. Press, 2008), 136.

4. John Kenneth Galbraith, *The Great Crash, 1929* (New York: Houghton Mifflin, 2009), 7.

5. Laurence Bergreen, *Capone: The Man and the Era* (New York: Simon and Schuster, 1994), 132.

6. Kathleen Morgan Drowne and Patrick Huber, *The 1920s: American Popular Culture through History* (Westport, CT: Greenwood Press, 2004), 153.

7. G. L. King, "Wampus Club's Thirteen Baby Stars Broadcast from KFI's Microphone," *Radio Digest,* Feb. 7, 1925.

8. "Stars Flock to Bay for Frolic: Los Angeles Studios Call Halt as Celebrities Migrate to Wampus Ball," *Oakland Tribune,* Jan. 20, 1924.

9. "Rockne Teaches Class at USC This Summer," *Southern California Trojan,* May 23, 1924.

10. Paul Lowry, "Knute Rockne in Our Midst," *Los Angeles Times,* July 8, 1924.

11. Elmer Henderson to Knute Rockne, telegram, Dec. 20, 1923, UADR 13/66, folder—Henderson, Elmer (USC, Univ. of Tulsa), 1924–1926, Athletics, Series 2. Correspondence and Subject Files, alphabetical (mainly 1924–1929), University Records, University of Notre Dame Archives.

12. Braven Dyer, "Knute Rockne Due Tomorrow," *Los Angeles Times,* July 6, 1924.

13. Lowry, "Knute Rockne in Our Midst," *Los Angeles Times,* July 8, 1924.

14. Richard J. Shmelter, *The USC Trojans Football Encyclopedia* (Jefferson, NC: McFarland and Co., 2014), 265.

15. Paul Lowry, "Henderson Emits Gloom," *Los Angeles Times,* Oct. 21, 1919.

16. Braven Dyer, "Knute Rockne Due Tomorrow," *Los Angeles Times,* July 6, 1924.

17. William R. LaPorte to Knute Rockne, Oct. 1, 1924, UADR 19/134, box 19, folder 134, UADR Athletic Directors Records, University of Notre Dame Archives.

18. Knute Rockne to William R. LaPorte, Oct. 7, 1924, UADR 19/134, box 19, folder 134, UADR Athletic Directors Records, University of Notre Dame Archives.

19. Karen Croake Heisler, *Fighting Irish: Legends, Lists, and Lore* (Champaign, IL: Sports Publishing LLC, 2006), 69.

20. "Notre Dame–40, Lombard–0," *Official 1924 Football Review, University of Notre Dame* (sports yearbook), 24, University of Notre Dame Archives website, http://archives.nd.edu/Football/Football-1924.pdf.

21. "Notre Dame Eleven Defeats Army," *New York Times*, Oct. 19, 1924, reproduced in *Official 1924 Football Review, University of Notre Dame* (sports yearbook), 29.

22. Robinson, *Rockne of Notre Dame*, 147–48.

23. New Amsterdam Theatre: History (website), http://newamsterdamtheatre.com/history.html.

24. "New Amsterdam Theatre: 1905," photograph at Shorpy Historic Pictures (website), http://www.shorpy.com/node/9430?size=_original.

25. Jerome Holtzman, ed., *No Cheering in the Press Box* (New York: Henry Holt and Co., 1978), 147.

26. Grantland Rice, "The Four Horsemen," *New York Herald Tribune*, Oct. 18, 1924.

27. Robinson, *Rockne of Notre Dame*, 154.

28. Holtzman, *No Cheering in the Press Box*, 147.

29. Billy Evans, "Coin Lured Famous Iowa Grid Mentor to Trinity," *Harrisburg (PA) Evening News*, Jan. 25, 1924.

30. "Heavy Trinity Eleven Wins with Small Score," *University of Richmond Collegian*, Oct. 24, 1924.

31. Warren W. Brown, "Notre Dame Gallops over Carnegie Tech," *Chicago Herald and Examiner*, Nov. 30, 1924, reproduced in *Official 1924 Football Review, University of Notre Dame* (sports yearbook), 43.

9. Go West, Young Man

1. Bob Pool, "City of Angels' First Name Still Bedevils Historians," *Los Angeles Times*, Mar. 26, 2005.

2. Kevin Starr, *Material Dreams: Southern California through the 1920s* (New York: Oxford Univ. Press, 1990), 132.

3. Jon Wilkman and Nancy Wilkman, *Los Angeles: A Pictorial Celebration* (New York: Sterling Publishing Co., 2008), 52.

4. Robert Sklar, *Movie-Made America: A Cultural History of American Movies* (New York: Vintage Books, 1994), 67.

5. U.S. Bureau of the Census, *15th Census of the United States, 1930,* Washington, D.C.: National Archives and Records Administration, 1930.

6. Leo Braudy, *The Hollywood Sign: Fantasy and Reality of an American Icon* (New Haven, CT: Yale Univ. Press, 2011), 72, 125.

7. "History: Rose Bowl Stadium Historical Facts," Rose Bowl: America's Stadium (website), http://www.rosebowlstadium.com/about/history.

8. Michelle L. Turner, *The Rose Bowl* (Mt. Pleasant, SC: Arcadia Publishing, 2010), 29, 37.

9. Schmidt, *Shaping College Football*, 17.

10. Richard Whittingham, *Rites of Autumn: The Story of College Football* (New York: Free Press, 2001), 153.

11. Associated Press, "Stanford to Play Notre Dame Here," *Los Angeles Times*, Nov. 25, 1924.

12. Robinson, *Rockne of Notre Dame*, 162.

13. Associated Press, "Notre Dame Opponent Still Sought," *Los Angeles Times*, Nov. 26, 1924.

14. Knute Rockne to William R. LaPorte, Dec. 8, 1924, UADR 19/134, box 19, folder 134, UADR Athletic Directors Records, University of Notre Dame Archives.

15. Associated Press, "Notre Dame Opponent Still Sought," *Los Angeles Times*, Nov. 26, 1924.

16. Sperber, *Shake Down the Thunder*, 169.

17. "That Football Trip," *Notre Dame Scholastic* 58, no. 11, Jan. 1925, 330.

18. Bill Henry, "Notre Dame Gridders Arrive Here Today for New Year's Battle," *Los Angeles Times*, Dec. 31, 1924.

19. "And They Call It a Five-Passenger Car!" (photo caption), *Los Angeles Times*, Jan. 4, 1925.

20. "That Football Trip," *Notre Dame Scholastic* 58, no. 11, Jan. 1925, 332.

21. Robert E. Burns, *Being Catholic, Being American*, vol. 1: *The Notre Dame Story, 1832–1934* (South Bend, IN: Univ. of Notre Dame Press, 1999), 364.

22. "That Football Trip," *Notre Dame Scholastic* 58, no. 11, Jan. 1925, 330.

23. "Immense Reception Planned for Irish," *Los Angeles Times*, Dec. 28, 1924.

24. "Irish Rooters Arrive," *Los Angeles Times*, Dec. 31, 1924.

25. "That Football Trip," *Notre Dame Scholastic* 58, no. 11, Jan. 1925, 330.

26. John B. Rae, "The Fabulous Billy Durant," *Business History Review* 32, no. 33 (Autumn 1958): 255–71.

27. "Motor Cars for 'Irish,'" *Los Angeles Times*, Dec. 28, 1924.

28. Hermine Lees, "History of St. Andrew Church," *The Tidings*, May 7, 2004.

29. Joseph Scott, "Notre Dame versus Stanford," *Notre Dame Scholastic* 58, no. 11, Jan. 1925, 350.

30. Walter Eckersall, "Card Gridders Arrive Today," *Los Angeles Times*, Dec. 28, 1924.

31. "Knute Rockne and Others," Bettman Collection, Editorial # 517296612, Getty Images (website), http://www.gettyimages.com/license/517296612.

32. Burns, *Being Catholic, Being American*, 1: 367.

33. John Charles Hibner, *The Rose Bowl 1902–1929: A Game-By-Game History of Collegiate Football's Foremost Event, from Its Advent through Its Golden Era* (Jefferson, NC: McFarland and Co., 1993), 132–37.

34. Joseph Scott, "Notre Dame versus Stanford," 350.

35. "Fantasy Football," Library Muse (weblog), Rauner Special Collections Library, Dartmouth University, https://sites.dartmouth.edu/library/2014/10/14/fantasy-football-2/.

36. "South Bend Celebrates Rockne Win," *Los Angeles Times*, Jan. 2, 1925.

37. "Coaches Laud Rockne," *Los Angeles Times*, Jan. 2, 1925.

38. "Grid Mentors Meet Scribes at Luncheon," *Los Angeles Times*, Jan. 3, 1925.

39. Braven Dyer, "Irish Will Not Take On Bears," *Los Angeles Times*, Jan. 3, 1925.

40. "That Football Trip," *Notre Dame Scholastic* 58, no. 11, Jan. 1925, 330.

41. "Trojans Accept Missouri Bid," *Los Angeles Times*, Dec. 3, 1924.

42. "USC to Wear Blue Uniforms," *Los Angeles Times*, Dec. 18, 1924.

43. "Bill Cole Ruled out of Game between USC and Bears," *Los Angeles Times*, Oct. 31, 1924.

44. Braven Dyer, "Officials Act in USC War Today," *Los Angeles Times,* Jan. 15, 1925.

45. Sperber, *Shake Down the Thunder,* 97, 122, 154, 187.

46. Braven Dyer, "USC Looking for New Coach," *Los Angeles Times,* Jan. 16, 1925.

47. Jim Lefebvre, *Coach for a Nation: The Life and Times of Knute Rockne* (Minneapolis, MN: Great Day Press, 2013), 354.

48. "Trojans Offer Coach Rockne Game Next Year," *Chicago Daily Tribune,* Jan. 7, 1925.

49. "Henderson Resigns as Trojans' Coach," *Chicago Daily Tribune,* Jan. 16, 1925.

50. Sperber, *Shake Down the Thunder,* 129, 186.

51. "Trojans Flirt with Rockne as Successor to Henderson," *Chicago Daily Tribune,* Jan. 14, 1925.

52. Ibid.

53. "Rockne Returns," *Chicago Daily Tribune,* Jan. 16, 1925.

54. Warren Bovard to Knute Rockne, telegram, Jan. 15, 1925, UADR 8/179, Director of Athletics, 1909–29 [1908–1931], University of Notre Dame Archives.

55. Braven Dyer, "Expect Resignation of Henderson This Morning," *Los Angeles Times,* Jan. 15, 1925.

56. "Henderson Resigns as Trojans' Head Coach," *Chicago Daily Tribune,* Jan. 16, 1925.

57. Sperber, *Shake Down the Thunder,* 187.

58. Knute Rockne to Warren Bovard, June 4, 1925, UADR 8/179, Athletics, Correspondence and Subject Files, University Records, University of Notre Dame Archives.

59. George Shaffer, "Rockne Spurns Coast Job; Gives Bill Spaulding Boost," *Chicago Daily Tribune,* Jan. 20, 1925.

60. "Rockne Returns," *Chicago Daily Tribune,* Jan. 16, 1925.

61. Sperber, *Shake Down the Thunder,* 180.

62. "Rockne Won't Leave Job," *Los Angeles Times,* Jan. 14, 1925.

63. Dyer, "USC Looking for New Coach," *Los Angeles Times,* Jan. 16, 1925.

64. "Henderson Resigns as Trojans' Head Coach," *Chicago Daily Tribune,* Jan. 16, 1925.

65. Shaffer, "Rockne Spurns Coast Job," *Chicago Daily Tribune,* Jan. 20, 1925.

10. A New Man in Charge

1. National Oceanic and Atmospheric Administration, National Weather Service (website), Online Weather Data, http://www.nws.noaa.gov/climate/xmacis.php?wfo=lot.

2. Bergreen, *Capone,* 143.

3. Nate Hendley, *Al Capone: Chicago's King of Crime* (Ontario: Five Rivers Chapmanry, 2010), 48.

4. Paul Sann, *The Lawless Decade: Bullets, Broads, and Bathtub Gin* (North Chelmsford, MA: Courier Corp., 2010), 111.

5. Curt Johnson with R. Craig Sautter, *The Wicked City: Chicago from Kenna to Capone* (Highland Park, IL: Da Capo Press, 1998), 180.

6. Bill Henry, Observations (column), *Los Angeles Times,* Jan. 14, 1925.

7. Bill Henry, Observations (column), *Los Angeles Times,* Feb. 18, 1925.

8. "U.S.C. Supporters Hope Jones Will Be Man to Bring Stop to California Grid Victories," *Los Angeles Times*, Feb. 8, 1925.

9. Paul Lowry, "Students in Tribute to Gloomy Gus," *Los Angeles Times*, Jan. 17, 1925.

10. Joe Jares, "Al Wesson—Hall of Fame Candidate," *USC Report*, Aug. 28, 2007.

11. Paul Lowry, "Name Howard Jones Coach at U.S.C.: Iowa Gridiron Mentor Succeeds Henderson," *Los Angeles Times*, Feb. 4, 1925.

12. "Howard Jones Made Coach of Trojan Eleven," *Chicago Daily Tribune*, Feb. 4, 1925.

13. Lowry, "Name Howard Jones Coach at U.S.C.," *Los Angeles Times*, Feb. 4, 1925.

14. Ibid.

15. Ibid.

16. "T. A. Jones Buys 2 Paper Mills," *Hamilton (OH) Daily News*, Dec. 5, 1925.

17. Howard Jones: Actor (1885–1941), Internet Movie Database (website), http://m.imdb.com/name/nm0428234/.

18. Henry, Observations (column), *Los Angeles Times*, Feb. 18, 1925.

19. Tucker, *Notre Dame vs. the Klan*, 185.

20. "The Klan Walks in Washington," *Literary Digest*, Aug. 22, 1925.

21. Tucker, *Notre Dame vs. the Klan*, 139.

22. Burns, *Being Catholic, Being American*, 1: 381.

23. Tucker, *Notre Dame vs. the Klan*, 110.

24. Ibid., 179–203.

25. Ibid., 209–10.

26. Robinson, *Rockne of Notre Dame*, 176.

27. Tucker, *Notre Dame vs. the Klan*, 186.

28. "Mrs. Howard Jones Files for Divorce," *New York Times*, July 28, 1925.

29. "Would Divorce Football Coach," *Evening Independent*, July 30, 1925.

11. "The Game Is On"

1. Randy Roberts, *John Wayne: American* (Lincoln, NE: Bison Books, 1997), 48, 52.

2. "Rufus B. von KleinSmid," About USC: Gallery of USC Presidents, University of Southern California (website), http://about.usc.edu/presidents/rufus-b-von-kleinsmid/.

3. Roberts, *John Wayne*, 52.

4. "Large Grid Squad Greets New U.S.C. Coach in Opening Workout," *Los Angeles Times*, Apr. 28, 1925.

5. "U.S.C. Football Men Out Today," *Los Angeles Times*, Apr. 27, 1925.

6. "Mrs. Howard Jones Freed," *New York Times*, Sept. 28, 1925.

7. Dave Feigenbaum, "Jones' Boys of '25 Prompt Tag of 'Thundering Herd,'" *Southern California Daily Trojan*, Oct. 23, 1951.

8. "Zane Grey Film Opens Monday at Million Dollar," *Los Angeles Times*, Mar. 12, 1925.

9. McCready Huston, *Salesman from the Sidelines: Being the Business Career of Knute K. Rockne* (New York: Ray Long and Richard R. Smith, 1932), 235.

10. Robinson, *Rockne of Notre Dame*, 177.

11. John McMahon, "The Day the Rock Was Baptized," *Notre Dame Scholastic* 98, no. 20, Mar. 29, 1957, 24–25.

12. Robinson, *Rockne of Notre Dame,* 176.

13. Lefebvre, *Coach for a Nation,* 369.

14. Dorothy V. Corson, "Notre Dame's Log Chapel: A Sacred Place Filled with Sacred Memories," The Spirit of Notre Dame: Notre Dame Legends and Lore (website), http://www3.nd.edu/~wcawley/corson/logchapel.htm.

15. McMahon, "The Day the Rock Was Baptized."

16. "Trojans May Yet Play Notre Dame," *Southern Californian Trojan,* Sept. 28, 1923.

17. "Henderson Resigns as Trojans' Coach," *Chicago Daily Tribune,* Jan. 16, 1925.

18. Sperber, *Shake Down the Thunder,* 190.

19. "N. Dame Cards Only One New Foe for 1926," *Chicago Daily Tribune,* Nov. 24, 1925.

20. Walter Eckersall, "Trojans, N. Dame May Clash in Chicago in '26," *Chicago Daily Tribune,* Nov. 25, 1925.

21. Peter N. Synodis, "Climate Influenced Rockne's Decision," *Southern California Daily Trojan,* Apr. 1, 1955.

22. "Gwynn Wilson Leaves for East to Secure Games," *Southern California Daily Trojan,* Nov. 25, 1925.

23. Jerry Crowe, "Rockne Had to Be Sold on the Idea," *Los Angeles Times,* Nov. 21, 1990.

24. John D. Hawke, "Remarks Before the Stonier Graduate School of Banking, Washington D.C., June 19, 2000," News Release 2000–46, Office of the Comptroller of the Currency, U.S. Department of the Treasury, June 20, 2000, http://www.occ.gov/static/news-issuances/news-releases/2000/nr-occ-2000–46.pdf.

25. Portrait of Harold Stonier, reproduced in Cameron Applegate, *"The Game Is On": Notre Dame vs. USC, A Fifty Year History of Football's Oldest Inter-Sectional Rivalry* (Los Angeles, CA: Two Continents Publishing, 1977), 34.

26. Synodis, "Climate Influenced Rockne's Decision," *Southern California Daily Trojan,* Apr. 1, 1955.

27. Applegate, *"The Game Is On,"* 33–34.

28. Jerry Crowe, "Rockne Had to Be Sold on the Idea," *Los Angeles Times,* Nov. 21, 1990

29. Applegate, *"The Game Is On,"* 33–34.

30. Robinson, *Rockne of Notre Dame,* 174.

31. Lowry, "Knute Rockne in Our Midst," *Los Angeles Times,* July 8, 1924.

32. Applegate, *"The Game Is On,"* 35.

33. "Gwynn Wilson Leaves for East to Secure Games," *Southern California Daily Trojan,* Nov. 25, 1925.

34. Applegate, *"The Game Is On,"* 35–36.

12. The Plastic Age

1. "Movie Producer Bankrupt: Benjamin P. Schulberg Lists Debts at $820,744 and Assets $1,420," *New York Times,* Oct. 22, 1925; David Stenn, *Clara Bow: Runnin' Wild* (New York: Cooper Square Press, 2000), 58.

2. Screen Siftings (column), *Lincoln Star,* Apr. 25, 1926.

3. "The Flapper and the Vampire: Clara Bow meets Bela Lugosi," Turner Classic Movies (website), http://fan.tcm.com/_Clara-Bow-38-Bela-Lugosi-Did-They-or-Didn39t-They/blog/6388259/66470.html?createPassive=true.

4. Passport of Florence Jane Dean, United States Department of State, May 14, 1917.

5. "Major William Dean," *Annals of Iowa,* 3rd series, 12, no. 8 (1921): 638.

6. "Hunt Owner of Mystery Auto," *Los Angeles Times,* Aug. 5, 1919.

7. "Recalls Leap to Death," *Los Angeles Times,* Nov. 4, 1920.

8. Marriage Certificate of Jane Dean and George Ridley, May 29, 1920, collection of Carolyn Jones O'Connell and Bernadette Vargas (daughter and granddaughter of Howard Jones respectively).

9. "Coach Jones and Wife on Honeymoon," *Los Angeles Examiner,* Apr. 3, 1926.

10. Lee Conti, On the Lookout (column), *Southern California Daily Trojan,* Apr. 6, 1926.

11. "Howard Jones and Wife Seek Happiness in New Ventures in Matrimony," *Iowa City Press-Citizen,* Apr. 2, 1926.

12. Juana Neal Levy, Society (column), *Los Angeles Times,* Apr. 2, 1926.

13. Braven Dyer, "Don Williams Best Quarterback Prospect since Days of Aubrey Devine, Says Jones," *Los Angeles Times,* May 9, 1926.

14. Braven Dyer, "Brice Taylor May Lose Berth on University of Southern California Football Team," *Los Angeles Times,* Apr. 25, 1926.

15. Braven Dyer, "Don Williams Best Quarterback Prospect," *Los Angeles Times,* May 9, 1926.

16. Roberts, *John Wayne,* 47, 49.

17. Braven Dyer, "Don Williams Best Quarterback Prospect," *Los Angeles Times,* May 9, 1926.

18. Ray Schmidt, "Kaer and 1926 USC," *College Football Historical Society Newsletter* 8, no. 2 (Feb. 1995), available at the LA84 Foundation's online Sports Library, http://library.la84.org/SportsLibrary/CFHSN/CFHSNv08/CFHSNv08n2h.pdf.

19. Ibid.

20. Sperber, *Shake Down the Thunder,* 217–19.

21. Robinson, *Rockne of Notre Dame,* 185–87.

13. The Greatest Game I Ever Saw

1. Bill Henry, "Irish Plan to Stage Workout," *Los Angeles Times,* Dec. 2, 1926.

2. Bill Henry, "Notre Dame Eleven Due to Arrive Here Tonight," *Los Angeles Times,* Dec. 3, 1926.

3. Bill Henry, "Irish Plan to Stage Workout," *Los Angeles Times,* Dec. 2, 1926.

4. Robinson, *Rockne of Notre Dame,* 187.

5. Henry, "Notre Dame Eleven Due," *Los Angeles Times,* Dec. 3, 1926.

6. Paul Lowry, "Irish Eleven Arrive Friday Night," *Los Angeles Times,* Nov. 29, 1926.

7. Braven Dyer, "Trojans Look Good in Drill," *Los Angeles Times,* Dec. 2, 1926.

8. "Irishmen Face Trojans as Grid Curtain Drops; 100,000 to See the Battle," *Notre Dame Scholastic* 60, no. 11, Dec. 3, 1926, 346.

9. Ibid.

10. Lowry, "Irish Eleven Arrive Friday Night," *Los Angeles Times,* Nov. 29, 1926.

11. Bill Henry, Observations (column), *Los Angeles Times,* Nov. 26, 1926.

12. "Trojans Have Slight Edge, Coaches Say" *Los Angeles Times,* Dec. 4, 1926.

13. "Tickets Gone for Big Game," *Los Angeles Times,* Nov. 17, 1926.

14. "KHJ Will Be on the Air Today with Grid Classic," *Los Angeles Times,* Dec. 4, 1926.

15. "Coaches Dine with Editors at Banquets," *Los Angeles Times,* Dec. 4, 1926.

16. "Sunshine Promised Tomorrow," *Los Angeles Times,* Dec. 5, 1926.

17. "Place Autos at Service of Notre Dame Eleven," *Los Angeles Times,* Dec. 5, 1926.

18. "Burlesques on Irishmen to Be Seen in Floats," *Southern California Daily Trojan,* Dec. 2, 1926.

19. Henry, "Notre Dame Eleven Due," *Los Angeles Times,* Dec. 3, 1926.

20. "Portrait of Knute Rockne and Son with Actress," Bettman Collection, Editorial # 517731006, Getty Images (website), http://www.gettyimages.com/license/517731006.

21. "About USC Spirit Leaders: How It All Started: Lindley Bothwell and the USC Yell Leaders," University of Southern California, Recreational Sports (website), http://sait.usc.edu/recsports/spirit/leaders/about/.

22. Football: Notre Dame vs. USC, 1926, Pathe Fox newsreel [negative], AATH 9181 F2, Notre Dame Athletics Collection: Audio-Visual, University of Notre Dame Archives.

23. "The Bears History: Uniform History," Chicago Bears (website), http://www.chicagobears.com/tradition/uniform-history.html.

24. Henry, "Notre Dame Eleven Due," *Los Angeles Times,* Dec. 3, 1926.

25. "The Otto Graham Myth and the Evolution of the Face Mask," Cleveland Browns (website), http://m.clevelandbrowns.com/news/article-1/The-Otto-Graham-Myth-and-the-Evolution-of-the-Face Mask/572726b4-eca8–4e21-aa17-b99b28e735f4.

26. "Detailed Account of How Irishmen Turned Back Herd," *Los Angeles Times,* Dec. 5, 1926.

27. Paul Lowry, "Notre Dame Beats U.S.C.," *Los Angeles Times,* Dec. 5, 1926.

28. "Detailed Account," *Los Angeles Times,* Dec. 5, 1926.

29. Braven Dyer, "Would Do as Jones Had to, Says Rockne," *Los Angeles Times,* Dec. 6, 1926.

30. Applegate, *"The Game Is On,"* 40.

31. "Detailed Account," *Los Angeles Times,* Dec. 5, 1926.

32. "Greatest Game Ever Saw, Says Rock to Jones," *Los Angeles Times,* Dec. 5, 1926.

33. Helen Sauber, "Homecoming Program Voted Successful by S.C. Alumni after Week of Festivities," *Southern California Daily Trojan,* Dec. 7, 1926.

34. "Theatrical Ball Scene of Gayety," *Los Angeles Times,* Dec. 5, 1926.

35. Irene Schmitz, "Victory Dance Is Climax of Alumni Week," *Southern California Daily Trojan*, Dec. 3, 1926.

14. What's All This Fuss about a Football Game?

1. David Stenn, *Clara Bow: Runnin' Wild* (New York: Cooper Square Press, 2000), 109.

2. Elinor Glyn, qtd. on title card, *It*, Paramount Pictures, 1927.

3. Stenn, *Clara Bow*, 50.

4. Braven Dyer, "Tappan Lands Regular Berth," *Los Angeles Times*, Oct. 18, 1927.

5. Stenn, *Clara Bow*, 110.

6. Howard Jones, "Watching Coast Elevens," *Los Angeles Times*, Oct. 30, 1927.

7. Stenn, *Clara Bow*, 111–14.

8. "Stork Visits Howard Jones," *Los Angeles Times*, Dec. 10, 1927.

9. Braven Dyer, "Trojans Leave Tomorrow for Notre Dame Game," *Los Angeles Times*, Nov. 21, 1927.

10. Paul Lowry, "Trojans Bolt Grid Classic," *Los Angeles Times*, Nov. 22, 1927.

11. Dyer, "Trojans Leave Tomorrow," *Los Angeles Times*, Nov. 21, 1927.

12. "Trojan Co-Ed Is Hostess at Cafe," *Southern California Daily Trojan*, Nov. 23, 1927.

13. Ralph Huston, On the Lookout (column), *Southern California Daily Trojan*, Nov. 23, 1927.

14. "Overflow of Trojan Spirit Shown in Notre Dame Rally; Starred by College Tableu," *Southern California Daily Trojan*, Nov. 23, 1927.

15. Karmi Wyckoff, "Gridders Will Get Plaudits," *Southern California Daily Trojan*, Nov. 22, 1927.

16. Huston, On the Lookout (column), *Southern California Daily Trojan*, Nov. 23, 1927.

17. Jake Shuken, "33 Trojans Thunder On to Chicago: Williams Is Out of Big Game," *Southern California Daily Trojan*, Nov. 22, 1927.

18. Braven Dyer, "Trojans Given Rousing Send-Off to Chicago," *Los Angeles Times*, Nov. 23, 1927.

19. "1924 Notre Dame Fighting Irish Football Team," Wikipedia (online encyclopedia), http://en.wikipedia.org/wiki/1924_Notre_Dame_Fighting_Irish_football_team.

20. John F. Swenson, "Chicagoua/Chicago: The Origin, Meaning, and Etymology of a Place Name," *Journal of the Illinois Historical Society* 84, no. 4 (Winter 1991): 235–48.

21. "Fighting Irish Back Home: Begin Work for Trojan Tilt," *Los Angeles Times*, Nov. 22, 1927.

22. Braven Dyer, "Pullman Tips," *Los Angeles Times*, Nov. 24, 1927.

23. Bill Harvey, "Trip, Loss, and Cold Barriers," *Southern California Daily Trojan*, Nov. 23, 1927.

24. Shuken, "33 Trojans Thunder On to Chicago," *Southern California Daily Trojan*, Nov. 22, 1927.

25. Dyer, "Pullman Tips," *Los Angeles Times*, Nov. 25, 1927.

26. Braven Dyer, "Jones Leads Trojan Squad into Chicago Today," *Los Angeles Times*, Nov. 25, 1927.

27. Braven Dyer, "Public Eye on Pigskin," *Los Angeles Times*, Nov. 26, 1927.

28. Fred Vandevender, "116,000 Fans to see Notre Dame Battle Trojans," *Los Angeles Examiner*, Nov. 23, 1927.

29. "Chicago Plans Rousing Welcome for U.S.C. Grid Team," *Los Angeles Times,* September 3, 1927.

30. Shuken, "33 Trojans Thunder On to Chicago," *Southern California Daily Trojan,* Nov. 22, 1927.

31. "Notre Dame Gridders Work on Plays for Trojan Clash," *Los Angeles Times,* Nov. 25, 1927.

32. "Jones to Speak at U.S.C. Alumni Dinner Friday," *Chicago Daily Tribune,* Nov. 24, 1927.

33. "Trojans Dine at Training Table; Visit at Banquet," *Chicago Daily Tribune,* Nov. 26, 1927.

34. "Irish 'Sad and Drury,'" *Billings Gazette,* Nov. 26, 1927.

35. "Football Experts Put Away the Groceries," *Huntington Press,* Nov. 30, 1927.

36. "U.S.C. Mentor at 'Mike' Tonight; Rockne, 'Pop' Warner, Tad Jones Also Speak," *Los Angeles Examiner,* Nov. 25, 1927.

37. "Grid Tutors to Speak Before Big Tilt," *Lincoln Evening Journal,* Nov. 22, 1927.

38. Associated Press, "Chicago Shows Trojan, Irish School Colors," *Los Angeles Examiner,* Nov. 26, 1927.

39. Advertisement for round-trip excursion train to the Notre Dame-USC game, leaving Indianapolis for Chicago at 12:40 A.M. on Nov. 26, 1927, offered by J. N. Lemon, division passenger agent, Big Four Route, *Indianapolis News,* Nov. 14, 1927.

15. See You in Chicago

1. "Grid-O-Graph to Display N.D. Game in Bovard," *Southern California Daily Trojan,* Nov. 23, 1927.

2. *Encyclopedia of Chicago,* s.v. "Soldier Field" (by Steven A. Riess), http://encyclopedia.chicagohistory.org/pages/1165.html.

3. John. P. Gallagher, "Notre Dame Gridders Prepare for Clash with Thundering Herd," *Los Angeles Times,* Nov. 20, 1927.

4. Ralph L. Power, "Fans Await Grid Broadcast," *Los Angeles Times,* Nov. 25, 1927.

5. "Fans to Hear Trojan Game," *Los Angeles Times,* Nov. 24, 1927.

6. George Strickler, "Irish Coach Prefers Dry Field for Game Saturday with S.C.," *Los Angeles Examiner,* Nov. 23, 1927.

7. Braven Dyer, "Irish Down Trojans," *Los Angeles Times,* Nov. 27, 1927.

8. Dyer, "Public Eye on Pigskin," *Los Angeles Times,* Nov. 26, 1927.

9. Walter Eckersall, "117,000 See Notre Dame Win," *Chicago Daily Tribune,* Nov. 27, 1927.

10. "Several Hundred S.C. Alumni Off for Eastern Tilt," *Southern California Daily Trojan,* Nov. 22, 1927.

11. Edward Burns, "Police, Ushers Make Traffic Job Look Easy," *Chicago Daily Tribune,* Nov. 27, 1927.

12. Fred Vandevendor, "116,000 Witness Great Game at Soldiers Field," *Los Angeles Examiner,* Nov. 27, 1927.

13. Irving Vaughan, "Here's Play by Play Story of East-West Epic," *Chicago Daily Tribune,* Nov. 27, 1927.

14. "Play-By-Play Story of Titanic Battle between Trojan and Irish Clans," *Chicago Daily Tribune,* Nov. 27, 1927.

15. Braven Dyer, "Irish Down Trojans," *Los Angeles Times,* Nov. 27, 1927.

16. "Notre Dame Victors by Single Point," *Ottawa Journal,* Nov. 28, 1927.

17. Dyer, "Irish Down Trojans," *Los Angeles Times,* Nov. 27, 1927.

18. "Drury, Trojans Hit Touchback Decision," *Chicago Daily Tribune,* Nov. 30, 1927.

19. "Play-By-Play Story of Titanic Battle," *Chicago Daily Tribune,* Nov. 27, 1927.

20. Harland Rohm, "Tired Victors Take Time Out to Eat, Cheer," *Chicago Daily Tribune,* Nov. 27, 1927.

21. "2,200 Persons Fete Rockne and Team at Dinner," *Chicago Daily Tribune,* Nov. 27, 1927.

22. Braven Dyer, "Thundering Herd Arrives Home This Morning," *Los Angeles Times,* Nov. 29, 1927.

23. "Jones Doesn't Back Official," *Harrisburg ((PA) Evening News,* Nov. 30, 1927.

24. "Football Men Given Big Cheer," *Southern California Daily Trojan,* Nov. 30, 1927.

25. Karmi Wyckoff, "Impromptu Rally to Welcome Varsity: Informal Reception Scheduled," *Southern California Daily Trojan,* Nov. 29, 1927.

26. "Football Men Given Big Cheer," *Southern California Daily Trojan,* Nov. 30, 1927.

27. "Drury, Trojans Hit Touchback Decision," *Chicago Daily Tribune,* Nov. 30, 1927.

28. "Pictures of Disputed Play Shown in Movie of Big Game," *Los Angeles Times,* Nov. 28, 1927.

29. "N.D. Game Films Meet Difficulties," *Southern California Daily Trojan,* Nov. 30, 1927.

30. "Film Show Delayed by Union Row," *Los Angeles Times,* Nov. 30, 1927.

31. "East Side, West Side Entertains," *Davenport Democrat,* Nov. 28, 1927.

32. "Actress Gets Run Down by Trojan Herd," *Los Angeles Times,* Dec. 6, 1927.

33. Stenn, *Clara Bow,* 112.

34. Brondfield, *Rockne,* 181.

35. Sperber, *Shake Down the Thunder,* 270.

36. Associated Press, "Notre Dame and S. California Sign 2 Year Home and Home Agreement," *Lancaster Eagle-Gazette,* Nov. 28, 1927.

37. Paul Lowry, "Trojans in 27–14 Win," *Los Angeles Times,* Dec. 2, 1928.

38. "Ruth Gets 3-Year Contract with New York Yankees at $70,000 a Year," *Allentown Morning Call,* Mar. 3, 1927.

39. Robert L. Carringer, *The Jazz Singer* (Madison: Univ. of Wisconsin Press, 1979), 194.

40. Brooke L. Blower, *Becoming Americans in Paris: Transatlantic Politics and Culture between the World Wars* (New York: Oxford Univ. Press, 2001), 93.

41. "Al Smith Campaign Ad," Corbis Historical Collection, Editorial # 534234786, Getty Images (website), http://www.gettyimages.com/license/534234786.

42. John Kobler, *Capone: The Life and World of Al Capone,* 2nd ed. (Boston, MA: Da Capo Press, 2003), 16.

43. Peter Winnewisser, *The Legendary Model A Ford,* 2nd ed. (Iola, WI: Krause Publications, 2006), 8.

44. "Miller Will Be Only Notre Dame Veteran Available for 1928," *Bismarck Tribune,* Dec. 9, 1927.

45. Lawrence Perry, "Knute Rockne Likely to Devise New Offense for Next Season," *Syracuse Herald,* Nov. 14, 1927.

46. "'Fighting Irish' as Applied to Notre Dame Teams OK," *Havre Daily News,* Oct. 13, 1927.

16. Win One for the Gipper

1. Sperber, *Shake Down the Thunder,* 284–86.

2. John P. Gallagher, "Rockne Sad and Gloomy: Sage of South Bend Says Notre Dame Will Be Lucky to Win Single Game This Year," *Los Angeles Times,* Sept. 30, 1928.

3. Sperber, *Shake Down the Thunder,* 286.

4. Francis Wallace, "Gipp's Ghost Beat Army," *New York Daily News,* Nov. 12, 1928.

5. Sperber, *Shake Down the Thunder,* 286.

6. Michael R. Steele, *The Fighting Irish Football Encyclopedia* (Champaign, IL: Sports Publishing LLC, 2003), 63–64.

7. Sperber, *Shake Down the Thunder,* 284.

8. John D. McCallum and Paul Castner, *We Remember Rockne* (Huntington, IN: Our Sunday Visitor, Inc., 1975), 68.

9. Culver, qtd. in "The Forgotten Trojans" by Ray Schmidt, *College Football Historical Society Newsletter* 3, no. 1 (Nov. 1989), available at the LA84 Foundation's online Sports Library, http://library.la84.org/SportsLibrary/CFHSN/CFHSNv03/CFHSNv03n1c.pdf.

10. Stenn, *Clara Bow,* 111.

11. Braven Dyer, Grid Gossip (column), *Los Angeles Times,* Sept. 30, 1928.

12. "Notre Dame Eleven on Way to Los Angeles," *Los Angeles Times,* Nov. 26, 1928.

13. Braven Dyer, "Niemiec Has Slight Hurt," *Los Angeles Times,* Nov. 29, 1928.

14. John Heisler, *"Then Ara Said to Joe . . .": The Best Notre Dame Football Stories Ever Told* (Chicago, IL: Triumph Books, 2007), 1.

15. McCallum and Castner, *We Remember Rockne,* 203.

16. Paul Zimmerman, Sport Postscripts (column), *Los Angeles Times,* July 29, 1941.

17. "Tucson Fetes Two Elevens," *Los Angeles Times,* Nov. 28, 1928; Dyer, "Niemiec Has Slight Hurt," *Los Angeles Times,* Nov. 29, 1928.

18. Dyer, "Niemiec Has Slight Hurt," *Los Angeles Times,* Nov. 29, 1928.

19. Braven Dyer, "Notre Dame Will Arrive Here Today for Battle with Thundering Herd Tomorrow," Nov. 30, 1928.

20. Dyer, "Niemiec Has Slight Hurt," *Los Angeles Times,* Nov. 29, 1928.

21. Paul Lowry, "Fighting Warriors on Edge for Titanic Gridiron Duel," *Los Angeles Times,* Dec. 1, 1928.

22. Dyer, "Notre Dame Will Arrive Here Today for Battle with Thundering Herd Tomorrow," *Los Angeles Times,* Nov. 30, 1928.

23. Braven Dyer, "Jones Drives Trojans Behind Locked Gates," *Los Angeles Times,* Nov. 27, 1928.

24. Braven Dyer, "Howard Jones Shifts Line-up," *Los Angeles Times,* Dec. 1, 1928.

25. Lowry, "Fighting Warriors on Edge," *Los Angeles Times*, Dec. 1, 1928.

26. "Trojans Favored to Collect Honors Today, Census among Local Sportsmen Indicates," *Los Angeles Times*, Dec. 1, 1928.

27. Paul Lowry, "Trojans in 27–14 Win," *Los Angeles Times*, Dec. 2, 1928.

28. Braven Dyer, "Here's the Play-by-Play Description of the Irish-Trojan Football Classic," *Los Angeles Times*, Dec. 2, 1928.

29. Applegate, *"The Game Is On,"* 49.

30. Dyer, "Here's the Play-By-Play Description of the Irish-Trojan Football Classic," *Los Angeles Times*, Dec. 2, 1928.

31. "Rockne Leaves for East; Son Seriously Ill," *Los Angeles Times*, Dec. 2, 1928.

32. Sperber, *Shake Down the Thunder*, 289.

33. "Rockne Leaves for East; Son Seriously Ill," *Los Angeles Times*, Dec. 2, 1928.

34. Paul Lowry, Rabbit Punches (column), *Los Angeles Times*, Nov. 6, 1928.

35. Fred Eisenhammer and Eric B. Sondheimer, *College Football's Most Memorable Games*, 2nd ed. (Jefferson, NC: McFarland and Co., 2010), 18.

36. "Trojans Will Receive Championship Grid Cup," *Los Angeles Times*, Dec. 28, 1928.

37. Paul Lowry, Rabbit Punches (column), *Los Angeles Times*, Dec. 8, 1928.

38. Howard Jones, "Overwhelming Evidence in Favor of Coast Football Cannot Be Disputed, Says Jones," *Los Angeles Times*, Dec. 3, 1928.

17. Capone's Last Game

1. Dan Satterfield, "St. Valentine's Day Massacre—The Real Weather That Day, Feb. 14, 2011," Dan's Wild Wild Science Journal (weblog), American Geophysical Union Blogosphere (website), http://blogs.agu.org/wildwildscience/2011/02/14/st-valentines-day-massacre-the-real-weather-that-day/.

2. John O'Brien, "The St. Valentine's Day Massacre," *Chicago Tribune*, Feb. 14, 2014.

3. John H. Lyle, "The St. Valentine's Day Massacre," *St. Petersburg Times*, Feb. 27, 1961.

4. "St. Valentine's Day Massacre" (photo gallery), Vintage Photos: Vintage Chicago Crime, *Chicago Tribune* (website), Feb. 7, 2014, http://galleries.apps.chicagotribune.com/chi-140207-st-valentines-day-massacre-pictures/.

5. Jonathan Eig, *Get Capone: The Secret Plot That Captured America's Most Wanted Gangster* (New York: Simon and Schuster, 2010), 191.

6. Ibid., 199.

7. O'Brien, "The St. Valentine's Day Massacre," *Chicago Tribune*, Feb. 14, 2014.

8. Douglas O. Linder, "Al Capone Trial (1931): An Account," Famous Trials Series, University of Missouri-Kansas City School of Law (website), http://law2.umkc.edu/faculty/projects/ftrials/capone/caponeaccount.html.

9. "The Crash of 1929," 1990, *American Experience*, transcript on Public Broadcasting Service website, http://www.pbs.org/wgbh/americanexperience/features/transcript/crash-transcript/.

10. Jennifer Rosenberg, "The Stock Market Crash of 1929," updated Feb. 26, 2016, About Education: Twentieth-Century History, 1920–1929, About.com (website), http://history1900s.about.com/od/1920s/a/stockcrash1929.htm.

11. Donald Crafton, *The Talkies: American Cinema's Transition to Sound, 1926–1931,* (Berkeley: Univ. of California Press, 1999), 168, 215.

12. Stenn, *Clara Bow,* 158.

13. Ibid., 114–68.

14. "The 1st Academy Awards: 1929," Oscars Ceremonies, Academy of Motion Picture Arts and Sciences (website), http://www.oscars.org/awards/academyawards/legacy/ceremony/1st.html.

15. Bronwyn Cosgrave, *Made for Each Other: Fashion and the Academy Awards* (New York: Bloomsbury Publishing, 2007), 4.

16. "The 1st Academy Awards: 1929."

17. "Menu" (from First Academy Awards Ceremony), photograph available on weblog of Kate Virtue, http://pinkvirtue.blogspot.com/.

18. Cosgrave, *Made for Each Other,* 5.

19. Stenn, *Clara Bow,* 159.

20. Cosgrave, *Made for Each Other,* 4.

21. Stenn, *Clara Bow,* 159.

22. "Fairbanks Turns Professor," *Los Angeles Times,* Feb. 7, 1929.

23. Full Cast and Crew, *Salute* (1929), Internet Movie Database (website), http://www.imdb.com/title/tt0020359/fullcredits?ref_=tt_cl_sm#cast.

24. "U.S.C. Football Stars' Status Periled by Film Stunt," *Los Angeles Times,* May 18, 1929.

25. Full Cast and Crew, *Salute* (1929).

26. Stenn, *Clara Bow,* 190.

27. "U.S.C. Football Stars' Status Periled by Film Stunt," *Los Angeles Times,* May 18, 1929.

28. Braven Dyer, "Howard Jones Signs New Five Year Contract," *Los Angeles Times,* Jan. 22, 1929.

29. "Jones Elected Coaches' Head," *Los Angeles Times,* Jan. 1, 1929.

30. "Howard Jones Will Conduct Grid School," *Los Angeles Times,* Feb. 15, 1929.

31. "Grid School Opens Today at U.S.C.," *Los Angeles Times,* July 21, 1929.

32. Braven Dyer, Grid Gossip (column), *Los Angeles Times,* Sept. 29, 1929.

33. Howard H. Jones and Al Wesson, *Football for the Fan* (Los Angeles, CA: Times-Mirror Press, 1929), 132.

34. Sperber, *Shake Down the Thunder,* 302.

35. Arthur J. Hope, *Notre Dame: One Hundred Years* (1943; rev. ed., South Bend, IN: Univ. of Notre Dame Press, 1999), ch. 28, available online at the University of Notre Dame Archives website, http://archives.nd.edu/hope/hope28.htm.

36. Sperber, *Shake Down the Thunder,* 301.

37. "Notre Dame Head Deplores Its Football Fame; Calls It Bubble and Tells of $750,000 Stadium," *New York Times,* Feb. 13, 1929.

38. Sperber, *Shake Down the Thunder,* 300.

39. "New Stadium at Notre Dame," *Cornell Daily Sun,* Feb. 22, 1929.

40. Sperber, *Shake Down the Thunder,* 300.

41. Knute Rockne to Rev. Charles O'Donnell, July 4, 1929, UPCO 7/63, Charles L. O'Donnell Papers, President 1928–1934: Rev. Charles O'Donnell CSC, University of Notre Dame Archives.

42. Knute Rockne to Rev. O'Donnell, telegram, July 1, 1929, UPCO 7/63, Charles L. O'Donnell Papers, President 1928–1934: Rev. Charles O'Donnell CSC, University of Notre Dame Archives.

43. Sperber, *Shake Down the Thunder*, 302.

44. Knute Rockne (resignation) to Rev. Matthew Walsh, 1927, UPWL19/17, Notre Dame President 1922–1928: Rev. Matthew J. Walsh, University of Notre Dame Archives.

45. Braven Dyer, "Grid Coaches Have So Many Coaches There's No Room for Substitutes on Bench," *Los Angeles Times*, Sept. 11, 1928.

46. Sperber, *Shake Down the Thunder*, 326.

47. 1929 Coaching Staff: Thomas Lieb, Thomas A. Mills, John Chevigny, John "Ike" Voedisch, Ass't. Coaches, *Official Football Review, University of Notre Dame, 1929* (sports yearbook), 16–17, University of Notre Dame Archives website, http://archives.nd.edu/Football/Football-1929.pdf.

48. Lawrence Perry, "Badgers to Have Hard Time Filling Tom Lieb's Shoes," *Appleton (WI) Post-Crescent*, Feb. 16, 1929.

49. "Thomas Lieb, Ass't. Coach," *Official Football Review, University of Notre Dame, 1929* (sports yearbook), 16.

50. "Phlebitis," 2014, Web MD (website), http://www.webmd.com/a-to-z-guides/phlebitis?print=true.

51. Robinson, *Rockne of Notre Dame*, 220–25.

52. Ted Vosburgh, "Three Year Probe Indicts American College Systems," *Madison (WI) Capital Times*, Oct. 24, 1929.

53. W. H. Cowley, "Athletics in American Colleges," *Journal of Higher Education* 1, no. 1 (Jan. 1930): 29–35.

54. John J. Miller, *The Big Scrum: How Teddy Roosevelt Saved Football* (New York: Harper Collins, 2011), 184–90.

55. John Sayle Watterson, *College Football: History, Spectacle, Controversy* (Baltimore, MD: Johns Hopkins Univ. Press, 2002), 120.

56. "Coach Says 'He-Man Game' Turning into 'Silk Stocking Fete,'" *Wilmington News-Journal*, June 18, 1927.

57. Ronald Austin Smith, *Pay for Play: A History of Big-time College Athletic Reform* (Champaign: Univ. of Illinois Press, 2010), 69.

58. Sperber, *Shake Down the Thunder*, 306.

59. "Rockne Resents Hints of Slack Eligibility Rules," *Los Angeles Times*, Apr. 23, 1927.

60. "Rockne Surprises," *Cornell Daily Sun*, Feb. 5, 1929.

61. Sperber, *Shake Down the Thunder*, 297.

62. Valentine S. Hoy, "Howard Jones: Immortal Coach," *Coronet*, Oct. 1954, 156.

63. Richard J. Shmelter, *The USC Trojans Football Encyclopedia* (Jefferson, NC: McFarland and Co., 2014), 268.

64. "Bovard Makes Strong Denial," *Los Angeles Times*, Oct. 24, 1929.

65. Scott Eyman, *John Wayne: The Life and Legend* (New York: Simon and Schuster, 2014), 34.

66. Sperber, *Shake Down the Thunder*, 251.

67. Claire Suddath, "Brief History of the Crash of 1929," Oct. 29, 2008, Time.com (website), http://content.time.com/time/nation/article/0,8599,1854569,00.html.

18. Another Bite of the Onion

1. "Notre Dame Cheered by 6,000," *New York Times*, Nov. 15, 1929.

2. "Getting Ready for the Trojans," *Official Football Review, University of Notre Dame, 1929* (sports yearbook), 68.

3. "New Rules to Guide Traffic at Soldiers' Field Tomorrow," *Chicago Daily Tribune*, Nov. 15, 1929.

4. Bert Demby, "Purdue and N.D. Face Stiff Tests," *Valparaiso (IN) Vidette-Messenger*, Nov. 15, 1929.

5. Paul Lowry, Rabbit Punches (column), *Los Angeles Times*, Nov. 12, 1929.

6. "Plan Big Send-Off for SC," *Los Angeles Times*, Nov. 12, 1929.

7. "Who Stole the Trojan War Flag?" *Los Angeles Times*, Nov. 15, 1929.

8. Paul Lowry, "Trojan Team Due to Arrive Today in Chicago," *Los Angeles Times*, Nov. 15, 1929.

9. Wes D. Gehring, *Joe E. Brown: Film Comedian and Baseball Buffoon* (Jefferson, NC: McFarland and Co., 2006).

10. Full Cast and Crew, *Maybe It's Love* (1930), Internet Movie Database (website), http://www.imdb.com/title/tt0021133/fullcredits?ref_=tt_cl_sm#cast.

11. Lowry, "Trojan Team Due to Arrive Today," *Los Angeles Times*, Nov. 15, 1929.

12. "Trojans on Short End," *Los Angeles Times*, Nov. 16, 1929.

13. Lowry, "Trojan Team Due to Arrive Today," *Los Angeles Times*, Nov. 15, 1929.

14. "Trojans Encounter Snow," *Chicago Daily Tribune*, Nov. 15, 1929.

15. Jack Gallagher, "Nation Eyes Tilt Today," *Los Angeles Times*, Nov. 16, 1929.

16. "Trojan Alumni Plan Grid Banquet for Team," *Chicago Daily Tribune*, Nov. 14, 1929.

17. Jack Gallagher, "Knute Rockne on Job Again," *Los Angeles Times*, Nov. 13, 1929.

18. Jack Gallagher, "Ramblers Prepare for Troy," *Los Angeles Times*, Nov. 14, 1929.

19. Allen J. Gould, "Play by Play of Fall of Troy," *Los Angeles Times*, Nov. 17, 1929.

20. "Mayor Jimmy Walker and E. J. Kelly, president of the South Park Board, at Soldier Field today watching the Notre Dame-U. of S. California football game, Chicago" (photograph), Nov. 16, 1929, LC-USZ62–96793, Miscellaneous Items in High Demand, Prints & Photographs Online Catalog, Library of Congress, http://www.loc.gov/pictures/item/89709558/.

21. "Notre Dame Confident," *Los Angeles Times*, Nov. 15, 1929.

22. "Notre Dame Team Cheered by 6,000," *New York Times*, Nov. 15, 1929.

23. Sperber, *Shake Down the Thunder*, 316.

24. "Notre Dame Confident," *Los Angeles Times*, Nov. 15, 1929.

25. "125 Moments: 1929 National Championship Season," Department of Athletics, University of Notre Dame Archives, http://125.nd.edu/moments/1929-national-championship-season/.

26. Gallagher, "Nation Eyes Tilt Today," *Los Angeles Times*, Nov. 16, 1929.

27. Paul Lowry, "S.C. Mentors Say Trojans Have Chance to Win," *Los Angeles Times*, Nov. 14, 1929.

28. "Resume of the Season," *El Rodeo*, 1930 (USC yearbook), University of Southern California, 129; and "Capt. John Law, Right Guard," *Official Football Review, University of Notre Dame, 1929* (sports yearbook), 20.

29. Steven Travers, *The USC Trojans: College Football's All-time Greatest Dynasty* (Lanham, MD: Taylor Trade Publishing, 2006), 28.

30. Braven Dyer, "Howard Jones Picks Trojans for Chicago Trip," *Los Angeles Times*, Nov. 11, 1929.

31. Gould, "Play by Play of Fall of Troy," *Los Angeles Times*, Nov. 17, 1929.

32. Robinson, *Rockne of Notre Dame*, 229.

33. Gould, "Play by Play of Fall of Troy," *Los Angeles Times*, Nov. 17, 1929.

34. McCallum and Castner, *We Remember Rockne*, 58.

35. Gould, "Play by Play of Fall of Troy," *Los Angeles Times*, Nov. 17, 1929.

36. Robinson, *Rockne of Notre Dame*, 229.

37. Gould, "Play by Play of Fall of Troy," *Los Angeles Times*, Nov. 17, 1929.

38. Tom Lewis, "Building All-Americans with Howard Jones," *Sports Story Magazine*, Oct. 1933, 55.

39. Don Maxwell, "Rockne Gives 1 Order; Boys Obey—and Win," *Chicago Daily Tribune*, Nov. 17, 1929.

40. Gould, "Play by Play of Fall of Troy," *Los Angeles Times*, Nov. 17, 1929.

41. Alan J. Gould, "Notre Dame Defeats Trojans 13–12," *Los Angeles Times*, Nov. 17, 1929.

42. Paul Lowry, "Jones Talk at Feast Stirring," *Los Angeles Times*, Nov. 17, 1929.

43. Robinson, *Rockne of Notre Dame*, 230.

19. After a Million Dreams

1. National Bureau of Economic Research, "US Business Cycle Expansions and Contractions," NBER website, http://www.nber.org/cycles.html.

2. "1930," July 19, 2008, Economic Populist (web forum), http://www.economicpopulist.org/content/1930.

3. Robert Shiller, "The Yale Tradition in Macroeconomics" (paper presented at the Economic Alumni Conference, New Haven, Apr. 8, 2011), 31.

4. Donald Rapp, *Bubbles, Booms, and Busts: The Rise and Fall of Financial Assets* (New York: Copernicus Books, 2009), 34.

5. Maury Klein, *Rainbow's End: The Crash of 1929:* (New York: Oxford Univ. Press, 2001), 244.

6. Braven Dyer, "Record Broken by Seat Sale," *Los Angeles Times*, Dec. 17, 1929.

7. "Rose Bowl to Be Enlarged," *Los Angeles Times*, Jan. 20, 1930.

8. Braven Dyer, "Irish Ban Rose Tilt; Jones Not Against It," *Los Angeles Times*, Nov. 26, 1929.

9. Richard D. White, *Will Rogers: A Political Life* (Lubbock: Texas Tech Univ. Press, 2011), 161.

10. "Irish Awarded Grid Laurels," *Los Angeles Times*, Dec. 1, 1929.

11. "Notre Dame Awarded Erskine Grid Laurels," *Los Angeles Times*, Jan. 4, 1930.

12. "Irish Awarded Grid Laurels," *Los Angeles Times*, Dec. 1, 1929; "Notre Dame Awarded Erskine Grid Laurels," *Los Angeles Times*, Jan. 4, 1930.

13. Associated Press, "Knute Rockne Gets Erskine Grid Award," *Brooklyn Daily Eagle*, Jan. 19, 1930.

14. "Rockne Away to Florida Resort," *Lincoln Star Journal*, Jan. 13, 1930.

15. Associated Press, "Rockne Drops Role as Grid Coach to Be a Family Man," *Appleton (WI) Post-Crescent*, June 5, 1930.

16. Paul Lowry, "Lions Acquire Ex-Irish Coach," *Los Angeles Times*, Feb. 9, 1930.

17. "Rockne Pupil at Georgetown," *Los Angeles Times*, Jan. 12, 1930.

18. "Interhall Football," *Official Football Review, University of Notre Dame, 1929* (sports yearbook), 52.

19. "Howard Jones' Father Dies at His Home," *Los Angeles Times*, Feb. 18, 1930.

20. "Trojan Coach Will Arrive Here Friday," *Los Angeles Times*, Mar. 13, 1930.

21. "Trojan Coaches Taking Informal Check on Southern California Football Prospects," *Los Angeles Times*, Aug. 24, 1930.

22. "Rockne's Return from Florida Is Delayed Again," *Chicago Daily Tribune*, Mar. 25, 1930.

23. "Ever See This Man Before?" *Los Angeles Times*, Mar. 19, 1930.

24. "Rockne to Take Test at Clinic," *Los Angeles Times*, Apr. 5, 1930.

25. United Press, "Coach Rockne Leaves for Mayo Clinic to Get Physical Tests," *San Bernardino County Sun*, Apr. 6, 1930.

26. "Capone Slips from Prison," *Los Angeles Times*, Mar. 18, 1930.

27. "'Scarface' Al Gives Self Up," *Los Angeles Times*, Mar. 22, 1930.

28. "Gang Leaders to Be Hounded," *Los Angeles Times*, Apr. 24, 1930.

29. "Capone Flies to Cuba for Brief Vacation," *Los Angeles Times*, Apr. 30, 1930.

30. "Knute Rockne to Play Conductor Again This Year," *Independent Record*, Jan. 31, 1930.

31. "Rockne in Shape to Coach Again; Leads Tour to Europe This Summer," *Uniontown (PA) Morning Herald*, June 10, 1930.

32. Watterson, *College Football*, 26.

33. Smith, *Pay for Play*, 31.

34. Associated Press, "May Abolish East-West Football Contests," *Los Angeles Times*, Jan. 28, 1930.

35. Russell J. Newland, "Intersectional Games Will Not Be Dropped," *Los Angeles Times*, Feb. 2, 1930.

36. "'Big Games' Criticized," *Los Angeles Times*, Mar. 9, 1930.

37. Klosinski, *Notre Dame, Chicago Bears, and "Hunk,"* 97.

38. Ibid., 94.

39. Darren Everson, "The Forgotten Ghosts of College Football," *Wall Street Journal*, Oct. 30, 2009, http://www.wsj.com/news/articles/SB10001424052748703792304574503761591504496.

40. Associated Press, "Notre Dame Faculty Head Cracks Down on Famed Coach," *Lincoln Star*, Nov. 27, 1929.

41. Gereon Zimmermann, "Notre Dame's Father Hesburgh," *Look Magazine*, Oct. 24, 1961, 147, 149.

42. McCallum and Castner, *We Remember Rockne*, 7, 8.

43. Sperber, *Shake Down the Thunder*, 328.

44. "Notre Dame's Grid Stadium Being Built," *Odgen Standard Examiner*, Aug. 31, 1929.

45. John Heisler, *100 Things Notre Dame Fans Should Know and Do Before They Die* (Chicago, IL: Triumph Books, 2013), 8.

46. Robinson, *Rockne of Notre Dame*, 239.

20. Divorce and Deception

1. "U.S.C. Fete Begins in Week," *Los Angeles Times*, May 25, 1930.

2. "Rufus B. von KleinSmid," About USC: Gallery of USC Presidents, University of Southern California (website), http://about.usc.edu/presidents/rufus-b-von-kleinsmid/.

3. "Huge S.C. Fund Details Given," *Los Angeles Times*, Mar. 9, 1930.

4. Steven B. Sample, *The University of Southern California at 125: Inventing the Future Since 1880* (Exton, PA: Newcomen Society of the United States, 2005), 13.

5. "Did You Know?" About USC, University of Southern California (website), http://about.usc.edu/facts/did-you-know/.

6. "Huge S.C. Fund Details Given," *Los Angeles Times*, Mar. 9, 1930.

7. Knute Rockne to Henry Dockweiler, Oct. 14, 1929, UADR 10/172, Dockweiler, Henry I., Director of Athletics, 1909–1929 (Harper, Rockne), University of Notre Dame Archives.

8. H. L. Mencken and George Jean Nathan, "Movie Morals," *Smart Set*, Dec. 1922, 47.

9. Stenn, *Clara Bow*, 112.

10. Roberts, *John Wayne*, 64.

11. Eyman, *John Wayne*, 34.

12. Trivia, *The Big Trail* (1930), Internet Movie Database (website), http://www.imdb.com/title/tt0020691/trivia?ref_=tt_trv_trv.

13. Scott Allen Nollen, *Three Bad Men: John Ford, John Wayne, Ward Bond* (Jefferson, NC: McFarland, 2013), 357.

14. Richard W. Slatta, *The Cowboy Encyclopedia* (New York: W. W. Norton and Co., 1996), 130.

15. Eymen, *John Wayne*, 46.

16. Donald Shepherd and Robert Slatzer, with David Grayson, *Duke: The Life and Times of John Wayne* (New York: Citadel Press Books, 1985), 79.

17. "Story of Wilson Retirement Confirmed," *Los Angeles Times*, June 27, 1930.

18. James Bacon, *Made in Hollywood* (New York: Contemporary Books, 1977), 204.

19. John P. Gallagher, "Deputy Commissioner Under Fire; Action Sought to End Asserted Gangster-Politician Pacts," *Los Angeles Times*, June 16, 1930.

20. "Rockne in Shape to Coach Again," *Uniontown (PA) Morning Herald*, June 10, 1930.

21. Sport Chatter (column), *Fitchburg (MA) Sentinel*, July 19, 1930.

22. "Howard Jones Departs," *Los Angeles Times*, June 6, 1930.

23. "Coliseum Contract Let," *Los Angeles Times*, Aug. 21, 1930.

24. David Coles, "Magnified Grandeur: The Big Screen, 1926–31," March 2001, In70mm.com, http://www.in70mm.com/newsletter/2001/64/grandeur.

25. Eymen, *John Wayne*, 59.

26. James Stuart Olson, *Historical Dictionary of the 1960s* (Westport, CT: Greenwood Publishing, 1999), 476.

27. Robinson, *Rockne of Notre Dame*, 241–42.

28. Associated Press, "Joe Savoldi's Knee Action Like Scythe," *Lincoln Evening Journal*, Oct. 28, 1930.

29. "Joe Savoldi, Full-back," *Official Football Review, University of Notre Dame, 1930* (sports yearbook), 26, University of Notre Dame Archives website, http://archives.nd.edu/Football/Football-1930.pdf.

30. Feg Murray, "The Plunging Bricklayer," *Los Angeles Times*, Nov. 2, 1930.

31. Bert M'Grane, "Notre Dame Rules Strict," *Los Angeles Times*, Nov. 29, 1930.

32. Associated Press, "Savoldi Seeks Annulment," *Chicago Daily Tribune* Nov. 11, 1930.

33. Bert M'Grane, "Notre Dame Rules Strict," *Los Angeles Times*, Nov. 29, 1930.

34. John P. Gallagher, "Irish Football Star Expelled," *Los Angeles Times*, Nov. 18, 1930.

35. Associated Press, "Savoldi Seeks Annulment," *Chicago Daily Tribune*, Nov. 11, 1930.

36. Huston, *Salesman from the Sidelines*, 9–13.

37. United Press, "Savoldi Seeks Annulment," *Chicago Daily Tribune*, Nov. 11, 1930.

38. Paul Mickelson, "Savoldi on Bench for Drake Game," *Los Angeles Times*, Nov. 16, 1930.

39. Irving Vaughan, "Notre Dame Dismisses Joe Savoldi," *Chicago Daily Tribune*, Nov. 18, 1930.

40. Robinson, *Rockne of Notre Dame*, 242.

41. Chris Willis, *Joe F. Carr: The Man Who Built the National Football League* (Lanham, MD: Scarecrow Press, 2010), 264.

42. Paul Mickelson, "Battered Irish Team on Way to Los Angeles," *Los Angeles Times*, Dec. 2, 1930.

43. Bert M'Grane, "Notre Dame Rules Strict," *Los Angeles Times*, Nov. 29, 1930.

44. Mickelson, "Battered Irish Team on Way to Los Angeles," *Los Angeles Times*, Dec. 2, 1930.

45. Eugene J. Young, *With Rockne at Notre Dame* (New York: Putnam, 1951), 139–40.

46. Bill Henry, "Rockne Sends Irish Through Secret Drills," *Los Angeles Times*, Dec. 5, 1930.

47. Young, *With Rockne at Notre Dame*, 140.

48. "Coast Coaches Favor Trojans over Rivals," *Los Angeles Times*, Dec. 6, 1930.

49. Edward Lawrence, "Trojans Not Only Ones Fooled by K. K. Rockne," *Los Angeles Times*, Dec. 7, 1930.

50. Associated Press, "Buck Bailey Picks S.C. to Defeat Notre Dame," *Los Angeles Times*, Dec. 5, 1930.

51. Earl Gustkey, "Rockne's Final Game," *Los Angeles Times*, Dec. 6, 1990.

52. "Trojans Meet Tonight for Annual Meal," *Los Angeles Times*, Dec. 5, 1930.

53. McCallum and Castner, *We Remember Rockne,* 146.

54. Applegate, *"The Game Is On,"* 56.

55. Lefebvre, *Coach for a Nation,* 435.

56. George Shaffer, "Defeat of Troy Brings Climax and Title," *Official Football Review, University of Notre Dame, 1930* (sports yearbook), 85.

57. "Jones Inactive During Gigantic," *Los Angeles Times,* Dec. 7, 1930.

58. Howard Jones, "Jones Praises Irish Players," *Los Angeles Times,* Dec. 8, 1930.

59. Lawrence, "Trojans Not Only Ones Fooled by K. K. Rockne," *Los Angeles Times,* Dec. 7, 1930.

60. Ibid.

61. Jones, "Jones Praises Irish Players," *Los Angeles Times,* Dec. 8, 1930.

62. Braven Dyer, "Notre Dame Warriors on Way to South Bend," *Los Angeles Times,* Dec. 8, 1930.

63. Young, *With Rockne at Notre Dame,* 145.

64. "Throngs Greet Gridiron Heroes of Notre Dame," *Chicago Daily Tribune,* Dec. 11, 1930.

65. "It's Notre Dame Hour Tomorrow in Chicago Loop," *Chicago Times,* Dec. 9, 1930.

66. Associated Press, "Notre Dame Crowd Riots," *Los Angeles Times,* Dec. 7, 1930.

67. "More Ado at South Bend," *Chicago Daily Tribune,* Dec. 11, 1930.

68. "False Rumor Leads to Trouble at Bank," *New York Times,* Dec. 11, 1930.

69. "Bank of U.S. Closes, State Takes Over Affairs," *New York Times,* Dec. 12, 1930.

70. "Surety Company Closes," *New York Times,* Jan. 1, 1931.

71. "Where Will Lehman Failure Fit in History?" Sept. 15, 2008, Marketplace (website), American Public Media, http://www.marketplace.org/2008/09/15/business/fallout-financial-crisis/where-will-lehman-failure-fit-history.

72. Federal Deposit Insurance Corp., *The First Fifty Years: A History of the FDIC, 1933–1983* (Washington, D.C.: FDIC, 1984), 33–35.

73. "The Bank Failure," *New York Times,* Dec. 13, 1930.

74. "Depositor Hangs Herself," *New York Times,* Jan. 1, 1931.

21. Flying into Destiny

1. Stefan Kanfer, *Groucho: The Life and Times of Julius Henry Marx* (New York: Vintage Books, 2000), 126.

2. Stenn, *Clara Bow,* 282.

3. Ibid., 212, 228–33.

4. Associated Press, "Graft Nest Torn Open," *Los Angeles Times,* Jan. 19, 1931.

5. Milton Friedman and Anna Jacobson Schwartz, *A Monetary History of the United States, 1867–1960* (Princeton, NJ: Princeton Univ. Press, 1963), 317.

6. *The Encyclopedia of Arkansas History and Culture* (online encyclopedia), s.v. "The Drought of 1930–1931" (by John Spurgeon), http://www.encyclopediaofarkansas.net/encyclopedia/entry-detail.aspx?entryID=4344.

7. "Dust Bowl 1931–1939." *Historic Events for Students: The Great Depression,* vol. 1, ed. Richard C. Hanes and Sharon M. Hanes (Detroit, MI: Gale, 2002), 168–85, available online at World History in Context (internet database), http://ic.galegroup.

com/ic/whic/ReferenceDetailsPage/ReferenceDetailsWindow?zid=a24f908894dee1
81373628d8d34f05c1&action=2&catId=&documentId=GALE%7CCCX3424800020&u
serGroupName=nysl_ro_ironhs&source=Bookmark&u=nysl_ro_ironhs&jsid=bdf5
90f2e5625e1437fdc903205149e0.

8. Kathy Weiser-Alexander, "20th Century History: Dust Bowl Days or the 'Dirty Thirties,'" *Legends of America* (online magazine), http://www.legendsofamerica.com/20th-dustbowl.html.

9. Alan Gould, "Football on the Decline," *Los Angeles Times,* June 15, 1931.

10. Sperber, *Shake Down the Thunder,* 322, 345, 346.

11. Mary Stuhldreyer, "Football Fans Aren't Human," *Saturday Evening Post,* Oct. 23, 1948, 22–23.

12. Associated Press, "Rockne to Be Overhauled," *Los Angeles Times,* Dec. 19, 1930.

13. Associated Press, "Knute Mum on Future Grid Plans," *Los Angeles Times,* Dec. 25, 1930.

14. "Knute Rockne Is Out Again," *The Danville (VA) Bee,* Jan. 1, 1931.

15. Arch Ward, "Notre Dame Head Defends Football; Irish Get Trophy," *Chicago Daily Tribune,* Dec. 12, 1930.

16. "Irish Coach May Quit," *Los Angeles Times,* Dec. 19, 1930.

17. Robinson, *Rockne of Notre Dame,* 257.

18. Don Woodard, *Black Diamonds! Black Gold! The Saga of Texas Pacific Coal and Oil Company* (Lubbock: Texas Tech Univ. Press, 1998), 227.

19. Sperber, *Shake Down the Thunder,* 237.

20. Edward Harrison, "News from 1931: New York Auto Show Special," Credit Writedowns (website), https://www.creditwritedowns.com/2010/01/news-from-1931-new-york-auto-show-special.html.

21. Huston, *Salesman from the Sidelines,* 114–15.

22. Re-creation of Knute Rockne Locker Room Speech, Knute Rockne at Spring Practice, 1920s, Fox Movietone, AUND C2941 VT, Notre Dame Audio-Visual and Oversize Graphics Collection, University of Notre Dame Archives.

23. Cliff Herd, 1930–1931 Scrapbook, University of Southern California Athletic Department Archives.

24. "Rockne Returns from Clinic in Great Shape," *Harrisburg (PA) Evening News,* Jan. 2, 1931.

25. Associated Press, "Notre Dame Gets Trophy of Football Champions," *Alton Evening Telegraph,* Jan. 7, 1931.

26. "Auto Show to Open in Splendor Today," *New York Times,* Jan. 3, 1931.

27. John A. Kiener, "Yarr Football Captain," *Notre Dame Scholastic* 64, no. 13, Jan. 16, 1931, 399.

28. Address by Knute Rockne to Studebaker Sales Organization, Detroit-Leland Hotel Banquet Room, Detroit-Leland Hotel, Detroit, MI, Jan. 20, 1931, digital copy in the collection of the author.

29. City Briefs (column), *Dubois (PA) Morning Courier,* Jan. 22, 1931.

30. Sport Chatter (column), *Fitchburg (MA) Sentinel,* Jan. 19, 1931.

31. Associated Press, "Rockne Says Grid Critics 'Sheltered' from Reality," *Kingsport (TN) Times,* Feb. 22, 1931.

32. Associated Press, "Says Auto Men Need Superiority Complex," *Appleton (WI) Post-Crescent,* Jan. 24, 1931.

33. United Press, "Rockne Attends the Omaha Auto Show," *Lincoln Evening Journal,* Jan. 24, 1931.

34. "Rockne Speech Lauded," *Los Angeles Times,* Feb. 1, 1931.

35. "Local Studebaker Agency Folk Attend Banquet Tuesday," *Corsicana Daily Sun,* Feb. 9, 1931.

36. "Rockne Forgetting Football on Trip," *El Paso Evening Post,* Feb. 11, 1931.

37. Associated Press, "'Bosh' Snorts Rockne," *Lincoln Star,* Feb. 13, 1931.

38. Associated Press, "Rockne Breaks Loose Again," *Los Angeles Times,* Feb. 13, 1931.

39. United Press, "Drake Toughest Team for Notre Dame," *Ames (IA) Daily Tribune,* Mar. 16, 1931.

40. "Knute Rockne in Retirement," *Los Angeles Times,* Feb. 14, 1931.

41. Bill Jauss, "Rockne Left a Legacy That Ranged Beyond the Field or Locker Room," *Chicago Tribune,* Feb. 28, 1988.

42. Braven Dyer, "Rockne Visits Loyola: Notre Dame Mentor Drops in on Opening of Spring Practice at Del Rey Institution," *Los Angeles Times,* Feb. 17, 1931.

43. John S. Daggett, "Radio for Day Rich in Variety," *Los Angeles Times,* Feb. 19, 1931.

44. Dyer, "Rockne Visits Loyola," *Los Angeles Times,* Feb. 17, 1931.

45. Braven Dyer, "Rumor Notre Dame May Break With Trojans," *Los Angeles Times,* Mar. 2, 1931.

46. "History of Studebaker Told," *Los Angeles Times,* Feb. 22, 1931.

47. Dyer, "Rockne Visits Loyola," *Los Angeles Times,* Feb. 17, 1931.

48. "Hear Knute Rockne," *Woodland (CA) Daily Democrat,* Feb. 18, 1931.

49. "Rockne Assures Ingram Success as Bear Mentor," *Los Angeles Times,* Feb. 20, 1931.

50. Associated Press, "Drake Hardest Team for Notre Dame," *Ames Daily Tribune,* Mar. 16, 1931.

51. "Industry's Leaders Preside over Meeting of Studebaker Dealers," *Atlanta Constitution,* Mar. 8, 1931.

52. "The Biltmore Ballrooms," Novare Events (website), http://novareevents.com/biltmore-ballrooms/.

53. Ralph McGill, "Atlanta Youngsters Meet Knute Rockne," *Atlanta Constitution,* Mar. 5, 1931.

54. "Rockne Will Fly to Miami Today," *Atlanta Constitution,* Mar. 5, 1931.

55. Robinson, *Rockne of Notre Dame,* 263.

56. Alan Gould, "Knute Rockne Gives Radio Interview about Propects at Notre Dame This Season," *Jacksonville Daily Journal,* Mar. 7, 1931.

57. Wallace, *Knute Rockne,* 254.

58. Associated Press, "Rockne Forsakes Business for Pleasure in Trip to Florida; Speaks over Radio," *Uniontown (PA) Morning Herald,* Mar. 7, 1931.

59. Gene Hinton, "Air Views," *Atlanta Constitution,* Mar. 15, 1931.

60. Huston, *Salesman from the Sidelines,* 20, 21.

61. "To Introduce Rockne Six," *Salem (OR) Daily Capital Journal,* Dec. 5, 1931.

62. John H. Helney, "Stutz Stresses New Line Points: Packard, Studebaker, Dodge, Hudson and Graham-Paige among Notable Exhibits," *Indianapolis News,* Feb. 3, 1928.

63. Huston, *Salesman from the Sidelines,* 132.

64. "320 Football Candidates Report for N.D. Spring Call," *Indianapolis News,* Mar. 24, 1931.

65. "Knute Rockne's Last Photograph," *Brooklyn Daily Eagle,* Apr. 4, 1931.

66. "Sports Managerships for Next Year Are Announced by Knute K. Rockne," *Notre Dame Scholastic* 64, no. 22, Mar. 27, 1931, 693.

67. McCallum and Castner, *We Remember Rockne,* 74.

68. Keith Ellis, Martha DeJernett House, and Bob Padgett, "From the Blue Hole to the Hall of Fame: The Life and Times of David 'Big Dave' DeJernett," The Chopping Block (website), http://www.hatchets.net/Hatchetnotes.htm.

69. United Press, "Negro Basketball Star Threatened in Letter," *Valparaiso (IN) Vidette-Messenger,* Mar. 14, 1931.

70. Michael R. Steele, *Knute Rockne: A Bio-Bibilography* (Westport, CT: Greenwood Press, 1983), 133.

71. United Press, "Speculating in Sports," *Hammond Times,* Mar. 30, 1934.

72. "How 'The Spirit of Notre Dame' Was Made," *Notre Dame Alumnus* 10, no. 1 (Oct. 1931): 13.

73. "Notre Dame to Carry On in Rockne Picture," *Sandusky (OH) Register,* July 5, 1931.

74. Elmer Layden and Ed Synder, *It Was a Different Game: The Elmer Layden Story* (Upper Saddle River, NJ: Prentice Hall, 1969), 78.

75. *Good News (1930),* Internet Movie Database (website), http://www.imdb.com/title/tt0020929/?ref_=fn_al_tt_1; *Good News (1947),* Internet Movie Database (website), http://www.imdb.com/title/tt0039431/?ref_=fn_al_tt_1.

76. Robinson, *Rockne of Notre Dame,* 262.

77. Roy Scholz, "Publicity Dept. More Than a Big Name—It's a Big Job," *Notre Dame Scholastic* 65, no. 5, Oct. 23, 1931, 17.

78. John A. Kiener, "Acquaintance Bares Secret of Rockne," *South Bend Tribune,* Mar. 30, 1975.

79. "To Introduce Rockne Six," *Salem (OR) Daily Capital Journal,* Dec. 5, 1931.

80. Robinson, *Rockne of Notre Dame,* 117.

81. Knute Rockne to Rev. Charles L. O'Donnell, Mar. 30, 1931, UPCO 7/59, Charles L. O'Donnell Papers, President 1928–1934: Rev. Charles O'Donnell CSC, University of Notre Dame Archives.

82. John D. Bybee, "The Rockne Crash: A Tragedy Marked by Discrepancies," 1931, Sedona Legend Helen Frye (website), http://www.sedonalegendhelenfrye.com/1931.html.

83. Charles Perry, "L.A.'s Oldest Eating Group Hams It Up," *Los Angeles Times,* Dec. 12, 2007.

84. "Breakfast Club to Fete Rockne," *Los Angeles Times,* Mar. 31, 1931.

85. "Rockne to Be Paid Tribute at Luncheon," *Los Angeles Times,* Apr. 2, 1931.

86. Bybee, "The Rockne Crash"; "Rockne's Tragic Death Stuns Sports World," *Los Angeles Times,* Apr. 1, 1931.

87. "Rockne Bids Mother Goodbye," *Decatur Evening Herald,* Apr. 2, 1931.

88. Wallace, *Knute Rockne,* 254.

89. Bybee, "The Rockne Crash."

90. Christy Walsh, "Happy Landings," *Notre Dame Alumnus* 9, no. 9 (May 1931): 301.

91. "Grid Coach Joked about Airplane Landing," *Scranton Republican,* Apr. 1, 1931.

92. Bybee, "The Rockne Crash."

93. Amtrak, "Kansas City, MO (KCY): Station History," Great American Stations (website), http://www.greatamericanstations.com/Stations/KCY.

94. Wallace, *Knute Rockne,* 254.

95. Knute Rockne to Bonnie Rockne, Western Union telegram, Mar. 31, 1931, photograph of telegram available at Notre Dame Monogram Club, Notre Dame Athletics (website), http://www.und.com/sports/monogramclub/spec-rel/100506aag.html.

96. Bybee, "The Rockne Crash."

97. "Coroner's Jury Investigates Fatal Crash of Plane," *Olean (NY) Times Herald,* Apr. 1, 1931.

98. Wallace, *Knute Rockne,* 256.

22. In the Depths of Despair

1. Studebaker Corporation of America, "The World Champion: Studebaker President Eight" (advertisement), *Brooklyn Daily Eagle,* June 16, 1930.

2. Carolyn Jones O'Connell, interview by the author, Fontana, CA, Jan. 16, 2010.

3. Ralph Huston, "Rockne's Tragic Death Stuns Sports World," *Los Angeles Times,* Apr. 1, 1931.

4. "Many Tributes Paid Knute Kenneth Rockne," *Ogden Standard-Examiner,* Apr. 1, 1931.

5. Huston, "Rockne's Tragic Death Stuns Sports World," *Los Angeles Times,* Apr. 1, 1931.

6. Carolyn Jones O'Connell, interview by the author, Fontana, CA, Jan. 16, 2010.

7. "Southern California Band and Glee Clubs Return from Long Tour in North," *Southern California Daily Trojan,* Apr. 7, 1931.

8. "Glick Beaten by Townsend," *Los Angeles Times,* Apr. 1, 1931.

9. "Elks Pay Tribute to Coach Rockne," *Los Angeles Times,* Apr. 2, 1931.

10. United Press, "Club Offers Rockne Last High Praise," *San Bernardino County Sun,* Apr. 2, 1931.

11. "Breakfast Clubbers Honor Knute Rockne," *Los Angeles Times,* Apr. 2, 1931.

12. "Sportsmen Laud Rockne's Memory," *Los Angeles Times,* Apr. 3, 1931.

13. Associated Press, "Notre Dame Stupefied," *Los Angeles Times,* Apr. 1, 1931.

14. Robinson, *Rockne of Notre Dame,* 266.

15. Brondfield, *Rockne* 18.

16. Associated Press, "Notre Dame Stupefied," *Los Angeles Times,* Apr. 1, 1931.

17. United Press, "Knute Rockne Back Home in Notre Dame," *Daily Notes* (Cannonsburg, PA), Apr. 2, 1931.

18. Associated Press, "Notre Dame Stupefied," *Los Angeles Times,* Apr. 1, 1931.

19. "Rockne's Family Informed of His Death by Radio," *Chicago Daily Tribune,* Apr. 1, 1931.

20. Sperber, *Shake Down the Thunder,* 355.

21. Brondfield, *Rockne,* 18.

22. Grantland Rice, "Rice Pays Tribute to His Friend," *Los Angeles Times,* Apr. 1, 1931.

23. Paul Lowry, Rabbit Punches (column), *Los Angeles Times,* Apr. 1, 1931.

24. Arch Ward, "Knute Rockne as I Knew Him," *Chicago Daily Tribune,* Apr. 2, 1931.

25. Charles E. Dorais, "Rockne Just Ambitious Boy Who Made Dreams Come True, Says Former Room-mate," *Los Angeles Times,* Apr. 3, 1931.

23. Valhalla Awaits

1. United Press, "Cannon Given Final Orders," *San Bernardino County Sun,* Apr. 3, 1931.

2. Wallace, *Knute Rockne,* 254–57.

3. United Press, "Knute Rockne Back Home in Notre Dame," *Cannonsburg (PA) Daily Notes,* Apr. 2, 1931.

4. United Press, "Avalanche of Telegrams," *Piqua (OH) Daily Call,* Apr. 1, 1931.

5. "Rockne's Widow en Route Home," *Lincoln (NE) Evening State Journal,* Apr. 4, 1931.

6. "Witnesses Tell Story of Airplane Crash That Killed Rockne," *Milwaukee Sentinel,* Apr. 1, 1931.

7. Harold Weissman, "Tragic Death of Rockne Brings Tribute by Millions," *Long Beach (CA) Independent,* Jan. 5, 1950.

8. "Body of Knute Rockne Taken to South Bend," *Chillicothe (MO) Constitution,* Apr. 1, 1931.

9. North American Newspaper Alliance, "Young Rockne Boys Stifle Their Grief," *Lincoln (NE) Evening State Journal,* Apr. 1, 1931.

10. "Body of Knute Rockne Taken to South Bend," *Chillicothe (MO) Constitution,* Apr. 1, 1931.

11. George Currie, "Only the Future Will Disclose Measure of Rockne's Greatness," *Brooklyn Daily Eagle,* Apr. 5, 1931.

12. "Sons of Noted Coach aboard Funeral Train," *Middletown (NY) Times Herald,* Apr. 1, 1931.

13. United Press, "Body Enroute to South Bend from Kansas," *Delphos (OH) Daily Herald,* Apr. 1, 1931.

14. "Rockne Funeral at South Bend," *Sedalia (MO) Democrat,* Apr. 1, 1931.

15. United Press, "Vice President of Notre Dame Meets Body of Rockne at Kansas City," *Lincoln (NE) Evening Journal,* Apr. 1, 1931.

16. "Hoover Sends Condolences to Rockne Widow," *Ogden (UT) Standard-Examiner,* Apr. 1, 1931.

17. United Press, "Sons Accompany Coach's Remains to South Bend," *Lincoln (NE) Evening State Journal,* Apr. 1, 1931.

18. "Famous Coach Home, Leaves Trail of Sorrow Behind," *Dubois (PA) Morning Courier,* Apr. 2, 1931.

19. "Knute Rockne Back Home in Notre Dame," *Cannonsburg (PA) Daily Notes,* Apr. 2, 1931.

20. Thomas Coman, "Rockne's Tragic Death Shocks Nation," *Notre Dame Alumnus* 9, no. 9 (May 1931): 294.

21. "Thousands in Chicago Pay Silent Tribute," *Los Angeles Times,* Apr. 2, 1931.

22. George Kirksey, "Riotous Grief Marks Arrival 'Death' Train," *San Bernardino County Sun,* Apr. 2, 1931.

23. "Notre Dame in Mourning for Knute Rockne," *Decatur Evening Herald,* Apr. 2, 1931.

24. "Famous Coach Home, Leaves Trail of Sorrow Behind," *Dubois (PA) Morning Courier,* Apr. 2, 1931.

25. Coman, "Rockne's Tragic Death Shocks Nation," *Notre Dame Alumnus* 9, no. 9 (May 1931): 293.

26. Paul Mickelson, "Heart-Sick City Pays Hushed Tribute to Its Dead Hero," *Lincoln (NE) Star,* Apr. 2, 1931.

27. "Historic South Bend Railroads and Stations: Union Station," South Bend's Historical Heritage (website), http://www.monon.monon.org/sobend/unionstation.html.

28. Coman, "Rockne's Tragic Death Shocks Nation," *Notre Dame Alumnus* 9, no. 9 (May 1931): 294.

29. Jimmy Corcoran, "Mrs. Rockne to Be Taken from Train to Avoid Crowds," *Belvidere (IL) Daily Republican,* Apr. 3, 1931.

30. Coman, "Rockne's Tragic Death Shocks Nation," *Notre Dame Alumnus* 9, no. 9 (May 1931): 296.

31. Ibid., 294, 295.

32. "Silent Homage Is Paid Today to Notre Dame Famous Coach," *Macon (MO) Chronicle-Herald,* Apr. 2, 1931.

24. When Autumn Comes

1. Art Cohn, Cohn-ing Tower (column), *Oakland Tribune,* July 28, 1941.

2. "Harold Escapes 'Feet First' to Play Golf," *Los Angeles Times,* Apr. 20, 1930.

3. Grantland Rice, "Loos Advises Playing Golf with Your Head," *Los Angeles Times,* Dec. 21, 1935.

4. J. Anita Foster, *I Caught a Fisherman: Pioneers of Virginia Lakes Resort 1923* (Angwin, CA: Elite Printing Co., 1968), 179.

5. "Ward Bond: Actor (1903–1960)," Internet Movie Database (website), http://www.imdb.com/name/nm0000955/?ref_=nv_sr_1.

6. "Harding-Jones Employee Housing, c. 1930," photograph in the George C. Crout Collection, Digital Archives, MidPointe Library System, Middletown, OH, http://www.midpointedigitalarchives.org/cdm/singleitem/collection/Crout/id/2893/rec/1.

7. Sid Ziff, "Nobody Knew Him," *Los Angeles Times,* Oct. 24, 1963.

8. Carolyn Jones O'Connell, interview by the author, Fontana, CA, Jan. 16, 2010.

9. "Son Hopes to Fill Dad's Shoes," *Los Angeles Times,* September 25, 1932.

10. Salvador "Sal" Mena, interview by the author, Holtville, CA, July 7, 2011.

11. Carolyn Jones O'Connell, interview by the author, Fontana, CA, Jan. 16, 2010.

12. Art Cohn, Cohn-ing Tower (column), *Oakland Tribune,* July 28, 1941.

13. Ambrose Schindler, interview by the author, Redondo Beach, CA, Sept. 14, 2005.

14. Jones, Jane Dean, Case No. 161265, Sept. 17, 1936, Los Angeles County Archives and Records Center, Los Angeles, CA.

15. Bernadette Vargas, interview by the author, Fontana, CA, Jan. 16, 2010.

16. Carolyn Jones O'Connell, interview by the author, Fontana, CA, Jan. 16, 2010.

17. The Golfer, "Ojai Tournament Next," *Los Angeles Times,* Apr. 14, 1931.

18. Paul Lowry, Rabbit Punches (column), *Los Angeles Times,* Aug. 12, 1931.

19. "Trojans End Annual Grid Grind Today," *Los Angeles Times,* Apr. 17, 1931.

20. "News of the Cafes," *Los Angeles Times,* May 8, 1931.

21. "S.C. Officials Leave," *Los Angeles Times,* June 3, 1931.

22. "Howard Jones Weds on Coast; Wife Marries in Chicago after Divorce," *Daily Iowan,* Apr. 2, 1926.

23. "Coaches Go to School Today," *Los Angeles Times,* June 22, 1931.

24. Braven Dyer, "Trojan Gridiron Machine Favored to Capture 1931 Pacific Coast Conference Crown," *Los Angeles Times,* Aug. 23, 1931.

25. "Jones Objects to Propaganda," *Los Angeles Times,* Sept. 8, 1931.

26. "Grid Stars Open Film Work Here," *Los Angeles Times,* July 28, 1931.

27. "Jones Will Complete Grid Pictures Today," *Los Angeles Times,* Aug. 21, 1931.

28. "Howard Jones's Scoring Play—No 46," *Los Angeles Times,* Aug. 23, 1931.

29. McCallum and Castner, *We Remember Rockne,* 133.

30. Braven Dyer, "Jones Plans New Shift for Trojan Grid Team," *Los Angeles Times,* Aug. 25, 1931.

31. George Kirksey, "Notre Dame Coaching Staff to Remain Unchanged Next Season," *San Bernardino County Sun,* Apr. 8, 1931.

32. Lawrence Perry, "Rockne Pupil Picked to Succeed Famous Mentor," *Appleton (WI) Post-Crescent,* Apr. 4, 1931.

33. "Hunk Anderson Named Notre Dame Grid Chief," *Chicago Daily Tribune,* Apr. 11, 1931.

34. "Hunk Anderson under Knife," *Los Angeles Times,* July 9, 1931.

35. Paul Mickelson, "Hunk Anderson Recovers," *Los Angeles Times,* July 16, 1931.

36. "St. Mary's Warriors Upset Trojans, 13–7," *Los Angeles Times,* Sept. 27, 1931.

37. "We Were Lucky to Win—Skip Madigan," *Los Angeles Times,* Sept. 27, 1931.

38. "Rockne Fans to Raise Fund," *Los Angeles Times,* Sept. 10, 1931.

39. "Notre Dame vs. Southern California," *Los Angeles Times,* Oct. 11, 1931.

40. Braven Dyer, "Baker Rejoins Trojans," *Los Angeles Times,* Oct. 13, 1931.

41. Braven Dyer, "Devine Praises Irish," *Los Angeles Times,* Nov. 11, 1931.

42. Braven Dyer, "Trojans Depart Tonight for Notre Dame," *Los Angeles Times,* Nov. 17, 1931.

43. "Hawkins Cleared by U.S.C.," *Los Angeles Times,* Dec. 6, 1931.

44. "Grid Row Nearing End," *Los Angeles Times,* Dec. 25, 1931.

45. "Apologies Demanded by Hawkins," *Los Angeles Times,* Dec. 19, 1931.

46. "Trojans 'Camera Shy,'" *Los Angeles Times,* Nov. 18, 1931.

47. Dyer, "Trojans Depart Tonight for Notre Dame," *Los Angeles Times,* Nov. 17, 1931.

48. Braven Dyer, "Star Will Be Set to Start Against Irish," *Los Angeles Times,* Nov. 19, 1931.

49. Braven Dyer, "Trojans' 16–14 Win All Time Thriller," *Los Angeles Times*, Nov. 28, 1951.

50. Dyer, "Star Will Be Set to Start Against Irish," *Los Angeles Times*, Nov. 19, 1931.

51. Dyer, "Trojans' 16–14 Win All Time Thriller," *Los Angeles Times*, Nov. 28, 1951.

52. Braven Dyer, "Trojans Stage Heavy Workout Despite Rain," *Los Angeles Times*, Nov. 20, 1931.

25. The Game of the Century

1. Robert E. Wright and Thomas W. Zeller, *Guide to U.S. Economic Policy* (Thousand Oaks, CA: CQ Press, 2014), 46.

2. James M. Rubenstein, *Making and Selling Cars: Innovation and Change in the U.S. Automotive Industry* (Baltimore, MD: Johns Hopkins Univ. Press, 2001), 196.

3. Aurel Schubert, *The Credit-Anstalt Crisis of 1931* (New York: Cambridge Univ. Press, 1991), 7.

4. John P. Gallagher, "Irish Mentor Gives Outfit Hard Workout," *Los Angeles Times*, Nov. 17, 1931.

5. "South Bend Game May Be Played on Dry Turf," *Los Angeles Times*, Nov. 21, 1931.

6. Joseph M. White, *Worthy of the Gospel of Christ: A History of the Catholic Diocese of Fort Wayne-South Bend* (Huntington, IN: Visitor Publishing, 2007), 163.

7. U.S. Congress, *Congressional Record*, 107th Cong., 1st sess., vol. 147, pt. 9, June 26, 2001–July 16, 2001 (Washington, D.C.: GPO, 2005), 12718.

8. Alison Skertic, "South Bend," *Indianapolis Monthly*, Aug. 2006, 102.

9. University of Notre Dame, "History," Notre Dame Stadium: Preserving the Traditions (website), http://stadium.nd.edu/history/.

10. Calculated from strut framing plan for Notre Dame Stadium, 1929, Osborne Engineering Company.

11. James Carmody, "Some Statistics on the New Stadium," *Notre Dame Alumnus* 9, no. 2 (Oct. 1930): 48.

12. Raymond Schmidt, *Shaping College Football: The Transformation of an American Sport, 1919–1930* (Syracuse, NY: Syracuse Univ. Press, 2007), 125.

13. University of Southern California, "History," About USC (website), https://about.usc.edu/history/.

14. Braven Dyer, Grid Gossip (column), *Los Angeles Times*, Nov. 15, 1931.

15. T. A. D. Jones, "Tad Jones and Alonzo Stagg Pick Notre Dame to Win Over Trojans in Grid Classic," *Los Angeles Times*, Nov. 20, 1931.

16. Braven Dyer, "Star Will Be Set to Start Against Irish," *Los Angeles Times*, Nov. 19, 1931.

17. John. S. Daggett, "Grid Classics Feature Radio," *Los Angeles Times*, Nov. 21, 1931.

18. "Rockne Debut Reveals Coach Was to Quit," *Los Angeles Times*, Dec. 6, 1931.

19. Paul Lowry, Rabbit Punches (column), *Los Angeles Times*, June 4, 1931.

20. Associated Press, "Irish Sign Five-Year Grid Pact with Carnegie Tech," *Los Angeles Times*, June 5, 1931.

21. Lawrence Perry, "Rockne Is Not Dismayed Over New Irish Standards," *Appleton (WI) Post-Crescent*, Mar. 19, 1931.

22. Sperber, *Shake Down the Thunder*, 302.

23. Ibid., 374–76.

24. Braven Dyer, "Stirring Trojan Rally Upsets Irish, 16 to14," *Los Angeles Times*, Nov. 22, 1931.

25. Bill Plaschke, "The Original Man of Troy," *Los Angeles Times*, Feb. 23, 2012.

26. "Graduating Seniors," *El Rodeo*, 1930 (USC yearbook), University of Southern California, 158.

27. Ambrose Schindler, interview by the author, Redondo Beach, CA, Sept. 14, 2005.

28. Bill Statz, "Howard Jones Birdcage Shift," Coach Somebody! (website), http://footballcoachessymposium.com/2014/09/howard-jones-birdcage-shift/.

29. Adam Augustyn, *The Britannica Guide to Football* (New York: Rosen Publishing, 2011), 64.

30. Dyer, "Stirring Trojan Rally Upsets Irish, 16 to 14," *Los Angeles Times*, Nov. 22, 1931.

31. Ambrose Schindler, interview by the author, Redondo Beach, CA, Sept. 14, 2005.

32. Notre Dame vs USC (part 5, 4th quarter) [negative, sound], 1931, AATH 10005 FC1 (game film), Notre Dame Athletics Collection: Audio-Visual, University of Notre Dame Archives.

33. Braven Dyer, "Trojans Turn Thoughts to Washington Game; Jones Told to Name Salary by Iowa Alumni," *Los Angeles Times*, Nov. 28, 1927.

34. Dyer, "Stirring Trojan Rally Upsets Irish, 16 to14," *Los Angeles Times*, Nov. 22, 1931.

35. Notre Dame vs USC (part 5, 4th quarter) [negative, sound], 1931, AATH 10005 FC1.

36. Dyer, "Stirring Trojan Rally Upsets Irish, 16 to14," *Los Angeles Times*, Nov. 22, 1931.

26. The Final Quarter

1. James Vautravers, "1931 College Football National Championship," TipTop25.com (website), http://tiptop25.com/champ1931.html.

2. Dyer, "Stirring Trojan Rally Upsets Irish, 16 to14," *Los Angeles Times*, Nov. 22, 1931.

3. Heartley Anderson, "Desperate Trojan Rally Vanquishes Irish," *Los Angeles Times*, Nov. 22, 1931.

4. Dyer, "Stirring Trojan Rally Upsets Irish, 16 to 14," *Los Angeles Times*, Nov. 22, 1931.

5. "Park Plans to Broadcast Trojan Clash," *Los Angeles Times*, Nov. 20, 1931.

6. "Mrs. Jones Hears Game," *Los Angeles Evening Herald*, Nov. 21, 1931.

7. "Three Big Games to Be on Air Saturday," *Lincoln Evening Journal*, Nov. 20, 1931.

8. "Broadcast Here of Irish-Trojan Go Thrills Many," *Montana Butte Standard*, Nov. 22, 1931.

9. "Today's Radio Programs," *Brooklyn Daily Eagle*, Nov. 21, 1931.

10. "Radio," *The Ottawa Journal*, Nov. 21, 1931.

11. Will Rogers, "Will Rogers Remarks," *Los Angeles Times*, Nov. 24, 1931.

12. Notre Dame vs USC (part 5, 4th quarter) [negative, sound], 1931, AATH 10005 FC1.

13. Edwin Pope, *Football's Greatest Coaches* (Atlanta: Tupper and Love, 1955), 132.

14. Dyer, "Trojans' 16–14 Win All Time Thriller," *Los Angeles Times*, Nov. 28, 1951.

15. John P. Gallagher, "Troy Players Happy Outfit," *Los Angeles Times*, Nov. 22, 1931.

16. Braven Dyer, "Midwest Still Stunned by Trojan Triumph," *Los Angeles Times*, November 23, 1931.

17. Gallagher, "Troy Players Happy Outfit," *Los Angeles Times*, Nov. 22, 1931.

18. Dyer, "Midwest Still Stunned by Trojan Triumph," *Los Angeles Times*, Nov. 23, 1931.

19. Pope, *Football's Greatest Coaches*, 132.

20. "Trojan Grid Squad Bare Heads at Rockne's Grave," *Los Angeles Times*, Nov. 22, 1931.

21. Pope, *Football's Greatest Coaches*, 132.

22. "Trojan Grid Squad Bare Heads at Rockne's Grave," *Los Angeles Times*, Nov. 22, 1931.

23. Dyer, "Midwest Still Stunned by Trojan Triumph," *Los Angeles Times*, Nov. 23, 1931.

24. Mal Florence, "Some Old Trojans Relive Their Biggest Win," *Los Angeles Times*, Oct. 23, 1981.

25. Associated Press, "Trojans Get Relaxation," *Brownsville (TX) Herald*, Nov. 23, 1931.

26. Florence, "Some Old Trojans Relive Their Biggest Win," *Los Angeles Times*, Oct. 23, 1981.

27. "Great Civic Welcome Planned for Trojans," *Los Angeles Times*, Nov. 24, 1931.

28. "Trojan Train Shifted to Early Hour," *San Bernardino County Sun*, Nov. 25, 1931.

29. Marian Rhea, "Trojan Women Acclaim Grid Heroes," *Los Angeles Examiner*, Nov. 25, 1931.

30. Associated Press, "30,000 at L.A. City Hall Greet Trojan Grid Men," *Santa Cruz Evening News*, Nov. 25, 1931.

31. "300,000 Cheer S.C. Grid Heroes in Wild Greeting," *Los Angeles Herald*, Nov. 25, 1931.

32. "Cheering Thousands Greet Trojans Today," *Los Angeles Examiner*, Nov. 25, 1931.

33. Marian Rhea, "Trojan Women Acclaim Grid Heroes," *Los Angeles Examiner*, Nov. 25, 1931.

34. Wendell Sether, "City Goes Wild as S.C. Gridiron Squad Returns," *Southern California Daily Trojan*, Nov. 30, 1931.

35. Associated Press, "Victory Football Given Mrs. Baker," *San Bernardino County Sun*, Nov. 26, 1931.

36. "Cheering Thousands Greet Trojans Today," *Los Angeles Examiner*, Nov. 25, 1931.

37. "Car Decorations for Parade Offered by Store," *Southern California Daily Trojan,* Nov. 24, 1931.

38. Bob Ray, "Tumultous Greeting Is Given Irish Conquerors," *Los Angeles Times,* Nov. 26, 1931.

39. "300,000 Cheer S.C. Grid Heroes in Wild Greeting," *Los Angeles Herald,* Nov. 25, 1931.

40. "City Cheers Trojan Heroes in Triumphal Homecoming," *Los Angeles Herald,* Nov. 25, 1931.

41. "300,000 Cheer S.C. Grid Heroes in Wild Greeting," *Los Angeles Herald,* Nov. 25, 1931.

42. Ray, "Tumultous Greeting Is Given Irish Conquerors," *Los Angeles Times,* Nov. 26, 1931.

43. "City Cheers Trojan Heroes in Triumphal Homecoming," *Los Angeles Herald,* Nov. 25, 1931.

44. "Cheering Thousands Greet Trojans Today," *Los Angeles Times,* Nov. 25, 1931.

45. "300,000 Cheer S.C. Grid Heroes in Wild Greeting," *Los Angeles Herald,* Nov. 25, 1931.

46. John S. Daggett, "Trojan Parade Will Be on Air," *Los Angeles Times,* Nov. 25, 1931.

47. "Cheering Thousands Greet Trojans Today," *Los Angeles Times,* Nov. 25, 1931.

48. "300,000 Cheer S.C. Grid Heroes in Wild Greeting," *Los Angeles Herald,* Nov. 25, 1931.

49. Ray, "Tumultous Greeting Is Given Irish Conquerors," *Los Angeles Times,* Nov. 26, 1931.

50. "300,000 Cheer S.C. Grid Heroes in Wild Greeting," *Los Angeles Herald,* Nov. 25, 1931.

51. Ray, "Tumultous Greeting Is Given Irish Conquerors," *Los Angeles Times,* Nov. 26, 1931.

52. Amce Newspictures, photograph of parade through downtown Los Angeles, Nov. 28, 1931, in the collection of the author.

53. Florence, "Some Old Trojans Relive Their Biggest Win," *Los Angeles Times,* Oct. 23, 1981.

54. Ray, "Tumultous Greeting Is Given Irish Conquerors," *Los Angeles Times,* Nov. 26, 1931.

27. Aftermath

1. Ray, "Tumultous Greeting Is Given Irish Conquerors," *Los Angeles Times,* Nov. 26, 1931.

2. John Scott, "Football Picture Magnet," *Los Angeles Times,* Dec. 10, 1931.

3. "Howard Jones Calls 1931 Trojan Football Team Greatest Eleven He Ever Coached," *Los Angeles Times,* Jan. 7, 1932.

4. Jones, Jane Dean, Case No. 161265, Sept. 17, 1936, Los Angeles County Archives and Records Center, Los Angeles, CA.

5. "Howard Jones Victim of Heart Attack," *Oakland Tribune,* July 28, 1941.

6. Carolyn Jones O'Connell, interview by the author, Fontana, CA, Jan. 16, 2010.

7. "Howard Jones' Son, Ex-Times Man, Weds," *Los Angeles Times,* June 25, 1948.

8. Carolyn Jones O'Connell, interview by the author, Fontana, CA, Jan. 16, 2010.

9. United Press, "'Mom' Rockne, Widow of Great Irish Coach, Dies," *Long Beach Independent Press-Telegram,* June 3, 1956.

10. Associated Press, "Rockne's Son Shot after He Entered Home," *Kokomo Tribune,* Jan. 22, 1951.

11. United Press International, "William Rockne, Rock's Son, Dies at South Bend," *Logansport (IN) Pharos-Tribune,* Nov. 8, 1960.

12. Associated Press, "Knute Rockne Jr. to Don Army Uniform Saturday," Feb. 10, 1943.

13. Photograph of tombstone of Knute Rockne Jr., Lincoln Charter Township Cemetery, Stevensville, MI, digital copy in the collection of the author.

14. Bob Wieneke, "Rockne's Son Dies at Age 82," *South Bend Tribune,* Aug. 11, 2008.

15. Mary Jean Rockne (1920–1992), Ancestry.com, http://records.ancestry.com/mary_jean_rockne_records.ashx?pid=37619206.

16. Craig Wolff, "Rockne Grandsons Feel Held Back by Their Name," *New York Times,* Apr. 18, 1983.

17. Tamara Jones, "Oklahoma Neighbors Recall Gunman's Bizarre Behavior," *Santa Cruz Sentinel,* Aug. 21, 1986.

18. "Hunk Anderson in Breakdown; Off to Clinic," *Los Angeles Times,* June 24, 1931.

19. Associated Press, "Elmer Layden to Succeed Hunk Anderson at Notre Dame," *Kokomo Tribune,* Dec. 8, 1933.

20. Donald J. Lechman, *Notre Dame vs. USC: The Rivalry* (Charleston, SC: History Press, 2012), 131.

21. Ben Yagoda, *Will Rogers: A Biography* (Norman: Univ. of Oklahoma Press, 2000), 310.

22. Associated Press, "Will Rogers—Wiley Post Killed—Craft Crashed at 'Top of the World,'" *Kokomo Tribune,* Aug. 16, 1935.

23. Stenn, *Clara Bow,* 231.

24. Ibid., 238.

25. Ibid., 240.

26. Richard O. Davies, *The Maverick Spirit: Building the New Nevada* (Reno: Univ. of Nevada Press, 1999), 169.

27. Stenn, *Clara Bow,* 269.

28. Ibid., 280.

29. Roberts, *John Wayne,* 95.

30. Bernard Brandon Scott, *Hollywood Dreams and Biblical Stories* (Minneapolis, MN: Augsburg Fortress Publishers, 1994), 74.

31. Michael Newton, *White Robes and Burning Crosses: A History of the Ku Klux Klan from 1866* (Jefferson, NC: McFarland and Co., 2014), 66.

32. Luciano J. Iorizzo, *Al Capone: A Biography* (Westport, CT: Greenwood Press, 2003), 96.

33. Thomas Joseph Jurkanin and Terry G. Hillard, *Chicago Police, an Inside View: The Story of Superintendent Terry G. Hillard* (Springfield, IL: Charles C. Thomas, 2006), 16.

34. United Press, "Scarface Al Capone, Man Who Had 500 Murdered, Dies at Miami Beach," *Lead (SD) Call Daily,* Jan. 26, 1947.

35. Stephen Moore, "What Really Ended the Great Depression?" *Orange County Register,* Oct. 10, 2014.

36. United Press, "Studebaker President Kills Self with Pistol," *Fresno Bee,* July 1, 1933.

37. Harold C. Burr, "Army-ND Game Too Big for Own Good," *Brooklyn Daily Eagle,* Dec. 31, 1946.

38. Tim Hyland, "Heisman Trophy Winners by School," College Football, About Sports, About.com (website), http://collegefootball.about.com/odtheheismantrophy/a/heisman-schools.htm.

A Response to Professor Murray Sperber

1. Sperber, *Shake Down the Thunder,* xx.

2. Ibid.

3. Ibid., 505.

4. Braven Dyer, "The Sports Parade," *Los Angeles Times,* Nov. 28, 1942.

5. John Hall, "The Creation," *Los Angeles Times,* Nov. 23, 1976.

6. "Indiana Gets Huskers' Place on N. Dame Card," *Chicago Daily Tribune,* Dec. 10, 1925.

7. The Atchison, Topeka and Santa Fe Railway System Timetables, Nov. 1, 1925, digital copy in the collection of the author.

8. Dyer, "The Sports Parade," *Los Angeles Times,* Nov. 28, 1942.

9. The Atchison, Topeka and Santa Fe Railway System Timetables, Nov. 1, 1925, digital copy in the collection of the author.

10. Paul Zimmerman, "Mark Kelly, Famed Ex-Sports Editor, Dies," *Los Angeles Times,* Dec. 6, 1952.

11. Brondfield, *Rockne,* 180.

12. Lechman, *Notre Dame vs. USC: The Rivalry,* 13.

13. McCallum and Castner, *We Remember Rockne,* 73.

14. Rockne, qtd. in Sperber, *Shake Down the Thunder,* xx–xxi.

15. Knute Rockne to Paul Schissler, telegram, Nov. 19, 1925, UADR 19/67, Schissler, Paul J. (Oregon State Agricultural College, Corvallis, OR) 1923–1925, Director of Athletics, 1909–1929 (Harper, Rockne), University of Notre Dame Archives.

16. Sperber, *Shake Down the Thunder,* 292.

17. "Story of Retirement of Wilson Confirmed," *Los Angeles Times,* June 27, 1930.

18. Sperber, *Shake Down the Thunder,* xxi; Gwynn Wilson to Knute Rockne, telegram, Dec. 5, 1925, UADR 19/131, Univ. of Southern California: Gwynn Wilson 1926, Director of Athletics, 1909–1929 (Harper, Rockne), University of Notre Dame Archives.

19. Sperber, *Shake Down the Thunder,* 202.

20. Ibid., 170.

21. Ibid., 222.

22. Huston, *Salesman from the Sidelines*, 79; Sperber, *Shake Down the Thunder*, 545.

23. Sperber, *Shake Down the Thunder*, 202.

24. Bill Plaschke, "Behind This Great Game Is a Great Woman," *Los Angeles Times*, Nov. 25, 2006.

25. Sperber, *Shake Down the Thunder*, xx.

Index